eBizguides

ZAMBIA

eBiZ guides

CREDITS

It is always good to know who worked hard for this guide.

Many talented people and many wonderful stories have gone into making it. Here is the list of those involved:

PRODUCTION

Producer: Pascal Belda

Regional Project Director: Melanie Rose Hardiman

Local Project Director: Wendy Fleury

Associate Production: Luis Aparicio

Advertising Agency Lusaka: D & C Saatchi & Saatchi

EDITION

Written and edited by eBizguides

Economic sections and sector overviews written by: Directory Publishers of Zambia (from Zambia Review 2006)

General Information section written by: Zambia National Tourist Board, eBizguides

Tourism & Leisure section written by: Zambia National Tourist Board, eBizguides

Art Director: Elisa Lopez Fuentes

Photos: pictures by eBizguides, Zambia National Tourist Board, Mopani Copper Mines, Luanshya Copper Mines, Chilanga Cement

ACKNOWLEDGEMENTS

We would like to thank the following people for their collaboration and support.

H.E. Mr Levy Patrick Mwanawasa, President of the Republic of Zambia, Dr J. Kanganja, Secretary to the Cabinet, H.E. Mr Anderson Chibwa, Zambia High Commissioner to the U.K., Mr Mulele, Permanent Secretary, Ministry of Tourism, Mr Chilipamushi, Permanent Secretary, Ministry of Commerce, Trade and Industry, Mr Chizyuka, Permanent Secretary, Ministry of Agriculture and Co-operatives, Mr Nkhata, Permanent Secretary, Ministry of Mines and Mineral Development, Mr Siakalenge, Director of Industry, Ministry of Commerce, Trade and Industry, Mrs Charity Lumpa, Zambia National Tourist Board, Mr Ephraim Belemu, Zambia National Tourist Board, Mr Gye Robinson, President, Zambia National Farmers' Union, Mr Francis Saudubray, Ambassadeur de France, Mr Graham Cleveland, Directory Publishers of Zambia.

We would also like to thank the heads of the following companies for their sponsorship and support, without whom this eBizguide would not have been possible:

Chilanga Cement Plc – Coppernet Solutions – D & C Saatchi & Saatchi – DHL – Lilayi Lodge – Luanshya Copper Mines Plc / Chambishi Metals Plc – Lusaka Stock Exchange Ltd – Michelangelo – Ministry of Agriculture – MNB Legal Practitioners – Mopani Copper Mines Plc – Mulungushi Village Complex – National Housing Authority – National Milling Corporation Ltd – National Pension Scheme Authority – National Savings and Credit Bank – Zambian Airways – Zambian Breweries Group Plc – Zambia Bureau of Standards – Zambia Telecommunications Company Ltd – Zambeef Products Plc – Zamnet Ltd – ZESCO – Directory Publishers of Zambia (Zambia Review 2006)

DISCLAIMER

World Investment News Inc, 1 Rue de la Tour de L'ille P O BOX 5415 Geneva 11 Switzerland

Customer Service: Tel: + 34 91 787 38 70, Fax. +34 91 787 38 89

Email: info@ebizguides.com, www.ebizguides.com

Printed by: China Printing Corporation

2nd Edition

ISBN: 84933978-9-x

How to use this guide?

The goal of eBizguides is to offer extensive economic and investment information on a country, with a focus on the top companies, while offering the best tourism and leisure information for your spare time. With this, we believe that our readers can get fully acquainted with the country, before investing in it long term.

This book comprises three major sections, which deal with general information, the country's economy and leisure.

General Information

Background information on the country is coupled with the main business resources available to you.

The Zambian Economy

This section of the book starts off with an in-depth look at the country's investment and legal framework, and the country's economy itself. Through personal interviews with the most important business people in the country, we then provide our readers with privileged information and sector analysis, including introductions written by key decision-makers in the sector, such as government ministers.

You will also find fact files of all the major corporations, outlining their business activities, key projects and any investment opportunities. We consider this to include some of the most invaluable information for business globetrotters.

Leisure

For you to fall in love with the country, we also showcase the best spots to visit, essential areas to discover, the top hotels and restaurants, and much more.

Icons

eBiz Recommended

These companies were particular favourites of our team during their stay; this stamp is mostly given to restaurants, hotels, and so on.

eBiz Recommended Partner

Our team has been interviewing the heads of many companies; when they choose to allocate this stamp to a company, it is because they themselves have received reliable service from the company.

Notice

This indicates that the information is important and something to take notice of when planning, or during, your stay.

Legends

Proverbs

These local phrases will help you to understand the popular culture in the country better. Perhaps you can even use them yourself.

Top Companies

This is a listing of the top companies that eBizguides encountered during their time in the country.

Blue boxes

This is useful insider information that will help you to assess the country, do business and enjoy your stay.

Contents

Did You Know?

Zambia has only 11 million inhabitants for a surface that is equal to the surface of France, the Netherlands, Belgium and Switzerland combined.

Livingstone was the capital of Zambia until 1935. When a more central location was needed, Lusaka was chosen to be the government administrative centre by a town planner from London. Lusaka was a desolate, windswept place at the time, and it was not envisaged that there would be any industrial development.

Zambia is the world's fourth largest producer of copper and the largest producer of cobalt.

Although Livingstone is very well known for making the Victoria Falls famous, he was almost totally unsuccessful in his own aims, failing to set up any trade missions or to convert Africans to Christianity.

Despite a large number of different ethnic tribes and languages (over 73), Zambia is one of the only African countries never to have suffered any wars or civil wars. Zambia is renowned for its peacefulness and safety.

40,000 years ago, the Zambezi River was falling into the Batoka Gorge, 90km away from the Victoria Falls. A long process of erosion resulted in the eight gorges that now form the river's slalom course after it has passed over the present Falls. Each gorge was once a great waterfall.

Zambia holds two thirds of Southern African water resources. 60% of the land is arable and only 15% is exploited.

Lake Tanganyika is the deepest of the Rift Valley lakes of Central / East Africa with a maximum depth of 1,470m. It is estimated to be about 15 million years old.

The main commercial street in Lusaka is named Cairo Road. During the British rule, the vision of Cecil Rhodes was to connect adjacent African possessions of the British Empire through a continuous line from Cape Town, South Africa, to Cairo, Egypt.

Although copper has been known and used for centuries in the Copperbelt area, the early European discovery was made by prospector William Collier who discovered copper on the site where he had shot a roan antelope in 1902; the first company to exploit the resources in Luanshya was called Roan Antelope Mining Corporation.

The Kariba Dam was one of the most ambitious undertakings in Africa. 34,000 people had to be relocated. It took five years, GB £78 million and a million cubic metres of concrete to build the wall 128m high that formed a lake of 5,200 km2.

Lake Tanganyka
TANZANIA
Lake Mweru
DEMOCRATIC REPUBLIC OF THE CONGO
Mpulungu
Kasama
Mafinga Hills
Lake Bangweulu
Luapula
ANGOLA
Solwezi
Mulfulira
Kitwe
Ndola
Kapiri Mposhi
Chipata
Kabwe
Mongu
LUSAKA
Zambezi
Lake Kariba
Zambezi
Livingstone
NAMIBIA
THE VICTORIA FALLS
ZIMBABWE
BOTSWANA
0 100 200 km
0 100 200 mi

Zambia Fact File

Name:	Zambia
Capital city:	Lusaka
Main cities:	Lusaka, Livingstone, Ndola, Kitwe
International airports:	Lusaka, Livingstone, Ndola
Time:	GMT + 2 hours
Currency:	Kwacha
Language:	English is the official language. There are 73 dialects and 7 vernacular languages
Phone code:	+260
Area:	752,614 sq. km
Border countries:	Angola, Democratic Republic of Congo, Malawi, Mozambique, Namibia, Tanzania, Zimbabwe
Population:	11 million
Population growth rate:	2.12%
Life expectancy at birth:	50 years
GDP:	Approx. US $7.1 billion
Growth rate:	4.3%

GENERAL INFORMATION

"Treat the days well and they will treat you well"
Zambian proverb

HISTORY

Archaeologists have established that in the northern African Rift Valley the civilizing process got under way at least three million years ago, and crude stone implements, similar to some of that age found in Kenya, have been found beside the Zambezi River.

Early stone-age sites have been unearthed in many parts of Zambia, the most significant being at the Kalambo Falls in the north and at Victoria Falls in the south.

The centuries between 1500 and 1800 AD saw many of the peoples of Zambia organized into chieftaincies or monarchies. The Chewa in the east, the Lozi in the west, and the Bemba and Lunda in the north were the largest of these, all established under the influence of, some as direct extensions of, the large and powerful Lunda Empire of the Mwata Yamvo in what is now southern Zaire. By the 18th century, the Empire was trading with the Atlantic coast, where the world economy was represented by the Swahili city-states from Somalia to south of the Zambezi delta. Copper, ivory and rhino horn had a ready market, as well as slaves.

THE EUROPEAN FACTOR

The wealth of the Indian Ocean trade was one of the elements that in the 15th century inspired the Portuguese, who had recently reconquered their country from Muslim Moors, to embark on their bold 'Voyages of Discovery'.

By 1515 the Portuguese had through the force of arms seized the Indian Ocean trade and, what is relevant to the course of events in Zambia, established themselves on the coasts of Mozambique and Angola.

Besides the influence brought to bear on Zambia by the Swahili and the Portuguese, the effects of the Dutch (and subsequently British) colonization of the Cape and its hinterland from 1652 onwards would also be felt.

The Freedom Statue on Independence Avenue symbolizes Zambia's liberation from the colonial rule

INVASIONS FROM THE SOUTH

Perhaps as a response to foreign intrusions in southern Africa, Shaka Zulu of the Nguni clan set about creating a centralized militaristic state in the early 19th century. Three of these groups were to make a forceful impact on Zambia.

One of these was a Sotho clan; its leader was Sebitwane. Another was Mzilikazi, one of Shaka's generals. After being defeated by the Dutch settlers in the Transvaal, he and his Ndebele invaded and conquered Western Zimbabwe.

The third was Zongendaba. He led his followers out of Shaka's domains in the 1820s. These Ngoni crossed the Zambezi in 1835 and went northwards as far as Lake Tanganyika where they settled for a while among the Bemba. In 1865, under Zongendaba's successor Mpenzeni I, they established themselves permanently in what is now Zambia's Eastern province.

Mzilikazi conquered Zimbabwe in 1837, while Sebitwane had crossed the Zambezi a few years previously and taken over territory just north of the Victoria Falls. From there he marched west to conquer the Lozi kingdom of the Upper Zambezi and founded his Kololo state.

In 1840, David Livingstone, a 27-year-old Scottish doctor, sailed from Britain to the Cape to work as a medical evangelist with the London Missionary Society. Meanwhile, Portugal was planning to consolidate its African territories by uniting Angola and Mozambique across the central plateau.

Unlike the Portuguese, the British knew nothing about the region and Livingstone was to explore the region to give the true picture. Livingstone started going on longer and longer journeys of exploration, receiving help from a wealthy Englishman named William Cotton Oswell; the two of them were the first Europeans to visit Lake Ngami in the middle of the Kalahari.

In 1851 Livingstone and Oswell crossed the Kalahari to visit Sebitwane, on the Upper Zambezi. It's here that Livingstone had his first sight of the slave trade. He and Oswell, who was also a staunch abolitionist, concluded that the only way to stop the trade would be through a new type of mission where a combination of Christianity and commerce would lead to civilization; in fact, a sort of Christian development programme under which slave trading would be replaced by 'legitimate' trade in, for instance, cotton, which grew in the area and for which there was a large market in Britain. Sebitwane, though scarcely interested in Christianity itself, agreed that Livingstone could establish a mission in his country, if only because it might afford him protection against his enemy Mzilikazi of the Ndebele, whose warrior kingdom bordered his own.

To establish the mission, all that remained was to find a suitable outlet to the sea. The most economical passage for anticipated cotton (and ivory) exports might have been through the Portuguese port of Luanda on the Atlantic, but it appeared to be an unsuitable route. Livingstone then convinced himself that the Zambezi could be 'God's Highway' to the Indian Ocean and, with the support from Sekeletu, Livingstone marched off eastwards down the river. He 'discovered', and named after Queen Victoria, the great waterfall, which the Kololo had already called Mosi oa Tunya (The Smoke that Thunders).

EMPIRE

By the end of the 19th century, the British imperialist Cecil John Rhodes, a millionaire businessman hungry for power, had been able to take over the whole of Zambia; he had persuaded the British government to grant his company, the British South African Company (BSAC), the licence to stake claim to African territory. In 1911 the territory was named Northern Rhodesia, its capital the town of Livingstone, overlooking the Victoria Falls. (In 1935 the seat of government was moved to Lusaka.)

Rhodes' ambition was to make Africa British from the Cape to Cairo (hence the name of Lusaka's main street, Cairo Road). Even though Zambia did not contain much mineral wealth – an important consideration for BSAC shareholders – the territory had to be occupied, if only to prevent the Portuguese from winning their age-old claim to the area. It was now that the country's borders came to be drawn, by agreement with other colonial powers.

Any BSAC hopes for substantial revenue from mining were soon dashed and to obtain income it imposed the Hut Tax (payable in cash) on all African males who had reached puberty. Tax revolts were suppressed with bullets, and defaulters had their houses burned down and were imprisoned if caught. Forced labour at a pittance by men trying to forestall these penalties became the order of the day – tens of thousands were sent to work in the South African or Southern Rhodesian mines; the railway between the Victoria Falls and Katanga (Zaire) was financed from the Hut Tax, which consistently turned a profit. Some 20,000 Zambians forcibly recruited as porters for the British forces in East Africa during the First World War perished of disease or debilitation.

By 1923, company rule had become an objectionable anachronism for the British Government, and in that year, the Colonial Office took over the territory, proclaiming it a protectorate where African interests would be paramount.

As far as Africans were concerned, Colonial Office rule may have been more benign, in a paternalistic way, than the Company's, but it was a form of apartheid under which they were subject to racial discrimination including pass laws and restrictions on the occupation of land, their political aspirations expected to be fulfilled through a revamped tribal system. Whites, meanwhile, were a privileged elite with a protected economic position and the beginnings of representative government. Persons of mixed blood and immigrants, mainly traders from what are today India and Pakistan, held an ambivalent place under this regime.

KING COPPER

The discovery and opening up during the late 1920s and

New government offices on Independence Avenue

1930s of the rich underground ore bodies along the Zambian Copperbelt were soon to make that small region – 120km long by 40km wide – one of the world's most concentrated and renowned mining areas.

Over the years, the industry came to be controlled by two large groups, the South African Anglo American Corporation and the Roan Selection Trust, with a predominantly US shareholding.

Exploitation of the reserves required a large labour force and Zambians from all over the territory were drawn to the Copperbelt. In 1948, the first African Mineworkers' Union was formed; in 1955 there was a 100% stoppage over pay conditions that lasted 58 days – ending with victory for the miners. The mining companies now started seriously, if slowly, to move Africans into management.

On the broad political front, African nationalist feeling had been growing since the 1939–45 world war, in which many Zambians fought for the Allies in Burma. By the end of the 1940s, the Northern Rhodesia African Nationalist Congress, led by Harry Nkumbula, had been formed out of various welfare associations initiated by the 'mission graduates' of the pre-war decades.

FEDERATION

The nationalist movement was given impetus in the early 1950s when the Colonial Office agreed to have Northern Rhodesia joined in a federation with Nyasaland (Malawi), a British 'protectorate', and Southern Rhodesia (Zimbabwe). Southern Rhodesia, under white settler rule, was bankrupt, and saw Northern Rhodesia, with its copper wealth, as a milk cow.

Zambian opposition to federation was not strong enough to prevent its imposition in 1953. During its 10 years of existence, the white settlers there built up an impressive economic structure.

In the mid fifties, the failed campaign against the Federation became a struggle for full independence. When battle-weary Nkumbula seemed inadequate to the task, his ANC split. Younger and more dynamic nationalists formed first the Zambia African National Congress (which was banned and its leaders imprisoned) and then, in 1958, the United National Independence Party. When he came out of detention, Kenneth David Kaunda, a charismatic activist, was given the leadership of the new party. UNIP engaged in a continuous and largely peaceful campaign for independence.

By 1960 the British government had acknowledged that the days of colonial (or minority) rule on the continent were coming to an end. The premier of the white-dominated Federation, Roy Welensky, threatened to declare unilateral independence from Britain, but was baulked. When Zambian trade unions, including now powerful miners, threw their weight behind UNIP, the nationalist momentum became unstoppable. Intense and often violent rivalry between Kaunda's UNIP and Nkumbula's ANC was eventually neutralized in a transitional coalition government.

INDEPENDENCE

The Federation was dissolved in 1963. In January the following year, Zambia's first universal adult suffrage elections were held and, though the ANC performed well in a few substantial areas, UNIP won convincingly, Kaunda becoming prime minister. On 24th October 1964, Zambia became an independent republic with him as president.

Kaunda remained in office for 27 years. Although during his early years great strides were made in the areas of education, health and infrastructure, his attempts to 'decolonize' the economy by nationalizing it completely produced only inefficiency, corruption and a disastrous decline.

His one-party participatory democracy, which gave UNIP sole power, soon fossilized into an autocracy maintained by police-state methods.

In 1990 an obviously collapsing economy, together with political frustration, led to serious food riots and an attempted military coup that had people dancing in the streets. When the disorders could be halted only with firearms, opposition to the regime became so deep and widespread and the demand for change so urgent that Kaunda had to concede.

DEMOCRACY

The one-party state was abolished and free elections were held in October 1991. Kaunda and UNIP were defeated 80% to 20% by the newly formed Movement for Multiparty Democracy, a broad coalition of different interest groups.

The MMD's Frederick Chiluba, a trade unionist who had been locked up by Kaunda, became Zambia's second president. He promised democratic, transparent and accountable governance, but inherited an empty treasury, a foreign debt of seven billion US dollars and a country in a worse state than it had been when it won its independence in 1964.

Upon assuming the presidency, Chiluba embarked on an economic reform programme. He abolished foreign exchange controls, passed new investment laws, set up a stock exchange, and embarked on a privatization programme, which at one point was dubbed by the World Bank as the best on the continent.

All this led to Zambia being courted enthusiastically by aid donors, and saw a surge in investor confidence in the country reflected in a growing number of investors.

But in the 1990s there was a cooling in relations with the donors amid negative perceptions of constitutional tinkering ahead of the November 1996 elections, which prevented former president Kenneth Kaunda from standing as a presidential candidate. The elections in 1996 saw blatant harassment of opposition parties.

In 2001 Chiluba announced he was going to amend the constitution and stand for a third term. The public outcry was immense amid increasing allegations of corruption. He finally agreed to stand down and named Levy Mwanawasa as his successor. After a very controversial election in December 2001, MMD won again and Mwanawasa was sworn in as president.

NATIONAL SYMBOLS

NATIONAL FLAG

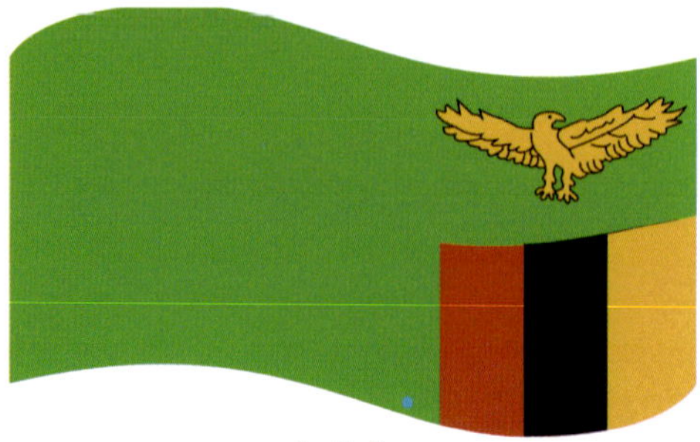

Zambia flag

The flag of Zambia was hoisted for the first time on 23rd October 1964, symbolizing patriotism and the nation's natural resources: an eagle in flight over three stripes of

THE NATIONAL ANTHEM

Stand and sing of Zambia, proud and free,
Land of work and joy in unity,
Victors in the struggle for the right,
We have won freedom's fight.
All one, strong and free.

Africa is our own motherland,
Fashioned with and blessed by God's good hand.
Let us all her people join as one,
Brothers under the sun.
All one, strong and free.

One land and one nation is our cry,
Dignity and peace 'neath Zambia's sky,
Like our noble eagle in its flight,
Zambia, praise to thee.
All one, strong and free.

Praise be to God,
Praise be, praise be, praise be,
Bless our great nation,
Zambia, Zambia, Zambia.
Free men we stand,
Under the flag of our land,
Zambia, praise to thee!
All one, strong and free.

red, black and orange on a green background. Red represents the struggle for freedom, black the people of Zambia, orange the country's mineral wealth and green the wildlife and environment. The eagle in flight symbolizes the freedom in Zambia and the ability to rise above national problems.

GOVERNMENT

The government of Zambia is elected in a multi-party general election every five years. Up until 1991, when the first multi-party elections were held, the country was ruled by Kenneth Kaunda in a one-party state. The Movement for Multiparty Democracy (MMD), and their leader Levy Patrick Mwanawasa, are now the ruling government for the second term. Their economic policy is to move Zambia from a centralized, state-driven economy to a more liberal open market economy that is private sector driven.

THE CONSTITUTION

The Republican Constitution has changed four times in 32 years.

Zambia became a republic immediately upon attaining freedom in October 1964. The constitution published on 25th August 1973 abrogated the original 1964 constitution. The new constitution and the national elections that followed in December 1973 were the final steps in achieving what was called a 'one-party participatory democracy'.

The 1973 constitution provided for a strong president and a unicameral National Assembly. National policy was formulated by the central committee of the United National Independence Party (UNIP), the sole legal party in Zambia. The cabinet executed the central committee's policy.

In accordance with the intention to formalize UNIP supremacy in the new system, the constitution stipulated that the sole candidate in elections for the office of president was the person selected to be the president of UNIP by the party's general conference. The second-ranking person in the Zambian hierarchy was UNIP's secretary general.

In December 1990, at the end of a tumultuous year that included riots in the capital and a coup attempt, President Kaunda signed legislation ending UNIP's monopoly on power. In response to growing popular demand for multi-party democracy, and after lengthy, difficult negotiations between the Kaunda government and opposition groups, Zambia enacted a new constitution in August 1991. The constitution enlarged the National Assembly from 136 members to a maximum of 158 members, accomplished an electoral commission, and allowed for more than one presidential candidate, who no longer had to be a member of UNIP. The constitution was amended again in 1996 to set new limits on the presidency (including a retroactive two-term limit, and a requirement that both parents of a candidate be Zambian born). The National Assembly comprises 150 directly elected members, up to eight presidentially appointed members, and a speaker. Zambia is separated into nine provinces, each administered by an appointed deputy minister who essentially performs the duties of a governor.

INTERNATIONAL RELATIONS

Zambia is a member of the Southern African Development Community (SADC); Common Market for Eastern and Southern Africa (COMESA); African Union (AU); African Development Bank (AfDB); Food and Agriculture Organization (FAO); Commonwealth; United Nations; International Labour Organization (ILO); World Trade Organization (WTO); World Bank; International Monetary Fund (IMF); Multilateral Investment Guarantee Agency (MIGA); World Health Organization (WHO); Non-Aligned Movement (NAM); New Partnership for Africa's Development (NEPAD); EU Economic Partnership Agreement; African Growth and Opportunity Act (AGOA).

EXECUTIVE POWER OF THE GOVERNMENT

Zambia is separated into nine provinces, each governed

by a minister appointed by the president: Central, Copperbelt, Eastern, Luapulu, Lusaka, Northern, North Western, Southern and Western. The chief of state and the head of government is the president, who appoints cabinet ministers from members of the National Assembly.

Zambian citizens of 18 years and over are eligible to vote. Zambia has a unicameral legislature. Legislative powers are vested in the 158-member National Assembly. Of these, 150 are directly elected by voters; the remaining eight are nominated by the republican president. Out of the 158, 17 are currently women.

THE JUDICIAL SYSTEM

The judicial system is based on English common law and customary law. Common law is administered by several High Courts, which have authority to hear criminal and civil cases and appeals from lower courts. Resident Magistrate's Courts are also established at various centres. Local courts mainly administer customary law, especially cases relating to marriage, property and inheritance.

Under the constitution of 1997, the Supreme Court is the highest court in Zambia and serves as the final court of appeal. The chief justice and other eight judges are appointed by the president. In consultation with the prime minister, the president also appoints the director of public prosecutions and the attorney general, the latter being the principal legal adviser to the government. The independence of the judiciary has been respected by the government. Trials in Magistrate's Courts are public. There is also an Industrial Relations Court, which handles and resolves labour disputes.

GOVERNMENT OFFICES

Ministry of Agriculture, Food and Fisheries
Mulungushi House, Independence Avenue
P O Box RW 50291, Lusaka
Tel: +260-1-251537/233/251962
Fax: +260-1-252029

Court of Justice

Ministry of Commerce, Trade and Industry
9th Floor, New Government Complex
P O Box 31968/34373, Lusaka
Tel: +260-1-228301/221184
Fax: +260-1-226673

Ministry of Communication and Transport
Fairley Road, Ridgeway
P O Box 50065, Lusaka
Tel: +260-1-251444/938/740/759
Fax: +260-1-253260

Ministry of Community Development and Social Services
Sadzi Road, off Kabelenga Road
Private Bag W252, Lusaka
Tel: +260-1-225327/221933
Fax: +260-1-221933

Ministry of Defence
Cabinet Office, Independence Avenue
P O Box RW 17X, Lusaka
Tel: +260-1-251211/264920
Fax: +20-1-254670/221339/253875

Ministry of Education
Jacaranda Road
P O Box 50093, Lusaka
Tel: +260-1-250855/227636
Fax: +260-1-222396

Ministry of Energy and Water Development
2nd Mulungushi House, Independence Avenue
P O Box 51254, Lusaka
Tel: +260-1-254636
Fax: +260-1-252339

Ministry of Environment and Natural Resources
Mulungushi House, Independence Avenue
P O Box 30055, Lusaka
Telephone: +260-1-252711/250186
Fax: +260-1-252952

Ministry of Finance and National Planning
Chimanga Road
P O Box 50062, Lusaka
Tel: +260-1-250544
Fax: +260-1-251204

Ministry of Foreign Affairs
Charter House, Independence Avenue
P O Box 50069, Lusaka
Tel: +260-1-252666/250240/252708
Fax: +260-1-250634/240/252867

Ministry of Health
Ndeke House, Haile Selassie Avenue
P O Box 30205, Lusaka
Tel: +260-1-253040/253050
Fax: +260-1-253187

Ministry of Home Affairs
Cabinet Office, Independence Avenue
P O Box 50997, Lusaka
Tel: +260-1-254261
Fax: +260-1-254336

Ministry of Information and Broadcasting Services
New Government Complex, Nasser Road
P O Box 50200, Lusaka
Tel: +260-1-253486/253965
Fax: +260-1-254013/252391/250524

Ministry of Labour and Social Security
New Government Complex, Nasser Road
P O Box 32186, Lusaka
Tel: +260-1-227640

Ministry of Lands
Mulungushi House, Independence Avenue
P O Box 30069, Lusaka
Tel: +260-1-252288/251927
Fax: +260-1-250130/253340

Ministry of Legal Affairs
Fairley Road
P O Box 50106, Lusaka
Tel: +260-1-251588/252045/7

Fax: +260-1-253695/253679

Ministry of Local Government and Housing
P O Box 34204, Lusaka
Tel: +260-1-253077
Fax: +260-1-252680

Ministry of Mines and Minerals Development
New Government Complex, Nasser Road
P O Box 31969, Lusaka
Tel: +260-1-235340
Fax: +260-1-251224

Ministry of Science, Technical Education and Vocational Training
Los Angeles Boulevard
P O Box 50464, Lusaka
Tel: +20-1-252541/252411
Fax: +260-1-252951

Ministry of Sports, Youth and Child Development
New Government Complex, Nasser Road
P O Box 50592, Lusaka
Tel: +260-1-227168
Fax: +260-1-223996

Ministry of Tourism
Kwacha House
P O Box 30575, Lusaka
Tel: +260-1-227645/223930
Fax: +260-1-225174

Ministry of Works and Supply
Government Road
PO Box 50236, Lusaka
Tel: +260-1-252366
Fax: +260-1-222360

GEOGRAPHY

Zambia takes its name from the Zambezi River, which rises in the north-west corner of the country and forms its southern boundary. The landlocked country lies between latitudes 10° and 18° south and longitudes 22° and 33° east.

Its neighbours are: Congo DR to the north and north-west, Tanzania to the north-east, Malawi to the east, Mozambique to the south-east, Zimbabwe to the south, Botswana and Namibia to the south-west and Angola to the west.

Zambia's 752,000 square kilometres makes it a large country about the size of France, the Netherlands, Belgium and Switzerland combined. It consists for the most part of a high plateau, with an average height of between 1,060 and 1,363 metres above sea level (3,500 and 4,500 ft). Isolated mountain ridges rise to more than 6,000 ft, with a peak above 7,000 ft on the eastern border called Nyika Plateau. Over most of the country the surface tends to be flat, broken by small hills, the result of countless ages of undisturbed erosion of the underlying crystalline rocks. These rocks contain the bulk of the country's wealth in the form of minerals and the 90-mile long corridor known as the Copperbelt, along the north-western part of the country, is the mainstay of the economy.

The level of the land falls southward from the Congo DR/Zambezi divide in the north towards the Zambezi depression in the south. The plateau is broken by the huge valleys of the Upper Zambezi and its major tributaries, of which the Kafue and Luangwa Rivers are the largest. One result of the plateau formation of Africa generally is the swift discharge of water towards the coast and the interruption of the rivers by waterfalls and rapids. This has made them of little value for transport over their length, but very suitable for hydroelectric schemes and white water rafting adventures.

With the exception of the Northern and Luapula provinces, which are part of the Congo DR basin, Zambia lies on the watershed between the Congo DR and Zambezi River systems. The three great natural lakes of the country, Bangweulu, Mweru and the southern end of Lake Tanganyika, are all in the north and are part of the headwaters of the Zaire River. Lake Tanganyika is the second deepest natural lake in the world.

Lake Bangweulu, which with its swamps covers an area of about 3,800 square miles, is drained by the Luapula

River. This river starts flowing south, then turns west and northwards to pass through Lake Mweru on its way to Congo DR.

Along the southern border of the country stretches Lake Kariba, the largest artificial lake in Africa and the second largest in the world. It is about 280km long and 40km across at its widest point.

NOTICE! **Zambia is one of the last countries to have "The Big Five": Buffalo, Elephant, Leopard, Lion and Rhino.**

NATURAL RESOURCES

Apart from its abundant wildlife, rivers and lakes, Zambia holds 6% of the world's copper reserves and is the fourth largest copper-producing nation in the world. Zambia is internationally recognized as a major producer of emeralds, aquamarines, amethyst and tourmalines and the quality of the gems is highly competitive with world markets.

Electricity is relatively cheap due to the abundance of hydroelectric power sources as well as reasonably large coal reserves. Most of the electricity is supplied from major hydropower stations located in the Kafue Gorge, Lake Kariba north bank and the Victoria Falls, as well as from the mini-hydropower stations in Lusiwashi, Musonda Falls, Chishimba Falls and Luzua. The domestic electricity supply is 240 volt, 50 hertz alternating current, with 415 volt single and three phase supply available for industrial use.

Water is provided principally by the civic authorities in all

The heavy rains from November to April turn Zambia into a beautiful green fertile land

cities and towns. Many residential properties are served by borehole systems.

CLIMATE

The general height of the land gives Zambia a more pleasant climate than that experienced in most tropical countries. There are three seasons – cool and dry from May to August, hot and dry from September to November, warm and wet from December to April.

Only in the valleys of the Zambezi and Luangwa is there excessive heat, particularly in October and, in the wet season, a high humidity.

In the warm wet season, frequent heavy showers and thunderstorms occur, followed by spells of bright sunshine. Plants grow profusely and rivers and streams fill up almost overnight.

During the cool dry season, night frosts may occur in places sheltered from the wind. The countryside dries up gradually and grass fires, fanned by high winds, are a feature of this time of the year. In depressions, radiation occurs on cloudless nights.

Temperatures rise high during the hot, dry season but new leaves appear on the trees before the start of the rains and new grass brightens the countryside. The main growing period of woody vegetation is between August and November.

While the rainfall pattern over the whole country is similar – between November and March – the amount of rain varies considerably. In the north of the country rainfall is 1,250mm (50 inches) or more a year, decreasing southwards to Lusaka where it is about 750mm (30 inches) annually. South of Lusaka rainfall is dictated more by the east and south-east trade winds, which have lost much of their humidity by the time they have reached so far inland. Rainfall in this area is between 500mm and 750mm (20 and 30 inches).

Except for very rare falls in August, rainfall is confined to the wet season, which sometimes starts as early as October and finishes as early as March. At the height of the wet season it rains on seven or eight days out of ten.

Average temperatures are moderated by the height of the plateau. Maxima vary from 15° C to 27° C in the cool season with morning and evening temperatures as low as 6° C to 10° C and occasional frost on calm nights in valleys and hollows which are sheltered from the wind.

In the cool season the prevailing winds, dry south-easterlies, come from the southern hemisphere belt of high pressure. Invasions of cold air from the south-east bring cloudy to overcast conditions. During the hot season maximum temperatures may range from 27° C to 35° C.

PEOPLE AND CULTURE

Zambia has over 73 different tribes, with a population of just about 11 million people, most of whom live in and around the urban centres. The population growth is at 3.7%.

Zambia has one of the lowest population to land ratios in Africa: only 11 million people in a country half the size of Europe.

About 46% of the population is under 15 years of age.

The employment opportunities offered in the post-independence era in the copper mines and associated industries led to a strong rural–urban migration. The result has been to make Zambia one of the most urbanized countries in Africa. About one fifth of the population lives on the Copperbelt to the north of the capital, but the biggest concentration of people is in Lusaka itself with an estimated population of over two million (which represents about 10% of the population). This has resulted in massive tracts of uninhabited land across the country.

With over 70 different tribes in Zambia, there is wide cultural diversity. Interestingly enough, however, it is one of the few countries in Africa with very little tribal animosity, and the existence of so many tribes has proved less of a political problem than in many other African states. The main tribes are the Lozi, the Bemba, the Ngoni, the Tonga, the Lunda, the Luvale and the Kaonde.

THE LOZI

The Lozi migrated into Western Zambia from the Luba Lunda Kingdom of Mwata Yamvwa in Zaire, which was one of the greatest central African chieftainships in the 17th and 18th centuries. Eventually they were conquered by the Makalolo from the south, themselves fleeing from the great Zulu conqueror, Shaka. They left their language, Sikololo, as the lingua franca of the Barotse plains and imposed much of their cultural tradition on the area. The Lozi people eventually rose up against them in 1864 and all but annihilated them. Their Chief is called the Litunga and they are essentially cattlemen. Every year they migrate to higher ground above the Barotse floodplains of the Zambezi in a grand ceremony called the Kuomboka.

THE BEMBA

Representing some 18% of the population, the Bemba, along with the Lunda, recognize an almost legendary place called Kola as their land of origin. Historically they were nomadic hunter-gatherers. Their paramount chief is called the Chitimukulu. When copper mining began in earnest on the Copperbelt, the Bemba-speaking people came down for jobs in force.

THE NGONI

Originally from South Africa, also fleeing the Great Shaka Zulu, the Ngoni migrated into Eastern Zambia and adopted the fighting tactics of Shaka. They conquered indigenous tribes there with ease. The day they crossed over the Zambezi was a momentous occasion marked by an eclipse of the sun and ceremonial beer drinking, stories of which are still told to this day. They ruled this area

There are more than 73 different tribes in Zambia

in peace until they were conquered by colonial government in 1897, with troops coming in from Nyasaland (Malawi). Their warlike festival of Nc'wala was suppressed until independence and then revived. Today the Ngoni speak Chichewa, the language of the people they conquered. Many of their cultural traditions remain and, at the annual independence celebrations every October, their dances are well known.

THE TONGA

Among the most numerous in Zambia, archaeological evidence proves their existence for at least 900 years in the Southern province. Six centuries ago, one of the areas where they now live, the Zambezi Valley, was a flourishing trade centre. Here there was brisk trade between the valley people and the Arabs, Chinese and Indians on the east coast of Africa. One form of currency used was a copper ingot cast in the form of a cross.

THE LUNDA

Now living in the Luapula area and North Western province, the Lunda people are descendants of the original Mwata Yamvwa chieftainship in Zaire.

THE LUVALE

Coming from the north of Lake Tanganyika, their first chief was a woman named Kenga Naweji. Descendants of these people are the Valuvale, Valuchase, Vambunda, Vachokwe and Vaviya tribes living in the North Western province. The Luvale were for centuries great travellers and traders; much of their culture recalls their contact with the Portuguese on the Angolan coast, 500 years ago.

THE KAONDE

The Kaonde People can be found in Solwezi, Kasempa and Chizera districts of the North Western province and in Kaoma in the Western province. The Kaonde, like the Lunda, are the descendants of the famous Luba Lunda Empire of Zaire. The Kaonde were among the first Zambian tribes to carry out the mining of copper, and archaeological evidence at the Kansanshi Mine in Solwezi dating back to the iron age period proves this.

WHITE ZAMBIANS

There are a small number of white Zambians who trace their families back to colonial immigrants who came over during British rule. Most regard themselves as Zambians rather than British. Many of the country's businesses are owned and run by white Zambians.

ASIAN ZAMBIANS

Like the white Zambians, many people of Asian origin came to Zambia during the colonial period. When the British ruled colonies in Africa and India, there was a large movement of labour from Asia to Africa. The Asian Zambians are an affluent group of people retaining a strong sense of Asian identity and culture.

NOTICE!

Despite a large number of tribes and languages (over 70), Zambia has never suffered any ethnic conflicts or civil wars. Zambians are reknown to be very peaceful

HEALTH AND EDUCATION

The government has a policy of universal free primary education and health care. Health facilities, however, are grossly inadequate with only half the required doctors needed to service the population.

Some 95% of primary school age children are enrolled at schools, with 20% continuing to secondary level and 2% of the 20 to 24 age group in tertiary level. Illiteracy is only 27% but the drop-out rate at schools is very high. In rural areas, the standard of education is hampered by lack of facilities, transport and teachers.

LANGUAGES

There are over 73 dialects spoken in Zambia, but the official language is English. All media and business is in

English and most Zambians speak it fairly well. Bemba is the next most commonly understood language, followed by Nyanja Tonga, Luvale, Lozi, Mambwe and Tumbuka.

While it is normal to speak English plus a local language, a number of Zambians speak fluently a number of local languages.

RELIGIONS

There is freedom of worship in Zambia with over 15 different churches. Christianity is followed by over 60% of the population.

There is also a large group of Hindus and Muslims originating from the Asian communities. At the same time, traditional African beliefs are widely adhered to.

PUBLIC HOLIDAYS

Thursday 1st January – New Year's Day
Friday 12th March – Youth Day
Friday 9th April – Good Friday
Saturday 10th April – Holy Saturday
Monday 12th April – Easter Day
Saturday 1st May – Labour Day
Tuesday 25th May – Africa Freedom Day
Monday 5th July – Heroes' Day
Tuesday 6th July – Unity Day
Monday 2nd August – Farmers' Day
Sunday 24th October – Independence Day
Monday 25th October – Public Holiday for Independence
Saturday 25th December – Christmas Day

NOTICE!

In most cases, if a holiday falls on a Sunday, the public holiday will be postponed to Monday.

The majority of Zambians are Christians and there are a significant number of Muslims and Hindus

BUSINESS HOURS

Government offices are open from 08h00 to 16h30, Monday to Friday. Some government offices are closed from 12h30 to 14h30.

Lunch hour for most companies is from 13h00 to 14h00. Most banks are open from 08h30 to 15h00, Monday to Friday. Only some are open on Saturday mornings.

Shops are generally open from 08h00 to 17h00, Monday to Friday, although some stay open until 19h00, and on Saturdays from 08h00 to 13h00, although some stay open until 17h00.

MONEY MATTERS

CURRENCY

Zambia's unit of currency is the kwacha. The kwacha has denominations of 20, 50, 100, 500, 1,000, 5,000, 10,000, 20,000 and 50,000 kwacha notes. Nobody uses ngwee coins any more as they are worthless.

Most used denominations are K500 and K1,000, K5,000, K10,000 and K20,000 notes.

The currency fluctuates quite regularly, usually from K3,000 for US $1 to K4,500 for US $1. The kwacha has had a tendency to appreciate in 2006 and is currently K3,400 for US $1.

There is no limit to the importation of foreign currency, provided it is declared on arrival through a currency declaration form. Zambia is also one of the rare countries with no exchange controls.

It's best to come into the country with either traveller's cheques or dollars or pounds, which can be exchanged at any of the many bureaux de change in the main towns.

The kwacha is the Zambian currency

Euros are not widely recognized and you might have some difficulty exchanging them. If you are offered an exchange on the black market at the borders, exercise extreme caution, as these people are notorious for cheating you without you even realizing it. Traveller's cheques attract a commission when changing to other currencies.

Inflation is still high but has been slowing down over the past two years. In 2005, the rate was 15%. For 2006, the estimated inflation rate is around 10%.

BANKS

Zambia has a number of international and local banks providing ATM services.

Barclays, Standard Chartered, Finance Bank and Zambia National Commercial Bank have ATM services. ATM machines can be found in all the major towns around the country.

NOTICE! See Business Resources section.

FOREX BUREAUX

Lusaka has many Forex bureaux, mostly located in Cairo Road and shopping malls like Arcades and Manda Hills. Dollars, euros, rands, pounds and most regional currencies can be exchanged for better rates than at the banks.
(See Business Resources section.)

CREDIT CARDS

Most hotels, restaurants, travel agencies and the bigger shops will take credit cards; however, they will charge a higher commission. Most of the bigger banks will advance local currency against a credit card. Standard Chartered, Barclays, Zambia National Commercial Bank (ZANACO) and Finance Bank have ATM machines which accept Visa cards for cash.

INDICATIVE PRICES

The cost of living in Zambia, and especially in Lusaka, can be very expensive if one wants to keep a westernized lifestyle as most products are imported.

Meal (high end)	K100,000
Housing (high end)	US $1,000
Bus fare	K2,000
Driver	K600,000 (monthly)
Maid	K500,000 (monthly)
Bottle of water	K1,500
Newspaper	K3,000
Taxi from town to Arcades	K20,000
1 hour in Internet café	K15,000

COMMUNICATIONS

FIXED LINES

The only phone operator is the state-owned company Zambia National Telecommunication Company (Zamtel). Their services have been improving over the past years but new lines are still difficult to obtain; it can take up to one month to get a phone line.

The international country access code for Zambia is 260. From inside Zambia, you dial 00 to get an international line followed by the country access code.

Public telephones are available in most public buildings, e.g. post offices, and there are phone and fax services along Cairo Road. International calls can also be made from a private home or large hotel. (Note the surcharge at hotels is quite high.)
Zamtel offers prepaid cards that can be used for landline phones (denomination K25,000 up to K250,000).

Rates per minute remain quite high for local calls (around K200 per minute) and most public phone services will charge you up to K2,000 per minute for calls or faxing. Rates are bound to improve in the years to come as Zambia is getting equipped with a fibre optic network.

In most northern provinces and remote parts of Zambia, only satellite phone is possible.

103: Local directory assistance
211: Zamtel recharge number and credit inquiry

Regional codes are:
Lusaka: 01
Livingstone: 02
Copperbelt: 03
Choma: 032
Chinsali: 04
Kabwe: 05
Chipata: 062
Petauke: 063
Chama: 064
Kaoma: 07
Kasemba: 08

RECOMMENDED PARTNER

Zamtel/ Cell Z
Head office (Ndola)
Provident House, P O Box 71630, Ndola
Tel: +260-2-612399
Fax: +260-2-615855

RECOMMENDED PARTNER

Lusaka Office
Cell Z Office, Church Road, Lusaka
Tel: +260-1-231996/ 256637

MOBILE PHONES

There are three mobile phone service providers, namely Celtel, MTN and Cell Z (Zamtel).

Although the entry price is very small (a SIM card can be bought for as little as K15,000), rates per minute are fairly high compared with other neighbouring countries. Recharge cards cost from K5,000 (around 1.2 units) to

Recharge cards for mobile phones and land lines are available

K100,000 (around 30 units). A unit is equal to a US dollar.

Recharge cards can be bought almost anywhere; however, small shops on the side of the roads will rarely have cards of higher denomination than K10,000.

Coverage is very good in urban areas, but the network doesn't reach all the provinces.

RECOMMENDED

MTN Zambia
Longolongo Road
P O Box 35464, Lusaka
Tel: +260-96-750750
Fax: +260-96-767100

RECOMMENDED

Celtel Zambia Limited
Celtel House, Nyerere Road, Woodlands
P O Box 320001, Lusaka
Tel: +260-1-250707
Fax: +260-1-250595
Website: www.celtel.com

A new company, Novitel, provides high quality, low-cost international phone calls and prepaid discount international calling services worldwide

Novitel
Provident House
P O Box 71630, Lusaka
Tel: +260-97-853717/95-853717
Email: telpatel@novitelonline.com
Website: www.novitel.net

SATELLITE PHONE

Satellite communication is compulsory in some areas, as remote parts of Zambia are not linked to the phone network and cell coverage is non-existent. Zamnet offers VSAT satellite services that can be installed easily and cost-effectively.

INTERNATIONAL CALLING CARDS

Novitel has an excellent international calling card with very competitive rates. The account can be recharged from anywhere in the world and calls can be made outside Zambia through the same card.

RECOMMENDED

Novitel
Provident House
P O Box 71630, Lusaka
Tel: +260-97-853717/ 95-853717
Email: telpatel@novitelonline.com
Website: www.novitel.net

INTERNET SERVICES

There are several Internet cafés in Lusaka, Livingstone and most major cities. Mostly found on Cairo Road or major shopping centres like Arcades and Manda Hills. The main Internet service providers are Zamtel, Zamnet, Coppernet and Microlink.

NOTICE!

Microlink Cyber Café in Arcades Shopping Centre is one of the fastest and most efficient wireless access Internet cafés.

Broadband and wireless access is developing very quickly in major towns and Internet connection is quite fast and efficient. In the remoter parts of Zambia, satellite Internet is possible.

RECOMMENDED PARTNER

Coppernet Solutions
Mukuba Pension House, Dedan Kimathi Road
P O Box 38671, Lusaka
Tel: +260-1-223333, 224444
Fax: +260-1-226666
Email: info@coppernet.zom
Website: www.coppernet.zm

RECOMMENDED PARTNER

Zamnet
P O Box 38299
Lusaka
Tel: +260-1-224149/59/227430/2

Email: sales@zamnet.zm

MAIL

Postal services are fairly well organized in Zambia and you should have no problem sending or receiving letters. In Lusaka, the main post office is located on Cairo Road.

For faster and international professional mail, choose courier services such as DHL, TNT or UPS.

Zambia Postal Services Corporation
Ndola (Headquarters), PO Box 71845
Tel: +260-2-613274
Cairo Road
Lusaka
Tel: +260-1-234407

NOTICE! **Find more addresses and phone numbers in the section Business Resources.**

BEFORE AND AFTER YOU ARRIVE

HEALTH AND SAFETY

Visitors from or passing through a yellow fever and cholera zone (most of tropical Africa and South America) must be able to produce a valid International Certificate of Vaccination. Air travellers who only pass through the airports of such a zone are exempt from the requirement. (See Health International/MARS and Speciality Emergency Services for medical rescue services.)

A yellow fever certificate is mandatory if you are travelling from an infected area. Vaccinations for cholera, tetanus and yellow fever are advised.

If you are visiting Zambia for a couple of weeks or so and don't plan to spend time staying in rural villages or poor urban neighbourhoods, or travelling by local transport, then no pre-departure vaccinations are necessary. In this case, malaria will be the greatest danger you will be facing, but can be avoided with proper precautions.

If you are planning on staying longer in the country, vaccinations are highly recommended. Yellow fever jabs are good for 10 years and confer high immunity. Yellow fever is a monkey disease but it can be spread by mosquitoes. Epidemics are very rare but the jab is a protection. You may be required to show your international immunization certificate as a proof of this when entering the country. Jabs against typhoid and hepatitis A and C are also advised if you are to stay for a long period of time.

Malaria is a common disease in Zambia. There is no vaccination for malaria and precautionary measures should be taken to minimize the risk: for a short stay, it is highly advisable to take anti-malarial tablets. Malaria is virulent in the low-lying areas of the country, which includes most of the good wildlife destinations. Take prophylactics two weeks before arrival and continue for two weeks after leaving.

For a long-term stay, tablets can be harmful to the liver and it is preferable to take preventive measures through sprays, mosquito nets etc.

High fever, headache, stiffness, pain in the joints and deep fatigue are the common symptoms of malaria. At any sign of the above symptoms, you should go for a malaria test and go to see a doctor.

NOTICE! **See Business Resources section for medical services.**

Tap water in the major towns is purified and perfectly safe to drink. In the more remote areas, always boil it first, except if you're staying at a lodge or hotel where drinking water is boiled already. However, bottled water is always preferable and available in all major towns.

Travellers should carry an adequate supply of their prescribed medicines with them, although chemists in the major centres now carry a wide range of medicines and first aid accessories. There are some emergency chemists open after hours and on Sundays in Lusaka.

SECURITY

For the most part, Zambians are very friendly and helpful and Zambia is one of the safest countries in Africa. As far as personal safety is concerned, one could easily hitch-hike alone throughout the country without a problem.

However, petty theft is as common as in any major city where unemployment is high. Be very aware when walking around carrying anything of value as there are master pick-pockets here and there. Never leave your vehicle unlocked and never change money on the streets. Carry minimum amounts of cash and keep it hidden or in a money belt. If possible, don't leave your car unattended. This is less of a problem in the rural areas.

ENTRY VISA REQUIREMENTS AND EXTENSIONS

Entry visa requirements for diplomats and United Nations personnel accredited to Zambia:

Gratis or official visas can be obtained at Zambian missions abroad or ports of entry on presentation of letters of accreditation.

Delegates coming to Zambia on confirmed government business:

Delegates from international organizations coming to Zambia can obtain entry visas at Zambian missions abroad or ports of entry provided they produce official invitation letters.

Tourists to Zambia:

All tourists will be issued with visas at ports of entry to Zambia or at Zambian missions abroad for a maximum of 90 days per year.

Private visitors:

Nationals of countries who require visas to enter Zambia for the purpose of visiting friends or relatives can be issued with visas at Zambian missions abroad or ports of entry for a maximum of 90 days per year.

Business visitors:

Nationals of countries who require visas coming as experts on business with organizations in Zambia can be issued with entry visas at ports of entry.

Transit visitors:

Nationals of countries who require visas can obtain them at Zambian missions abroad or ports of entry. A transit visa is valid for seven days.

Referred Visas:

Countries whose nationals do require a visa to enter Zambia: Benin, Burkina Faso, Cameroon, Chad, China, Cote D'Ivoire, Gabon, Gambia, Ghana, Greece, Guinea Bissau, Guinea Conakry, Hong Kong, India, Iran, Lebanon, Liberia, Mali, Niger, Nigeria, Pakistan, Papua New Guinea, Saudi Arabia, Senegal, Sierra Leone, South Korea, Sri Lanka, Turkey, United Arab Emirates.

Countries whose nationals do not require a visa to enter Zambia:

Nationals of all Commonwealth countries do not require visas to enter Zambia except for the following countries which, on a reciprocal basis, require visas:
Australia, Britain, Gambia, Ghana, India, New Zealand, Nigeria, Mozambique, Sri Lanka, Sierra Leone, Pakistan, Papua New Guinea, Ireland, Romania and forme Republic of Yugoslavia, which has signed visa abolition agreements with Zambia.

NOTICE!

As requirements do tend to change and vary from country to country, we strongly advise you contact your nearest Zambian Mission for all entry requirements.

RE-ENTRY VISAS

Private and business visitors wishing to visit neighbouring countries are issued with re-entry visas valid for seven days at internal immigration offices or border posts before departure from Zambia.

Holders of employment and entry permits are issued with re-entry visas valid for a maximum period of 90 days at internal offices. However, British nationals resident in Zambia holding entry permits are on a reciprocal basis exempted from re-entry visa requirements.

VISA FEES

British Nationals

Single entry – UK £35 (at port of entry), UK £33 (at London Zambian mission)
Double/multiple entry – UK £45
Transit – UK £35
Re-entry – K5,000
Day tripper – US $10.00

Other Nationals

Single entry – US $25.00
Multiple entry – US $80.00
Double entry – US $40.00
Transit entry – US $25.00
Re-entry – K5,000

Visas fees, unless authorized otherwise, must be paid in US dollars and British pounds only. Visa application forms can be downloaded from www.zhci.org.uk.

EXTENSION OF VISA

Visitors to Zambia are only allowed to stay in Zambia for a maximum period of 90 days in one year. To extend the length of stay, visitors need visa extension permits, which can be quite costly:

For tourists and private visitors: visiting permit (K500,000). To be applied for 30 days before the end of the 90-day period.

For business people and others: temporary permit (K2,000,000).

DEPARTURE TAX

Departure tax is US $20 (international flights) and US $5 (domestic flights), payable in hard currency (kwacha or dollars) on the day of departure at Lusaka International Airport. Traveller's cheques are not acceptable.

CUSTOMS

Travellers may, for their own consumption, import 2.5 litres of duty free beer, wine or spirits and 400 cigarettes or 500g of tobacco.

The following items may be imported into Zambia without incurring customs duty:

400 cigarettes or 500g of tobacco; one bottle of spirits and wine and 2.5 litres of beer (unopened); 1oz bottle of perfume.

Souvenirs may be exported without restriction but it is illegal to export from Zambia any article made from wild animal skins, ivory, shell, claw, horn, tooth or feathers of any protected creature. Offenders will have goods confiscated and heavy fines imposed.

Game trophies such as tooth, bone, horn, shell, claw, skin, hair, feather or other durable items are subject to export permits.

For further information on duty free, please contact the Directors General of Customs and Excise in Lusaka.

Information on customs can be obtained at:

Zambia Revenue Authority
Lusaka, Zambia
Tel: +260 1 229214/19
Fax: +260 1 227821
Website: www.zra.org.zm

NOTICE!

There are very strict laws concerning what you can take out of Zambia. Any products made from crocodile, elephant, rhino, tooth can only be exported with a licence and strict permit.

GETTING THERE AND AROUND

GETTING THERE

By Air

From Europe:

British Airways has regular services to Lusaka, flying from Heathrow Airport on Mondays, Wednesdays and Fridays and returning to London on Tuesdays, Thursdays and Saturdays.

From Africa:

African carriers flying to Lusaka include Air Zimbabwe, Ethiopian Airways, Air Malawi, Kenya Airways, South African Airways, Interair, Nationwide Airlines, Comair and Regional Air.

Many tourists fly directly to Victoria Falls with South African Airways or Nationwide Airlines.

From South Africa:

Interair flies directly to Ndola International Airport from Johannesburg three times a week.

Nationwide Airlines flies Johannesburg / Livingstone / Lusaka three times a week.

South African Airways flies to Johannesburg every day. Zambian Airways has recently opened a route to Johannesburg, flying six days a week for a better rate than South African Airways.

By Road

The most fabulous way of entering Zambia by road is over the Victoria Falls Bridge from Zimbabwe. The main route between Lusaka and Bulawayo, from where you can reach Harare, crosses the border here.

The other main border points with Zimbabwe are Chirundu and Kariba, where you cross between Zambia and

Lusaka International Airport

Zimbabwe over the massive Kariba Dam.

From Malawi, the main crossing point is east of Chipata, on the main road between Lusaka and Lilongwe.

The only crossing point between Zambia and Botswana is the ferry across the Zambezi River at Kazungula, about 60km (37 miles) west of Victoria Falls. From Namibia, buses run from Windhoek to the Namibian outpost town of Katima Mulilo. From here you can cross the border into Zambia, go over the Zambezi on a ferry, then go via Sesheke to Livingstone.

The Tanzanian entry point is through the Tunduma/Nakonde border post onto the Great North Road.

Access from Congo DR is via the Lumbumbashi to Chingola road.

There is no access from Angola as yet.

Road borders all open at 06h00 and close at 18h00 except Victoria Falls, which closes at 20h00.

To bring a vehicle into Zambia you must obtain a temporary import permit (TIP) at the border or, depending on the

Zambia Railways links Livingstone to Kitwe

country of origin, a carnet de passage. If the driver is not the owner of the vehicle they must have a letter from the owner authorizing the use of the vehicle in Zambia. You must also purchase third party insurance at the border. Have your vehicle papers on hand at all times as roadblocks are fairly frequent.

By Bus

There are buses from Dar es Salaam and Mbeya in Tanzania to the border, where Zambian buses can be caught to the Copperbelt and Lusaka. From Malawi, a private bus company runs the Lilongwe to Lusaka route. Booking in advance is essential. (See Listings section for buses.)

Intercape Mainliner and Translux have services to and from Johannesburg in South Africa. Their combined timetables make daily departures possible.

By Boat

Zambia is one of the five countries bordering Lake Tanganyika and a ferry operates from Burundi to Tanzania to Zambia and back once a week, arriving at and leaving the port of Mpulungu every Friday.

By Train

You can catch a train from South Africa to Victoria Falls in Zimbabwe, then take the ferry train across the bridge to Livingstone (two trains daily) and another train to Lusaka, the Copperbelt or the Northern province.

From Dar es Salaam in Tanzania, the TAZARA line runs through to Kapiri Mposhi, where you can catch another train to Lusaka or Kitwe on the Copperbelt. Customs and immigration are conducted on board.

Passenger trains in Zambia are run by Zambia Railways and Tanzania Railways.

Zambia Railways run the 'Zambezi Express' three days a week from Livingstone to Lusaka and three days a week a through train from Livingstone to Kapiri, Mposhi to Ndola to Kitwe. ZR trains are pretty ill maintained and often run very late.

Tanzania Zambia Railways runs the line from New Kapiri Mposhi (2km from the ZR stop) to Dar es Salaam TAZARA (8km from Dar es Salaam TRC station). There are domestic trains and twice a week (departing Tuesdays and Fridays) through trains, the 'Mukuba Express' and 'Kilimanjaro Express'.

Take the train more for the experience and adventure than as an efficient way to reach your destination!!

GETTING AROUND

By Air

Zambian Airways/Airwaves is the major carrier of tourist and business people within Zambia. They fly to all major tourist destinations in Zambia year round, connecting to and from all major international carriers.

Zambian Airways flies to Livingstone, Ndola, Mfue, Chipata, Harare and Johannesburg.

Proflight is another scheduled flight airline offering good regular service. They fly to Livingstone, Ndola, Chingola, Solwezi, Mfue, and shuttle twice weekly to Lower Zambezi. Many other air charter companies can organize internal flights around Zambia. Rates are much more expensive, but during low season when there are fewer scheduled flights, it's sometimes the only way to get to your destination. Charter flights are also much more able to access the remotest parts of Zambia.

See Business Resources section for a listing of airlines and air charter companies.

By Bus

All the bus companies are privately owned but prices are relatively standardized and most services run fairly regularly. Minibuses are available for shorter runs and tend to be faster and slightly more expensive than regular buses.

Crowded conditions and long hauls over potholed roads make travelling by bus wearisome. The buses are fairly old and most of the time the advertised 'air conditioning' is broken, but the conditions are fairly decent and relatively clean.

Long-range buses frequently leave from Lusaka to all the main towns. CR Coach will take you to Chipata, Livingstone, Ndola and Mongu.

There are buses from Dar es Salaam and Mbeya in Tanzania to the Copperbelt and Lusaka, as well as from Lilongwe and Harare to Lusaka. Other privately owned companies run domestic services over a number of routes.

The main bus station is located behind the Cairo Road Shoprite.

Local town minibuses are painted blue and can be jumped on at pretty much any juncture. They're not expensive and you can always find a minibus that won't cost too much to buy all the seats in it to get your own private minibus to wherever you want to go, but you'll have to negotiate so be sharp about the value of money.

By Taxi

There are many taxis available in Lusaka (blue Toyota Corollas). Prices are negotiable but remain high. It's better to negotiate the price for the day of the week.

As an example, Arcades to the town centre will cost you around K15,000 after negotiation.

By Road

Zambia has 38,763km of roads, 8,200km of which are tarred and another 8,000km all-weather gravel road. The rest range from reasonable to bad dirt roads.

In Zambia, one drives on the left hand side of the road. The general speed limit on national highways is 100km/h, secondary roads 100km/h and in urban built up areas 65km/h unless otherwise indicated. Visiting drivers must hold an International Driver's Licence.

The best way of getting around is undeniably by vehicle, preferably a 4WD. Avoid driving at night if possible as there are no road markings and potholes, and animals cross the roads when least expected.

Sections of the major routes to the north, south, east and west are nearly always undergoing pothole repairs.

Petrol is available at most of the major towns, but gets more expensive as you get further from the railway line. If travelling in the more remote areas, be sure to take extra supplies, as availability is not always guaranteed. If it's an emergency, try the local markets. They sometimes have bottles of petrol for sale.

Be sure to have all your vehicle papers on hand as you're bound to encounter a few roadblocks, and if you ever need to stop, pull well off the road.

Vehicle Permits

To bring a vehicle into Zambia you must obtain a temporary import permit (TIP) or, depending on the country of origin of the vehicle, a carnet de passage. If the driver is not the owner of the vehicle, they must have a letter of authorization from the owner for use of the vehicle in Zambia. Your local AA office should be consulted before leaving for Zambia to check whether any of these conditions have changed. Otherwise, write to the Controller of Customs and Excise.

Car Hire

There are many car hire companies in Lusaka, Ndola and Livingstone offering a small range of vehicles. Some offer a flat weekly rate but most charge a daily rate plus mileage, insurance and petrol. Most cars come with a chauffeur and are thus expensive. You can find long-term car hire from individuals or very small (unofficial) car rental companies for much cheaper rates.

NOTICE! **See Business Resources section.**

MISSIONS AND EMBASSIES

ZAMBIAN EMBASSIES ABROAD

Angola

106/108, Rua Rei Katyavala Maculusso

P O Box 1496, Luanda, Angola

Tel: +244-2-331145/31241

Fax: +244-2-331241

Belgium

469 Avenue Molière, 1050 Brussels

Tel: +32-2-3435646

Fax: +32-2-3474333

Botswana

Zambia House, 1118 Queens Road, The Mall

Tel: +267-351951

Fax: +267-353952

Email: zamhico@megabw

China

5 Dongsijie, San Li Tun, Beijing

Tel: +86-10-65321778/653221554

Fax: +86-10-65321891

Email: zamem@public.bta.net.en

Democratic Republic of Congo

54-58 Avenue de L'Ecole, Gombe

BP 1144, Kinshasa

Tel/Fax: +243-8845106

Ethiopia

Old Airport Area, Higher 23 Kebele 12

PO Box 1909, Addis Ababa

Tel: +251-1-711302

Fax: +251-1-711566

Email: zam.emb@telecom.net.et

Germany

Axel-Springer-Str. 54a

10117 Berlin

Tel: +49-30-2062940

Fax: +49-30-20629419

Email: BotschafvinSambia@t-online.de

India

C-79, Anand Niketan, New Delhi 110 021

Tel: +91-23101289/24101292

Fax: +91-24101520

Email: zambiand@sify.com

Japan

10-2 Ebara I-Chome,Shinagwa-Ku, Tokyo 142

Tel: +81-3-34910121

Fax: +81-3-34910123

Email: zamet@crisscross.com

Kenya

Nyerere Road,

PO Box 48741, Nairobi

Tel: +254-20-24850/2724796/2724799

Fax: +254-20-271894/2710664

Email: zambiacom@swiftkenya.com

Malawi

Area 40/2,

P O Box 30138, Lilongwe 3

Tel: +265-782635/782590

Fax: +265-782114/784349

Email: zambia@malawi.net

Mozambique

Avenida Kenneth Kaunda 1286,

P O Box 4655, Maputo

Tel: +258-1-492452/491307

Fax: +258-1-491893

Email: zhcmmap@zebra.uem.mz

Namibia

22 Sam Nujoma Drive/Mandume Ndemufayo Road

P O Box 22882, Windhoek

Tel: +264-61-26461-237610/1

Fax: +264-61-228162

Nigeria

Plot 767, Off Pnama Crescent, Minister's Hill, Maitana

PMB 5055, WUSE, Abuja

Tel: +234-9-2347060
Fax: +234-9-2348855

Russia
Prospect Mira 52 A, Moscow
Tel: +7-095-6810752/6885001/6885083
Fax: +7-095-6885092
Email: zambiana@online.ru

South Africa
Sanlan Building, 353 Festival Road,
P O Box12234, Hatfield 0028, Pretoria
Tel: +27-12-3261847
Fax: +27-12-3262140

Sweden
Engelbrektstgatan 7
PO Box 26013, Stockholm
Tel: +46-8-799040
Fax: +46-8-796850
Email: info@zambiaembassy.se
Website: www.zambiaembassy.se

Switzerland
17-19 Chemin Du Champ-D'Anier, 1209 Le Petit-Saconnex, Geneva
Tel: +41-22-7885330/1
Fax: +41-22-7885340

Tanzania
5 & 8 Ohio/Sokoine Drive,
PO Box 2525, Dar es Salaam
Tel/Fax: +255-22-2125529
Email: zhcd@raha.com

United Kingdom
Zambia House, 2 Palace Gate, London W8 5NG
Tel: +44-207-5896655
Fax: +44-207-5811353

United States of America
9th Floor, 800 Second Avenue, NY-10017
Tel: +1-212-8885770
Fax: +1-212-8885213
Email: zambia@un.int

United States of America
2419 Massachusetts Avenue, Washington DC
Tel: +1-202-2659717
Fax: +1-202-3320826
Email: zambia@tmn.com

Zimbabwe
48 Union Road, Zambia House
PO Box 4698, Harare
Tel: +263-4-773777/81
Fax: +263-4-773782
Email: zambia@primenetzw.com

FOREIGN EMBASSIES IN ZAMBIA

Angola
6660 Mumana Road
P O Box 31595, Lusaka
Tel: +260-1-290346/291142
Fax: +260-1-292592/5

Botswana
5201 Pandit Nehru Road, Diplomatic Triangle
P O Box 31910, Lusaka
Tel: +260-1-250555/250019/252058
Fax: +260-1-253895

Canada
United Nations Avenue
P O Box 31313, Lusaka
Tel: +260-1-250833
Fax: +260-1-254176
Email: lsaka@paris03.x400.gc.ca

China
United Nations Avenue
P O Box 31975, Lusaka
Tel: +260-1-253770/252410
Fax: +260-1-251157

Cuba
5574 Magoye Road, Kalundu
P O Box 33132, Lusaka
Tel: +260-1-291308/80

Fax: +260-1-291586

Cyprus (Consulate)
P O Box 32922, Lusaka
Tel: +260-1-262931
Fax: +260-1-263004

Denmark
Ndeke House Annexe, Haile Selassie Avenue
P O Box 50299, Lusaka
Tel: +260-1-254277/254182/253750
Fax: +260-1-254618

Egypt
United Nations Avenue, Longacres
P O Box 32458, Lusaka
Tel: +260-1-250229/254149

Germany
5209 United Nations Avenue
P O Box 50120, Lusaka
Tel: +260-1-250644/251259/251262
Fax: +260-1-254014

France
4th Floor, Anglo American Building, 74 Independence Avenue
P O Box 30062, Lusaka
Tel: +260-1-251322/251340
Fax: +260-1-254475

Greece (Consulate)
5 Joseph Mwila Road, Fairview
P O Box 31587, Lusaka
Tel: +260-1-231064/20

India
1 Pandit Nehru Road
P O Box 32111, Lusaka
Tel: +260-1-253159/60
Fax: +260-1-254118
Email: indiazam@zamnet.zm

Ireland (Development Corporation Office)
6663 Katima Mulilo Road, Olympia Extension
P O Box 34923, Lusaka
Tel: +260-1-291124/290650
Fax: +260-1-290482

Italy
Plot No 5211 Embassy Park, Diplomatic Triangle
P O Box 31046, Lusaka
Tel: +260-1-250755/250783
Fax: +260-1-254929
Email: italyzam@zamnet.zm

Japan
5218 Haile Selassie Avenue
P O Box 34190, Lusaka
Tel: +260-1-251555
Fax: +260-1-253488

Kenya
5207 United Nations Avenue
P O Box 50298, Lusaka
Tel: +260-1-250722/ 250742/250751
Fax: +260-1-253829

Korea
Private Bag E35, Lusaka
Tel: +260-1-239415/286335

Libya
Los Angeles Boulevard
P O Box 35319, Lusaka
Tel/Fax: +260-1-251239

Malawi
5th Floor, Woodgate House, Cairo Road
P O Box 50425, Lusaka
Tel: +260-1-228296-8
Fax: +260-1-223353

Mozambique
Plot 9592 Kacha Road, Northmead
P O Box 34877, Lusaka
Tel: +260-1-220333
Fax: +260-1-220345

Namibia
6968 Kabanga Road, Rhodes Park
P O Box 30577, Lusaka
Tel: +260-1-252250/250968
Fax: +260-1-252497

Netherlands
Plot 5208, United Nations Avenue
P O Box 31905, Lusaka
Tel: +260-1-253819/ 253590/253994
Fax: +260-1-253733/ 250220

Nigeria
Pandit Nehru Road
P O Box 32598, Lusaka
Tel: +260-1-253177/ 253365/253268
Fax: +260-1-253560

Norway
65 Bird Cage Walk, Haile Selassie Avenue
P O Box 34570, Lusaka
Tel: +260-1-252188/252625
Fax: +260-1-253915

Poland
Protea House, Chachacha Road
P O Box 30529, Lusaka
Tel: +260-1-224448

Portugal
23 Yotam Muleya Road, Woodlands
P O Box 33871, Lusaka
Tel: +260-1-253720/ 260296
Fax: +260-1-253893/6

Romania
Chancery: 2 Leopards Hill Road, Kabulonga
PO Box 33871, Lusaka
Tel: +260-1-262239

Russia
Plot No 6407, Diplomatic Triangle
P O Box 32355, Lusaka
Tel: +260-1-252128/252120/252183
Fax: +260-1-253582

Somalia
377A Kabulonga Road
P O Box 34051, Lusaka
Tel: +260-1-262119/263944

South Africa
26D Cheetah Road, Kabulonga
Private Bag W369, Lusaka
Tel: +260-1-260999
Fax: +260-1-263001

Sweden
Haile Selassie Avenue, opposite Ndeke House
P O Box 30788, Lusaka
Tel: +260-1-251249/251711
Fax: +260-1-254049

Switzerland (Consulate)
Lumumba Road
P O Box 31189, Lusaka
Tel: +260-1-223838

Tanzania
Ujamaa House, 5200 United Nations Avenue
P O Box 31219, Lusaka
Tel: +260-1-253222/253320/23/24
Fax: +260-1-254861

United Kingdom
Diplomatic Triangle, 5210 Independence Avenue
P O Box 50050, Lusaka
Tel: +260-1-251133
Fax: +260-1-253798

United States
Independence Avenue (Corner of United Nations Avenue)
P O Box 31617, Lusaka
Tel: +260-1-250955
Fax: +260-1-252225

Zimbabwe
4th Floor, Memaco House, Cairo Road
P O Box 33491, Lusaka
Tel: +260-1-254006

European Communities Delegation
Plot 4899, Los Angeles Boulevard
P O Box 34871, Lusaka
Tel: +260-1-250711/251140/255583/250179/255585
Fax: +260-1-252336/ 250906
Email: delegation-zambia@cec.eu.int
Website: www.delzmb.cec.eu.int

NOTICE! For those countries not featured, please contact the Ministry of Foreign Affairs in your own country for updates on the Honorary Consul who represents you in Zambia.

INTERNATIONAL ORGANIZATIONS

Agency for International Development
US Embassy
Independence Avenue (Corner of United Nations Avenue)
P O Box 31617, Lusaka
Tel: +260-1-229326

Common Market for Eastern and Southern Africa (COMESA)
The Comesa Centre, Ben Bella Road
P O Box 30051, Lusaka
Tel: +260-1-229725/32
Fax: +260-1-225107/228849
Email: secgen@comesa.int
Website: www.comesa.int

European Union
Plot 4899, Los Angeles Boulevard
P O Box 34871, Lusaka
Tel: +260-1-250711/251140/255583/250179/255585
Fax: +260-1-252336/ 250906
Email: delegation-zambia@cec.eu.int
Website: www.delzmb.cec.eu.int

International Monetary Fund (IMF)
5199 United Nations Avenue
P O Box 50846 Lusaka
Tel: +260-1-254716
Fax: +260-1-253485

United Nations Development Programme (UNDP)
P O Box 31966, Lusaka
Tel: +260-1-250800

World Bank
Anglo American Building, Independence Avenue, Lusaka
Tel: +260-1-250516/ 250480

World Health Organization (WHO)
P O Box 32346, Lusaka
Tel: +260-1-255039/253688/255398

Traveling through Zambia by train, a poetic way to get the African experience

BUSINESS RESOURCES

" Wisdom can come even from a small anthill"
Zambian proverb

ADVERTISING AGENCIES

Captive Promotions
Plot 2398, Longolongo Road
Post Net Private Bag E835, Kabulonga Box 149, Lusaka
Tel: +260-1-222443/96-730261
Email: captive@zamtel.zm

RECOMMENDED PARTNER

D&C Saatchi & Saatchi
Former 1st Alliance Bank, 64 Chachacha Road, Lusaka
Tel: +260-1-235530-1
Fax: +260-1-235532

Young & Rubicam
Zone F, 2nd Floor, Comesa Centre, Ben Bella Road
P O Box 32497, Lusaka
Tel: +260-1-228489-91
Fax: +260-1-225173

AIRLINES

Air Malawi
Zone D, Comesa Centre, Ben Bella Road
P O Box 36384, Lusaka
Tel: +260-1-228120
Fax: +260-1-228124
Email: airmalawi@zamnet.zm

Air Zimbabwe
Chachacha Road
P O Box 35191, Lusaka
Tel: +260-1-225431/271148

Avocet Air Link
P O Box 32056, Lusaka
Tel: +260-1-229261/233422
Fax: +260-1-229261

British Airways
Holiday Inn, Church Road
P O Box 32006, Lusaka
Tel: +260-1-254984/255320
Fax: +260-1-250623
Email: contactba.1.zambia@britishairways.com
Website: www.ba.com

Many companies offer air charter services to reach remote regions of Zambia

Kenyan Airways
Comesa Centre, Ben Bella Road
Tel: +260-1-228908
Airport Office
P O Box 31856, Lusaka
Tel: +260-1-271042

RECOMMENDED PARTNER

Proflight
Stand 15b, Private Hangars,
Lusaka International Airport
P O Box 30536, Lusaka
Tel: +260-1-271036
Fax: +260-1-271139
Website: www.proflight-zambia.com

South African Airways
Intercontinental Hotel
P O Box 34150, Lusaka
Tel: +260-1-254350
Airport Office
Tel: +260-1-271101
Email: saa@zamnet.zm

TAAG-Angolan Airlines
1st Floor North Exchange Building, Central Park, Cairo Road
P O Box 37731, Lusaka
Tel: +260-1-238634
Fax: +260-1-222401

RECOMMENDED PARTNER

Zambian Airways
Lusaka International Airport
Tel: +260-1-271230/271342
Intercontinental Hotel Office
P O Box 310277, Lusaka
Tel: +260-1-258586/8
Fax: +260-1-256589
Ndola Office
Tel/Fax: +260-2-621466
Kitwe Office
Tel/Fax: +260-2-231316
Email: Zambian-airways@zamnet.zm

BANKS

African Banking Corporation Zambia Limited
4th Floor National Savings and Credit Bank Building, Cairo Road
P O Box 39501, Lusaka
Tel: +260-1-234541
Fax: +260-1-234542
Email: abcz@africanbankingcorp.com
Website: www.africanbankingcorp.com

Barclays Bank Zambia
Kafue House, Cairo Road
P O Box 31936, Lusaka
Tel: +260-1-228858
Fax: +260-1-226185

Cavmont Capital Bank Limited
Mezzanine Floor, Anchor House, Sepele Road
P O Box 38474, Lusaka
Tel: +260-1-229508/12/224280/6/7
Fax: +260-1-224304/224313

Central Bank of Zambia
Cairo Road
P O Box 30080, Lusaka
Tel: +260-1-228888
Fax: +260-1-222375
Email: pr@boz.zm
Website: www.boz.zm

Finance Bank
Chinika House, Cairo Road
P O Box 37102, Lusaka
Tel: +260-1-229733-40
Fax: +260-1-223359
Email: fbz@financebank.co.zm
Website: www.financebank.co.zm

Indo-Zambia Bank Ltd
Cairo Road
P O Box 6907, Lusaka
Tel: +260-1-224653/225080
Fax: +260-1-225090
Email: izb@zamnet.zm

Intermarket Discount House
Farmers' House, Corner of Cairo and Church Road
P O Box 35832, Lusaka
Tel: +260-1-227227/8/220927/9
Fax: +260-1-227227/8/220927/9
Website: www.intermarket.co.zm

Investrust Bank Plc
Plot No. 4527/8, Freedom Way
P O Box 32344, Lusaka
Tel: +260-1-238733/235284
Fax: +260-1-235497/237060
Email: fcn@investrustbank.co.zm

National Savings and Credit Bank
Plot 248B, Cairo Road
P O Box 30067, Lusaka
Tel: +260-1-227534
Fax: +260-1-223296

Most banks and Forex bureaux are located on Cairo Road

Stanbic Bank
Woodgate House, Nairobi Place, Cairo Road
P O Box 31955, Lusaka
Tel: +260-1-229285/6/229071/3/224809
Fax: +260-1-225380

RECOMMENDED
Standard Chartered Bank
Standard Chartered House, Cairo Road
P O Box 32238, Lusaka
Tel: +260-1-229242
Email: customer.first@zm.standardchartered.com

Zambia National Commercial Bank
Main Branch, Zimco House, Cairo Road
P O Box 33611, Lusaka
Tel: +260-1-229592/221358
Fax: +260-1-224005/6
Email: lumbweb@zanaco.co.zm
Website: www.zanaco.co.zm

NOTICE!
For more information see finance section

CARGO

Global Logistics Limited
7437 Mungwi Road
P O Box 30101, Lusaka
Tel: +260-1-243581/253584/243595
Fax: +260-1-243559

Hill & Delamain
P O Box 30899, Lusaka,
Tel: +260-1-241182/2446444/51
Fax: + 260-1-241616/260964/247216
Email: hdcargo@zamnet.zm
Kitwe Office
P O Box 21752, Kitwe
Tel: +260-2-210680

RECOMMENDED
Kuehne & Nagel
Plot 8131, Corner Kasombola and Mwembeshi Roads, Light Industrial Area
P O Box 34040, Lusaka
Tel: +260-1-287870/287742
Fax: +260-1-287871
Cell: +260-96-755777
Email: juwayhir.weltin@kuehne-nagel.com

CATERERS

Intercontinental Hotel
Haile Selassie Road
P O Box 32201, Lusaka
Tel: +260-1-250000/250600
Email: Lusaka@interconti.com
Website: www.intercontinental.com

Taj Pamodzi Hotel
Corner of Church Road and Addis Ababa Drive
P O Box 35450, Lusaka
Tel: +260-1-250995/254455
Fax: +260-1-254005
Website: www.tajhotels.com

Gerritz Restaurant
26 Chaholi Road, off Addis Ababa Road, Lusaka
Tel: +260-1-253639

COMMUNICATIONS

RECOMMENDED PARTNER
Zamtel/ Cell Z
Head Office (Ndola), Provident House
P O Box 71630, Ndola
Tel: +260-2-612399
Fax: +260-2-615855
Lusaka Office
Cell Z Office, Church Road
Tel: +260-1-231996/256637

RECOMMENDED
MTN Zambia
Longolongo Road
P O Box 35464, Lusaka
Tel: +260-96-750750
Fax: +260-96-767100

Celtel Zambia Limited
Celtel House, Nyerere Road, Woodlands
P O Box 320001, Lusaka
Tel: +260-1-250707

Fax: +260-1-250595

Website: www.celtel.com

Novitel

Provident House

P O Box 71630, Lusaka

Cell: +260-97-853717/95-853717

Email: telpatel@novitelonline.com

Website: www.novitel.net

Zambia Postal Services Corporation

Ndola (Headquarters)

P O Box 71845, Ndola

Tel: +260-2-613274

Lusaka Office

Cairo Road, Lusaka

Tel: +260-1-234407

Website: www.zampost.co.zm

Post Net Zambia

Arcades Shopping Centre, Great East Road, Lusaka

Tel: +260-1-252617

CONFERENCE FACILITIES

Fairview Hotel

Church Road

Private Bag E186, Lusaka

Tel: +260-1-222604

Email: Fairview@zamnet.zm

Hotel Edinburgh

Obote Avenue, Kitwe

Tel: +260-2-222444

Fax: +260-2-225036

Email: edinburgh@microlink.zm

Intercontinental Hotel

Haile Selassie Avenue

P O Box 32201, Lusaka

Tel: +260-1-250000/250600

Email: Lusaka@interconti.com

Website: www.intercontinental.com

Mulungushi Conference Centre offers modern facilities in a quiet environment in the heart of Lusaka

Lalayi Lodge
Off Kufue Road (Lilayi Turnoff), Lusaka
Tel: +260-1-279022-5
Fax: +260-1-279026
Email: lilayi@zamsaf.co.zm
Website: www.lilayi.com

RECOMMENDED
Mulungushi Conference Centre
Great East Road
P O Box 37157, Lusaka
Tel: +260-1-290270

Mulungushi Village
Lusemfwa Road
P O Box 37157, Lusaka
Tel: +260-1-291416/292629
Fax: +260-1-290830
Email: mvc@zamnet.zm
Website: www.mulungushivillage.com

RECOMMENDED
Sun International / Royal Livingstone
P O Box 50151, Livingstone
Tel: +260-3-321122
Fax: +260-3-322225
Email: sunint@coppernet.zm or zamres1@sunint.co.za

RECOMMENDED
Taj Pamodzi Hotel
Church Road
P O Box 35450, Lusaka
Tel: +260-1-250995/254455
Fax: +260-1-254005
Website: www.tajhotels.com

COURIER EXPRESS

RECOMMENDED PARTNER
DHL International
Corner of Makishi Road
to Parirenyatwa Road
P O Box 31395, Lusaka
Tel: +260-1-228212
Lusaka International Airport
Tel: +260-1-271465

FedEx Express
4174 Nangwenya Road, Rhodes Park, Lusaka

DHL offices on Makishi Road

Tel: +260-1-252189/252191

Fax: +260-1-252585

Mercury Couriers

P O Box 33333, Lusaka

Tel: +260-1-239872

CONSULTANTS / ACCOUNTANTS

BDO Spencer Steward Zambia Chartered Accountants

Stand No. 2374, Bata Boulevard Showgrounds

P O Box 35139, Lusaka

Tel: +260-1-250222/250631/254166

Fax: +260-1-254623

Email: administrator@bdo.co.zm

CYMA Chartered Accountants and Management Consultants

4th Floor, Electra House, Cairo Road

P O Box 38298, Lusaka

Tel: +260-1-231960

Fax: +260-1-236779

Email: cyma@zamtel.zm

Deloitte and Touche

Kafue House, Cairo Road

Central Post Office and Western Union services on Cairo Road

P O Box 30030, Lusaka
Tel: +260-1-228677
Fax: +260-1-228744

Ernst and Young
Development House, Corner of Chachacha and Katondo Roads
P O Box 32385, Lusaka
Tel: +260-1-237785
Fax: +260-1-227022

Grant Thornton Chartered Accountants
5th Floor, Mukuba Pension House, Dedan Kimathi Road
P O Box 30885, Lusaka
Tel: +260-1-227722/28/226683/223476
Fax: +260-1-223774
Email: gt@gt.com.zm

KPMG
Corner of Nkwazi and Chachacha Roads
P O Box 31014, Lusaka
Tel: +260-1-228875

DRY CLEANERS

Classique Cleaners
Cairo Road, North End, Lusaka
Tel: +260-1-227042/223343
Fax: +260-1-220769
Email: classiq@coppernet.zm

Lusaka Dry Cleaners
Chiparamba Road
P O Box FW 236, Lusaka
Tel: +260-1-235409
Fax: +260-1-235409
Email: lussteam@zamnet.zm

Multiserv Dry Cleaning
Arcades Shopping Centre, Great East Road, Lusaka
Tel: +260-95-883749

FOREX BUREAUX

Delta Bureau de Change
P O Box 34277, Lusaka
Tel: +260-1-238803
Email: unitran@pop3.zamnet.zm

Unifinance Bureau de Change
Cairo Road
P O Box 35495, Lusaka
Tel: +260-1-237575
Email: bcm@zamnet.zm

Runnymede Bureau de Change
Arcades Shopping Centre, Great East Road, Lusaka
Tel: +260-1-256669

HAIR AND BEAUTY

Jasmine Beauty Parlour
5A Omelo Mumber Road, Rhodes Park, Lusaka
Cell: +260-97-807752/773580

Le Soleil
Zambezi Road, Roma Extension, Lusaka
Tel: +260-1-212437
Cell: +260-95-802533/97-802533
Email: pilatus@zamnet.zm

Salon La Chic Hair Care
Shop 9, Hotel Intercontinental Shopping Arcade
P O Box 31170, Lusaka
Tel: +260-1-250000/250617 Ext. 2170

Salon Namel
Manda Hill Shopping Complex, Lusaka
Tel: +260-1-255513

Scruples Hair and Beauty Salon
Arcades Shopping Centre, Great East Road, Lusaka
Tel: +260-1-256608

HEALTH CLUBS /SPORTS

Active Bodies
Great East Road
P O Box 34040, Lusaka
Tel: +260-1-290285

Bowling Alley
Arcades Shopping Centre, Great East Road, Lusaka
Tel: +260-1-256601/2

Chrismar Hotel
Los Angeles Boulevard
P O Box 36043, Lusaka
Tel: +260-1-253036/253605
Fax: +260-1-252569
Email: chrismar@zamnet.zm
Website: www.chrismar.co.zm

Intercontinental Hotel
Haile Selassie Avenue
P O Box 32201, Lusaka
Tel: +260-1-250000/250600
Email: Lusaka@interconti.com
Website: www.intercontinental.com

Holiday Inn
Church Road
P O Box 30666, Lusaka
Tel: +260-1-251666
Fax: +260-1-253529
Email: holinn@zamnet.zm
Website: www.holiday-inn.com/lusakaridgeway

Lusaka Golf Club
Los Angeles Boulevard
P O Box 31254, Lusaka
Tel: +260-1-250697

Polo Club
Nangwenya Road, Lusaka
Tel: +260-1-255200

Chainama Hills Golf Club
Kamloops Road, Lusaka
Tel: +260-1-290073

Millennium Village Complex
Birdcage Walk, Longacres, Lusaka
Tel: +260-1-228842
Fax: +260-1-228665
Email: lafico@coppernet.zm

Taj Pamodzi Hotel
Church Road
P O Box 35450, Lusaka
Tel: +260-1-250995/254455

HOTELS

NOTICE!

See Tourism and Leisure section.

INSURANCE

Madison Insurance Company Zambia
Plot 255 Kaleya Road
P O Box 37013, Lusaka
Tel: +260-1-295311
Fax: +260-1-295320
Email: Madison@zamnetzambia.com
Website: www.madisonzambia.com
Ndola Office
P O Box 73842, Ndola
Tel: +260-2-619019/617714

Nico Insurance
1131 Parirenyatwa Road, Fairview
P O Box 32825, Lusaka
Tel: +260-1-222862/226547
Fax: +260-1-222863

Professional Insurance
Cairo Road
P O Box 34264, Lusaka
Tel: +260-1-220219/227509
Fax: +260-1-222863
Email: nicozam@zamnet.zm

The Alliance Française: to mix culinary pleasures with language skills!

Zambia State Insurance Corporation
Premium House, Independence Avenue
P O Box 30894, Lusaka
Tel: +260-1-229343/57
Email: zisc@zisc.co.zm
Website: www.zsic.co.zm
Kitwe Office
P O Box 20217, Kitwe
Tel: +260-2-226865

Zigi Insurance Company Limited
5th Floor Mukuba Pension House, Dedan Kimathi Road
P O Box 37782, Lusaka
Tel: +260-1-226835/231757
Email: zigi@zamnet.zm
Kitwe Office
12 Kantana Street, Kitwe
Tel: +260-2-222130

INTERNET PROVIDERS

RECOMMENDED PARTNER

Coppernet Solutions
Mukuba Pension House, Dedan Kimathi Road
P O Box 38671, Lusaka
Tel: +260-1-223333, 224444
Fax: +260-1-226666
Email: info@coppernet.zom
Website: www.coppernet.zm

Microlink
Farmers' House, Cairo Road
P O Box 35681, Lusaka
Tel: +260-1-222764
Website: www.microlink.zm

UUNET Zambia
3rd Floor NSCB Building, Cairo Road, North End, Lusaka
Tel: +260-1-223715
Fax: +260-1-223716
Email: elisha@zm.uu.net

Website: www.uunet.co.zm

Zamtel
Head Office (Ndola), Provident House
P O Box 71630, Ndola
Tel: +260-2-612399
Fax: +260-2-615855
Lusaka Office
Cell Z Office, Church Road
Tel: +260-1-231996/256637

RECOMMENDED PARTNER

Zamnet
P O Box 38299
Lusaka
Tel: +260-1-224149/59/227430/2
Email: sales@zamnet.zm

INTERNET CAFÉS

Coppernet Solutions
Silicon House
P O Box 22149, Kitwe
Tel: +260-2-245700/245011
Fax: +260-2-245734
Email: sales@coppernet.zm

Zone Internet Café
Arcades Shopping Centre, Great East Road, Lusaka
Tel: +260-1-256747

LANGUAGE CENTRES AND INTERNATIONAL SCHOOLS

Alliance Française
Alick Nkhata Avenue
P O Box 30948, Lusaka
Tel: +260-1-253467
Email: afl@microlink.zm

The International School of Lusaka
6945 Nangwenya Road, Ridgeway
PO Box 50121, Lusaka
Tel: +260-1-252291/253959
Fax: +260-1-252865/250351

Email: isladmin@zamnet.zm

LEGAL SERVICES

MNB Legal Practitioners
5th Floor, Godfrey House, Longolongo Road
P O Box 34207, Lusaka
Tel: +260-1-236920/236921
Fax: +260-1-236134
Email: mnb@zamnet.zm

MNB Legal Practitioners
1st Floor, Mukuba Pension House, President Avenue
P O Box 20817, Kitwe
Tel: +260-2-231863
Fax: +260-2-231862
Email: mnbkitwe@zamnet.zm

Musa Dudhia & Co, Advocates and Notaries
Comesa Centre, 2nd Floor, Zone C, Ben Bella Road
P O Box 31198, Lusaka
Tel: +260-1-228426-30
Fax: +260-1-227188/222603
Email: musadud@zamnet.zm

MEDIA

The Post Newspaper
Bwijinfumu Road
Private Bag E352, Lusaka
Tel: +260-1-226027/226493/231093

Times of Zambia Newspaper
Freedom Way, North End
P O Box 30394, Lusaka
Tel: +260-1-229076

RECOMMENDED PARTNER

Directory Publishers of Zambia
54 Independence Avenue
P O Box 30963, Lusaka
Tel: +260-1-257133
Fax: + 260-1-257137
Email: dpzsales@coppernet.co.zm
Website: www.yellowpages.co.zm
Publishing House for the official Zambia Telephone

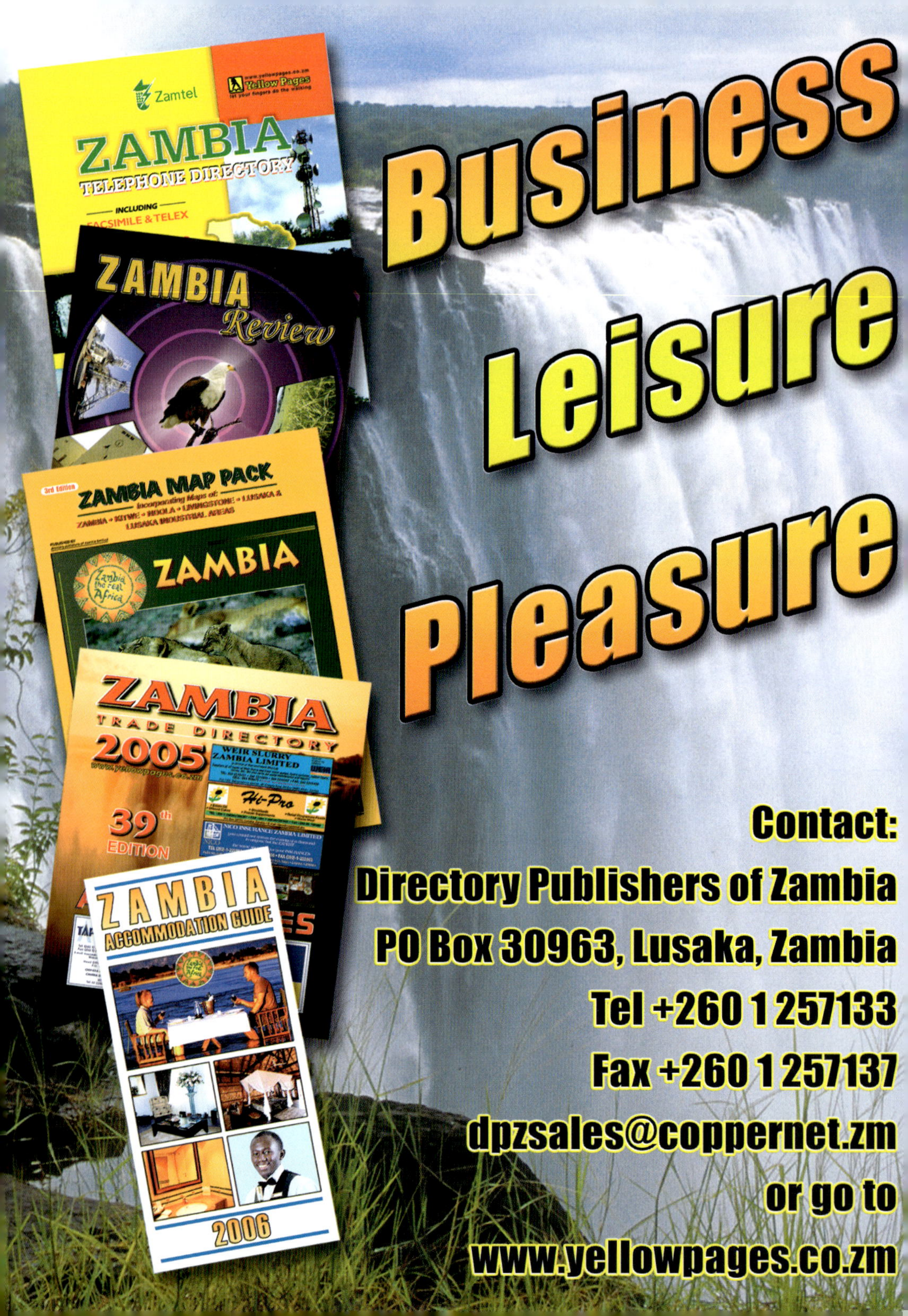
Zamtel
Yellow Pages
ZAMBIA
TELEPHONE DIRECTORY
INCLUDING
FACSIMILE & TELEX
ZAMBIA
Review
3rd Edition
ZAMBIA MAP PACK
ZAMBIA
ZAMBIA
TRADE DIRECTORY
2005
39th
EDITION
ZAMBIA
ACCOMMODATION GUIDE
2006
Business
Leisure
Pleasure
Contact:
Directory Publishers of Zambia
PO Box 30963, Lusaka, Zambia
Tel +260 1 257133
Fax +260 1 257137
dpzsales@coppernet.zm
or go to
www.yellowpages.co.zm

Directory and the On-Line Phone Book, the Zambia Trade Directory, the Zambia Review, the Zambian Accommodation Guide, the Zambia Map Pack and the official SADC Directory.

RADIO STATIONS

Radio Phoenix
12th Floor, Zimco House, Cairo Road
Private Bag E702, Lusaka
Tel: +260-1-226841/226652/236790
Fax: +260-1-226839
Email: rphoenix@zamnet.zm

MEDICAL SERVICES

Ambulance Service/Speciality Emergency Services
Lusaka
Tel: +260-1-273302
Kitwe
Tel: +260-2-211182

RECOMMENDED

Care For Business Medical Centre
Addis Ababa Drive, Lusaka
Tel: +260-1-254396-8/252917
Email: cfbmedic@zamnet.zm

Premium Medical Services
Administration Office
Chisango Rd and Polonalio Miti Steet
P O Box 35177, Lusaka
Tel: +260-1-226469
Fax: +260-1-229058
Medical Clinic
Premium House, Independence Avenue, Kamwala
Tel: +260-1-222288/222047

Nchanga North Haulage International Ltd
Chingola
Tel: +260-2-344333/313833/310237

Kitwe Polyclinic
Kitwe
Tel: +260-1-230593

K G Dental Surgery
5459 Kariba Road, Kalundu, Lusaka
Tel: +260-1-292219

Stellalfie Dental Surgery
21 Matandani Close, off Lubuto Road, Rhodes Park
P O Box 5020, Lusaka
Tel: +260-1-251313
Cell: +260-96-431329
Email: sadental@zamtel.zm

Link Pharmacies
Manda Hill Shopping Centre, Great East Road, Lusaka
Tel: +260-1-256605-6
Arcades Shopping Centre, Great East Road, Lusaka
Tel: +260-1-255556

Vikay Pharmacy
Cairo Road
P O Box 34562, Lusaka
Tel: +260-1-232724

OFFICE SUPPORT

Business Connexion Zambia
82 Kabundi Road, Riverside, Chingola
Tel: +260-2-351231

CompDisc and Office Suppliers Limited
P O Box 31153, Lusaka
Tel: +260-1-236284
Cell: +260-97-775151
Fax: +260-1-227319
Email: compdisc@zamnet.zm

RECOMMENDED

Computer Express
Carousel Shopping Centre, Lumumba Road
P O Box 32367, Lusaka
Tel: +260-1-225035/232753
Fax: +260-1-232752

Infotech
Kenneth Kaunda House, Cairo Road, Lusaka
Tel/Fax: +260-1-236987

Email: info@infotec.co.zm
Website: www.infotech.co.zm

InkTec
Showgrounds, Lusaka
Tel: +260-1-256649

Necor Zambia
Lonrho House, Cairo Road, Lusaka
Tel: +260-1-229782
Fax: +260-1-226772
Website: www.necor.co.zm

Planet Book
Arcades Shopping Centre, Great East Road, Lusaka
Tel: +260-1-256714
Email: planet@zamtel.zm

REAL ESTATE

Anderson and Anderson
P O Box 30263, Lusaka
Tel: +260-1-227244
Fax: +260-1-222433
Email: Anderson@zamnet.zm

Dez Rez
11 Nkana West, Mwamuna House
P O Box 20622, Kitwe
Tel: +260-2-231012

Homenet Hollywood Kabulonga
Corner of Bishops and Roan Road, Kabulonga, Lusaka
Tel: +260-1-260849/50
Tel: +260-1-263686
Email: kabulonga@homenetzambia.com

The Comesa Centre is a large office complex near Kafue road

Homenet Hollywood Manda Hill
Manda Hill Shopping Centre, Great East Road, Lusaka
Tel: +260-1-255747/8/3
Fax: +260-1-255747
Email: mandahill@homenetzambia.com
Website: www.homenetzambia.com

Knight Frank
Anglo American Building, Independence Avenue, Lusaka
Tel: +260-1-250538
Fax: +260-1-254717
Email: kfzam@knightfrank.co.zm
Website: www.knightfrank.com/zambia

Promark Estate
P O Box 37218, Lusaka
Tel: +260-1-265107/180
Email: promark@coppernet.zm

National Housing Authority
4668 Chilufya Mulenga Road
P O Box 50074, Lusaka
Tel: +260-1-254154/251663
Fax: +260-3-253396

REMOVALS

AGS Frasers International Removals
Mukatasha Road, Plot No. 7242, Industrial Area, Lusaka
Tel: +260-1-286666/905
Fax: +260-1-286656
Email: ags@zamnet.zm
Website: www.ags-worldwide-movers.com

Elliott International
Plot 5286, Mungwi Road
Postnet # 399, Private Bag E 891, Lusaka
Tel: +260-1-243574/5/96-860501/95-880003
Fax: +260-1-243576
Email: elliott@zamnet.zm
Website: www.elliott.co.zm

CAR HIRE

AVIS Rent A Car
Holiday Inn Garden Court, Church Road
P O Box 38645, Lusaka
Tel: +260-1-251642/251652/97-773978
Fax: +260-1-252201
Ndola Aiport
Airport Road, Ndola
Tel: +260-2-620741/97-800741
Email: avis@zamnet.zm

Gemistar Travel and Tours
Plot No. 4623, Mwaimwena Road, Rhodes Park, Lusaka
Tel: +260-1-254834/256422-3/97-806364/97-887438
Fax: +260-1-254899
Email: gemistar@zamtel.zm

Hensons Used Cars and Rentals
Plot No. 10489, Manchinchi Road, Olympia
P O Box 50360, Lusaka
Tel: +260-1-292227/96-755036
Fax: +2260-1-294624

Hertz
Intercontinental Hotel, Haile Selassie Road
P O Box 34035, Lusaka
Tel: +260-1-256778-80
Fax: +260-1-256778

Limo Car Hire
21 Lilayi Road, off Kafue Road, Lusaka
Tel: +260-1-278628/97-743145
Fax: +260-1-278628
Email: limohire@zamnet.zm

Taiwo Car Hire
Great East Road
P O Box 36224, Lusaka
Tel: +260-1-291283

Unitravel Tours
Los Angeles Boulevard, Longacres, Lusaka
Tel: +260-1-250914
Fax: +260-1-250944

Email: unitravel@coppernet.zm

Long-term private rental

Mrs L. Lucheta

Tel: +260-97-799960

SECURITY

Mint Master Security Zambia Ltd

2 Chaholi Road, Rhodes Park

P O Box 31034, Lusaka

Tel: +260-1-252630/254439

Fax: +260-1-254433

Email: mintlsk@zamnet.zm

Ndola Office

Tel: +260-2-621603

Fax: +260-2-620702

Safetech

Plot 7305, Kambala Road

P O Box 32677, Lusaka

Tel: +260-1-287236/38

Fax: +260-1-286360

Email: vvidmar@safetech.co.zm

Website: www.ssi-group.com

SUPERMARKETS

Castle Supermarket

Kafue Road, Lusaka

Tel: +260-1-224896

Melissa Supermarket

Chozi Road, Northmead Shopping Centre

P O Box 32154, Lusaka

Tel: +260-1-265375

Shoprite Checkers

NHS Building, Cairo Road

P O Box 37226, Lusaka

Shoprite, a supermarket chain from South Africa found everywhere in the country

Arcades, one of the two ultra modern shopping malls with shops and cinema

Tel: +260-1-231706

Shoprite Checkers
Great East Road, Manda Hill Shopping Centre
P O Box 37226, Lusaka
Tel: +260-1-251155/ 255410

RECOMMENDED

Super Spar
Arcades Shopping Centre, Great East Road, Lusaka
Tel: +260-1-256523/256610
Fax: +260-1-256623

TAXIS

Dial-A-Cab
Metered Cabs
Tel: +260-95-773937/96-222222/97-773937

Mr Oliver Lindengwe
Lusaka
Cell: +260-97-607011

Mr Penias
Lusaka
Cell: +260-97-705845

Mr Mose
Cell: +260-97-778663
Ndola to Kitwe

INVESTMENT & LEGAL FRAMEWORK

"When a mother advises her child, an orphan within earshot should also take the advice"
Zambian proverb

WHY DO BUSINESS IN ZAMBIA?

Zambia is a multi-party democracy and provides a market-oriented, liberalized economic environment in a strife-free, multicultural society. The Zambian government welcomes investors and has designed a package of incentives aimed specifically at creating a sound investment climate for increased domestic economic growth.

A UNIQUE PLACE TO INVEST

Zambia offers potential investors a generally positive investment climate in which the maintenance of macro-economic stability and the creation of an enabling environment for private sector activity, industrial growth, export promotion and foreign direct investment (FDI) is a prime concern. Furthermore, the country boasts a democratic Westminster-style government as well as an investment-friendly and export-oriented incentive package for business.

As a landlocked country, Zambia pursues a policy of regional cooperation in order to maximize the use of transport infrastructure and institutional capacities. The country is well positioned within southern and central Africa to exploit the regional Southern African Development Community (SADC) and Common Market for Eastern and Southern Africa (COMESA) markets, with which it has good political as well as economic relations, reinforced by a number of important trade agreements.

Ports most frequently used include Durban in South Africa, Dar es Salaam in Tanzania and Walvis Bay in Namibia (a closer route for Zambian imports and exports), with the route to the port of Beira in Mozambique being

Lusaka offers a modern and reliable infrastructure

another option. Goods may be transported by rail or road from all ports since infrastructure is in good condition. While there are no major waterways, Mpulungu Port on Lake Tanganyika is an inland port linking Zambia to Burundi.

The country is resource rich in terms of mineral wealth as well as the presence of plentiful arable land, abundant water, affordable electricity from coal reserves as well as hydroelectric power, and a pleasant climate and topography. There exist opportunities to further develop the downstream processing of natural resources in areas such as textiles, agro-industries and gemstone processing.

Zambia offers both stability and security for investors, with a government that promotes investment and continues to facilitate access to key stakeholders, investment promotion institutions and agencies. Labour costs are competitive, with the labour force comprising skilled as well as semi-skilled workers.

Investments are protected and private property rights guaranteed through the Investment Act, which states that investments may not be expropriated unless parliament has passed an Act relating to the compulsory acquisition of that property, in which event full compensation at market value and free transfer of the funds in the currency in which the investment was made are guaranteed. Furthermore, investors are guaranteed that investments will not be adversely affected by any changes to the Investment Act for a period of seven years.

Zambia belongs to the Multilateral Investment Guarantee Agency (MIGA) and has signed multilateral, regional and bilateral investment protection agreements with a number of countries. In the event of disputes, arbitration may be sought through the Zambia High Court, the International Centre for the Settlement of Investment Disputes (ICSID) or the United Nations Commission on International Trade Law (UNCITRAL). Investment in the stock market is protected by the Securities Act 1993.

Trademark protection is adequate, and patent laws conform to the requirements of the Paris Convention for the Protection of Industrial Property, to which Zambia is a signatory. Furthermore, Zambia is a signatory to a number of international agreements on patents and intellectual property, including those of the World Intellectual Property Organization (WIPO), Paris Union, Berne Union, African Regional Industrial Property Organization (ARIPO), and the Universal Copyright Convention of UNESCO.

There is no legal distinction between foreign and domestic investors, except in the case of the retail sector. Foreign investment in the Lusaka Stock Exchange (LuSE) is not restricted, and the privatization process is likewise open to foreign bidders. While there are no requirements for local content, equity, financing, employment or technology transfers, companies seeking licences or concessions or investors bidding for privatized companies are encouraged to commit to local participation.

Government is cognizant of current challenges to increased investment in the country, such as the high cost of entry for investors wishing to establish new businesses and delays in acquiring land and in getting work permits. Initiatives under way to tackle these obstacles include the ongoing effort to review the Investment Act in order to make operational a one-stop centre to reduce bureaucratic procedures for investors to obtain required authorizations. In addition, planned legal reforms include the strengthening of commercial law and property rights.

POSITIVE STEPS TAKEN TO PROMOTE TRADE AND INVESTMENT

Structural reforms and macroeconomic policy objectives are backed by the International Monetary Fund (IMF) and World Bank, with market-focus economic strategies encouraging broad-based growth and private sector development:

- Removal of all forms of consumer subsidies.
- Removal of price controls.
- Deregulation of interest and foreign exchange rates.
- Strengthening of the financial markets through the stock exchange.

- Abolition of foreign exchange controls.
- Reduction of tariffs to a maximum of 25%.
- Zero tariffs on exports to countries belonging to the Common Market for Eastern and Southern Africa's free trade area.
- Repatriation of up to 100% of after-tax profits by foreign investors.

DOMESTIC LAWS

Zambia's policy regime is very liberal. The policy framework provides a very strong standard for the treatment of investors and the functioning of markets.

The legal and regulatory regime comprises the Zambia Constitution Act, Investments Act, Companies Act, labour laws, foreign investment treaties, taxation Acts such as the Incomes Act, the Immigration and Deportation Act, the Customs and Excise Act, Export Processing Zones Act, Tourism Act, court system, etc.

THE INVESTMENT ACT

The Investment Act is the principal instrument for promoting and facilitating investments as well as coordinating government policies on investment in the country. The Investment Act provides for the formation of the Zambia Investment Centre (ZIC) as an institution responsible for promoting, coordinating government policies on and facilitating investment in Zambia. The Investment Act is currently being reviewed to make it more investor friendly.

THE PRIVATIZATION ACT

The Privatization Act is the principal legal instrument for the government divestiture programme. The Act gives the Zambia Privatization Agency (ZPA) the responsibility for all government privatization issues. So far 259 companies out of a working portfolio of 283 have been privatized.

The privatization programme is yet another window of investment opportunities for private investors.

THE EXPORT DEVELOPMENT ACT

In a quest to increase the country's revenue base through the promotion of non-traditional exports, government enacted the Export Development Act 1985 as amended by Act No. 29 of 1994. The Act provides for the formation of the Export Board of Zambia as a corporate body that deals with all matters relating to export promotion.

The functions of the Export Board are outlined below:

- To represent the interests of exporters to government and its agencies and to recommend policies in relation to trade promotion, development of export production and to the regulation of export trade.
- To advise exporters, potential and existing, on export markets and trade information; on quality, supply and pricing of export products; on existing export regulations, export incentives and available technical assistance.
- To promote the development of exports in general and of specific products by liaison with missions and organizations in export markets, by trade fair participation, by undertaking trade missions and by other promotional activities.
- To develop, or assist in developing, Zambia's human resource in export production and marketing through various training activities for officials, managers and technicians in the export sector.

THE ZAMBIA EXPORT PROCESSING ZONES ACT (ZEPZA)

The Export Processing Zones Act came into effect in November 2001, providing for the establishment of export processing zones and their licensing and regulation. The Act also provides for the establishment of the Export Processing Zones Authority, a corporate body that is mandated to carry out the functions of the export processing zones as outlined in the Act.

In order to enhance the country's investment climate, the Export Processing Zones Authority will carry out, among others, the following functions:

• To facilitate the development of export processing zones.
• To facilitate the development of export processing zones by developers and investors.
• To administer, control and regulate export processing zones and to ensure compliance with the Act and any other laws relevant to the activities of export processing zones.
• To monitor and evaluate the activities, performance and development of enterprises in export processing zones.

COMPETITION AND FAIR TRADING ACT

The Competition and Fair Trading Act came into force in February 1995. This law was designed to prevent anti-competitive and restrictive business practices and promote consumer welfare. The Act deals with agreements and concerted practices of enterprises and organizations that are appreciably anti-competitive, and the abuse of market power by enterprises that are dominant within their market. The Act also deals with consumer welfare and protection issues.

The Competition and Fair Trading Act led to the formation of the Zambia Competition Commission, an autonomous corporate body under the Ministry of Commerce, Trade and Industry. The Competition Commission strives to foster the development of a competitive, efficient, fair and informed Zambian market.

The functions of the Competition Commission are as follows:

• To encourage competition in the economy.
• To strengthen the efficiency of production and distribution of goods and services.
• To secure the best possible conditions for the freedom of trade.
• To expand the base of entrepreneurship.
• To protect consumer welfare.

INVESTMENT LEGISLATION

Companies seeking to obtain investment certificates to set up new business, or expand, rehabilitate or modernize existing enterprises in Zambia must complete a standard application form and submit it to the Investment Centre once certain requirements are met, including payment of a processing fee of K1,280,000 (inclusive of VAT).

The projects approval committee of the Investment Board meets every month to consider applications for investment certificates. It is required that promoters submit sufficient detailed information to enable the Investment Centre to form an informed opinion on the project. The applications should be submitted at least a week before the consideration date. This is to enable the Centre to evaluate the investment proposal before presenting it to the Board for consideration. Once an application has been approved a certificate fee of K7,670,000 (inclusive of VAT) is charged before collection of the investment certificate.

GENERAL BUSINESS INCENTIVES

The Zambian government has designed a package of incentives aimed specifically at establishing a suitable environment for increased domestic industrial growth, export promotion, the development of market-oriented production management and private sector development. The Investment Act 1993, as amended in 1996, regulates matters such as investment incentives and investment guarantees.

Income tax allowances and deductions are extended to a number of sectors, including agriculture, manufacturing, mining and the hospitality industry. Expenditure on research, technical education, or any further training related to a company's specific business activity is also tax deductible. Where double taxation agreements exist between Zambia and another country, the foreign tax payable by the investor to the other country is allowed as a credit for that investor against Zambian tax.
Investors pay 15% income tax on income from non-tradi-

The Zambia Investment Center is promoting Zambia as an investment destination

tional exports and one-seventh of the normal 35% corporate income tax rate in the first five years of operation for rural enterprises. Income from farming is taxed at a rate of 15%. Buildings used for manufacturing, mining or hotels qualify for a wear and tear allowance of 5% of the cost, plus an initial allowance of 10% of the cost in the year in which the building is first used.

Tax incentives relating to investments on the Lusaka Stock Exchange (LuSE) include a reduction of corporate income tax to 33%, no restrictions on foreign ownership and shareholding levels and no capital gains tax.

Export incentives are also offered. Special exemption from duty and sales tax on imports and machinery is extended to exporters of non-traditional products with net foreign exchange earnings, tourism investment with foreign exchange earnings in excess of 25% of the gross annual earnings, and agro-related products for export.

Customs duty has been reduced on a wide range of raw materials and selected intermediate goods used in manufacturing, as well as various other products affecting different sectors of the economy. (Consult the relevant sections for sectoral incentives in mining, manufacturing, tourism and agriculture.) Excise duty on electricity has been reduced from 10% to 7%, and there is no duty on eligible goods traded within the COMESA free trade area among member states.

MINING SECTOR INCENTIVES

Zambia's rich diversity of mineral resources encompasses metals, gemstones, a variety of industrial minerals and potential energy resources such as uranium, coal and hydrocarbons, with investment opportunities ranging from large-scale mining operations to smaller prospects. There are promising prospects for further exploration and exploitation in areas other than traditional copper and cobalt.

Zambia's investor-friendly mineral policy is enshrined in the Mines and Minerals Act 1995, which greatly simplifies licensing procedures, placing minimum reasonable constraints on prospecting and mining activities and allowing international arbitration to be written into development agreements if need be. The Environmental Protection and Pollution Control Regulations 1997 provide a framework for responsible development.

Investors in the mining industry are guaranteed:

- Secure title to mining rights.
- Stability of the fiscal regime.
- Foreign exchange retention.
- Right to market mine products.
- Right to assign (right to trade the mining right).
- Stability in environmental management.
- International arbitration.
- Freedom of commercial operation.

Minerals in the ground are vested in the president on behalf of the state, with the right to explore or produce minerals authorized by a licence granted under the Mines and Minerals Act. The Mines Development Department is responsible for issuing permits and licences. The Department also monitors all mineral exploitation activities, including prospecting, and carries out mapping and surveying.

Licences and permits issued include those for both large and small-scale mining, prospecting, retention licences, gemstone licences, gemstone sales certificates, artisans' mining rights and reconnaissance permits. Documents that are necessary when applying for these permits include: a statement of mineral deposit in the mining area; topographical maps of the area; certificate of incorporation and articles of association; programme of operations and estimated costs; photocopies of passports of directors and shareholders; bank statements and reference letters from applicants' banks.

INVESTMENT INCENTIVES AND TAX RELIEF FOR MINING COMPANIES

The government adopts a supportive role in encouraging private sector initiatives and further investment in the industry. Mining companies carrying out mining operations in the production of copper and cobalt are taxed as follows:

- Corporate tax rate – 25%
- Dividends, interest and management fees – 0%
- Royalties – 0.6%

Furthermore, mining losses are allowed to be carried forward for a period of 20 years, and the restriction of offsetting losses against profits for mines with a common owner (which are not adjacent) has been removed so that 100% of losses can be offset. Copper and cobalt price participation fees are tax deductible. Mines are exempt from payment of customs duty on consumables and mineral royalties up to a cap of US $16 million in the first year and US $15 million per year for the next four years thereafter. There is no payment of excise duty on electricity consumed, and duty-free importation of capital equipment and utility vehicles is provided for. They are also deemed to be a '1975 new mine' and allowed 100% deduction of capital expenditure in the year incurred.

AGRICULTURE SECTOR INCENTIVES

The agricultural sector also has the potential to drive economic growth in Zambia, and agricultural policy aims at increasing private sector participation in production, processing and marketing of agricultural and horticultural products and commodities with minimal government interference. At present, only 15% of Zambia's 60 million hectares of arable land is under cultivation.

Developments in the area of agricultural inputs, such as fertilizers, farm equipment and animal feed, also have significant potential, as does the packaging of agricultural produce for export – in particular, high-value exports such as coffee and flowers, which require high-quality packaging. There is also scope in the domestic marketing of foods such as flour, cooking oil and pork products.

The government has provided the following incentives and allowances for agriculture:

- 15% income tax on agricultural concerns.
- 100% tax allowance for land development and conservation.
- Capital expenditure on farm improvements qualifies for an allowance of 20% per annum for the first five years.
- A substantial rate of depreciation allows farm machinery to be rapidly written off against tax.
- Dividends payable to farmers are tax exempt for the first five years of operation.
- Special development allowances for growing crops such as tea, coffee, banana plants, citrus fruit trees or other similar plants or trees.
- Customs duty exemptions on selected capital machinery and equipment used exclusively for agriculture.
- Reduced duty on/duty free imports of certain raw materials.

Exporters are able to gain assistance from the Export Board of Zambia as well as the Zambia Export Growers' Association, which may help with export procedures as well as in finding potential markets.

Workshop from the Ministry of Finance

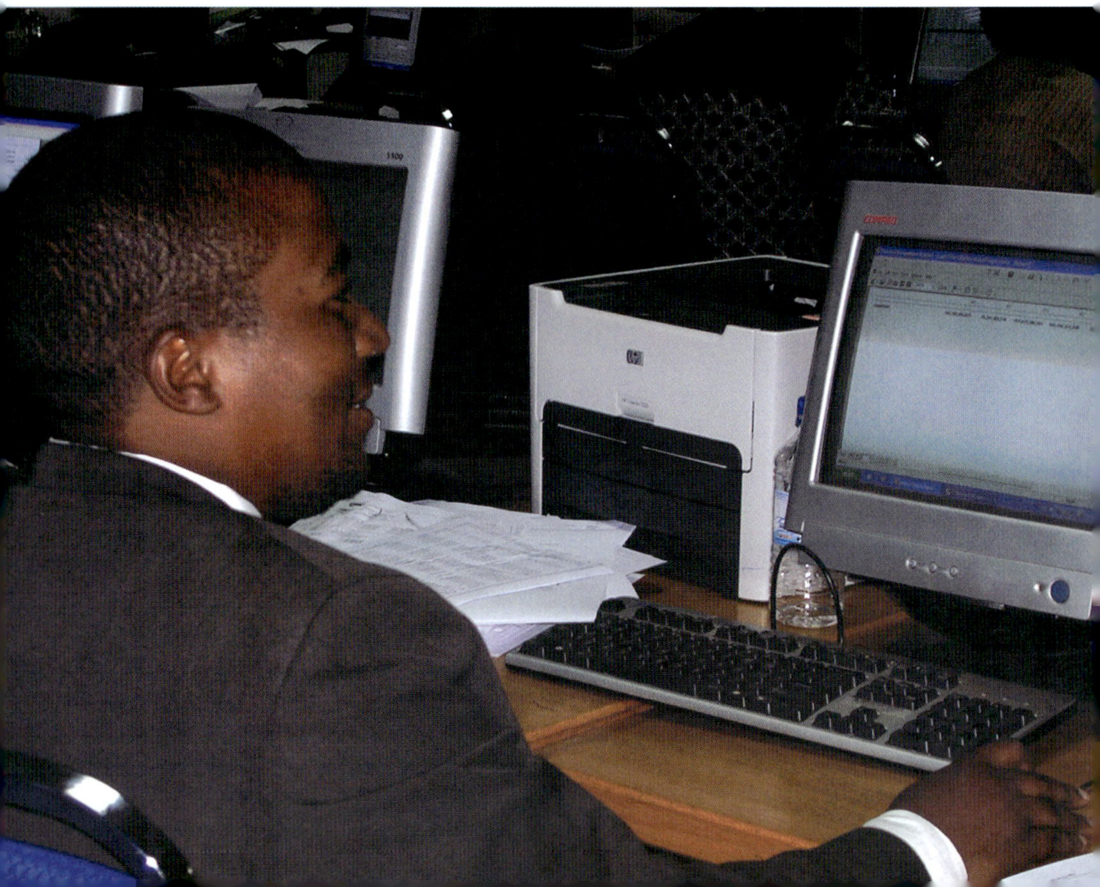

MANUFACTURING SECTOR INCENTIVES

Manufacturing activity is led by the private sector, with government playing a proactive, facilitative role. An important sector as regards Zambia's macroeconomic strategy for encouraging broad-based economic growth, manufacturing accounts for almost a quarter of the country's gross domestic product and about 10% of employment. Important investment areas include agro-processing, wood and leather products, food processing, textile production and mineral products.

Zambia has a fairly wide manufacturing base and well-developed infrastructure, with opportunities available in several subsectors:

- Food processing and beverages.
- Clothing and textiles.
- Leather and leather products.
- Wood and wood products, paper products and packaging.
- Processing of metals, including the smelting and refining of copper.
- Engineering products.
- Processing and polishing of gemstones and jewellery making.
- Agro-processing, including fertilizers, soil conditioners, pesticides and herbicides.
- Plastic and glass containers.
- Chemicals, pharmaceuticals and personal hygiene products.
- Refining of petroleum.
- Cement and explosives.

In the 2004 budget, a lot of leeway was given to the sector by reducing import duties on most raw materials and intermediate goods from 15% to 5%. Most capital equipment is already duty free and the importation of capital equipment for industrialization continues to be facilitated by government. Production costs for local manufacturers are being cut so as to keep industries competitive internationally and to safeguard them against undervalued imports.

The current policy of government is to, as much as possible, move away from taxing capital goods to make investment less costly. Forklifts are capital equipment used by many industries, including production processes. As such, customs duty on forklifts was reduced from 15% to 5% in 2005.

In recognition of the need to protect industry from cheap imports, promote local manufacturing and preserve employment, customs duty on imported chalk was increased from 15% to 25% in 2005. The measure is expected to raise K144 million. Furthermore, export duty at the rate of 25% on unprocessed timber and scrap metals exported has been introduced in order to encourage the export of value added timber products and has the added benefit of creating employment. The export duty on scrap metal is meant to stimulate local recycling of waste metal and to encourage the growth of the local foundry industry.

In accordance with the Southern African Development Community (SADC) Protocol on Trade, which calls for the establishment of a free trade area by the year 2012, Zambia has implemented tariff reductions on items in Category B, the bulk of which are intermediate products.

OTHER INVESTMENT OPPORTUNITIES AND INCENTIVES

The country's tourism assets, which cover spectacular scenery, one of the largest concentrations of game in Africa, a colourful cultural heritage and major attractions such as Lake Kariba and the Victoria Falls, have enormous potential for further, intensified development. Opportunities exist in game ranching, provision of high quality accommodation, transport services, adventure holiday packages, organized tours and outdoor sports facilities.

The amended Investment Act 1996 offers a number of incentives for developing tourism infrastructure. This includes generous income tax allowances for hotels on wear and tear and similar allowances on machinery used for tourism purposes.

Investment opportunities also exist in the energy sector, including the development of the Itezhi-Tezhi and Kafue Gorge Lower hydroelectric projects, and the Zambia–Tanzania and Zambia–Namibia interconnectors. Other promising opportunities are those in the services sector, including business, education, health, construction, transport and financial services.

The establishment of industrial parks is planned and an export processing zone (EPZ) has been established. Intraregional growth hubs are being created with improved and integrated transportation and other infrastructure in order to stimulate trade and investment. These comprise the Zambia–Malawi–Mozambique Growth Triangle, Mtwara Development Corridor and Beira Development Corridor.

Zambia Revenue Authority

The setting up of public–private partnerships to exploit the abundant natural resources in these development areas is also foreseen. This is in line with SADC's policy of promoting cross-border trade through the integration of transport networks, and will benefit several provinces of Zambia by promoting the development of local agriculture, fisheries, tourism and mining.

New listings on the LuSE enjoy the following incentives:

- Discount of 2% from a normal corporate tax rate applicable to each sector for a period of one year.
- A further discount of 5% over and above the 2% available for those companies that have more than 33% of their shares taken up by Zambians for a period of one year.

INVESTMENT GUARANTEES

Zambia is signatory to the Multilateral Investment Guarantee Agency, which guarantees foreign investment protection in cases of war, strife, disasters, other disturbances or expropriation. The Investment Act assures investors that no investment of any description can be expropriated unless parliament has passed an Act relating to the compulsory acquisition of that property. Also, in the case of expropriation, full compensation shall be made at fair market value and shall be convertible at the then current exchange rate. In addition, investors are guaranteed that investments will not be adversely affected by any changes in the Investment Act for a period of seven years.

INTERNATIONAL LAWS AND AGREEMENTS

The promotion of trade is vital to Zambia in its efforts to find additional regional and international markets for its products, and the country is signatory to a number of bilateral, regional and multilateral trade agreements. Trading partners within southern Africa include: Republic of South Africa, Malawi, Zimbabwe and the Democratic Republic of Congo, with reciprocal promotional and protection of investment protocols having been signed. Important international trading partners include EU countries such as Germany and the United Kingdom.

Foreign investment is having many positive effects on Zambia and its economy. A number of EU countries – in particular the United Kingdom – have also made substantial investments in Zambia, as has South Africa. Relations between Asia and Africa are also significant, and are facilitated through the Africa–Asia Business Forum.

Zambia is a member of the following regional and international organizations:

South African Development Community (SADC); Common Market for Eastern and Southern Africa (COMESA); African Union (AU); African Development Bank (AfDB); Food and Agriculture Organization (FAO); Commonwealth; United Nations (UN); International Labour Organization (ILO); World Trade Organization (WTO); World Bank; International Monetary Fund (IMF); Multilateral Investment Guarantee Agency (MIGA); World Health Organization (WHO); Non-Aligned Movement; New Partnership for Africa's Development (NEPAD); EU Economic Partnership Agreement; African Growth and Opportunity Act (AGOA).

TAXATION

Zambia's tax system is focused on stimulating growth in the economy while bringing in sufficient resources to finance development and sustain its operations.

Established in 1994, the Zambia Revenue Authority (ZRA) assesses and collects taxes and duties on behalf of the government, facilitates international trade, and advises government on aspects of tax policy. General information on taxation is available from the ZRA Advice Centre.

All individuals receiving an income from a source within Zambia, whether they are resident or non-resident, are liable to pay tax. A foreign resident business undertaking pays tax only if business is conducted in Zambia through a permanent establishment. A company is resident in Zambia for tax purposes if the company is incorporated or formed in Zambia or the central management and control of the company's business or affairs is exercised in Zambia. Companies are taxed on trading profits as well as interest and dividends, if those dividends are paid in Zambia.

In partnerships, the taxable income of the partnership is first determined on the basis that it is a separate, taxable person. After income has been apportioned among the partners according to the partnership agreement, partners are individually assessed on their respective share of the partnership income.

Double taxation agreements have been concluded with Botswana, Canada, Denmark, Finland, France, Germany, India, Ireland, Italy, Japan, Kenya, Netherlands, Norway, Romania, South Africa, Sweden, Switzerland, Tanzania, Uganda, the United Kingdom and the United States.

Zambia's business tax rate is among the lowest in the region. Income tax rates, including reduced tax rates and tax incentives, are as follows:

- Personal income tax – a maximum of 37.5%.
- Corporate tax – normal corporate tax at 35%; chemical manufacture of fertilizer 15%; farming and non-traditional exports 15%; copper and cobalt mining 25%.
- Banking and financial institutions – 35% up to K250 million; 45% above K250 million; 15% withholding tax.
- Trusts, deceased or bankrupt estates – 35%.

For the first five years of operation, rural enterprises enjoy one seventh of the normal income tax of 35% and dividends paid out of farming profits are tax exempt. There is a 100% tax allowance for land development and conservation, and capital expenditure on farm improvements qualify for an allowance of 20% per annum for the first five years. A substantial rate of depreciation allows farm machinery to be written off rapidly against tax.

From 2005, in addition to paying reduced corporate tax of 25%, companies carrying out mining operations in the production of copper pay no tax on dividends, interest or management fees, and only 0.6% on royalties. They are also deemed to be a '1975 new mine' and allowed 100% deduction of capital expenditure in the year incurred.

During 2005, the top rate of Pay As You Earn (PAYE) was reduced from 40% to 37.5%. Furthermore, the exemption threshold was raised from K260,000 to K280,000 per month.

Annual income tax rates as of 1st April 2005 are as follows:

- First K3,360,000 at 0%.
- Next K8,640,000 at 30%.
- Next K48,000,000 at 35%.
- Balance at 37.5%.

Other tax amendments in the 2005 budget saw the exempt portion on terminal benefits increase from K5 million to K10 million, thus giving additional relief to retirees and related persons at the time of retirement, redundancy or loss of employment. Furthermore, the tax credit applicable to persons with disabilities was increased from K18,000 to K36,000 per annum; this relief is in addition to the new tax-free threshold of K280,000 per month.

For businesses, turnover tax income by any person carrying on consultancy business with an annual turnover of K200 million or less was removed during 2005 to prevent tax planning. The requirement for tax clearance certificates for traders, which was repealed in 2001, has been reintroduced, and is a prerequisite for traders wishing to obtain a trading licence or be registered as a supplier of goods and services. Furthermore, the Property Transfer Tax Act has been amended so as to require the production of a property transfer tax clearance certificate before change of ownership of shares is effected.

In 2005, the penalty for late submission was increased from 170 penalty units (K30,600) to 1,000 penalty units (K180,000) per month or part thereof for individuals, and from 340 penalty units (K61,200) to 2,000 penalty units (K3,600,000) per month or part thereof for companies.

VALUE ADDED TAX

The value added tax (VAT) system was introduced in July 1995 to replace a manufacturing and retail sales tax. VAT is invoice-based and operates on the destination principle, where goods and services are taxed in the country of consumption and not of origin.

Special tax refunds are granted to tourists and commercial exporters, and a range of favourable incentives to investors. Qualifying goods do not pay import VAT, and the VAT deferment scheme on capital goods and specified raw materials allows the payment of import VAT to be deferred and offset against input tax due on those items. It is possible to recover tax on capital purchases before trading commences through monthly VAT returns, and excess input tax over output tax is not held as a credit against future liabilities but is repaid.

Amendments to VAT-related legislation during 2005 included the following:

- Removal from cash basis of accounting, for VAT purposes, of all businesses except members of the Association of Building and Civil Engineering Contractors (ABCEC).
- Steeper fines in lieu of prosecution for VAT registered cash traders or retailers not using a cash register.
- Introduction of legislation for tourist refund and commercial exporters' schemes.
- Revision of the requirement to attach input tax schedules to VAT returns in order to include the VAT number of suppliers among required details.
- Amendments to ensure that VAT can only be claimed when it is incurred in relation to stock items that are not VAT exempt.

VAT has three main classifications of goods and services that ultimately determine liability to tax. These include standard rate at 17.5%, zero rate and exempt.

Following the decision by the government in 2004 to exempt agricultural products for VAT purposes, the majority of such products destined for export became uncompetitive as the VAT incurred in Zambia in the process of production and distribution could not be claimed back by the exporters. Consequently, in 2005 the government standard-rated fresh edible vegetables and other agricultural products sold predominantly in export markets.

With medical supplies and drugs being VAT-exempt, VAT incurred by local manufacturers on purchases of manufacturing inputs could not be claimed back, thereby rendering locally produced medical supplies and drugs uncompetitive in comparison to imported finished products. In order to redress this, and in line with the government's policy to lower the cost of medical supplies, the 2005 budget saw the government zero-rating medical supplies and the supply or importation of medical equipment designed solely for prosthetic use.

SETTING UP COMMERCIAL COMPANIES

Business in Zambia is undertaken by companies, trusts, partnerships and individuals. A business name must be registered or a company incorporated through the registrar of companies. This involves name clearance and submission of articles of association with details of directors in triplicate. Both foreign and locally registered companies require annual audits, with foreign companies also obliged to lodge annual financial statements with the registrar of companies.

LIMITED COMPANY

Requires a minimum of two directors above the age of 18, one of whom must be resident in Zambia. If the company has more than two local directors, at least half of them must be resident in Zambia.

FOREIGN COMPANY

Required within 28 days of the establishment of a place of business in Zambia to lodge with the registrar of companies a list of company directors, a certified copy of its memorandum or any other document defining the constitution of the company, and the name and address of a local representative. Branches or subsidiaries of foreign

Zambia is an excellent investment destination

companies operating in the country may be regarded as Zambian companies provided the company has a physical location or owns immovable property in Zambia. The legal liability of the parent company is limited to the amount of capital committed, together with any guarantees provided. Investors face no restriction on the amount of interest, profit, dividends, management fees, technical fees and royalties that they are allowed to repatriate. Income earned by foreign nationals may also be externalized without difficulty. While investors may borrow to invest in Zambia, some financial institutions do not provide loans to non-residents unless a wholly owned Zambian company participates in the business.

The Companies Act No. 24 of 1995 governs the registration of companies in Zambia. Registration is done at the

Office of the Registrar of Companies. Any two or more persons can incorporate a company under the Companies Act. These persons are required to submit the following documents:

- Application for name clearance, in order to avoid use of an existing or similar name.
- Application for incorporation by subscribing the names of directors and secretaries of the company.
- Articles of the company.
- Statutory declaration as to compliance with the Companies Act.
- Signed consent to act as director or secretary by each person named in the company's application.
- Declaration of guarantee, if a company is limited by guarantee.

The minimum share capital of a company is K500,000. The law requires that half the directors of the company be resident in Zambia.

All companies are required to submit annual returns with the registrar of companies within three months after the end of the financial year or one month after the annual general meeting if it is held within three months after the financial year.

The Companies Act allows foreign companies to register with the registrar of companies within 28 days of setting up or acquiring an established place of business. The documentation required may be obtained from the Office of the Registrar of Companies.

TRANSFER OF CAPITAL AND PROFITS

A foreign investor who has registered foreign capital with the Bank of Zambia is entitled, in respect of a business enterprise to which the investment certificate relates, to transfer out of Zambia in foreign currency on payment of the relevant taxes:

- Dividends or after-tax income
- The principal and interest of any foreign loan
- Management fees, royalties and other charges in respect of any agreement; or
- The net proceeds of sale or liquidation of the business enterprise.

IMPORT AND EXPORT RULES AND REGULATIONS

IMPORT PROCEDURES

Company incorporation: All businesses engaging in both domestic or international trade are required by law to be registered with the Patents and Companies Registration Office, an executive agency of the Ministry of Commerce, Trade and Industry. Registration is either by a business name, a public or private company (therefore being incorporated in Zambia) or a foreign company.

The minimum capital required to register a public or private company is K2 million. Registration fees (inclusive of name search, forms, processing of application forms) are as follows:

- K19,500 (for registering a business name).
- K139,000 minimum for registering a company (depending on share capital the fee increases by K5,000 increments for each additional K200,000 of share capital).
- K294,000 (for a foreign company).

CUSTOMS CLEARANCE AND VALUATION

In order to clear goods through Customs, an importer must present the usual commercial documents such as bill of lading, airway bill and commercial invoice. The import declaration form is used for statistical purposes, and no fee is required. For goods to be cleared at the border, the importer uses the Zambia Revenue Authority (ZRA) form CE20, the standard form for entry and exit. Zambia is using the Automated System for Customs Data and Management (ASYCUDA). Customs clearance can be accomplished within hours, however incomplete forms and other difficulties, e.g. lack of supporting documents, can result in substantial delays.

TARIFF STRUCTURE

Zambia applies tariffs on the c.i.f. (cost, insurance and freight) basis. Customs tariffs are calculated on the basis of the dutiable value, based on the WTO Agreement on Customs Valuation. Most tariffs are ad valorem, but a few specific tariffs remain. Zambia uses the international harmonized system. Zambia's 2001 tariff schedule is structured around four tiers: 0%, 5%, 15% and 25% rates of duty. Virtually all raw materials and most industrial or productive machinery fall within the 0% and 5% tariff categories, while most imported intermediate goods are subject to 15%, and imported final products are rated at 25%. Zambia's simple average import tariff is about 14%.

OTHER LEVIES AND CHARGES

Zambia levies excise duties on certain products at rates ranging from 10% to 125%. The excise duty is collected on cane and beet sugar and some derivatives, beverages, tobacco and some derivatives and substitutes, and petroleum products.

The value added tax (VAT) of 17.5% applies to goods and services of domestic production and those that are imported. VAT is levied on the c.i.f. value plus customs tariff. Exemptions from VAT include social services such as health, education and funeral services.

IMPORT RESTRICTIONS

Import prohibitions are maintained for environmental, health and security reasons. Import licensing is required for most agricultural products. Zambia does not currently apply trade sanctions.

SANITARY AND PHYTOSANITARY REGULATIONS

Sanitary and phytosanitary regulations are applied to imports of live animals, plants and seeds. A sanitary certificate from the exporting country is required as a prerequisite to the issuance of the veterinary permit. Food imports must satisfy the provisions of the Food and Drugs Act 1978, which contains packaging and labelling requirements for food. There are also standards for maize samp, rice and bread.

EXPORT PROCEDURES

As is the case with import procedures, all businesses engaging in trade are required to register with the Patents and Companies Registration Office.

Exporters must complete an export declaration form (standard customs authority form ZRA CE20), mainly for statistical purposes. An original commercial invoice and a packaging list for shipment should accompany the form. An airway bill or bill of lading for transportation of exports should be obtained either from the freight forwarder or the transporter being used. Zambia has no export taxes, charges or levies.

If there are preferences that are being claimed in the exporting market (e.g. reduced tariffs), then an appropriate stamped certificate of origin from the ZRA is required. COMESA, SADC, EU and AGOA textiles have different certificates of origin.

If the goods are covered by the Veterinary Department, a sanitary/phytosanitary certificate is needed. A phytosanitary certificate is obtained from the Mount Makulu Research Station for seeds, stems and fruits.

A very limited number of goods require a special export permit. Gemstone exports require a permit from the Ministry of Mines; timber requires a timber verification certificate from the Forestry Department. Additional information on exports may be obtained from the Export Board of Zambia.

LABOUR LAWS

The Department of Labour, which falls under the Ministry of Labour and Social Security, is responsible for formulation of labour policy. The department administers the statutes governing employer–employee relations. The major pieces of legislation relating to the labour market in

Zambia include:

1) The Employment Act (Cap 268), providing for the basic employment contractual terms such as:

- Minimum contractual age.
- Establishment of employment contracts.
- Settlement of disputes arising from such contracts of employment.
- The appointment of labour officers and other staff for the administration of the Act.
- Certain conditions of employment such as ordinary leave, sick leave, maternity, redundancy and welfare of employees.

2) The Industrial and Labour Relations Act (Cap 269), providing for:

- The conduct of industrial relation.
- The establishment of workers/employers organizations, their registration and administration.
- Collective bargaining.
- Settlement of disputes through conciliation and arbitration by the Industrial Relations Court, established under the Act.
- Consultative machinery.

The Zambia Federation of Employers (ZFE), an umbrella organization for employers, articulates the interest of employers. ZFE is represented at the Tripartite Labour Consultative Council, a body comprising the representatives from the Ministry of Labour and Social Security and the unions (through an umbrella body, the Zambia Congress of Trade Unions (ZCTU)).

3) The Minimum Wages and Conditions of Employment Act (Cap 276)

This Act enables the Minister to determine minimum conditions of employment for categories of employees not effectively covered through collective bargaining. Such employees include general workers, drivers and clerks.

4) Employment of Young Persons and Children Act (Cap 274)

The Act provides protection for young persons and children in the employment relationship. It is the major law against child labour and abuse.

5) Employment (Special Provisions) Act (Cap 270)

This is an enabling Act and may be activated only when a state of emergency is in place. Under this Act various regulations may be promulgated with regard to labour and employment.

The above-mentioned Acts may be purchased from Government Printers.

WORKING CONDITIONS

BASIC SALARIES, WAGES AND ALLOWANCES

There are normally two categories of employee, namely the unionized and non-unionized (management) staff. Conditions of service for non-unionized employees are normally fixed by top management, while those for unionized employees are negotiated through collective bargain/agreement. As indicated above, the Minimum Wage and Conditions of Work Act provides for machinery for determining statutory minimum wages and other conditions of employment in industries or companies where conditions of employment are not regulated by free collective bargaining.

Allowances which are commonly added to the basic salary include:

- Housing
- Transport
- Children's medical expenses and education
- Water, electricity, holiday travel (usually for senior management staff)

All allowances are taxable at the same rate as the basic salary.

Other common non-cash benefits may include:

- Transport to and from work
- Subsidized meals in staff canteen
- Sporting and recreation facilities

PENSIONS AND LIFE INSURANCE

Membership of a pension scheme may be a condition of employment and most employers maintain a pension scheme for their employees with the National Pensions Scheme Authority (NAPSA). Employers may establish or join other pension schemes under the Pension Scheme Regulation Act.

MEDICAL COVERAGE AND MATERNITY BENEFITS

Employers are obliged, by the Minimum Wages and Conditions of Employment Act, to grant an employee full pay should illness make the employee unable to work, subject to production of a certificate from a registered physician. The maximum period for which such benefit may be given is three months at full pay, followed by three months at half pay. Some employers provide health and medical coverage through membership to private clinics to which the employee and employer contribute equally. The Act also requires that maternity leave for female employees be paid up to 90 days, provided such female employees have worked for a minimum of 24 months with their employers.

HOUSING

The Employment Act requires employers to provide to employees one of the following:

- Housing or housing allowance in lieu thereof;
- House loan or advance towards the purchase or construction of a house; or
- Guarantee facility for a mortgage.

WORKING HOURS

The normal working hours are 40 hours per week for office workers and 45 hours per week for factory workers. Office hours are normally from 08h00 to 17h00 Mondays to Fridays and 08h00 to 13h00 on Saturdays (for most companies outside the retail sector).

The normal weekly hours should not exceed 48 hours under the Minimum Wages and Conditions of Employment Act. Overtime work should be paid at one-and-a-half times the normal rate and twice the normal rate on weekends and public holidays.

PAID HOLIDAYS

Employers are obliged, under the Minimum Wages and Conditions of Employment Act, to grant paid leave of absence of not less than 24 days annually. It is, however, a normal practice for employers to provide employees with more leave days than that prescribed in the Act depending on the rank and nature of the employee's job.

SPECIAL LEAVE

Employers are obliged, under the Minimum Wages and Conditions of Employment Act, to grant an employee seven days' paid leave on the death of an employee's spouse, child, mother or father. The Act also obliges the employer to provide for a funeral grant for a standard coffin, cash and mealie meal in the event of death of an employee, spouse, registered child or dependant of the employee.

TERMINATION OF EMPLOYMENT

A contract of employment may be terminated under Zambian law through:

- Resignation or dismissal
- Normal retirement or medical discharge
- Expiry of contract
- Redundancy
- Frustration, such as death

An employer is obliged, under section 26A of Statutory Instrument No. 15 1997, to afford an employee the opportunity to be heard prior to termination of the con-

tract of employment if the termination is on grounds related to the employee's conduct or performance. This obligation on the part of the employer is in conformity with the International Labour Organization Convention. The Zambian law further provides for the minimum benefits payable to the affected employee, and requires payment of full wages for an employee declared redundant until the redundant benefits are paid.

REDUNDANCY BENEFITS

The employer is obliged to pay at least one month's notice and redundancy benefits of not less than two months' basic salary for each completed year of service.

ACCESS TO LAND

A new Land Act (No. 29 of 1995) came into force in 1995. There are two categories of land in Zambia. These are:

State land
State land comprises only 6% of land in Zambia. The land is zoned into residential, commercial or industrial use by the district councils according to their jurisdictions.

Customary land
Approximately 94% of all land in Zambia is held under this system of tenure. Such land falls under the jurisdiction of the traditional chiefs.

SYSTEM OF TENURE

There are only two types of tenure in Zambia. These are leasehold and customary tenure. Zambia has no freehold system of tenure.

The leasehold tenure runs for 99 years and is renewable for a further 99 years. Further renewal is possible if there is no breach of the conditions in the existing agreement. Land in the customary area can be converted to leasehold, thus allowing it to be used as collateral.

Under the 1995 Act, land now has a value and can be sold even without improvement on the land.

LAND ACQUISITION AND TRANSFER

A non-Zambian can acquire land under the following conditions:

- He/she is a permanent resident in Zambia.
- He/she is an investor within the meaning of the Investment Act or any other law permitting investment in Zambia.
- In exceptional cases by presidential consent in writing.
- If a person registers a company under the Companies Act, with no less than 75% Zambian shareholding. The title deed will be issued in the name of the registered company.
- Under a short-term tenancy of not more than 5 years.
- If the person is granted concession or right under the National Parks and Wildlife Act.

Before land can be bought or sold state consent must be obtained. The consent is issued by the commissioner of lands on application. If consent is not granted within 45 days of filing the application, the application is deemed to be granted.

If consent is refused, the reasons for refusal must be furnished to the applicant within 30 days.

ACQUISITION OF LAND IN A CUSTOMARY AREA

In order to acquire land in a customary area you will require:

- The written consent of the area chief.
- Approval of the district council in the area.
- Additional approval from the director of national parks and wildlife if the land is situated in a game management area.

These approvals once obtained should be submitted to the relevant district council, which in turn will submit the documents to the commissioner of lands. The commissioner will then make a formal offer to the applicant.

The letter of offer will stipulate among other conditions:

The consideration fee

This is not a fixed amount and is dependent upon locality, services provided by the state or council and other related factors.

Survey requirements

This can be carried out by a private or governmental surveyor. Submission of a legal diagram or plan attached to the lease agreement is a mandatory requirement prior to issuance of a certificate of title.

Preparation fee

The Office of Commissioner of Lands charges fees for preparation of a lease. These fees are fixed by statutory instrument, but are subject to change.

Registration fee

Fees charged by the Lands and Deeds Registry before a lease is registered and certificate of title issued.

Property transfer tax

Under the Property Transfer Tax Act, if land is purchased from a private person then currently 2.5% of the value of the land is paid to the Zambia Revenue Authority by the vendor. No tax is payable where land is acquired from the state.

Upon acceptance of the offer and payment of these charges, a 99-year lease to transfer the title will be prepared. If the land is already surveyed the title deeds will be issued within 60 days; if not surveyed then the process can take up to three months or more.

ALIENATION OF STATE LAND

Acquisition of land in an area designated as state land will require consent of the relevant district council. Land which does not fall within the jurisdiction of any council can be alienated upon direct application to the commissioner of lands.

The commissioner of lands will then make a formal offer to the applicant, which will contain similar conditions to those for an application to acquire land situated in the customary area.

PURCHASE OF PRIVATE LAND

Land in private ownership can be bought and sold and title deeds issued by the commissioner of lands. In all instances, state consent will have to be obtained by the vendor before title deeds can pass to the purchaser.

INFORMATION ON LAND AVAILABILITY

- Offices of the Commissioner of Lands, which are in all provinces.
- Council and commissioner of lands advertisements in national press.
- Real estate agents.
- Zambia Investment Centre in liaison with Ministry of Lands.
- Direct contact with chief and district council.

All investors are advised to contact the Zambia Investment Centre for further enquiries or directly contact the commissioner of lands.

INVESTMENT DIRECTORY

Agricultural and Commercial Show Society of Zambia
Show Grounds
P O Box 30333, Lusaka
Tel: +260-1-253415/245558
Fax: +260-1-254898

Association of Building and Engineering Contractors
P O Box 31776, Lusaka
Tel: +260-1-224462

Bankers Association of Zambia
P O Box 31936, Lusaka
Tel: +260-1-224005
Fax: +260-1-224006

Clothing and Allied Industries Association of Zambia
P O Box 72464, Ndola
Tel: +260-2-650172

The Commissioner of Lands
Independence Avenue
P O Box 30069, Lusaka
Tel/Fax: +260-1-250130

Copperbelt Agricultural and Commercial Show Society
Show Grounds, Ndola Road
P O Box 20944, Kitwe
Tel: +260-2-227205/225008/230611
Fax: +260-2-227033
Email: cacss@zamnet.zm

Economics Association of Zambia
3rd Floor, Kulima Tower
P O Box 38006, Lusaka
Tel: +260-1-225305
Fax: +260-1-225306

Export Board of Zambia
Kwacha House 1st floor
P O Box 30064, Lusaka
Tel: +260-1-228107/224790
Fax: +260-1-222509
Email: bzint@zamnet.zm
Website: www.ebz.co.zm

Lusaka Chamber of Commerce
Room 126, 1st Floor, Farmer's House, Cairo Road
P O Box 37887, Lusaka
Tel: +260-1-224114/224134
Fax: +260-1-224134

Leather Industries Association of Zambia
P O Box 3922, Lusaka
Tel: 260-1-222210/225797

Lusaka Chamber of Commerce and Industry
Farmer's House, 1st Floor(Central Park)
P O Box 37887, Lusaka
Tel: +260-1-224114
Tel/Fax: +260-1-224134

Lusaka Stock Exchange
3rd Floor Exchange Building, Central Park, Cairo Road
P O Box 345223, Lusaka
Tel: +260-1-228537/94
Fax: +260-1-225969
Email: luse@zamnet.zm
Website: www.luse.co.zm

Ministry of Commerce, Trade and Industry
New Government Complex, Independence Avenue
P O Box 31968, Lusaka
Tel: +260-1-228301-9
Fax: +260-1+226673/221475
Email: comtrade@zamnet.zm

Partnership Forum
Lusaka
Tel: +260-1-238733/228735
Fax: +260-1-237060

Private Sector Development Association
P O Box 33850, Lusaka
Tel: +260-1-291018/293914/220515/6
Fax: +260-1-291039
Email: psda@action.co.zm

Textile Producers of Zambia
P O Box 71846, Ndola
Tel: +260-2-650821
Fax: +260-2-650111

Women Entrepreneurs in Industry & Business in Zambia
c/o BIMZ Limited
P O Box 50514, Lusaka
Tel: +260-1-245558

Zambia Association of Chambers of Commerce and Industry
Lusaka Show Grounds
P O Box 30844, Lusaka
Tel: +260-1-252369/253020

Fax: +260-1-224006/252483
Email: zacci@zamnet.zm

Zambia Association of Manufacturers
P O Box 1992, Lusaka
Tel: +260-1-242761/242786/242779
Fax: +260-1-242785

Zambia Export Growers Association
Airfreight Village, Lusaka International Airport
P O Box 310245, Lusaka
Tel: +260-1-233295/271166
Fax: +260-1-271161

Zambia Export and Import Bank
P O Box 33046, Lusaka
Tel: +260-1-229504/222304
Fax: 260-1-222313

Zambia Indigenous Business Association
Plot 3780, Chilubula Close, Olympia Park
P O Box 33736, Lusaka
Tel: +260-1-232555
Fax: +260-1-235875

Zambia Institute of Marketing
Cooperative House Annex, Chachacha Road
P O Box 32180, Lusaka
Tel/Fax: +260-1-232604
Email: zim@zamnet.zm

Zambia International Trade Fair
P O Box 71058, Ndola
Tel: +260-2-655513/655520
Fax: +260-2-651704
Lusaka Office
Tel/Fax: +260-1-220870
Cell: +260-96-920464
Email: zitf2000@coppernet.zm

Zambia Investment Centre
6457 Los Angeles Boulevard
P O Box 34580, Lusaka
Tel: +260-1-255241/2/3
Fax: 260-1-252150
Email: invest@zamnet.zm

Zambia National Farmers' Union
Lusaka Show Grounds
P O Box 3095, Lusaka
Tel: +260-1-252649
Fax: +260-1-252649

Zambia National Tourist Board
Century House, Cairo Rd
P O Box 30017, Lusaka
Tel: +260-1-229087-90
Fax: +260-1-225174
Email: zntb@zamnet.zm

Zambia Trade and Investment Enhancement Project
55 Independence Avenue
P O Box 39398, Lusaka
Tel: +260-1-251177/251127
Fax: +260-1-251141
Email: ronblack@coppernet.zm

Zambia Tourism Council
Tourism Council, Holiday Inn Cottage, Church Road
P O Box 36561, Lusaka
Tel: +260-1-252859
Fax: +260-1-255377

ZAMBIAN ECONOMY

"Today's small trees will be tomorrow's great forest"
Zambian proverb

BACKGROUND

Zambia began a transition from socialism to market-oriented democracy in the early 1990s, when an ambitious programme of economic liberalization was initiated. This is helping to unlock the country's vast potential, with the government committed to creating an enabling environment in which business can flourish and economic growth generates improvements in both social and physical infrastructure.

While mining and agriculture underpin the economy and continue to reap economic rewards, a growing number of secondary industries are springing up. Tourism is another valuable asset, and the country's abundant wildlife, outstanding national parks and natural attractions offer a tantalizing taste of the 'real Africa'.

Since the 1990s the Zambian economy has been characterized by market-oriented policies, with the country becoming increasingly integrated into the world economy. No longer a command-type economy based on import substitution, the structural adjustment programmes and stabilization policies of the past 14 years have contributed to a more outward looking attitude characterized by trade liberalization and the promotion of exports within a stable macroeconomic context.

Market liberalization, deregulation and privatization have served to enhance competition, efficiency and openness in commerce and industry. The role of the state has been considerably reduced, with private sector activity encouraged through the provision of an enabling environment and investment stimulated through several attractive incentive schemes. Furthermore, foreign direct investment is not confined to resource-based sectors, but encompasses transport, telecommunications and utilities.

Reforms which have been enacted include the abolition of foreign exchange controls, the deregulation of interest and foreign exchange rates, removal of price controls and consumer subsidies, reform of land tenure, reduction of tariffs and embargoes to open up domestic markets, a programme of privatization for many parastatals, and the strengthening of financial markets through merchant banking and the stock exchange. After tax profit, dividends and capital may be repatriated up to 100% without restriction, and there is statutory protection of investments.

Fiscal discipline in order to maintain macroeconomic stability has been a priority in recent years, with the spotlight on reform of the budgeting and spending systems. This was a prerequisite for securing a new Poverty Reduction and Growth Facility (PRGF) with the International Monetary Fund (IMF), as well as reaching the completion point under the Heavily Indebted Poor Countries (HIPC) Initiative. A new PRGF programme has subsequently been put in place and is set to run until 2007.

POVERTY REDUCTION STRATEGY AND MILLENNIUM GOALS

For the seventh consecutive year, the growth in national output is expected to be positive on account of output growth in the construction, tourism, trade, manufacturing and mining sectors during 2005.

Zambia's good macroeconomic performance under the PRGF, coupled with progress in social sectors such as health and education, led to its attainment of the enhanced HIPC initiative completion point in April 2005. As a result of this and the G8 agreement in July 2005, Zambia is to benefit from approximately US $5.3 billion in debt relief. As such, budgetary resources that would have been needed to service external debts are available for poverty-reducing expenditure in the social and economic sectors – amounting to some US $100 million per annum from 2006.

The country is presently faced with the twin challenges of HIV/AIDS and an over-reliance on copper mining. Furthermore, Zambia's social and physical infrastructure must be improved, both for economic development and to reduce poverty. Despite these challenges, and against a backdrop of rising international oil prices, the economy has performed remarkably well, with positive GDP growth registered every year since 1999. Zambia has the potential for further economic diversification and expansion, with present economic policies aimed at promoting broad-based growth and consolidating economic as well as political stability.

The process will be facilitated through the effective implementation of Zambia's fifth National Development Plan, which covers the period 2006 to 2010, succeeding the Poverty Reduction Strategy Paper (PRSP) and Transitional National Development Plan. Donors, in consultation with the Zambian government, are designing a joint assistance strategy for Zambia in order to improve donor harmonization in support of the national development plan and reduce the burden on government.

Furthermore, the United Nations Development Programme (UNDP) is assisting the Zambian government in developing a national long-term vision outlining development targets for the year 2030.

MAJOR ACHIEVEMENTS IN 2005

As stated in the government's 2005 budget, Zambia's macroeconomic objectives for 2005 were to attain a real GDP growth rate of at least 6%, year-end annual inflation of 15%, and a build up in gross international reserves equivalent to 1.3 months' cover of imports of goods and non-factor services.

For the most part, these targets were reached, with impressive macroeconomic developments registered during the year despite negative factors such as high oil prices on the international market, disruptions of fuel supply from the Indeni refinery and high domestic food prices arising from a shortfall in maize production following erratic rainfall during the 2004/05 agricultural season.

Zambia is trying to reduce its dependnce on copper exports by diversifying the economy

Macroeconomic achievements for 2005 include:

- Increased real sector activity
- Improved external sector performance
- Containment of expansion of monetary aggregates
- Decline in commercial banks' nominal lending interest rates
- Deceleration of inflation
- A sharp drop in the stock of external debt
- Improved balance of payments inflows following attainment of the enhanced HIPC completion point

Real GDP growth is estimated at about 4.3% in 2005, with positive economic growth driven by continued investments in the mining, manufacturing, tourism and construction sectors. While growth of 4.3% is slightly lower than the announced economic objectives, this may be attributed to the adverse supply-side developments listed above.

ECONOMIC GROWTH IN KEY SECTORS

MINING

The traditional focus of the Zambian economy has been mining and quarrying, in particular the mining and refining of copper and cobalt. The country holds 10% of the world's known reserves of copper and is ranked among the top producers of copper internationally. Zambia is also the world's largest cobalt producer. These metals made the country one of the most prosperous in southern Africa between 1965 and 1975, accounting for 95% of export earnings and contributing 45% of government revenues. Despite difficulties in the 1980s and 1990s, the sector has seen a turnaround in recent years, particularly in the copper mining subsector. This is due to factors such as improved production techniques, increased capital investment and substantially higher copper prices on international markets.

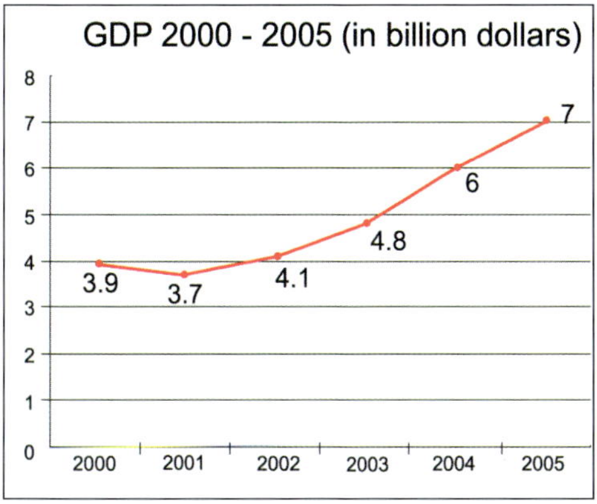

AGRICULTURE

Significant developments in the agricultural sector have identified it as a major engine for attaining broad-based economic growth as well as protecting the social sector. Food security is a key issue, and a great deal of this sector is involved in subsistence farming. The country's fertile tracts of land produce crops such as maize, sorghum, millet and cassava, which are mainly for domestic consumption. Export crops comprise sugar, coffee, groundnuts, rice and cotton as well as horticultural produce.

TOURISM

Tourism is another area of great economic potential for Zambia, which is home to spectacular national parks and game reserves of international standing. While growth in tourism has been boosted through improved marketing and investments by the private sector, resulting in substantial increases in tourist numbers, the sector neverthe-

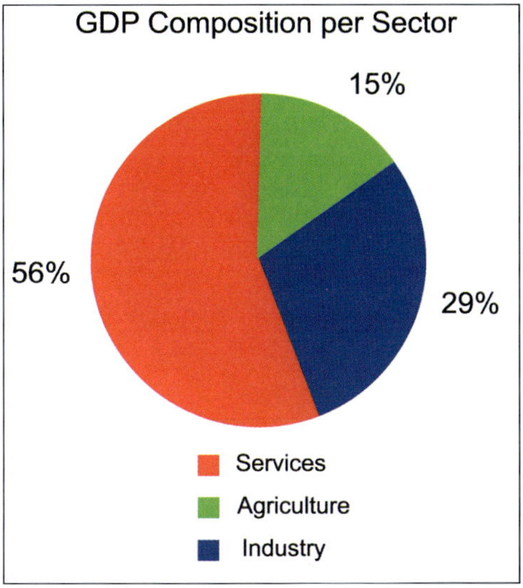

less remains largely underdeveloped, with the provision of hospitality services, accommodation and other tourism-related infrastructure earmarked for development.

MANUFACTURING

Zambia's secondary industries have considerable growth potential and their development is vital to economic diversification. In 2004, the manufacturing sector contributed 11% to the country's GDP, with the most important subsectors being food processing, beverages and tobacco, as well as leather and textiles. Secondary processing of metals takes place, including the smelting and refining of copper, and has led to the manufacturing of metal products and the development of vehicle assembly plants. Fertilizers, chemicals, explosives, and construction materials such as cement are also produced. Petroleum is refined, and there is an active oil industry.

BALANCE OF TRADE

External trade has been progressively liberalized since the early 1990s in response to the phenomenon of globalization. Government incentives to develop export industries in favour of import substitution have led to improved foreign exchange earnings.
Trade barriers have been substantially reduced and quantitative restrictions eliminated. With trade procedures and documentation becoming further standardized and simplified, export permits are no longer necessary. While export licences are required, they are little more than a formality, and import controls are only maintained for health, security and associated reasons. Both export and import licences are issued by commercial banks.

Customs duties are now the main trade policy instrument, and even these have been substantially reduced over the years to support private sector development and strengthen export competitiveness. Tariffs range from 0% to 5% for most basic raw materials, 15% for intermediate goods, and 25% for final products and capital goods.

Zambia's most successful traditional exports remain its metals and minerals, in particular copper and cobalt. There has been steady growth of non-traditional exports (NTEs) such as primary agricultural products, floriculture, sugar, gemstones, timber, electricity, cement and textiles.

Principal imports include foodstuffs, crude oil, chemicals, machinery, iron, steel and manufactured goods, inclu-

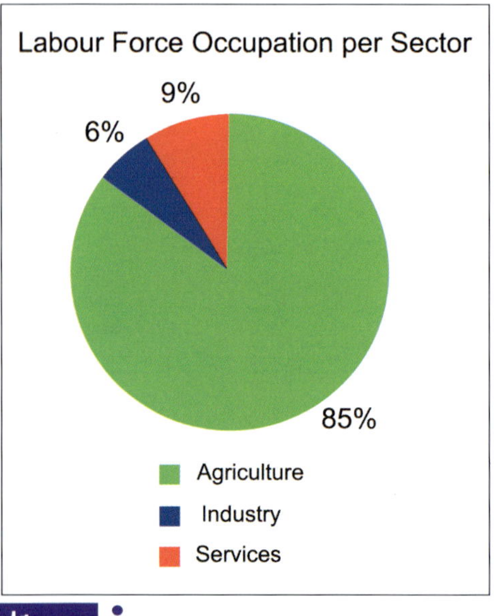

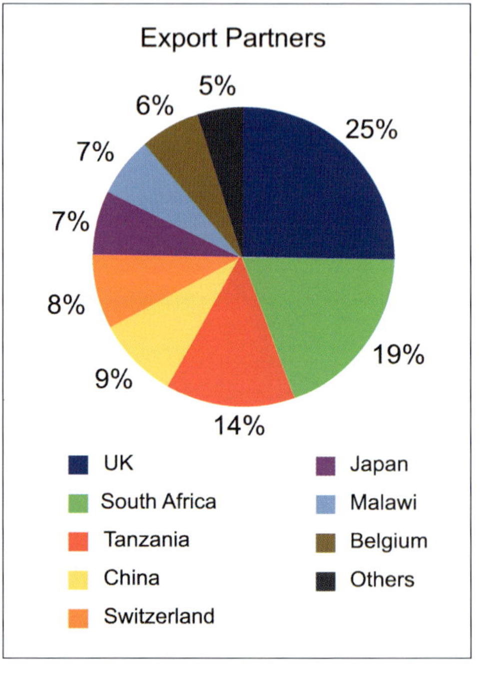

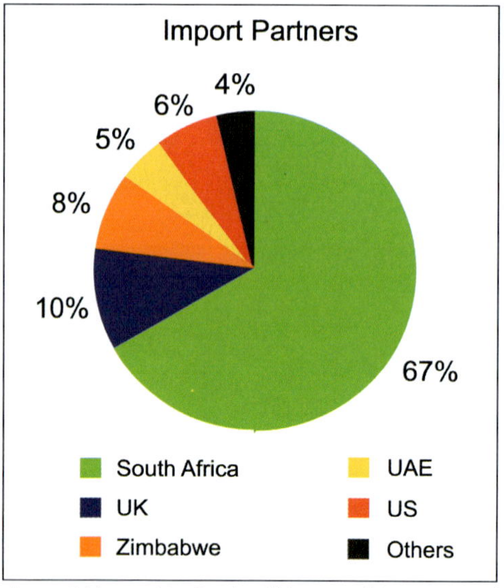

ding vehicles, with South Africa supplying most of Zambia's imports.

Zambia's leading trade partners are the European Union (EU) countries, such as Germany and the United Kingdom. There is also international trade with Japan and the United States of America (USA), and regional trade with South Africa, Zimbabwe, Malawi and the Democratic Republic of Congo.

INFLATION AND INTEREST RATES

Developments in nominal interest rates were mixed, with lending interest rates falling while savings rates moved upwards. The weighted average Treasury bill yield rate declined from 18.1% in December 2004 to 16.6% in 2005. As regards lending, the commercial banks' weighted average lending base rate and the average lending rate declined to monthly averages of 28.2% and 35.4% respectively in 2005 from 29.8% and 37.1% in 2004.

Further success was achieved in bringing down inflation, with the annual overall inflation rate standing at 15.9% at the end of 2005 compared with 17.5% at the end of 2004, which is broadly in line with the end of December 2005 inflation objective of 15%. The drop in inflation is mainly on account of a decrease in annual non-food inflation to 14% in December 2005 from 18.9% in December 2004, due to factors such as the fall in annual broad money between January 2005 and November 2005, and the appreciation of the kwacha exchange rate against other currencies. For 2006, the objective is to reduce inflation further to single digits.

FOREIGN EXCHANGE AND BALANCE OF PAYMENTS

The strengthening of the kwacha during the year to November 2005 saw the monthly average Bank of Zambia mid-exchange rate gaining by 28.9% to K3,393.33 per US dollar from K4,771.31 per US dollar in December 2004, which compared favourably relative to the appreciation of 2.7% over the same period in the previous year. The kwacha's gain was on account of the increased supply of foreign exchange arising from a favourable external sector performance, especially as regards export earnings, prudent fiscal management and reduced debt service payments as a result of Zambia reaching the enhanced HIPC completion point.

The performance of the external sector in 2005 was more favourable than expected. The overall balance of payments deficit narrowed by 21.3% to minus US $274 million in 2005, compared to minus US $348 million in 2004. This was on account of an improvement in the capital and financial account balance by 135% to US $552 million from US $235 million in 2004, resulting from a 24.4% growth in project grants to US $306 million in 2005, as well as an 11.7% increase in foreign direct investment to US $334 million. Increased external capital inflows have partly resulted from the rise in investor and donor confidence following attainment of the HIPC completion point in April 2005.

However, the current account deficit widened to US $826 million in 2005 from US $583 million in 2004. This follows the deterioration in the services account by 17.2% to minus US $252 million and the deficit in the income account by 42.7% to minus US $605 million in 2005.

The value of merchandise imports increased by 19.7% to US $2,068 million, with a growth in import volume mainly due to recapitalization and new investments in the mining sector.

Merchandise exports increased by 17.8% to US $2,095 million, largely as a result of the increase in the value of copper exports brought about by a rise in both export volumes and prices.

Preliminary estimates indicate that non-traditional exports registered strong growth in 2005, with earnings increasing by 18.0% to US $571 million. Accounting for this strong performance were burley tobacco, coffee, copper wire, electrical cables, fresh flowers, fresh vegetables, gemstones, scrap metal, cotton yarn, cotton lint and sugar exports.

As a result of favourable external sector developments, gross international reserves as at 11th November 2005 represented 2.3 months' cover of imports of goods and non-factor services. This was well in excess of the objective of at least 1.3 months' cover by end of December 2005.

REGIONAL EXPANSION AND DEVELOPMENT

The growth of GDP in sub-Saharan Africa reached 5.4% in 2004. While the IMF expected growth to slow to 4.8% in 2005, predictions for 2006 have been revised up to 5.9% which, if achieved, will be the strongest expansion in sub-Saharan Africa since the early 1970s. This growth is underpinned by strong global demand, structural reform, better domestic macroeconomic policies and fewer conflicts in the region. Nevertheless, growth will need to be above 7% per annum to meet the United Nations' Millennium Development Goals (MDGs) by 2015.

State-of-the-art brewery in Lusaka

INVESTING IN A BRIGHTER FUTURE

Total investment pledges during 2005 amounted to US $313.9 million compared with US $39.5 million the previous year. This comprises US $159.1 million in the mining sector and pledges of US $109.5 million, US $18.6 million and US $12.1 million in the manufacturing, tourism and service sectors respectively. Pledges in construction were US $7.5 million while the agriculture and transport sectors received US $3.6 million and US $3.3 million. The pledges were expected to generate 7,919 jobs compared with 5,567 jobs during the same period in 2004.

PRIVATIZATION

Zambia began a comprehensive privatization programme in the early 1990s. One of the most effective elements in Zambia's economic reform programme, the divestment of government interests in parastatal companies, is integral to private sector development and participation. Positive developments have included increased production capacity as well as improved standards of production, with companies capturing new export markets and thus earning increased foreign exchange. The programme has also led to an influx of major international investors who have further invested in other large projects outside the privatization programme. As such, local companies are able to benefit from the existence of strong foreign players.

Lusaka Stock Exchange

Privatization has also created thousands of local shareholders in various companies, with some 60% of companies and units having been sold to Zambians. Concurrently, privatization has served as an employment creator and has prevented the liquidation of many enterprises.

Privatization has taken place at an impressive rate and the country's privatization programme is acknowledged as being one of the most successful in terms of the World Bank's Poverty Reduction Growth Facility. Some of the multinationals that have invested in Zambia include Anglo American, Unilever, Tate & Lyle, Commonwealth Development Corporation, South African Breweries, National Grid, Midlands Power, China Non-Ferrous Metals and Lonhro.

Public sector assets that have been sold encompass both blue chip corporations as well as smaller companies in diverse areas such as telecommunications, mining, manufacturing, chemicals, railways, tourism, agriculture and financial services. Privatized companies that have been listed on the Lusaka Stock Exchange (LuSE) are Chilanga Cement, Zambia Sugar, Zambian Breweries, Rothmans, National Breweries, Pamodzi Hotel, BP Zambia, Shoprite Checkers and ZAMEFA.

CURRENT DEVELOPMENTS

Initially involving the divesture of approximately 150 state-owned enterprises, this number has increased to 284 as many of these enterprises have been split and their operating units sold independently. As at end of November 2005, a total of 262 companies had been privatized, leaving a balance of 22 out of a total working portfolio of 284 companies. Notable companies that were privatized in 2005 include Kafue Textiles as well as Monarch, a company involved in the manufacture and engineering of metallic building products.

The ZPA is presently involved in the following privatization operations:

- The partial privatization of Zambia National Commercial Bank (ZANACO) through the sale of 49% of its shares. Of the remaining shares, 25% will be retained by government, 25.8% will be held in trust with the ZPTF, and 0.2% will continue to be held by the existing minority shareholders.
- Negotiations with the preferred bidder for Ndola Lime Limited are at an advanced stage.
- Commercialization of the national electricity utility, Zambia Electricity Supply Corporation (ZESCO) is at an advanced stage, with most reform measures having been undertaken.
- The Zambian government together with the Zambia Industrial and Commercial Show Society Limited (ZICSSL) are inviting expressions of interest for the sale of a 51% shareholding in Mukuba Hotel Limited.
- The sale of at least 70% shares by competitive tender of Maamba Collieries Limited (MCL), Zambia's principal coal producer, has been approved and bids have closed.
- ZPA has sold 49 of the 51 Engineering Services Corporation of Zambia Limited (ESCO) properties and is currently working on the sale of the Mbala and Kaputa units.
- Following the approval of the granting of concessions for the railway line and platforms previously used by Njanji Commuter Services Limited to the private sector, technically and financially qualified investors interested in providing rail transport services within Lusaka are being sought.
- A strategic equity partner is being sought for Zambia State Insurance Corporation Limited (ZSIC), the country's premier insurance company.
- Government has approved the sale of 100% shares in Nitrogen Chemicals of Zambia Limited (NCZ).
- The lease for Ngoma Lodge in Kafue National Park is under negotiation.

FUTURE OPPORTUNITIES

Other companies being considered for future privatization include: Zambia Telecommunications Company Limited (ZAMTEL); Zambia Postal Services Corporation (ZAMPOST); Tazama Pipeline; Zambia Educational Publishing House; Mulobezi Railway; Contract Haulage; Tanzania-Zambia Railways Limited (TAZARA); Zambia National Building Society (ZNBS); State Lotteries Board; National Airports Corporation; and Kariba Minerals Limited.

AGRICULTURE

"A cow does not find its own horns heavy"
Zambian proverb

OVERVIEW

Almost 60% of Zambia is classified as having medium to high potential for agricultural production, and only 15% is currently under cultivation. Well supplied with rivers and lakes, Zambia has 45% of southern Africa's water resources. Agriculture has long been overlooked as a sector and its huge economic potential is largely untapped. Despite such a small proportion of cultivated land, Zambia's agricultural sector continues to help strengthen the country's economy and provide employment opportunities for its citizens. Over two-thirds of the country's workforce is engaged in agriculture, forestry and fisheries.

There are opportunities for growth if the country's natural assets are to be fully utilized. For example, while tobacco, cotton and coffee are seen as lucrative cash crops, their production can be largely increased. It is essential that traditional farmers become more commercially oriented if agricultural output is to be increased.

Food security is another key component of Zambia's agricultural policy. With farming unavoidably dependent upon rainfall and weather patterns, unfavourable conditions may result in poor crop production, reduced output and subsequent food shortfalls. As a result, the government has periodically been required to import maize meal in order to counter high local prices of staple foods.

In 2005 the government pledged K8 billion in support of out-grower schemes for the production of certain

Agriculture's importance in the economy is growing

Maize is the major crop in Zambia

cash crops and a further K1.5 billion for dairy production. As part of its farm block development and investment scheme, K14 billion was allocated for the infrastructural development of these blocks, placed strategically in specific areas of the country throughout its nine provinces.

SECTOR PERFORMANCE

The agriculture sector accounts for over 15% of Zambia's Gross Domestic Product (GDP) and makes a significant contribution towards the country's foreign exchange earnings. The sector's contribution to

MINISTRY OF AGR

ZAMBIA ..rich and ferti

Two-thirds of Zambia is classified as medium to high potential to agriculture production, and only 15% is currently under cultivation. Well supplied with rivers and lakes, Zambia has 45% of southern Africa's water resources.

ULTURE AND CO-OPERATIVES

nd offers excellent opportunities for investment..

Agriculture has long been overlooked as a sector and its huge economic potential is largely untapped. As such, government has given priority to fast-tracking agriculture development, with assistance given to both large and small-scale farmers.

Mulungushi House, P.O. Box 50197
Tel: +260-1-254645 Fax: +260-1-254083 Ridgeway, Lusaka-Zambia

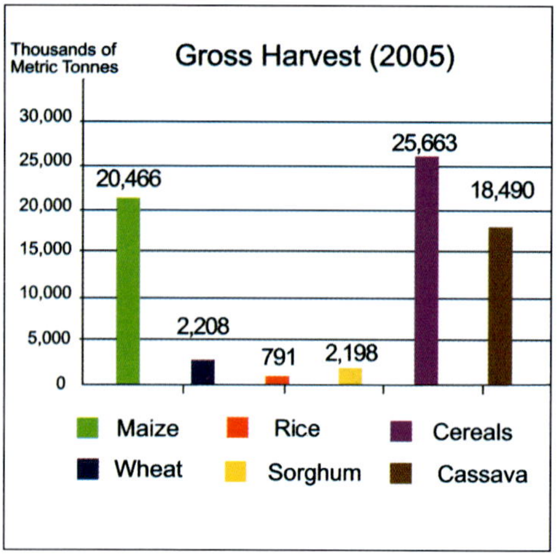

Zambia's non-traditional exports (NTEs) has increased by 36% over the last half decade, more than half of which can be attributed to export earnings of agricultural products.

The agriculture, forestry and fishing sector performed very well during 2004, with value added increasing by 4.5%. This was attributed in large part to continued favourable weather conditions, supportive government policies, private sector investment, and reduced electricity tariffs for irrigation farming. Furthermore, the prices of agricultural commodities on world markets have risen significantly – particularly for sugar, coffee, tobacco and cotton.

In 2005 there were less favourable weather conditions and lower than expected rainfall. In October 2005 Zambia declared a national disaster due to drought conditions and publicly noted its need for food aid to bridge crop production gaps resulting from the harsh weather conditions.

The sector has also been affected by the appreciation of the kwacha by almost 40% in 2005, making exports more difficult.

AGRICULTURAL SUBSECTORS

MAIZE

Maize production during 2004 reached 1.2 million tonnes, approximately double the size of the previous year's production. The bumper harvest has resulted in the strategic reserve of over 60,000 tonnes of maize, the staple crop. Accordingly, the price of maize dropped significantly during the year. However, in 2005 production dropped to 866,000 tonnes due to a partial drought.

Formal maize exports in 2004 amounted to about US $33,897,578, representing a substantial increase. The drastic increase in maize exports was due to an increase in demand for maize and the lifting of export bans on maize in Zambia.

The major market for white maize was Malawi, accounting for 47% of exports, followed by Zimbabwe at 35% and the Democratic Republic of Congo at 15%. A major constraint in maize exports continues to be the restrictions imposed on its exportation.

In 2005 a ban on all maize exports was imposed due to the maize deficit induced by the partial drought.

Data released by the Ministry of Agriculture and by cooperatives show a food surplus of 266,000 tonnes and a maize surplus of 185,000 tonnes over the 2004/05 consumption period.

WHEAT

In 2005, the production of wheat reached 136,833 tonnes, representing an increase of 65% over the production in 2004. Two crops of wheat a year are produced in rotation with cotton and soybeans. Greater focus has been given to the production of irrigated winter wheat. Local demand for wheat is exceeding 10,000 tonnes per year.

NUTS AND SEEDS

Groundnuts are produced for the export market, and there is ample room to expand the local production and processing of this lucrative product. There are also opportunities to increase production of cashew nuts, which are presently grown in Western province. Demand for vegetable oil from processed soybeans and sunflower seeds is increasing. Sunflower production averages 15,000 metric tonnes and soybean production has reached 60,000 metric tonnes, with the area planted to this crop likely to increase.

SUGAR

Zambia's 'white gold', sugar, is one of the country's most valuable export commodities, and is processed for the domestic market and exported to regional and international markets, in particular the EU.

The local sugar industry has been successfully privatized. This initiative has been led by Zambia Sugar, which is by far the largest manufacturer in the country. Zambia Sugar is among the least expensive producers of refined sugar in Africa and is listed on the Lusaka Stock Exchange. Zambia Sugar mills and refines its own sugar cane from its Nakambala Estate, as well as sugar cane from a number of out-growers, at its refinery in Mazabuka. Sugar cane is also grown and processed by Kalungwishi Sugar Estates in the Kasama district of Northern province and the recently opened Consolidated Farms Limited on the outskirts of Lusaka. Both these estates and their refineries produce sugar solely for the domestic market.

COFFEE

Coffee is grown in the Zambian highlands. The main markets are Japan, UK, South Africa, USA, Dubai and Germany. While the country is a relatively small producer, demand has been increasing due to the high quality of coffee produced, and there is scope to increase production to service niche markets in Europe.

COTTON

Since the initiation of major agricultural reforms and privatization of the industry in the early 1990s, Zambian cotton production and processing has grown rapidly. Cotton now ranks as one of the most important sources of crop income among small farmers and agribusiness firms in key agricultural production regions of the country. Production is largely undertaken by out-growers and the subsector is led by two companies – Clark Cotton, which has a ginnery in Chipata, and Dunavant. The increase in production led to another ginnery being built in Eastern province.

Zambia's ginning capacity was approximately 180,000 metric tonnes in 2005, with 144,300 metric tonnes produced in 2004 compared with some 32,000 metric tonnes before the industry was privatized.

Cotton is currently among the highest foreign exchange earners of non-traditional exports.

TOBACCO

Zambia produces as well as processes both burley and Virginia tobacco, with Central and Eastern provinces being the most favourable for the crop. Out-grower schemes have led to an increase in commercial production, and there is scope for small-, medium- and large-scale farmers. The Tobacco Association of Zambia gives assistance to tobacco growers, with help also coming from major world buyers.

Zambian tobacco has received a grade of high quality and flavour, and increased demand has resulted in substantial increases in production. This is being fuelled to some extent by a reduction in cultivation in Zimbabwe, with Zambian tobacco being similar to that grown in Zimbabwe and therefore being able to fill the gap. Production of Virginia tobacco rose to 23,000 metric tonnes in 2005 from 14,000 metric tonnes in 2004, and has the potential to increase further, helped to some extent by the influx of Zimbabwean tobacco farmers and better yields being obtained. Burley also grew significantly due to an increase in the number of growers and greater activity by the tobacco buying companies.

The Tobacco Association of Zambia anticipated that production in 2006 would reach 50,000 metric tonnes in

Since 2000, many Zimbabwean farmers have settled in Zambia to grow tobacco

total, and the value of exports would rise to US $83 million.

HORTICULTURE AND FLORICULTURE

Production of fresh vegetables and flowers for the local market and export has increased in recent years. Floriculture is now one of Zambia's leading non-traditional exports, with the Netherlands being the primary market. The UK is the main importer of Zambia's vegetables. The industry is an excellent example of the benefits of agricultural diversification.

Both floriculture and horticulture do exceedingly well in Zambia's temperate climate. One of the prime areas of expansion has been in the growing of roses, which are exported to the EU, with tropical fruits and vegetables also featuring prominently. The pre-packing of vegetables adds value to exports.

Medium- and large-scale commercial farmers have invested in year-round irrigated production of horticultural products as well as fresh flowers. An additional 40

Floriculture is a growing subsector

hectares of flowers was grown in 2005. There has been a marked increase in the export of horticultural products, especially with the mushrooming of out-grower schemes.

The sector is constrained by costly airfreight charges caused by high aviation fuel costs, and the sector has recently been affected by the appreciation of the kwacha. Potential in that area is still great but highly dependent on the development of irrigation methods.

FORESTRY

Forestry products consist mainly of softwood and hardwood timber harvested from natural forests and commercial plantations, with other products such as honey and beeswax. Forests and plantations cover some 66% of Zambia, with the majority of commercial plantations in the Copperbelt.

The privatization of the Zambia Forest and Forestry Industries Limited (ZAFFICO) has opened up the market for softwood. Similarly, the privatization of Zambezi Saw Mills has increased the participation of private enterprise in the hardwood sector. A number of privately owned saw-milling companies supply the market. Adding value to exports, processed timber is promoted ahead of raw timber produce. Products include plywood, furniture, carvings and curios, which are exported to South Africa and Namibia. There is a need to certify forests in Zambia if forestry products are to penetrate the European market.

LIVESTOCK AND DAIRY

The livestock industry, which comprises the production of beef, poultry, pork, mutton and lamb, has experienced mixed fortunes. While grazing conditions suit a variety of livestock, distribution is uneven and some areas are subject to tsetse fly. The eradication of livestock diseases is a top priority for this sector, with outbreaks of foot and mouth having proven problematic and CBPP continuing to be endemic. A large proportion of the industry remains at subsistence level, with beef and dairy cattle raised for domestic use. The cattle population is declining.

The leading company in beef production, processing and distribution in Zambia is Zambeef Products, listed on the stock exchange. Other beef producers include Keembe Meat Corporation, Realmeat and Galaunia Holdings.

Dairy farming is carried out by commercial, semi-commercial and traditional farmers, and is a subsector with considerable growth potential. Processors in Zambia include Zammilk (Zambeef Products Plc), Finta, Parmalat and Diamondale, among others.

FISHERIES

Commercial production of freshwater fish occurs in the northern, western and southern parts of the country as well as along major rivers and lakes. Development programmes are focused on conservation and research in order to improve yields, with private sector involvement comprising fish farming, marketing and distribution.

While fish is traditionally sold in its dried form, large amounts are now being frozen due to improvements in transportation and refrigeration facilities. Fish is processed at Mpulungu and exported by Tanganyika Cold Storage Exports.

OPPORTUNITIES IN EXPORT AND INVESTMENT

Sharing borders with eight other countries, Zambia is centrally situated as a gateway to both southern and central Africa. This location is strategically advantageous by placing Zambia in a position to exploit the growing regional markets of SADC and COMESA, and be an active participant in regional and international agricultural trade initiatives. Furthermore, rail and road infrastructure connects Zambia to regional markets as well as ports in Tanzania, Mozambique, Botswana, Angola, Namibia and South Africa. International air cargo services are also utilized, with Lusaka International Airport serving as a hub to connect Zambian products to global markets.

The country's climatic diversity – ranging from temperate to tropical – is able to support a variety of agricultural and horticultural produce. Export potential of this produce is huge, and while the sector has become increasingly productive due to profitable private sector investment, there is still massive potential for large-scale investment in commercial farms.

Agricultural exports have in the past tended to be dominated by maize. However, non-traditional exports, such as sugar, tobacco, cotton, horticultural and floricultural products, hides and wood are becoming increasingly lucrative in terms of export earnings, finding profitable markets in the EU. Furthermore, higher prices in global markets for commodities such as sugar, coffee, cotton and tobacco have resulted in these agricultural subsectors increasing their profit margins.

Zambia's total non-traditional export (NTE) earnings have registered strong growth over the last three years. Between 2004 and 2005 NTE earnings rose nearly 18% to US $571 million. This was attributed to increased export earnings of burley tobacco, coffee, fresh flowers, fresh vegetables, cotton yarn, cotton lint and sugar exports and to diversification in the agricultural sector.

Both traditional and non-traditional agricultural exports have historically been exported in their raw, unprocessed form. There is therefore considerable potential in the downstream processing of agricultural produce. Private enterprise is able to take advantage of the gap that exists in the market through investment in processing plants, either as stand-alone units or in conjunction with agricultural initiatives. There is also room for joint ventures between those involved in agricultural production and manufacturing industries concerned with food processing. This includes ventures between investors and farmers, with small-scale enterprises able to be transformed into profitable concerns with external financial backing.

DEVELOPMENT PROGRAMMES

The central theme of government programmes is to encourage both large-scale and small-scale farming, as well as enterprise diversification. In this regard, the establishment and expansion of large-scale farming is being facilitated through the creation of properly surveyed and demarcated farming blocks as a way of encouraging large investments and job creation. In order to raise employment and self-employment in rural areas, large-scale investment in commercial farming and out-grower schemes is being encouraged. Developments during 2005 included K14 billion provided for the commercialization of agricultural land for farming blocks, starting with Nansanga Farm Block.

Concerning small-scale farming, the government is putting additional emphasis on the provision of inputs on a timely basis in order to encourage out-grower schemes, especially for export crops. The Crop Marketing Authority (CMA) facilitates the procurement and distribution of agriculture inputs to targeted areas. Resettlement schemes are supported, with government continuing to improve the land tenure system as well as strengthening rural infrastructure and extension services. In 2005 the government allocated K8 billion for out-grower schemes for tobacco, coffee, cotton, paprika and cashew nuts.

Packaging for export of vegetables to Europe

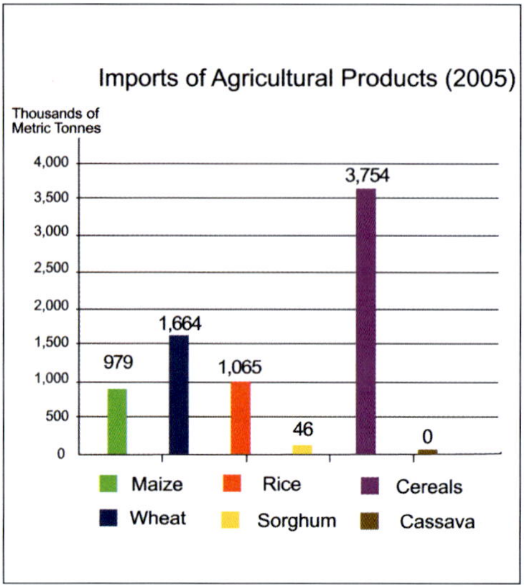

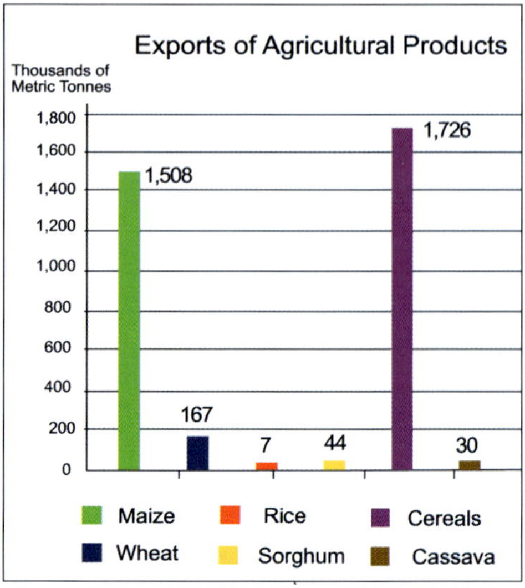

A comprehensive programme to boost the development of the agricultural sector has been developed, which includes a package of special incentives. The government has in recent years facilitated private sector investment, especially in the cultivation of cash crops such as cotton, paprika and tobacco. Furthermore, Zesco developed a scheme that reduced electricity tariffs by 50% for irrigation farming.

NOTICE! See Investment and Legal Framework section.

MAIN COMPANIES

AMIRAN AGROCHEMICALS

157 Freedom Way
P O Box 31744, Lusaka
Tel: +260-1-227-749/227-751
Fax: +260-1-224-954
Email: amiran@zamnet.zm
Website: www.amiran-zambia.com

Activity: Agrochemicals
Date of Creation: 1963
Employees: 45-50
Amiran Ltd was established in 1963 in Lusaka and has over 40 years of operation in and commitment to the Zambian market and nation. Amiran Ltd is a member of Balton CP Group of Companies and has around 45 to 50 employees.

Amiran was the pioneer company to introduce drip irrigation to the farming community in Zambia. Amiran gives the growers optimum solutions for drip irrigation systems in vegetable crops, coffee plantations, and banana and other orchards. The improvement of yield and quality under fertigation (irrigation + fertilization) systems is tremendous.

Amiran has developed in Zambia the Family Drip System (FDS). This low-cost system is suitable mainly for rural farmers who do not have an electricity supply at their farm. The irrigation is by gravity and one system can irrigate up to 1,000m^2. Most vegetable crops can be grown irrigated by the FDS. Many farmers in Zambia start to grow tomatoes using the FDS and upgrade after one or two seasons to a pressurized drip irrigation system.

Amiran provide and install earth dam lining to farmers and other customers to build reservoirs for agricultural and landscaping purposes. It is mainly used for reservoirs for drip irrigation purposes and fish ponds.
Amiran Ltd (Zambia) is the sole agent of the Israeli greenhouse manufacturers Azrom Ltd, and Amiran builds gre-

enhouse projects as turnkey projects. This includes all corresponding components such as greenhouse structures, greenhouse covers, computerized irrigation systems, including water recycling systems and coco-pit fibres as a growing medium.

Amiran has also supplied and installed poultry equipment to training institutes such as boarding schools and higher learning institutions for self-sufficiency and food surplus for sale.

COFFEE BOARD OF ZAMBIA

Mr Benny Zimba
Board Secretary
Showgrounds, Lusaka
Tel: +260-1-252850/252170
Fax: +260-1-252170
Email: coffee@zamnet.zm; coffee@iwayafrica.com
Activity: Coffee-related activities
Date of Creation: 1989
Turnover: US $15 million
Employees: 7

At present Zambia is a relatively small producer of coffee, with industry performance having been uneven due to declining coffee prices. The coffee produced is nevertheless of high quality and there is scope to increase production to service niche markets in Europe.

The Coffee Board of Zambia (CBZ) was established in 1989 to regulate the promotion, growing and marketing of coffee in Zambia. The Coffee Board of Zambia's main role is to finance coffee producers' projects and undertake the marketing for Zambian coffee; this is mostly done at specialized coffee fairs and very specific roadshows in places such as the US, Japan or Scandinavian countries.

Another role of the CBZ is experimenting, investigating and conducting research in areas relating to coffee. The

Milling maize and wheat

coffee inspector ensures strict compliance with relevant provisions of the Coffee Act by monitoring all coffee growers in Zambia.

The industry expects to generate about US $10.2 million from a projected yield of 6,800 tonnes of coffee in 2006, according to CBZ inspector Sunday Silongwe in an interview at the 78th Agricultural and Commercial Show in Lusaka. There are currently 70 large-scale coffee growers and 500 small-scale producers in Zambia, mainly in the Luapula, Northern, Copperbelt and Central provinces.

The CBZ is highly involved in the Copperbelt Economic Diversification Program, which is a project of the Global Development Alliance implemented in support of economic diversification in the Copperbelt. It is a US $2.6 million public & private partnership with an initial project framework of three years. The alliance partners include Development Alternatives, Inc. (DAI), Zambia Coffee Growers Association (ZCGA), Cheetah Zambia Ltd, Stravendale Farm Ltd, Konkola Copper Mines (KCM), Amiran Ltd, and the Zambia Agribusiness Technical Assistance Center (ZATAC).

The overall objective is to expand and strengthen private, market-oriented agro-enterprises (producer-group enterprises) and commercial out-grower production schemes. The project emphasizes activities that unlock and add value at the smallholder production level in order to increase the volume of high-value agro-products sold domestically, regionally and internationally so that smallholder income, and subsequently wealth, is increased.

"The vision of the CBZ is to increase production of high quality Arabica coffee through support to emergent and established large-scale farmers and support to out-grower schemes."
Mr Benny Zimba, Board Secretary

Zambeef is the leading producer, processor and distributor of beef in Zambia

DUNAVANT ZAMBIA

Mr Patrick Nyumbu
Country Project Manager
Mzilikazi Road, Lusaka
Tel: +260-1-1-286137
Email: cotton@zamnet.zm; wilsonr@dunavant.co.zm
Website: www.dunavant.com

Activity: Cotton merchandising

Dunavant Enterprises, Inc. is a privately owned company, with cotton merchandising as its primary business. Dunavant is one of the largest cotton merchandisers in the world, handling in excess of four million bales of US and foreign cotton per year. Their involvement in the cotton industry includes ginning and warehousing operations throughout the world. Dunavant owns a commodities trading company, various real estate development companies, a truck brokerage company that serves as agent for approximately 5,000 trucks used to haul cotton to domestic mills and to ports for export, and various other entities.

Dunavant has offices in the major cotton producing areas of the United States. Foreign offices include: Geneva, Switzerland; Guatemala City, Guatemala; Hong Kong, China; Sao Paulo, Brazil; Buenos Aires, Argentina; Lusaka, Zambia; Asuncion, Paraguay; Moree, Australia; Obregon, Mexico. In what is now the former Soviet Union, Dunavant has offices in Ashgabad, Turkmenistan; Dushanbe, Tajikistan; and Tashkent, Uzbekistan. With buying offices located in all major cotton producing areas, the price they receive is solid, based on up-to-the-minute information and flexibility that only a marketing network as vast as Dunavant's can offer. That price is backed by a record of performance and reliability.

Dunavant Cotton has been working in Zambia for several years and has a strong presence in Mumbwa. The distributors deal individually with Dunavant and have contracts for the inputs that they receive. Dunavant previously only provided inputs for cotton production, but in conjunction with CLUSA (Cooperative League USA) and FAO (Food and Agriculture Organization of the UN) in the 2002/03 season inputs for maize and legumes were also supplied. The distributors choose who they work with independent of Dunavant. The distributor distributes the inputs to the chosen farmers and is responsible for repayment of the credit individually.

Dunavant Cotton has partnered with the US government in an innovative programme designed to alleviate the impact of HIV/AIDS on its employees and residents in the surrounding communities. Dunavant Zambia Ltd was in 2004 nominated for the US Secretary of State's Award for Corporate Excellence due to its efforts to promote both public health and economic growth in Zambia.

LIVESTOCK DEVELOPMENT TRUST

7 Addis Ababa Drive, Rhodes Park, Woodlands
Private Bag 173, Lusaka
Tel: +260-1-251772/213648
Fax: +260-1-251802
Email: ldt@zamnet.zm

Activity: Livestock development

The Livestock Development Trust (LTD) was set up on 17th October 2002. It is a private and public sector partnership that seeks to promote environmentally friendly livestock development initiatives for all livestock farmers in a gender-sensitive and participatory manner.

It seeks to attain profitable livestock-led farming systems that improve productivity and add value to production through transfer of skills, information and technology, and improving credit and market access.

The LTD raises funds through the commercial management of livestock, through the provision of contractual, consultancy and specialist services and also through grants and donations. It imports practical and theoretical managerial skills and knowledge to course participants in order to enhance productivity in the livestock sector.

The LDT offers a two-year certificate course and tailor-made and demand-driven short courses.

LDT promotes the utilization of animal draft power technologies countrywide.

LDT runs a number of institutions dealing with livestock: Mochipapa Development and Research Centre (undertakes livestock-based research activities); Keembe Piggery (sources quality breeding stock and supports training in pig production); Palabana Dairy Training Institute (serves as a practical training base for all dairy courses and is a source of breeding stock to smallholder dairy farmers in Zambia); and Balmoral Vaccine Production Unit (supporting government disease and control programmes).

MARKET ACCESS TRADE AND ENABLING POLICIES (MATEP)

Mr Scott Simons
Chief of Party
3828 Parliament Road, Olympia Park
PostNet Box 246, Private Bag E10, Lusaka
Tel: +260-1-291569/290698
Fax: +260-1-291569
Email: scott_simons@dai.com; matep@dai.com

Activity: Trade of agriculture exports

The Market Access Trade and Enabling Policies (MATEP) project is a five-year USAID project designed to increase Zambia's exports of agricultural and natural resource products into regional and international markets.

It is a result-oriented project that is intended to make exports happen. MATEP is initially focusing on eight product value chains and on tourism. The value chains are horticulture, paprika, honey, coffee, livestock, cotton, maize and cassava. Exports of these eight, plus tourism, offer the greatest potential for growth over the project horizon, as well as for impact on Zambia's economy and population, owing to interventions of the project. MATEP will also assist stakeholders in responding to opportunities in other value chains as they arise.

The project has four closely interlinked components to achieve its export objective: trade and enabling policy, market access, tourism and finance.

The trade and enabling policy component focuses on domestic policies and regulations that constrain Zambia's exports as well as on regional and international trade agreements under which exports can grow. MATEP works closely with the Zambia Private Sector Development (PSD) programme.

The market access component focuses on identifying foreign markets into which Zambia can sell and on working with exporters to successfully complete transactions in those markets. MATEP targets both regional markets and more distant markets in Europe, America and Asia for Zambia's exports.

"With the finance component, MATEP uses investment capital and technical assistance to promote short-term and medium-term lending to exporting enterprises by piloting innovative lending partnerships with financial sector institutions."
Mr Scott Simons, Chief of Party

NANGA FARMS

Mr Raymond Strover
General Manager
P O Box 670079, Lusaka
Tel: +260-3-230260/251895/230260
Fax: +260-3-251971
Email: nanga@zamnet.zm

Activity: Coffee farm

Nanga Farms is situated on the banks of the Kafue River in the Southern province of Zambia. The farm produces fine quality washed Arabica coffee grown at an altitude of around 1,000m. The coffee plantation is intensively managed on 220 hectares, is fully irrigated and is replanted on a seven- to eight-year cycle, maintaining a young plantation and quality crop at its best. Harvesting of the crop is carried out from March to October, which employs up to 400 local residents on a seasonal basis. The whole crop passes through a wet processing plant where it is fermented and washed before being naturally dried under shade.

Annual production ranges from 300 to 400 tonnes of

green beans, all of which is available for export.

In the year 2000, the farm established the first coffee out-grower scheme in the Southern province for small-holder farmers in the surrounding area in an effort to improve their standard of living. The smallholders are provided with seedlings from Nanga, which also provides extension and back-up services. This small group of dedicated farmers, who call themselves the Lukama Development Association, at present has eight members, each with between 500 and 1,200 trees. The group will expand each year, as will the number of trees grown by each farmer. Once in production all their coffee will be processed and marketed by Nanga with the proceeds paid directly to the farmers.

The resident labour force is well catered for on the farm with a modern clinic staffed by two qualified nurses, good brick housing and ablutions, a local school, social centre and sports facilities. The farm also has a health, safety and environmental committee that looks after the health and safety interests of the labour force and the environment. Seasonal employees are transported in from local villages on a daily basis to pick coffee during the harvesting season, providing employment during a period of the year when there is little alternative source of income.

NATIONAL MILLING CORPORATION

Mr Peter Cottan
Managing Director
Cairo Road,
P O Box 31980, Lusaka
Tel: +260-1-222451/225977
Fax: +260-1-237073/226467
Email: peterc@nmc.co.zm

Activity: Agro-business

National Milling Corporation (NMC) is a subsidiary of the American-based company Seaboard Corporation, a diversified international agribusiness and transportation com-

National Milling Corporation, Zambia's pride nationwide

pany engaged in a wide range of activities, including meat processing, cargo shipping, commodity merchandising, sugar production, citrus fruit growing and electric power generation.

In Africa, South America and the Caribbean, Seaboard maintains 13 flour, maize and feed milling operations with a combined productive capacity of over 1.5 million metric tonnes of finished product per year. The African mills are located throughout the continent – Sierra Leone, Nigeria, Republic of Congo, Democratic Republic of Congo, Angola, Lesotho, Mozambique, Zambia, Kenya and Uganda.

In Zambia, National Milling Corporation was bought by Seaboard Corporation in 1999 following the privatization of the parastatal company.

The company operates four maize mills, one wheat mill and one stockfeed mill in four locations around the country and has a production capacity of 23 tonnes per hour for maize, 10 tonnes per hour for flour and 10 tonnes per hour for stockfeed. National Milling Corporation has recently converted its facilities for bulk handling.

NMC has strengthened its leadership on the market and has developed the strongest distribution network in Zambia, with 20 depots around the country providing maize and flour at 'Lusaka prices' to its consumers around Zambia.

The NMC has developed strategic partnerships with the farmers and created incentive schemes to increase yields and improve the quality of wheat produced. By developing four different grades of wheat quality (premium, A, B and C), National Milling Corporation has a better control of the quality of flour produced. NMC produces high protein and high quality flour that is ideally suited to the baking of bread and pastries.

The internal demand for wheat and maize should continue to grow steadily over the coming years. Over the next 12 months, the flour mill capacity will be increased by 50%, the maize mill by 30% and the stockfeed mill by 20%. The company is also looking to increase its exports in the region, and more particularly into DRC.

"NMC has strengthened its leadership on the market and has developed the strongest distribution network in Zambia."
Mr Peter Cottan, Managing Director

MPONGWE DEVELOPMENT CO. LTD

Mpongwe Development
P O Box 90599, Luanshya
Tel: +260-2-510604/217298
Fax: +260-217298

Date of Creation: 1984
Employees: 560

Mpongwe is the largest agricultural producer in Zambia, and is also the largest commercial arable farm in Africa. It has 15,000 hectares of land devoted to crops, of which 4,500 hectares are irrigated.

The Mpongwe Development Company in Zambia was founded in 1984, with the Commonwealth Development Corporation (CDC) as one of its original investors. In 1990, CDC assumed ownership and, 15 years later, the company is now trading profitably. Between 2001 and 2004, CDC Group has invested GB £650 million in private sector businesses in Africa, Asia and South America.

Mpongwe produces around 100,000 tonnes of wheat, soya and maize a year and also has small coffee and cattle operations. In 2005, Mpongwe met about 50% of Zambia's total soya demand, 20% of its wheat requirements and about 5% of the country's maize needs. More than 95% of the coffee crop is exported. MDC contributes 5% of the nation's requirement of maize, 40% of Zambia's requirement of wheat and 80% of the soybean requirement.

A plan to increase wheat production by converting another 1,000 hectares of rain-fed fields to irrigation was recently approved. The current manager has agreed to provide US $4m of additional equity to finance this expansion. In 2006 Mpongwe expects to increase coffee production to 1,400 metric tonnes from 1,030 metric tonnes in 2005.

Thanks to continued investment from CDC, Mpongwe employs 560 staff and provides substantial benefits to the local community. These include an active social responsibility programme that includes substantial financial support for local schools and medical facilities, thousands of seasonal jobs at harvest-time and new and improved housing, shops and a bank.

Mpongwe Development Corporation is a committed ethical business that processes coffee and maize in Zambia for local consumption. Profits from the mushroom project are recycled to fund local primary schools and rural health centres.

SEED CO

Mr David Clemence
Managing Director
Makeni Road
P O Box 35310, Lusaka
Tel: +260-1-272520/272521
Fax: +260-1-273390
Email: seedco@seedco.co.zm

Activity: Production of seeds

Seed Co Ltd has been actively involved in the production of quality seeds. The merger of two associations in 1983 (Seed Maize Association and Crop Seeds Association) resulted in the formation of the Seed Co-operative Company of Zimbabwe which consolidated the activities of both. Administration, planning, production, processing and distribution of all seeds was much more efficient with this new organization.

At a landmark meeting in May 1996, the Seed Co-op members agreed to a public flotation of the organization which led to the raising of Z $45 million in new shares and the quoting of Seed Co Ltd on the Zimbabwe Stock Exchange in July of the same year.

Flotation funding was used to increase seed conditioning capacity and small packing, create an export division, establish an export processing zone, as well as the purchase of another research station at Kadoma. Kadoma Research Centre, Seed Co's second research facility, was purchased in 1996, providing an invaluable site for the evaluation of varieties needed in the smallholder farming sector.

Regional expansion now extends to wholly owned operations in Zambia, Botswana and Malawi, with a majority shareholding in SEMOC in Mozambique. Recently, a research and technical agreement with Syngenta has been concluded. In addition, the formation of Syngenta Seedco Pty Ltd South Africa, in which Seed Co Ltd holds a 49% share, has been created. Seed research, production and distribution are being actively pursued in each of these countries in order to extend Seed Co's business interests in Africa. An East African business unit has recently been established in Nairobi, Kenya.

In Seed Co four critical research aspects are constantly being evaluated: new varieties, better than the currently available seed products, are constantly being assessed in terms of yield, quality, disease tolerance and agro-ecological adaptability. These criteria are paramount, and breeding methods are carefully planned with specific breeding goals established. It can take up to 12 years for a new maize hybrid to be released from when the initial breeding project is started to having product on the shelf for sale.

TOBACCO ASSOCIATION OF ZAMBIA

Dr J. Masinja
Managing Director
Mungoi Road, Plot 5055, Lusaka
Tel: +260-1-286635/286636
Fax: +260-1-286635

Activity: Tobacco

The overall objective of the Tobacco Association of Zambia (TAZ) is to foster development of the tobacco industry in Zambia and to protect the interest of tobacco growers. The association is responsible for representation of tobacco farmers in agro-related fora. It also represents the tobacco farmers in negotiations for tobacco prices and general marketing of the crop.

TAZ's mission is to promote and foster the development of the flue-cured tobacco industry in Zambia in a representative and fully inclusive and equal manner for the benefit of the tobacco growers, their employees, their customers and the Republic of Zambia, whilst at all times acting within the law.

Each grower who is a member of the association has equal rights and responsibilities within the TAZ constitution, irrespective of size of enterprise, which currently varies from less than one hectare to more than 200 hectares.

Through its newsletters, TAZ updates its members on seeds, general agronomy, Integrated Pest Management (IPM), soil protection and fertilizers, water resource management, fuel/barn efficiency, reforestation, and minors' and women's interests in tobacco growing.

TAZ will enter into a mutually beneficial partnership with its tobacco buyers irrespective of whether or not there is an equity share for TAZ as long as it is for the long-term benefit of TAZ members and the entire tobacco industry.

"TAZ, being the representative of the majority of the flue-cured tobacco growers in Zambia, is dedicated to providing assistance in every facet of production, research and sale of tobacco and is committed to the expansion and development of its grower base. Recognized as an asset to the people and the government of Zambia, TAZ will maintain and improve its position among the tobacco growing and exporting nations of the world."
Dr J. Masinja, Managing Director

YORK FARM

Mr Nigel Pollard
General Manager
York Farm, 5km south of Lusaka
P O Box 30829, Lusaka
Tel: +260-1-274020/22
Fax: +260-1-274023
Email: npollard@yorkfarm.co.zm

Activity: Agro-business
Date of Creation: 1960
Turnover: US $22 million
Employees: 3,500

York Farm was established in the 1960s and started exporting baby vegetables in the mid 1980s and roses in the late 1980s. The company is continually upgrading its production facilities, staff training and development.

In addition to supplying produce to the local markets, York Farm is now focused on the production of organic and conventional export quality vegetables. The farm is ideally positioned to supply leading international supermarkets, and exports some 3,300 tonnes of high quality vegetables annually to its customer base in the UK, Europe, South Africa and New Zealand.

The 1,200 cultivable hectares of this 1,800-hectare estate benefit from Zambia's almost humidity-free, temperate tropical climate during the dry season, which allows a wide range of crops to be grown under irrigation. During the rainy season, production is supplemented by protected cropping under the company's 12 hectares of greenhouses.

The main crops are mangetout, sugar snap peas, fine and bobby beans, baby corn, courgettes, baby carrots, tender stem broccoli and leeks, as well as different types and varieties of chillies. York Farm concentrates on the production of baby varieties for a number of reasons: they are popular forms of convenience food in high demand, of high value and thus lend themselves well to being air-freighted quickly to their destinations overseas.

York Farm has recognized the international demand for foodstuffs that are the freshest possible, and has correspondingly adapted its procedures to this. All crops are picked fresh daily, selected, washed, prepared and packed for export within the same 24-hour period. Once the products reach the pack-house they enter a 'cold chain' which remains unbroken right up to the final consumer. In line with modern requirements, York Farm is regularly audited by various quality assurance protocols, and has achieved accreditation with EUREPGAP, Nature's Choice Gold, BRC and HACCP, and ECOCERT.

"Commitment to the highest quality standards, together with provision of reliable delivery, has enabled York Farm to establish firm export links with many UK and Continental supermarkets."
Mr Nigel Pollard, General Manager

ZAMBIA AGRICULTURAL AND COMMERCIAL SHOW

Mr Michelo
Managing Director
P O Box 30333, Lusaka
Tel: +260-1-250222
Fax: +260-1-250631
Email: acsz@zamnet.zm
Website: www.acsz.co.zm

Date of Creation: 1919

The Zambia Agricultural and Commercial Show, which is organized by the Agricultural and Commercial Society of Zambia (ACSZ), is the country's premier annual show, held in the capital city, Lusaka, for five days ending on Farmers' Day, a public holiday observed on the first Monday of August.

The first show was held in 1919 and has been held every year thereafter with the exception of 1921, 1941, 1946 and 1966. During this period the venue has changed three times, from the Kafue riverbank site in Lusaka where the National Institute of Public Administration stands today, and since 1951 to its permanent home in the present day Showgrounds.

The show is the climax of district and provincial agricultural shows, which are held in the proceeding eight weeks, and so only the best of the agriculture products grown by small-scale farmers are finally exhibited at the show.

Exhibitors at the show have over the years included companies from Botswana, Burundi, Zimbabwe, Tanzania, Malawi, Kenya, South Africa, Namibia, Sweden, Holland, Norway, Egypt, England, Pakistan, India, China, France and Germany.

"The Zambia Agricultural and Commercial Show has truly become a leading southern African regional meeting place for investors and business people looking for opportunities and development."
Mr Michelo, Managing Director

ZAMBIA EXPORT GROWERS ASSOCIATION

Mr Luke Mbewe
Chief Executive Officer
Airfreight Village, Lusaka International Airport
P O Box 310245, Lusaka
Tel: +260-1-271166/271080
Fax: +260-1-271167
Email: zega@zegaltd.co.zm; zega@zamnet.zm
Website: www.zambiaexportgrowers.com

Activity: Farming association
Date of Creation: 1984

The Zambia Export Growers Association (ZEGA) was formed in 1984 as a non-profitmaking association to promote the interests of all growers wishing to export fresh horticultural produce. As a professional and independent body, ZEGA aims mainly to provide an efficient and adequate airfreight service to exporters, coordinate the buying of inputs and the organization of technical assistance, assist with information on marketing opportunities, lobby government and other bodies on behalf of grower–exporters and provide technical support and horticultural/floricultural training to members.

The industry has 30 direct exporters and the association is membership driven. In 2005 exports of fresh produce amounting to 10,060 tonnes were exported with an export value of over US $50 million. The area under flower production is about 195 hectares, of which 145 hectares are for roses and the rest for summer flowers. The export vegetables are normally grown in open fields under drip irrigation. Over 15,000 people are employed in the industry.

The product mix consists of cut flowers and vegetables. Over 60 varieties of roses and a variety of summer flowers are produced. Roses normally account for about 95% of cut flower production with the rest being summer flowers. Speciality vegetable exports include baby corn, courgettes, mangetout (snow peas), fine beans, sugar snaps, baby carrots, chillies, spring onions and okra. Some of the vegetables are organically grown, with good prospects of expanding production due to increasing European demand for organically grown produce. An out-grower scheme of small-scale vegetable growers has been put in place and this programme, too, has great potential to expand.

Horticultural production is not limited to large and medium-sized companies. Smallholder farmers also have opportunities to export crops under out-grower schemes. The major markets for Zambian rose exports are the Netherlands and the United Kingdom. Zambia also has a small market share in South Africa, particularly during the off-season period between May to September. The vegetables, which are grown according to the terms of the ZEGA code of practice, are mainly sold to prestigious European supermarkets.

Another ZEGA initiative has been the establishment of the Horticultural Training Trust to complement farm training with residential certificate and diploma courses in export horticulture.

ZAMBIA NATIONAL FARMERS' UNION

Mr Guy N. H. Robinson
President
ZNFU Stand, Showgrounds, Lusaka
Tel: +260-1-252649/255769
Fax: +260-1-252648
Email: kushiya@iwayafrica.com

Activity: Farmers' union

The ZNFU is one of the oldest associations in Zambia. ZNFU has existed under various names almost since the first large-scale farms were established in Zambia in the early 1900s.

Before independence in 1964, the ZNFU was called Rhodesia National Farmers' Union. After independence, the name became Commercial Farmers' Bureau. By 1992, this name had become outdated and misleading. Until independence, the membership had been almost entirely confined to large-scale farmers. Since then, there has been a steady growth of small-scale farmers' membership. This accelerated in the early 1980s, encouraged by a policy of keeping the annual subscription at a low level and by an entry qualification which accepts any person or organization engaged in the business of farming in Zambia.

The mission of the ZNFU is to promote and protect the interests of members as farmers, individuals, corporations/companies and other organizations involved in the business of farming in order to achieve sustainable economic and social development.

This mission statement sets out the ground rules for ZNFU activities and identifies not only what activities the ZNFU is engaged in, but also the core beliefs or guiding principles that underpin its activities and where it is heading. All objectives and strategies of the ZNFU are derived from the mission statement.

ZNFU is politically neutral or non-partisan. The ZNFU has a strict policy requiring members to resign any leadership posts within the ZNFU upon entering national politics.

"This is an organization made up of farmers and led by regularly elected leaders who are farmers as well. Investors are welcome and if they are serious they will definitely do good business in Zambia."
Mr Guy N. H. Robinson, President

ZAMBIA SUGAR

Mr Paul de Robillard
Managing Director
Mazabuka
Tel: +260-3-231109/+260-1-246137
Fax: +260-3-231112
Email: pderobillard@zamsugar.zm

Activity: Production of sugar

Zambia Sugar is located in the Mazabuka area on the Kafue Flats. These agricultural fields are business investments split among the commercial farmers that make up the Mazabuka farming belt today. Zambia Sugar Plc is a public listed company on the Lusaka stock exchange.

Zambia Sugar operates a sugar mill and the largest sugar estate in Zambia. The company cultivates sugar cane on some 11,000 hectares of land, from which about 190,000 tonnes of sugar is produced annually. Zambia Sugar exports around 75,000 tonnes of sugar per year to the EU and regional markets. Zambia Sugar also acquires sugar from other important farms in the region such as Nanga Farms Plc, owned by the Commonwealth Development Corporation (CDC), and Ceres Farms Ltd.

The sugar estate and mill rely on water from the neighbouring Kafue Flats. The farmers realize that maintaining the fresh water resource is of vital importance to them, but also to others in the region like fishermen, city dwellers in Lusaka and the hydropower plant at Kafue Gorge. The Zambia Sugar agricultural estate is almost exclusively reliant on the Kafue Flats wetland water resource for irrigation. The company has built canals that run from pump stations on the riverbanks to the sugar estate where the channelled water is released to the farms by way of furrow (surface) irrigation. For Zambia Sugar, water from the Kafue Flats wetland system is critical.

Zambia Sugar is one of the commercial farms represented in the partnership with WWF and the local community to establish Mwanachingwala Conservation Area; the company has contributed 3,000 hectares to the conservancy authority. Zambia Sugar has also contributed to the development of infrastructure in the MCA with labour, equipment, logistic support, materials and fuel.

The company has been involved in the reintroduction of game; Zambia Sugar contributed works worth US $10,000. The company has also demonstrated its commitment to the local community by grading community roads. In order to reduce water consumption and improve water quality in the waterways, Zambia Sugar has actively implemented a discharge water recycling system in its plantation.

ZAMBIA SEED COMPANY

Mr Ben Zulu
Managing Director
Buyantanshi Road
P O Box 35441, Lusaka
Tel: +260-1-243762/248025
Fax: +260-1-2245736
Email: zamseed@zamnet.zm

Activity: Seed production
Employees: 78

The Zambia Seed Co. Ltd of Lusaka (ZAMSEED) was founded in 1981 to produce, process and market agricultural and horticultural seeds. The company makes a point of knowing that its seeds will succeed in the importing countries.

The company employs 78 people and in 2005 generated over US $1 million in revenue, 1% of which was generated by exports to the Democratic Republic of Congo and Malawi.

The company has based its success on exporting selected varieties of seed that will adapt to the growing conditions of importing countries. ZAMSEED therefore looks at popular varieties of seeds growing in border areas, thus eliminating trial and error arrangements.

The good performance of the different varieties of seed has led to repeated purchases by numerous customers. ZAMSEED has historically exported fresh seed, enhancing the seed quality. The products are always exported in quality packages and provided with the necessary labelling requirements as demanded by the importer. The tender prices offered are normally competitive, often below local market prices.

The company always provides after sales service, especially on the Malawi market. In terms of the difficulties it has encountered, ZAMSEED stated that there are often nationalistic tendencies in many countries to protect local companies which inhibit it from penetrating potential export markets. Also, many importing governments mandate official trials of varieties in the potential importing country before they allow exports in.

ENERGY & MINING

"Firewood for cooking an elephant is collected by the elephant itself"
Zambian proverb

ENERGY

ELECTRICITY

Zambia has abundant energy resources, with a hydropower resource potential estimated at 6,000 megawatts (MW), although the installed capacity is presently around 1,715MW. Generation is mainly from Kariba North Bank (600MW), Victoria Falls (108MW) and Kafue Gorge (900MW). In addition, there are six smaller hydropower stations, namely Lisiwasi, Chishimba Falls, Musonda Falls, Itezhi-Tezhi, Mulungushi and Lunsemfwa, which contribute to the national grid and also supply outlying areas.

The major distribution network falls under the state-owned Zambia Electricity Supply Corporation (ZESCO), the national electricity utility, which is currently undergoing a process of commercialization. ZESCO operates and maintains a high voltage transmission system, is responsible for all electric power imports and exports in the country, and provides retail services to all but the largest mining customers in the Copperbelt region. The corporation provides over 70% of electricity generation in Zambia, serving some 250,000 retail customers and employing about 4,000 workers.

During 2004, Kariba North Bank (KNB) power station and ZESCO were merged to create one strong utility company. This was in order to reduce Zambia's energy costs, which would have risen by 30% had they remained two separate entities.

Power station in the Copperbelt

The mining sector is by far the largest consumer of electricity in Zambia, followed by industry and commerce. While the main distributor of electricity is ZESCO, the Copperbelt Energy Corporation (CEC), which is a privatized electricity utility, is responsible for the distribution of electricity in the Copperbelt region. Its cost-effective transmission and distribution network consists of 808 kilometres of overhead line and over 30 high voltage substations, with voltages operating up to 220KV. CEC buys most of its power from ZESCO, which it supplements with a 220KV interconnector to the DRC and 80MW emergency gas turbine generator.

Future Developments

The country has for many years exported electricity to its neighbouring countries, including South Africa, Botswana, Namibia and Tanzania, and remains among the countries with the lowest cost of energy in the region with huge untapped potential for further exports.

Regional cooperation is aimed at averting an anticipated energy shortfall in the region by 2007. The Zambezi River Basin, and hydropower initiatives such as the Itezhi-Tezhi, Batoka and Kafue projects, have the potential to generate an additional 11,000MW to boost regional energy supplies.

During 2005, increasing energy demands from the mining sector and rising regional electricity exports resulted in a shortfall in electricity, with Zambia having to spend some US $1 million per month on electricity imports. The country is in the process of upgrading its hydroelectricity power stations, with a US $140 million power rehabilitation project being undertaken by ZESCO due for completion by 2008. In addition to these capacity extensions in progress, there are plans under way to build two hydropower plants on the Kafue River to be located at Itezhi-Tezhi dam (120MW) and Kafue Gorge Lower (600MW).

PETROLEUM

While Zambia has no known oil or gas reserves, its downstream oil industry plays an important role in the economy. The 1,720-kilometre long Tazama pipeline, which is jointly owned by Zambia and Tanzania, allows the importation of crude oil into Zambia. Indeni Petroleum Refinery – the only inland refinery in east and central Africa – refines the crude oil that is distributed into the market by international companies operating in Zambia. These include British Petroleum (BP), Total Zambia Limited, Caltex Oil, Engen and Kobil Oil Zambia Limited.

The energy sector in Zambia is guided by the national energy policy and regulated by the Energy Regulation Board, which is the sole licensing authority for all the operators in the energy sector in Zambia. In liaison with other statutory bodies like the Zambia Competition Commission, the Energy Regulation Board undertakes to investigate and monitor the levels and structures of competition within the energy sector. In conjunction with the Environmental Council of Zambia, the board also formulates measures to minimize the environmental impact of the production and supply of energy, storage and use of fuels, and enforces such measures by attaching appropriate conditions to the licences held by the oil marketing companies.

Total Zambia has grown to be one of the leading petroleum companies and has been operating in Zambia since 1950. Total Zambia has a 21% market share of the petroleum industry in the country. In September 2005 Total acquired the shares of Mobil Zambia. Other actors include BP Zambia, Caltex Oil and Shell, through its local distributor Spectra Oil.

WATER SUPPLY

Zambia is blessed with abundant water resources, which cover some 11,890 square kilometres of the country's total area. Water resources comprise lakes – particularly Lake Tanganyika, Kariba Dam and lakes Bangweulu and Mweru – as well as a number of rivers. The country's main river is the Zambezi; other important rivers are the Luangwa, which joins the Zambezi from the north-east, and the Kafue, which flows from Zambia's north-western highlands. Kariba Dam, a major supplier of Zambia's water needs, is 280 kilometres in length, has a surface

area of 5,580 square kilometres and holds 185 billion cubic metres of water.

Urbanization, as well as demands from the mining and other manufacturing industries, has prompted increasing demand on Zambia's water and sanitation services. While the country has more than adequate water, it needs to be used more efficiently for sustainable and environmentally safe usage.

The privatization of water treatment and sewage services is being considered, and the construction of new plants is to be undertaken by private/public sector initiatives. The National Water Supply and Sanitation Council (NWASCO) regulates water supply and sanitation service providers with the aim of ensuring improved and sustainable service delivery. To achieve this goal, it concerns itself with the setting of quality and service standards, regulating the levels of capital expenditure associated with meeting these standards, evaluating efficiency levels, giving incentives for improved performance and penalizing defaulters for negligence.

A US $60 million joint agreement has been signed between the Zambian and Danish governments to execute a five-year water sector support programme, which began in December 2005. The programme focuses on delivering improved and sustainable water supply and sanitation services to the country's inhabitants while also building or enhancing capacity at local and central levels to manage major investments in the water sector efficiently and effectively. The programme will initially be implemented in Western, Lusaka and Southern provinces.

Access to safe drinking water in Zambia is currently at 51%, with the country committed to achieving the target of 74% access to safe drinking water by 2015 in line with the UN's Millennium Development Goals.

MINING

The country's vast mineral reserves include an estimated 10% of the world's known reserves of copper and 34% of its cobalt. The Copperbelt alone contains a total mineral resource of at least 2 billion metric tonnes. In addition to huge reserves of copper and cobalt, Zambia also possesses a variety of precious and semi-precious minerals, such as amethysts, aquamarines, emeralds, gold, silver, diamonds and selenium. Other known mineral resources, which are largely underexploited, include marble and granite as well as ferrous metals. Minerals that can be profitably quarried for use in the manufacturing, building and agricultural industries are clay, limestone, gypsum and phosphate.

GROWTH IN THE MINING SECTOR

During 2004 positive growth of 13.7% was recorded in the mining sector. Total copper production rose by 15.7% to 409,000 metric tonnes, compared with 353,594 metric tonnes in 2003. Robust copper production continued in 2005, with the Ministry of Mines and Minerals Development estimating output during the year at some 550,000 metric tonnes. This figure is expected to rise to over 600,000 metric tonnes during 2006.

Higher international metal prices coupled with improved production meant copper exports increased by 9% to 384,000 metric tonnes in 2004. Due to these higher copper prices, the value of exports rose by 62% from US $607 million in 2003 to US $985 million in 2004. Cobalt receipts were US $118 million in 2004 compared with US $62 million in 2003.

This positive climate is the driving force behind further mineral explorations and large-scale mining is expected to expand with the coming on board of Kansanshi Mine in the North Western province and the securing of new strategic shareholders in the Konkola Copper Mines (KCM) and Luanshya Mines. The mine at Kansanshi is already invigorating the local economy, resulting in the building of new infrastructure such as roads and electricity. In 2005, total investment pledges in the mining sector accounted for US $159.1 million, and came from British, Canadian, Indian and Singaporean nationals.

COPPER AND COBALT

After independence in 1964, the copper industry was seen as being so central and strategic to the country that a programme of nationalization was begun. Zambia's two main mines were nationalized in 1969, with copper production and refining being carried out by large state-run enterprises. These parastatals contributed massively to government revenue during the early 1970s when copper prices were high and the economy of Zambia was booming, and copper production reached a record high of some 750,000 metric tonnes a year. Zambia's copper industry began to decline following a drastic drop in the selling price of copper in the mid 1970s. Political change in 1991 led to a thorough restructuring of the mining sector. The adoption of a more outward-oriented and free market approach to production, together with an investor-friendly legislative framework and incentive scheme, raised hopes of a revitalized copper industry within a more diversified economy.

The privatization of the ZCCM and other state-owned mines and refining plants has resulted in a resurgence in the mining sector. Old mines have been reopened and new mines launched, and production has increased dramatically. Many international mining companies have entered the industry, attracted by strong international copper prices and the government's efforts to create a favourable business climate.

Presently, all mining companies are carrying out major projects to increase their production. From a total of 257,000 metric tonnes produced in 2000, copper production has increased during each subsequent year to reach approximately 550,000 metric tonnes in 2005.

After extraction from the ground, the copper needs to be processed

More than one billion tones of ore has been mines from the Copperbelt

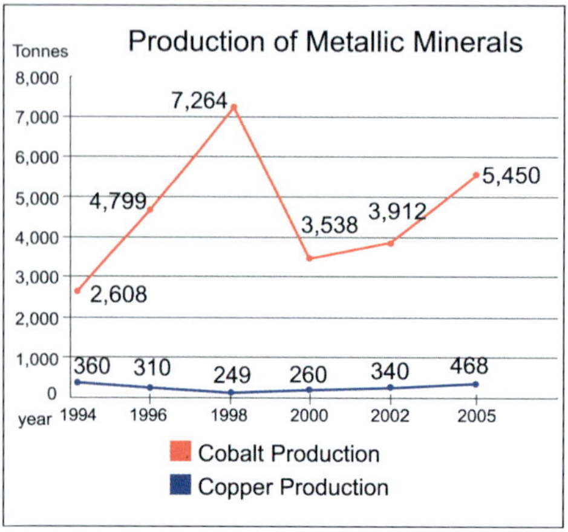

Current Mining Operations

Zambia Consolidated Copper Mines (ZCCM), an integrated copper and cobalt producer formed in 1982 with the merger of Roan Consolidated Mines and Nchanga Consolidated Copper Mines, has been one of the principal players in the Copperbelt mining industry. Privatization of ZCCM began in the mid 1990s, and by the end of 2000 most of its assets had been privatized by a variety of international companies.

Presently the largest producer on the Copperbelt, Konkola Copper Mines (KCM) was created from the privatized assets of ZCCM, consisting of the Konkola and Nchanga divisions and the Nampundwe pyrite mine. KCM also runs the Nkana smelter, Zambia's most important copper-producing factory. In 2003, KCM undertook a complete technical and strategic review, putting in place a new 20-year mine plan and related business plans, and in 2004 rising copper prices helped the mining giant fund rehabilitation work to increase its output.

KCM's expansion programme is aimed at increasing output by 20% in 2006, representing some 300,000 metric tonnes of finished copper.

A new acid plant with the capacity to produce 500 metric tonnes of acid per day is in its last phase of construction at Nchanga Mine. The acid plant will supply sulphuric acid for copper production, thus significantly reducing sulphuric acid imports into Zambia.

The expansion of the Nkana Smelter at a cost of US $125 million will increase the smelter capacity to 300,000 metric tonnes annually.

Furthermore, the Konkola Deep Mining Project (KDMP) aims to deepen the Konkola mine in Chililabombwe to access 250 million metric tonnes of copper ore at 4% contained copper at a cost of US $400 million. This makes it the largest single investment in Zambia and is poised to increase the life of the mine to 2032.

Zambia's privatization programme has resulted in First Quantum Minerals (FQM) Limited and Glencore International AG acquiring the Mufulira and Nkana divisions of ZCCM through Mopani Copper Mines (MCM). The joint venture provided for the upgrading and development of these properties, consisting of the Mufulira underground copper mine, smelter and refinery and the Nkana underground copper mine and cobalt plant.

The country's second largest copper producer, MCM, increased its production by 25% in 2004, reaching 159,657 metric tonnes. An expansion programme is forecast to increase the output of finished copper to 203,000 metric tonnes in 2006. Furthermore, the installation of new smelting technology will increase capacity from 650,000 to 850,000 metric tonnes of copper concentrate annually. The MCM copper mine developments, including the construction of a leaching plant, a new acid plant and the upgrading of its smelter, are expected to cost in the region of US $273 million.

First Quantum Minerals also owns and operates the Bwana Mkubwa copper mine located south-east of Ndola in the Copperbelt. Located 30 kilometres away in the DRC, the Lonshi mine is also exploited by FQM as part of its Bwana Mkubwa operation. BM draws its feedstock from Lonshi, which has proven reserves of 225,000 tonnes of acid-soluble copper. Bwana Mkubwa produced 41,456 metric tonnes of copper in 2004 and 140,200 metric tonnes of sulphuric acid.

FQM owns 80% of the Kansanshi open pit mine in Solwezi, North Western province. Copper production is estimated to reach 147,500 tonnes in 2006 following the setting up of a multimillion dollar pressure-leach project. An average production of 145,000 metric tonnes per annum is forecast for the 2006/2009 period.

Bwana Mkubwa and Kansanshi are two of the lowest cost mines in the world.

Equinox Resources owns the Lumwana open pit mine in North Western province, situated 220 kilometres north-west of the Copperbelt in Solwezi. Lumwana comprises two major deposits, Malundwe and Chimiwungo, which represent the largest known Zambian copper resource outside of the Copperbelt. These two ore bodies are rich in copper, with other metals such as gold, cobalt, silver and uranium also present.

Construction has started in 2006 and production is scheduled to begin by 2007. Output production will be of 140,000 metric tonnes of copper and 2,300 ounces of gold. The Lumwana mine contains up to 269 million metric tonnes of ore grading 8% copper and has an estimated lifespan of 18 years.

J&W Investments has an 85% stake in the Luanshya and Baluba copper mines, formerly owned by the defunct Roan Antelope Mining Company of Zambia (RAMCOZ). Renamed Luanshya Copper Mines, J&W plans to invest over US $32 million into operations over a five-year period. The two operations have a combined annual capacity of 50,000 metric tonnes of copper and 900 metric tonnes of cobalt.
Baluba mine, which has a lifespan of over 20 years, con-

tains cobaltiferous ore and total reserves estimated at 32,500,000 metric tonnes grading 2.48% copper and 0.17% cobalt. Substantial investments are being made in order to achieve a 35% production increase in 2006, with LCM aiming to increase production capacity to 67,500 metrics tonnes from 50,000 metric tonnes in 2005, and increase its workforce to 3,000 people.

J&W Investments has also taken over Chambishi Metals, a cobalt and copper refining company producing 4,500 metric tonnes of cobalt per annum by treating ore from the Kitwe dumps and offering toll treatment facilities.

Chambishi Mine, which has copper reserves of approximately 33 million metric tonnes, is owned 85% by China Non-Ferrous Metals Corporation. In 2004, the mine produced 49,054 metric tonnes of 40% copper concentrate and planned to produce 65,000 metric tonnes of concentrate in 2005, building up to 120,000 metric tonnes. An additional resource has been discovered which may contain over 100 million metric tonnes.

A number of other companies mine Zambia's rich copper and cobalt reserves. The Chibuluma Mine is owned by Metorex Limited and ZCCM-IH. Some 20,000 metric tonnes of ore per month are mined underground at Chibuluma West and then transported to the Chibuluma South concentrator for treatment. It was planned to raise this to 40,000 metric tonnes per month by 2006.

There are proven reserves of 135,000 tonnes grading 2.1% copper at Chibuluma West and approximately 8 million tonnes at 3.6% copper at Chibuluma South. The mine should eventually produce 7,000 and 14,000 metric tonnes annually at Chibuluma West and Chibuluma South.

Metorex also owns Ruashi Holdings in DRC, and is looking for additional prospects in the DRC and Zambia to triple output in the next five years. The company is presently constructing a copper smelter.

DIVERSIFICATION OF THE MINING SECTOR

For the past 60 years the Zambian economy has been heavily reliant on the mining of copper and cobalt and, despite the positive steps taken to diversify the industrial and manufacturing base, the reliance remains.

Zambia is naturally rich with other mineral resources, most of which are underexploited. The European Union and various other development institutions and banks are supporting private sector development through several programmes including the Mining Sector Diversification Program. The programmes aim at enhancing small-scale mining, reducing Zambia's dependence on copper and cobalt, increasing the range of minerals extracted for export, and developing downstream industries in mineral processing to add value to the exports.

OTHER MINERAL RESOURCES

A variety of precious and semi-precious gemstones are found in deposits scattered across the country. Many of these deposits are known to be of a very high quality and thus huge investment opportunities exist in the prospecting and mining of these minerals. In the last 15 years there has been a new emphasis on the mining of semi-precious stones, which are sold in bulk to realize incomes of appreciable value. While gemstones have traditionally been exported in their rough form, their polishing and processing is a growth industry with great investment potential. Zambia's main markets for exporting gemstones are South Africa, the Far East, USA and Switzerland.

EMERALDS

Presently, Zambian emeralds account for some 20% of the world's supply and account for approximately 80% of gemstone exports by value. International demand is high due to the excellent quality of the country's emeralds, which are a rich, deep colour and tend to have very few inclusions.

The largest mining concession in the area is operated by Kamakanga Gemstone Mine (Kagem), with the

Kamakanga mine producing emeralds of a very high quality.

Grizzly Mining exports rough gemstones to India, Israel, Japan and Europe. Since starting operations in 1999, the company has invested more than GB £4.5 million in modern machinery and other mining equipment.

OTHER GEMSTONES

Amethysts, with their rich reddish-purple colour, are mined in the Kalomo region in Southern province. South of Lusaka rodolite garnets are present in alluvial deposits, while malachite is found in the Copperbelt mines. Aquamarines exist in the Central and Western regions, and tourmalines near Serenje in Central province. Almandine garnets are mined north of Chipata. Other gems, such as rubies and sapphires, have also been found.

Most diamond mining takes place in the western parts of Zambia, with the greatest concentrations of alluvial diamonds being found in the western Kabompo.

Tourmaline is mined at the Kumanga mine in the Mkushi area by Gemstone Marketing & Consultancy Limited, with

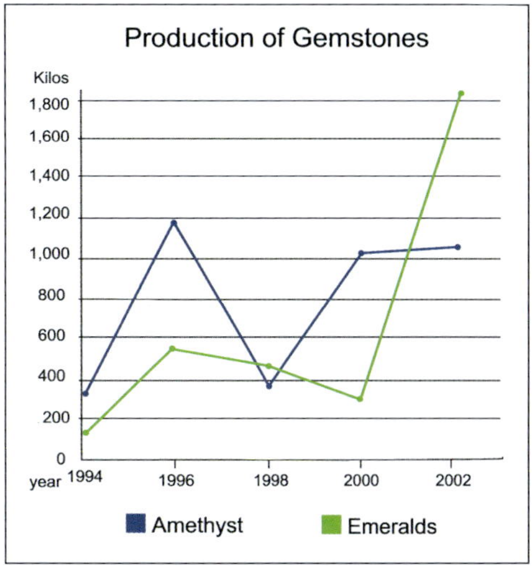

KCM is currently the largest producer on the Copperbelt

the 15 pockets of tourmaline mined ranging from pink, bicoloured pink-green and green, to the dark blue-green identified in kimberlite mineral clusters on Mulonga Plain in the Western province.

GOLD AND SILVER

Gold is found predominantly along the Mwembeshi Belt, located in the Central and Eastern provinces, as well as in North Western province. There are occurrences of silver on the Copperbelt, where it is produced at a number of copper mines. Silver has also been found in other regions, including Nyimba and Petauke in Eastern province, the Kafue National Park and the Umba River area.

Zambia's most important gold mine is Dunrobin Gold Mine, 120 kilometres west of Lusaka. A project to extract gold from slag at Dunrobin mine is under way. Silver is produced at Silver King Mine. Prospecting and exploration for gold, silver and diamonds occurs throughout the country.

ENERGY MINERALS

Coal is mined at the Maamba Colliery in the Gwembe Valley by South African Benicon Mining at Maamba Collieries Limited (MCL). This consists of two opencast mines in the Kanzize and Izuma basins with an annual capacity of between 600,000 and 800,000 metric tonnes of saleable coal. The MCL area has an estimated total of 78.2 million metric tonnes of coal reserves. It is estimated that the reserves could last for a further 96 years.

Uranium deposits exist in a variety of geological environments in Zambia. Exploration to unlock the country's significant reserves has focused on potential mineralization in the Copperbelt, Karoo Age sandstone and the gneiss domes region of North Western province. Agip and Cogema have identified uranium in southern Zambia as well. The Australian company Junior Haddington International Resources has a licence over the Siavonga region, which hosts several small deposits, with an estimated resource for this area being 6,400 metric tonnes of uranium oxide.

INDUSTRIAL, CONSTRUCTION AND AGRO-MINERALS

Feldspar is found in pegmatites, which are also rich sources of tin and gemstones. Sites that have been identified include the Northern, North Western and Eastern provinces, the Pemba area, the Serenje and Siavonga region and Lukusashi west and south.

Zambia has some valuable pure white marble deposits in Lusaka and other provinces. Lusaka boasts marble quartzite and light pink marble, as well as plain and dark greens and salmon pink. There are large granite reserves, with those at Itezhi-Tezhi and Kalomo usually speckled black or grey, with a rare blue granite found in Solwezi. Clay deposits occur throughout the country, with important deposits located at Serenje, Chama, Solwezi, Kasanka, Chingola, Mkushi and the Luano Valley.

The Copperbelt also has mining of silica. Fluorite is located in the Shangwa Hills region. While graphite reserves have not been quantified, they are known to exist in a number of areas. Tantalite occurs in Southern province and in Petauke district.

Zambia's only producer of lime, the Ndola Lime Company on the Copperbelt, supplies local manufacturing, agricultural and construction industries. It also exports to South Africa, the DRC, Zimbabwe, Malawi, Namibia and Tanzania.

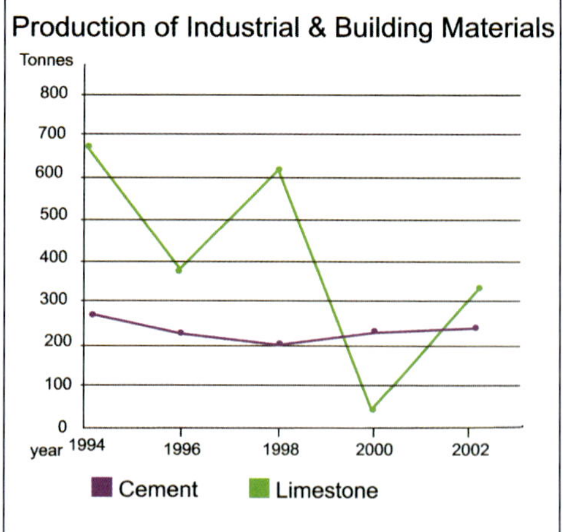

CURRENT MINERAL EXPLORATION

Prospecting is carried out in areas of proven underexploited potential, as well as in new areas.

Caledonia Mining is involved in further exploration at the Nama Project in the northern Copperbelt, where an extensive copper oxide deposit has been discovered. Caledonia is also involved in the Mulonga Plain Joint Venture Diamond Project in the Western province, where kimberlite mineral clusters have been found.

Prospecting for nickel is being carried out in and around Munali, south of Lusaka, in a joint venture between Falconbridge and Albidon, with some 4.1 million tonnes grading 1.35% nickel and 0.95g per tonne gold having been identified by early 2005.

A subsidiary of African Eagle Resources Plc, Katanga Resources Ltd is prospecting for copper, zinc, lead, gold and manganese in the Lunga, Mkushi, Sasare, Nyimba and Kampumba areas. Incorporating the old Mkushi Copper Mine, the Mkushi licence is believed to contain at least 30 million tonnes grading 1.25% copper.

Mwembeshi Resources, a subsidiary of Zambezi Resources, holds prospecting rights in central and eastern Zambia, where a variety of mineral deposits are currently being defined. Broad areas of mineralization have been discovered at Mulofwe Dome in the Chongwe district, with silver, copper, gold, bismuth and cobalt having been identified.

The Mining Sector Diversification Program aims at lessening Zambian's dependence on copper.

ZAMEFA transforms copper into copper wires, power cables, building wires and telecommunication cables

MAIN COMPANIES

BOC GASES ZAMBIA LTD

Mr J van Rooyen
Managing Director
P O Box 70252, Ndola
Tel: +260-2-621607/611803
Fax: +260-2-614651
Email: jvr@boc.com.zm

Activity: Gases
Date of Creation: 1998
Employees: 105

BOC Gases Zambia was established in 1998 when Afrox bought 70% of the shares of Zambia Oxygen Company (Zamox) and the Zambian government retained the remaining 30%.

BOC Gases is a major Zambian local manufacturer, importer and supplier of bulk liquid gases and compressed cylinder gases, welding products (arc and gas), Handigas and safety products.

BOC Gases owns and operates branches throughout Zambia located in Ndola, Lusaka, Kitwe, Chingola, Kabwe and Choma. In addition to the branches, it has appointed distributors to further enhance the geographic spread. The fleet includes bulk tankers for the safe and efficient distribution of oxygen, nitrogen, carbon dioxide and liquid petroleum gas. In addition to the bulk tankers it operates a fleet of cylinder and goods delivery vehicles, small delivery vehicles and various others.

Supporting the drive into neighbouring countries, BOC participated in a trade mission to Congo (DRC) as part of an official Zambian Export Board delegation. In January 2006 a sales branch with filling facilities in the DRC in Lubumbashi was established. BOC Gases also exports liquid petroleum gas to Malawi, Botswana and Zimbabwe.

BOC Gases Zambia has entered into an exclusive supply agreement with a global safety equipment manufacturer and supplier to support the safety business portfolio, and all equipment supplied conforms to international safety quality standards. Welding consumables sold by BOC Gases conforms to the relevant AWS and SABS standards. Afrox gas equipment is manufactured in South Africa, conforming to strict international values.

"BOC Gases Zambia will be the leading manufacturer and supplier of industrial and medical gases, welding products, consumables and related processes and services in Zambia."

Mr J van Rooyen, Managing Director

BP

Mr Crem Mapfumba
General Manager
Mukumba Pension House, Dedan Kimathi Road
P O Box 31999, Lusaka
Tel: +260-1-223847
Fax: +260-1-227118
Email: cremion.mapfumba@zm.bp.com
Website: www.bp.com

Activity: Oil

Although Zambia has as yet no known oil or gas reserves and consequently no upstream oil exploration and production, its downstream oil marketing industry is well developed and plays a key role in the development of the national economy.

The country's petroleum product needs are met from both processed imports and locally refined feeds from the Indeni oil refinery at Ndola. The import sources are mainly South Africa, Tanzania, Mozambique and Namibia. The consumption of petroleum products has been growing steadily over the past two years at an average of 10% year on year. This growth also signifies the good performance obtaining in the economy.

BP Zambia, as with all other oil marketing companies, plays a significant role in the Zambian oil industry, and so far holds a combined retail and commercial market share of above 40%. The company has 57 service stations throughout the country, the majority of which are in the urban areas of Lusaka and the Copperbelt. The fuel storage, handling and distribution capacity of BP Zambia is commensurate with its size in the market.

Of BP Zambia's commercial portfolio, the mining segment is the biggest. BP is also a significant participant in the aviation industry, with support and modern infrastructure at all major operating airfields in the country. As a public listed company – the only public listed oil company in Zambia so far – BP Zambia provides a platform for broader-based economic association and involvement.

"As a responsible corporate citizen, BP Zambia also invests in areas of health, safety and the environment (HSSE) and in areas of education and entrepreneurial development. For its staff, BP has been, and still is, the forerunner in employee wellness programmes."

Mr Crem Mapfumba, General Manager

CHIBULUMA SOUTH MINE LTD

Mr Ed. Mounsey
General Manager
P O Box 260499, Kalulushi
Tel: +260-2-239158
Fax: +260-2-239179
Email: chibfin@coppernet.zm
Website: www.metorexgroup.com
Activity: Copper mining
Date of Creation: September 1997

Vat leach plan

Capital: US $32m capital employed

Turnover: US $37m per annum

Employees: 460

The Chibuluma South mine is situated 12km south of the town of Kalulushi, which is approximately 12km west of Kitwe, one of the metropolitan and industrial centres of the Zambian Copperbelt. The current mining area is Chibuluma South, a new ore body developed to replace Chibuluma West near the town of Kalulushi, where mining ceased in February 2005 after 50 years of continuous mining operations.

The Chibuluma South mine is owned by Metorex (85%) and ZCCM-IH (15%). The reserve at Chibuluma South is around 8 million tonnes at 3.6% copper, and the inferred resource near Chibuluma South at the Chifupu prospect is over 1 million tonnes grading at 2.9% copper.

The Metorex Group has evolved by assembling a portfolio of profitable mining companies with a commodity mix and good growth prospects. The group has a record of sustained profitability, despite the cyclical nature of commodity prices. The group has a mix of commodities which offer counter-cyclical protection during economic cycles. Metorex's current mining activities are in antimony, coal, copper, gold and fluorspar. The Metorex Group head office is situated in Rosebank, Johannesburg, South Africa, from where it presently owns and manages six mining and processing companies throughout southern and central Africa.

The group is operated on a decentralized management but centralized logic basis. Each company operates as a self-standing, independent unit, responsible to Metorex for the attainment of its budget and the implementation of the strategic plans agreed upon at board level.

At Chibuluma South, access to the sulphide ore body was started in December 2003. Progress has been hampered by poor ground conditions, but in June 2005 reached competent ground, thus increasing the rate of advancement. The design tonnage of 40,000 tonnes per month is planned to be achieved in June 2006.

COPPERBELT ENERGY CORPORATION PLC

Mr Neil Croucher
Chief Executive Officer
23rd Avenue, Nkana East
P O Box 20819, Kitwe
Tel: +260-2-244000
Fax: +260-2-244040
Email: crouchern@cec.com.zm
Website: www.copperbeltenergy.com

Activity: Power transmission
Date of Creation: 1997
Employees: 350

Copperbelt Energy Corporation (CEC) was formed on 21st November 1997 during the privatization of the power division of the then core mining conglomerate of Zambia, Zambia Consolidated Copper Mines (ZCCM). CEC is a public limited company incorporated under the Companies Act (Cap 388) and is quoted on the Lusaka stock exchange (LuSE).

CEC is a privately owned company that transmits and distributes electrical energy to Zambia's critical mining industry based in the Copperbelt province. The mines consume about 60% of Zambia's energy and CEC's power system therefore handles close to 70% of Zambia's total electricity demand. CEC's transmission and distribution network consists of 808 kilometres of overhead lines and 36 high-voltage substations. CEC buys most of its power on long-term contracts from ZESCO.

CEC's system is maintained to the highest international standards of reliability and availability. To ensure that power continues to flow in an emergency, the company operates 80MW of emergency gas turbine plants in selected substations of their network. It has a well-equipped control centre operating 24 hours a day and also provides a high degree of network duplication.
CEC also serves the region by operating an interconnector with the DRC, through which power is wheeled to Zambia, Zimbabwe and South Africa. CEC's regional importance is expected to grow significantly in the coming years with new interconnection projects to supply countries with shortages of electricity in the region. Zambia is positioning itself as a power corridor to the south and the east, and CEC will have an important role in the development of the world's largest hydropower scheme on the Inga River in DRC.

The expansion of CEC's portfolio also includes the provision of telecommunication services in the Copperbelt and the company has recently launched a fibre optic network as part of a diversified growth programme.

"Copperbelt Energy Corporation is expecting to grow by 50% in the next five years and is looking into new areas of development such as power generation."
Mr Neil Croucher, Chief Executive Officer

EQUINOX COPPER VENTURES LIMITED

Mr Noel McNee
Operations and Technical Manager
Riverside, Kitwe
Tel: +260-1-220146/235479/238657
Fax: +260-1-220146
Email: equinoxkitwe@coppernet.zm
Website: www.equinoxminerals.com

Activity: Mining and exploration

Equinox is an international exploration and mine development company, dual listed on the Canadian (Toronto) and Australian stock exchanges. Equinox has active programmes in Zambia, Australia and Peru.

Equinox is developing into a mid-tier copper mining company to produce cash flow to sustain further exploration and growth, maximizing shareholder returns through capital appreciation. The company's primary focus is the development of the 100% owned Lumwana Copper

Project in Zambia. Equinox is progressing towards its objective to operate Africa's largest copper producing mine.

Situated 220km north-west of the renowned Zambian Copperbelt, Lumwana hosts a measured and indicated mineral resource of 269 million tonnes of ore grading at 0.8% copper. This represents one of the largest copper projects anywhere in the world currently advancing towards production. The optimized development plan envisages processing 20 million tonnes per year of ore to produce copper concentrates over a 17-year mine life.

The Definitive Feasibility Study (DFS) was completed in late 2005 by Equinox and its consultants. The DFS now forms the basis for the Lumwana project implementation. Annual production will average 150,000 tonnes (330 million pounds) of copper metal over the life of the mine, with over 188,000 tonnes (415 million pounds) being produced per year in the initial five-year period. Pre-production capital cost estimates total US $453 million and operating cash costs average US $0.70 per pound of copper produced and US $0.63 per pound during the initial five-year period.

In addition, Lumwana hosts an inferred resource of a further 632 million tonnes grading 0.6% copper, a uranium resource containing almost 22 million pounds of uranium oxide, and exploration potential at Lumwana represented by more than 25 high-priority copper and uranium targets that warrant further investigation. There is significant potential to extend the proposed mine life and there is further opportunity for additional revenue from credit metal by-products of cobalt, sulphuric acid and uranium.

Apart from Lumwana, Equinox controls 100% of prospective tenements covering 19,300 square kilometres, located predominantly in the Copperbelt, and referred to as the Zambezi Project. Equinox controls extensive ground positions over three of the four mineralized domes in Zambia.

FIRST QUANTUM

Mr Geoff Chater
Managing Director
800-543 Granville Street, Vancouver, Canada
Tel: +1-604-688-6577
Email: info@first-quantum.com
Website: www.first-quantum.com

Activity: Mineral exploration, development and mining

First Quantum Minerals Ltd is a growing mining and metals company whose principal activities include mineral exploration, development and mining.

The company produces LME grade A copper cathode, copper in concentrate, gold and sulphuric acid. The company's operations in Zambia include the 100% owned Bwana Mkubwa SX/EW facility and sulphuric acid plants, the 80% owned Kansanshi open pit copper-gold deposit, and it holds 17% of Mopani Copper Mines. First Quantum also holds strategic investments in the Nkana underground copper mine and cobalt refinery (16.9%) and the Mufulira underground copper mine, smelter and copper refinery (16.9%) in Zambia.

In the Democratic Republic of Congo, First Quantum operates the 100% owned Lonshi open pit copper mine which provides oxide copper ore for processing at Bwana Mkubwa, a 100% interest in the newly discovered Frontier copper-cobalt deposit, and 11,000 square kilometres of exploration rights.

The Kansanshi project is located in the North Western Province of Zambia, in Solwezi. Kansanshi is one of the oldest known mines in Zambia. The total production from the Kansanshi deposit to date is approximately 80,000 tonnes.

An additional expansion of the sulphide circuit is being developed for 2008 to increase the sulphide treatment capacity to 12 million tonnes of sulphide ore to maintain annual finished copper production of 145,000 tonnes as oxide ore is depleted and sulphide ore grades begin to fall. The 100% owned Bwana Mkubwa SX/EW facility is located near Ndola. Built in 1998 at a cost of US $30 million and expanded in 2002 for an additional US $25 million, Bwana Mkubwa is a proven low-cost copper producer and a showcase operation for First Quantum in Zambia.

Acid production in 2005 was 260,796 tonnes, of which 134,633 tonnes were produced at Ndola and 126,163 tonnes at Solwezi. Of the total acid produced, 32,601 tonnes were sold externally and 85,330 tonnes were consumed at Kansanshi. Annual acid production capacity at Ndola and Solwezi is 146,000 tonnes per site.

GEMFIELDS HOLDINGS LTD

Mr Alok Sood
CEO
P O Box 22550, Kitwe
Tel: +260-2-212735/217002
Fax: +260-2-216551
Email: alok.sood@gemfields.co.uk

Activity: Gemstone mining
Employees: 95

Gemfields is an independent gemstone mining and prospecting company with a primary focus in Zambia. The company currently owns three Zambian emerald mines, namely Kamakanga, Mbuva and Chibolele, and has entered into a conditional option agreement in relation to a fourth, Arinus. Gemfields also owns a series of prospecting licences covering a substantial part of the prospective emerald areas in the Zambian Ndola Rural Emerald Restricted Area (NRERA). The company also owns a 50% interest in Kariba Minerals which operates a Zambian amethyst mine. Gemfields Zambia also trades on AIM since November 2005.

Following first production, Gemfields intends to enhance profitability through downstream integration of gemstone cutting, polishing and distribution. The current business and strategy of the company originated in 2000 when it identified a significant opportunity in the gemstone industry and it has since pursued the primary objective of acquiring and developing coloured gemstone mines. The company has actively sought to acquire interests in Zambian gemstone mines and mining and prospecting licences, particularly within the emerald mining sector due to the high quality and value of Zambian emeralds.
The company plans to focus on developing existing mining interests in the NRERA and acquiring and progressing further gemstone interests in Zambia. The directors believe that opportunities exist to acquire additional emerald mines and to develop the company's existing licences and to further enhance profitability through economies of scale. The directors intend that the company's proposed emerald mining operations will be supported by a wholly owned gemstone cutting and polishing business, based in Jaipur, India, which will process a proportion of the emeralds produced by the mines operated by the company. The balance will be sold as rough emeralds to dealers.

"The company has been actively involved in exploring opportunities in the gemstone sector in Zambia since 2000, with a strategy to develop its existing emerald and amethyst mining interests and to acquire and progress further gemstone assets in Zambia. Gemfields' target for 2006 will be to operate using modern open-pit mining techniques along with a high specification emerald recovery plant."
Mr Alok Sood, CEO

KAGEM MINING LTD

Mr S. K. Bhattacharya,
CEO
Light Industrial Area
P O Box 21657, Kitwe
Tel: +260-2-212101/216845
Fax: +260-2-216324
Email: kagemm@coppernet.zm
Website: www.zamnet.zm/kagem.html

Activity: Gemstone mining
Date of Creation: 1984
Employees: 350
Zambia is one of the three largest emerald producing countries in the world and is reputed for producing the finest emeralds with the least inclusions. Kagem Mining Ltd is the largest well-developed emerald mine in Zambia and Africa. Kagem was incorporated in 1984 as a joint venture between the government of Zambia, with a 55% stake, and Hagura Mining Limited, which holds 45%.

Hagura Mining has invested more than US $25 million to rehabilitate the mine. The company operates a large (43sq.km) excavation site located near Ndola, in the Copperbelt. The mine has a 50-year life span. In 2006, Kagem Mining will be extracting US $22 million-worth of emeralds.

Kagem's emeralds are sold at auctions through closed tender. Buyers from around the world attend these auctions conducted in Lusaka.

As the largest gemstone mining operation in the country, Kagem Mining Ltd is modern, efficient, experienced and has high ambitions for the future. Kagem exports 100% of its production, mainly in rough emeralds, to India, Israel, Geneva, the UK and the USA. An expansion programme is under way to establish downstream industries, such as cutting and polishing, to add value to the rough stones. The company has recently bought new machinery and plans to cut and polish 10% to 15% of its production in the coming years.

"Our emeralds are the world's most sought-after gems! We are able to encompass any potential buyer in terms of supplying the best quality of Zambian emeralds."
Mr S. K. Bhattacharya, CEO

KARIBA MINERALS LIMITED

Lyapa Manza
General Manager
Kakota Road,
P O Box 37080, Lusaka
Tel: +260-1-287043
Fax: +260-1-287041
Email: karmin@uudial.zm

Activity: Mining and export of amethysts
Date of Creation: 1984
Turnover: US $2.3m
Employees: 345
Kariba Minerals' (KML) core business is mining and export of rough amethyst from its high-class deposits mine at

Miners preparing for a blast underground

Mapatizya mining area in Kalomo district.

The mine was first operated by a Lonrho-owned company called Northern Minerals Limited which was incorporated in 1960. In 1984 the government of Zambia, in conjunction with Lonrho (Africa), bought out the shareholders of Northern Minerals and renamed the company Kariba Minerals. In April 2004, Lonrho sold its entire 50% shareholding to Gemhouse Online, which is the present partner with the government in a joint venture arrangement.

KML's market share is estimated at over 90% of amethyst originating from Zambia. It is one of the largest individual producers in the world, and hosts some of the biggest deposits of high-grade amethyst on the planet.

The mine has been worked for a period exceeding 30 years at varying production levels influenced by levels of investment and the dictates of market demand. Success at KML has placed Zambia on the world map as a source of high-value amethyst and the share market of the Zambia official exports is just over 90%. This indicates that there is no local competition at present.

KML has a 10-year gemstone licence which was issued on 7th May 1997 and will expire in 2007 for an area of 250 hectares. The licence area is divided into six amethyst prospects, of which two to four are mined concurrently depending on geological and equipment constraints. Amethyst is processed into rough knocked products and transferred to the Lusaka facility for grading and preparation for the market.

Growth has been achieved in the company through an increase in production capacity over the past years. While grades mined have fallen over the same period, the company has taken advantage of economies of scale inherent in amethyst by mass-producing in the lower grade. Production has increased from levels of 36,000kg per annum 10 years ago to as much as 240,000kg of knocked amethyst at present.

KONKOLA COPPER MINES PLC

Mr Augustine Seyuba
Vice President-Corporate Relations
Fern Avenue
Private Bag KCM 2000, Chingola
Tel: +260-2-0021/350026
Fax: +260-2-351357
Email: augustine.seyuba@kcm.co.zm
Website: www.kcm.co.zm

Activity: Mining of copper
Date of Creation: 2000
Turnover: US $700m
Employees: 10,000

Konkola Copper Mines (KCM) is a mining company based in the Copperbelt province of Zambia. The company is currently the largest mining house in Zambia. KCM is part of Vedanta Resources Plc, a metals and minerals group with operations in India, Australia and Zambia. Listed on the London FTSE 250, Vedanta became the strategic equity partner in KCM in November 2004.

The company's business is to mine and process copper from the Nchanga mine in Chingola and Konkola mines in Chililabombwe and pyrite from Nampundwe mine, 40km west of the capital city, Lusaka. KCM operates smelter and refinery operations at Kitwe, also in the Copperbelt.

Vedanta's primary reason for undertaking this investment was the prospect of substantial long-term profitability, which every company exists to achieve, but also the opportunity to make a crucial contribution to the Zambian economy, as well as to contribute financially and socially to the wellbeing of the many thousands of people with whom KCM interacts.

KCM aims to produce 500,000 tonnes of copper a year, and become a world-class quality and cost-competitive copper producer and a role model for safety, environment and corporate social responsibility.

KCM accounts for one-sixth of the country's gross

domestic product (GDP) and contributes one-third of the country's export earnings. KCM has approximately 10,000 permanent employees. KCM has established a small business development unit that supports ex-miners in forming small and medium-sized enterprises (SMEs) and assists them in conducting business with the company.

"KCM is pressing forward with its major task of mining expansion and in becoming Zambia's most outstanding company in the mining industry."
Mr Augustine Seyuba, Vice President Corporate Relations

KONNOCO LTD (TEAL)

Mr Tim Williams
General Manager
Zambia Regional Office, 21 Mpezeni Ave
P O Box 21048, Kitwe
Tel: +260-2-230738/230739
Fax: +260-2-230740
Email: tim@tealmining.com
Website: www.tealmining.com

Konnoco (Zambia) Limited is a wholly owned subsidiary of TEAL Exploration and Mining Incorporated, a Toronto stock exchange listed company, and holds the exclusive rights to the Konkola North Copper Project through a large-scale mining licence that was issued in May 1997 and expires in May 2020.

Extensive exploration drilling was undertaken by the previous owners. Having acquired the data from these drilling programmes, TEAL identified inferred mineral resources of 78.8 million tonnes at 2.14% copper. This resource is contained within the east and south limb areas of the project. Historic records and more recently drilled results relating to other areas of the project indicate two further inferred mineral resources of approximately 107 million tonnes at grades of 2.30% copper and 63 million tonnes at grades of 3.88% copper respectively.

Within the south limb, TEAL intends to focus initially on the development of a high-grade region of the resource and re-equipping of existing infrastructure, which includes the No. 2 shaft, a 423-metre-deep vertical shaft, two ventilation shafts and three ore haulage levels. At the east limb, TEAL is considering various options to access the mineralization. The Konkola North Copper Project is adjacent to the existing Konkola Copper Mines Plc (KCM), which has existing operational mining infrastructure.

Once a feasibility study has been done and a mine development decision has been taken by Konnoco, TEAL will subscribe for new Konnoco shares so as to equity finance one-third of the total financing requirements for mine development. Thereafter, ZCCM-IH has the right to a 15% to 20% equity interest in Konnoco, of which 5% will be a free carried interest. ZCCM-IH's residual 10% or 15% 'paying' equity interest will obligate ZCCM-IH to fund its share of equity to develop a mine, although ZCCM-IH may elect to be debt funded by TEAL.

LUANSHYA COPPER MINES/CHAMBISHI METALS

Mr Jerry Gorman,
Chief Executive Officer (Africa)
P O Box 21151, Kitwe
Tel: +260-2-744002/744555
Fax: +260-2-744400
Email: jerryg@chambishi.com.zm

Date of Creation: 2004
Employees: 3,500

The cobalt metal production at Chambishi started in 1978. J&W Investments took Avmin's stake in Chambishi Metals, a copper and cobalt refining company, in July 2003 and Luanshya Copper Mines Plc in January 2004.

An investment programme of US $32 million over a five-year period was started, and J&W Investment took over. Since 2004, the production capacity of Luanshya Copper Mines has significantly increased following the substantial investment in a new state-of-the-art processing facility to extract copper and cobalt from the waste slag generated over a long period from Nkana Smelters in the Zambian Copperbelt since the early 1930s.

The new partnership between Luanshya Copper Mines and Chambishi Metals Plc has enabled synergies and significant economies of scale: the newly refurbished mine provides cobalt and copper feedstock to Chambishi Metals Plc, producing by-products of copper and cobalt for the telephone and battery industry. Chambishi Metals currently processes 50,000 tons of copper per year and 20,000 tons of cobalt per year.

The cobalt production process has been ISO 9001:2000 accredited, and today the Chambishi cobalt metal enjoys a share in all the sectors of the cobalt market due to its consistent superior quality through continuous process improvement.

Chambishi Metals and Luanshya Copper Mines provide employment for approximately 3,500 people. The empowerment of Zambian men and women has been made possible through a commitment to training in all aspects of operations right through to top management. Schools and apprenticeship technical training within the community have been established to help with business development and the acquisition of the skills needed to operate small businesses. Luanshya Copper Mines has also taken over the community hospital and other social and sporting amenities.

MOPANI COPPER MINES

Mr Tim Henderson
Chief Executive Officer
P O Box 22000, Kitwe
Tel: +260-2-247000
Fax: +260-2-247445
Email: mopani@mopani.com.zm

Activity: Mining
Employees: 8,200 employees (direct), 9,400 (contract)

Mopani Copper Mines (MCM) is a Zambian registered company owned by Carlisa Investments Corporation (a joint ven-

ture company comprising Glencore International AG and First Quantum Minerals Limited) and ZCCM-IH.

MCM copper, as quoted on the London metal exchange, is considered amongst the purest copper in the world. MCM spent US $485 million up to the end of 2005 with another US $229 million committed for 2006, making MCM the largest investor in Zambia. MCM is committed to increasing production and reducing the cents-per-pound cost of copper and cobalt through the consistent use of internationally acceptable management and mining practices.

In April 2000, MCM purchased the ZCCM assets at Mufulira Mine (comprising of underground mine, concentrator, smelter and refinery) at the northern extension of the Zambian Copperbelt and at Nkana Mine (underground mine, concentrator and cobalt plant) in the centre of the Zambian Copperbelt.

Mufulira refinery is the largest copper refinery in Africa with the capacity to produce in excess of 250,000 tonnes of finished copper per year. A programme is currently under way to rebuild and modernize the Mufulira metallurgical complex. This will comprise a new primary smelting furnace, a matte-settling furnace, a sulphuric acid plant, an oxygen plant and an update of the associated infrastructure. Currently, MCM's smelter has the capacity to process about 410,000 tonnes of concentrate a year. New technology, known as Isasmelt, will be installed in early 2006 at the Mufulira smelter by the Swiss firm Xstrata to dramatically increase the capacity for processing copper concentrate to 650,000 tonnes a year. The new furnace will be a top-blown, submerged-lance vessel in which concentrate will be smelted to a matte containing about 60% copper. The capital involved and the operating costs are relatively low.

MCM is also erecting a sulphuric acid plant, which is being constructed by Grinaker LTA. The first phase is currently being erected and will treat the fugitive gases from the furnace side of the smelter to produce about 850 tonnes per day of acid.

MCM employs just over 8,200 direct employees, with a contract labour strength of 9,400. MCM has created approximately 5,500 new jobs since inception.

"MCM is also committed to social programmes and the company owns and operates medical and educational facilities which rank among the best in the country. The company has comprehensive malaria control and HIV/AIDS programmes."

Mr Tim Henderson, Chief Executive Officer

NDOLA LIME COMPANY

Mr J. M. Chongo
Managing Director
P O Box 70057, Ndola
Tel: +260-2-610951/610953
Fax: +260-1-615275
Email: jchongo@ndolalime.co.zm
Website: www.ndolalime.co.zm

Activity: Lime mining
Date of Creation: 1931
Turnover: US $18m
Employees: 372

Ndola Lime Company was originally founded on 10th January 1931 as the Northern Rhodesia Lime Company Limited and is a wholly owned subsidiary of the Zambia Consolidated Copper Mines Investment Holding (ZCCM). The company is located 10km south-east of Ndola City in the Copperbelt province.

As the name suggests, Ndola Lime produces lime. Lime is an alkali and is one of the more important industrial chemicals that has many roles, all of them vital. Undoubtedly, there is no other material in commerce that has more diverse uses and varied functions as lime. Lime is used as quicklime, hydrated lime, limestone and agro-lime. Ndola Lime has two quills which at the moment produce 500 tonnes of quicklime per day, but it wants to double the production by the end of 2006.

The company operates a limestone quarry, crushing plant, annular shaft and rotary kilns, a hydrating plant and related support infrastructure.

The quicklime is used in the copper and cobalt mines to modify pH and at present this represents 90% of the business of Ndola Lime. The other markets for the lime are increasing: the hydrated lime is used in sugar refineries; the agro-lime is used to balance fertilizers in the north of the country; and the limestone is used in the metallurgical business by mixing with copper.

The company's mission statement is to convert Ndola Lime Company Ltd into a world-class market leader in the safe and efficient production of limestone products that continually meet and exceed customer requirements to the benefit of shareholders, employees and other stakeholders.

"The company has expansion plans towards Congo, therefore the whole market will increase considerably. In the medium run, the company wants to produce cement, which has a similar production process to lime."
Mr J. M. Chongo, Managing Director

NITROGEN CHEMICALS ZAMBIA

Mr Mwinga
Chief Executive Officer
Kafue
Tel: +260-1-312279/311879
Fax: +260-1-311706

Activity: Industry (manufacture and trading of explosives)
Date of Creation: 1967

The principal activity of Nitrogem Chemicals Zambia (NCZ) is the manufacture and trading of explosive grade ammonium nitrate, chemical fertilizers and industrial chemicals. It is also engaged in trading of the manufactured products.

The company was incorporated in 1967 and has three complexes. In 1970 the ammonium nitrate plant was constructed and 11 years later in 1981 the company added the nitric acid plant, the ammonium nitrate fertilizer plant, the ammonium sulphate plant and a compound fertilizer plant blending imported potassium and phosphate fertilizers. The latest complex constructed is a sulphuric acid plant commissioned in 1983.

Zambia enjoys an ideal climate for fertilizer manufacturing and has more advantages than disadvantages over its immediate neighbours. The primary objective of privatization of NCZ is therefore to promote a viable and competitive fertilizer manufacturing industry in Zambia. This has been demonstrated through the government's commitment to the development of agriculture and a number of policy initiatives related to fertilizer policy.

"NCZ is well poised to take advantage of the government's commitment to agriculture development."
Mr Mwinga, Chief Executive Officer

TOTAL ZAMBIA

Mr McCarthy
Manager/Director
P O Box 31724 , Lusaka
Tel: +260-1-242887
Website: www.total.com

Activity: Oil

Total Zambia Limited is an affiliate of the multinational petroleum group Total, with business activities in over 130 countries spread widely around the world. The Total group is the world's fourth largest international oil and gas company and the first in Africa.

The Total group is involved in the entire chain of the oil industry from exploration, development, production of oil, gas and chemicals to refining and distribution.
Total Zambia has grown to be one of the leading petroleum companies and has been operating in Zambia since 1950. Its business activities are widely spread in every part of the country, with a concentration in Lusaka, the Copperbelt, Solwezi and Livingstone. Its portfolio of commercial consumers includes the mining companies, road construction companies, big fleet transporters, breweries and farmers, to mention but a few. Total Zambia has a network of 46 service stations located in all the provinces of the country.

Apart from the main white oil products, Total Zambia deals in all lubricants including specialized ones for the mining, cement, sugar and brewery industries. Other products include bitumen, LPG, insecticides and car care products. Total Zambia has a 21% market share of the petroleum industry in the country.

A key strategy that drives the company's leading position is its complete commitment to international standards of safety, quality and respect for the environment in its business. Investment in industrial and personal safety campaigns each year produces a continued reduction in work-related accidents.

Total Zambia has extended its service package to include diversification services at its service stations. Convenience shops and car care services have been developed at a number of service stations.

"Total Zambia is fully involved in sustainable development for the communities where it operates, particularly in respect to health, education, women and youth development."
Mr McCarthy, Manager/Director

ZESCO LIMITED

Mr Rhodnie Sisala
Managing Director
Stand No 6949, Great East Road
P O Box 33304, Lusaka
Tel: +260-1-362711
Fax: +260-1-222753
Email: rpsisala@zesco.co.zm
Website: www.zesco.co.zm
Activity: Energy production and distribution
Date of Creation: 1970

ZESCO is wholly owned by the Zambian government through the Ministry of Finance and the Ministry of Energy & Water Development.

ZESCO was incorporated in 1969. In 1972, ZESCO took over several municipal undertakings, including Livingstone and Ndola. In late 1972, it took over Kabwe, Luanshya, Mufulira, Kitwe and Chingola. The effect of these takeovers was to enlarge the company area of supply to cover the whole of Zambia, except the Copperbelt mines which remained under the Copperbelt Power Company (CPC).

ZESCO generates, acquires, transmits and supplies electricity as a public undertaking. ZESCO has three major power stations: Kafue Gorge, Kariba North Bank and Victoria Falls. ZESCO also has smaller hydropower stations concentrated in the northern part of the country, namely at Musonda, Chisimba, Lunzua and Lusiwasi.

Due to the deterioration of the plants, ZESCO has been running the Power Rehabilitation Program (PRP) during the past few years. This programme refurbishes the plants to improve reliability, efficiency and in some cases increase the generation capacity of the three major generating stations.

As the bulk consumption of energy has increased tremendously in the last decade, ZESCO developed partnerships with foreign companies such as Sinohydro of China to develop specific power stations and FARAB of Iran to develop a hydropower station at Itezhi-Tezhi Dam.

Although electricity exports decreased in 2005, this was because of the PRP. ZESCO is going to increase its generation capacity for the year 2006 and is expected to increase exports. The Zambia-Tanzania-Kenya interconnector project is at an advanced stage of discussion and will considerably boost exports.

ZCCM INVESTMENTS HOLDINGS PLC

Mr W. S. Musama
Company Secretary
5309 Dedan Kimathi Road, Mukuba Pension House
P O Box 30048, Lusaka
Tel: +260-1-221023/220540
Fax: +260-1-220449/220727
Email: corporate@zccm-ih.com.zm
Activity: Investment holding company in mining operations

In 1969, the two major copper mining companies in Zambia, Nchanga Consolidated Copper Mines and Roan Consolidated Mines, were 51% nationalized; they were

reorganized in 1974 under management appointed by the government, and merged into ZCCM in 1982.

In 2000, the copper industry began its first full year of private operation since 1968, after the government completed privatization of the Zambia Consolidated Copper Mines (ZCCM) assets.

ZCCM was transformed into an investment company, ZCCM Investments Holdings Plc (ZCCM-IH), and retained shareholdings ranging from 10% to 20% in the newly created mining companies. These changes facilitated certainty of production through the inflow of significant capital equipment, additional management/technical expertise and the provision of adequate working capital.

Since the year 2000, the company has been involved in the resolution of historic liabilities arising from the predecessor company, ZCCM Limited. It is the intention of the company to refocus on the future and identify new viable opportunities to enhance its portfolio.

The company aims to seek equity partners, local and external, possessing appropriate competence and skills to manage the ventures successfully. This action is intended not only to contribute to national employment creation but also to expand and provide a sustainable investment portfolio to meet future challenges as an investment holding company.

The challenge of the present investment portfolio is hinged on the continued reduction of unit operating cost and continued realization of favourable selling prices. To this end, it is noted that efforts are being made and the various units within the portfolio have recorded notable successes.

FINANCE

"A dog does not bark with a bone in its mouth"
Zambian proverb

OVERVIEW

Since the early 1990s, a macroeconomic programme of market liberalization, deregulation and privatization has created a commercial climate characterized by enhanced competition, efficiency and openness. The implementation of structural reforms has continued, with more recent emphasis on improving public expenditure management and financial accountability, addressing the problems of the state-owned non-bank financial institutions, and removing the bottlenecks to private sector development.

Financial services play a vital role in facilitating all aspects of economic activity, and considerable growth has been seen in commercial banks and insurance providers following the liberalization of the sector in 1991. The establishment of the Lusaka Stock Exchange and the repeal of the Exchange Control Act in 1994 have greatly strengthened the capital market.

Despite these developments, the role of the financial sector in the economy has been constrained by challenges such as low financial intermediation, high costs of funds and an underdeveloped money and capital market. A Financial Sector Development Plan has been formulated to help achieve the aim of a stable, sound and market-based financial system that supports the efficient mobilization and allocation of resources necessary to achieve economic diversification, sustainable growth and poverty reduction.

HIPC COMPLETION POINT

Scheduled to run until 2007, the Poverty Reduction and Growth Facility (PRGF) arrangement approved by the IMF reflects a significant improvement in the country's fiscal discipline, macroeconomic environment and direction of economic policies in general, opening the way for enhanced balance of payments and budgetary support from donors. In 2005 Zambia reached the HIPC completion point, thus qualifying for a reduction in its external debt stock by US $3.9 billion up to the year 2023. Furthermore, the G8 countries agreed to cancel 100% of the debt owed by 18 African countries, including Zambia, under the Multilateral Debt Relief Initiative.

MONETARY DEVELOPMENTS

During 2005, monetary policy remained focused on achieving the inflation target of 15%. A tight monetary policy was implemented to contain annual reserve money and broad money growth rates by 10.5% and 14.8% respectively. Furthermore, to contain banking system domestic credit expansion to levels consistent with the economic growth objective and provide enough credit to the private sector, net domestic financing of the government budget was programmed not to exceed 1.6% of GDP, while net domestic credit and net private sector credit were projected to grow by 18% and 22.3%.

The annual overall inflation rate at 15.9% in December 2005 was below the end-2004 inflation rate of 17.5%. This was despite a number of supply side setbacks, such as high international oil prices, disruptions of fuel supply from the Indeni refinery and high domestic food prices arising from a maize shortfall. As such, the annual overall inflation out-turn in December 2005 is broadly in line with the inflation objective of 15%. The decline in annual overall inflation was largely attributed to the drop in annual non-food inflation to 14%. The drop in non-food inflation can also be attributed to the pass-through effects of the appreciation of the kwacha against other currencies, largely driven by favourable external sector performance, reduced external debt service and increased balance of payments support inflows following the attainment of the enhanced HIPC completion point. For 2006, the objective is to reduce inflation further to single digits, which requires the continued implementation of prudent budget management by government and the containment of broad money expansion.

Reduction of inflation in 2006 should also be assisted by the reduction of the prices of petroleum products, the continued slowdown in money supply growth and the pass-through effects of the appreciation in the kwacha against major traded currencies to domestic prices of consumer goods and services in the economy.

Zambia
National
Commercial
Bank
Limited

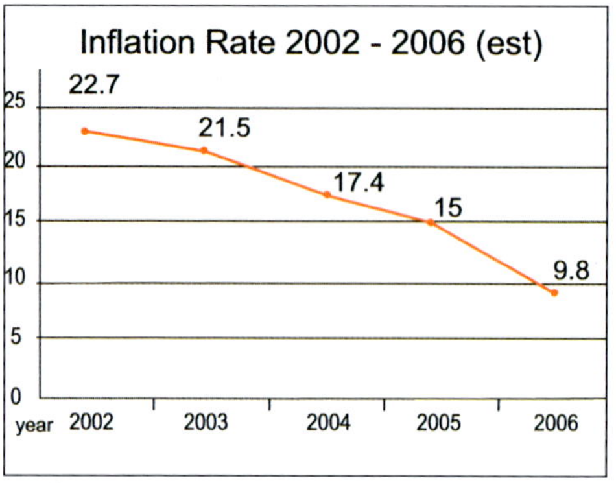

BANKING AND FINANCIAL SERVICES

Zambia's banking and financial system has undergone a process of modernization and streamlining. The regulatory framework has been strengthened and dealings in the market are facilitated by automated and computerized services. The country's central bank, the Bank of Zambia (BoZ), operates in line with international best practices.

The BoZ's subsequent focus has been on formulating and implementing monetary and supervisory policies that will ensure the maintenance of price and financial system stability. This is achieved by licensing, supervising and regulating the activities of banks and non-bank financial institutions so as to promote the safe, sound and efficient operation and development of the financial system.

The broad-based inter-bank foreign exchange system introduced during 2003 has led to improved foreign exchange market operations as well as a more transparent pricing mechanism. The auctioning of foreign exchange on behalf of exporters is now carried out by commercial banks which BoZ has appointed as primary dealers and market makers. During 2004, directives were drafted to strengthen the fight against money laundering in the banking and non-banking financial sector.

The evolution towards large financial conglomerates with integrated product development is slowly blurring the traditional boundaries between banks and non-bank financial institutions. Developed by BoZ and other stakeholders, the comprehensive Financial Sector Development Plan (FSDP) is expected to help construct an efficient financial system adequate to meeting the challenges of economic development.

COMMERCIAL BANKS

There are currently some 15 registered commercial, investment and merchant banks operating in Zambia. The most important commercial banks are Standard Chartered, Stanbic, Barclays Bank, Zambia National Commercial Bank (ZNCB) and Finance Bank Limited. As part of the government's privatization programme, 49% of the equity in ZNCB is to be sold to a strategic investor. Smaller banks include Investrust Bank, Merchant Bank, Cavmont Merchant Bank, Bank of China and Citibank, a wholesale commercial institution specializing mostly in large-scale projects. Indo-Zambia Bank, a successful joint venture between Zambia and India, concentrates on foreign exchange dealings, treasury operations and risk management functions.

All of Zambia's commercial banks participate in the Zambia Interbank Payment and Settlement System (ZIPSS) and the Real Time Gross Settlement (RTGS) implementation project launched during 2004. The banking sector is faced with several challenges, with key recommendations under the Financial Sector Development Plan (FSDP) including the following:

• Enhancing the quality of supervision through the development of internal capacity.
• Introducing a rule-based BoZ intervention to enable prompt corrective action and reduce the effects of regulatory forbearance.
• Revising liquidation procedures for failed banks and strengthening bankruptcy laws.
• Establishing a credit reference bureau to enhance credit culture.
• Enhancing consumer protection mechanisms.

BANKING SECTOR DEVELOPMENTS IN 2005

The overall condition and performance of the banking sector in the year 2005 was satisfactory. The sector continued to be adequately capitalized, with all banks meeting the minimum capital requirements of 5% for primary capital and 10% for regulatory capital. The ratio of gross non-performing loans to total assets was at 2.8%. The banking sector's earnings and liquidity position were also acceptable, with the ratio of liquid assets to total deposits and short-term liabilities at 70.3%. Developments in nominal interest rates were mixed, with lending interest rates falling while saving rates edged upwards.

The weighted average Treasury bill yield rate (WATBR) declined from 18.1% in December 2004 to 16.6% in November 2005. On the lending front, commercial banks' weighted average lending base rate (WALBR) and the average lending rate (ALR) declined to monthly averages of 28.2% and 35.4% respectively in November 2005, from 29.8% and 37.1% in December 2004.

The average savings rate (ASR) for amounts above K100,000 and the 30-day deposit rate for amounts above K20 million edged slightly upwards to 5.8% and 8.6% respectively.

NON-BANK FINANCIAL INSTITUTIONS

Non-bank Financial Institutions (NBFIs) complement the role of banks in the financial system. Originally established and funded by government, most Development Finance Institutions (DFIs) in Zambia have been closed, with the exception of the Development Bank of Zambia (DBZ), which was recapitalized by the government in 1994/95 and restructured in 2002.

Leasing companies are commercial ventures that are established under the Companies Act, and their principal activity is the provision of asset-based finance.

Housing Finance Institutions (HFIs), which traditionally provide banking services and mortgage lending, have tended to take two major forms – namely, building societies and employer-sponsored housing loan schemes. However, the generally unsatisfactory performance and financial status of the building society industry has

The Central Bank of Zambia

limited the contribution of housing finance institutions in the economy.

The collapse of most of the subsidized and publicly funded rural finance institutions in the mid 1990s created a gap in the provision of financial services to the low-income households in the rural and peri-urban areas. Microfinance Institutions (MFIs) have risen to fill this gap, and offer financial services such as small loans and savings facilities.

Restructuring of NBFIs under the Financial Sector Development Plan (FSDP) is focused on development of finance institutions, housing finance institutions and rural banking institutions, as well as developing a regulatory framework for microfinance institutions. Furthermore, a legislative framework is being established to provide for effective regulation and supervision of DFIs, HFIs, rural banks and MFIs.

These developments are particularly important with regard to the National Savings and Credit Bank (NSCB) and the Development Bank of Zambia (DBZ). The NSCB has been recapitalized and its outstanding obligations cancelled. Both banks are to become fully compliant with the BFSA and incorporated under the Companies Act in 2006. In order to protect depositors' funds and ensure reduction of operating costs, BoZ continues to monitor the Zambia National Building Society (ZNBS).

PERFORMANCE OF NBFIS IN 2005

While the overall performance of the NBFIs sector proved satisfactory, some institutions struggled to meet their minimum regulatory capital requirements.

Building societies continued to register a positive performance in 2005, recording a profit before tax of K4,097 million. The sector's increased earnings are due to the rapidly expanding mortgage portfolio, with the aggregate mortgages increasing by 72% to K25,256 million. This can be attributed to a reduction in lending rates over the period.

Generally, the microfinance sector performed fairly well during 2005, being adequately capitalized and having a satisfactory asset quality and earnings performance. Total assets of the sector stood at K74,500 million, representing an increase of 55% over 2004. The growth in assets was financed by an increase in capital and reserves due to two new microfinance institutions (MFIs) being licensed by BoZ during the period under review.

INSURANCE

PENSIONS AND SOCIAL SECURITY

The regulation of pension schemes in Zambia is provided for under the National Pension Scheme Act through the Pensions and Insurance Authority (PIA). Legislation developed to rationalize and strengthen pension schemes in Zambia led to the establishment of a new national pension scheme and amended administrative and financial aspects of the civil service and local authority pension schemes.

The Zambia National Provident Fund has been transformed into the National Pension Scheme Authority (NAPSA), which is now responsible for regulating both existing and new occupational pension schemes and covers all regularly employed persons in the private and parastatal sectors.

The advent of private occupational pension schemes dates to 1993. Managed by Zambia State Insurance Corporation (ZSIC) and administered by various insurance companies, these schemes now cover some 40% of employees in the formal sector. Employers remain liable for contributions to the national pension scheme, whether their employees are members of privately run pension funds or not.

Up to 1991, the insurance sector was dominated by the state-owned Zambia State Insurance Corporation. The liberalization of the sector during the 1990s has seen the arrival of numerous players and the competition significantly increased bringing new standards, lower prices, but also big failures.

Lusaka Stock Exchange

Zambia State Insurance Corporation has undergone a complete restructuring after years of financial indiscipline and unpaid claims. The company now operates on a healthy and clean balance sheet and remains Zambia's leading insurance company with a large portfolio of investments.

Other key players in the sector are Madisson Insurance, Professional Insurance, Nico Insurance, African Life Insurance Company, ZIGI Insurance and Goldman Insurance. These companies offer a wide and competitive range of services both in life and non-life insurance and are in the process or splitting their life insurance business from their non-life insurance business following amended legislation. Competition has significantly improved the level of service and the time of claim settlement. However, the problem of a lack of a re-insurance company is still hindering the sector.

Under the Financial Sector Development Plan (FSDP), key recommendations to develop the insurance industry include: upgrading the legal and regulatory framework to International Association of Insurance Supervision (IAIS) standards; enhancing the quality and independence of the insurance regulatory office; harmonizing legislation affecting insurance businesses; developing a policy on insurance of national assets; realigning health insurance regulations; and establishing an indigenous reinsurance company.

THE STOCK EXCHANGE

The Lusaka Stock Exchange (LuSE) was rated the 14th best performing stock exchange in the world by Standard and Poor's in Top 25 Exchanges of 2004, posting returns of 71.6% in US dollar terms, third in Africa after Egypt and Ghana, and the best in southern Africa.

Established in 1993, the exchange has played a key role in fostering economic transformation in the country. The LuSE is made up of stockbroking corporate members and is incorporated as a non-profit limited company. Currently the member brokers are Stockbrokers Zambia Limited, Intermarket Securities Limited and Pangea/EMI Securities. As of December 2005 there were 13 listed and 12 quoted companies on the stock exchange.

The listed companies include:

- British-American Tobacco Plc
- ZCCM-Investment Holdings Plc
- BP Zambia Plc
- Zambia Sugar Plc
- Chilanga Cement Plc
- Standard Chartered Bank Plc
- Zambeef Products Plc
- Metal Fabricators of Zambia Plc
- Farmers' House Plc
- Pamodzi Hotels Plc
- Shoprite Holdings Limited (RSA)
- National Breweries Plc
- Zambia Breweries Plc

The quoted companies include:

- Barclays Bank of Zambia Plc
- Cavmont Capital Holdings Plc
- Investrust Bank Zambia Plc
- Zambia National Commercial Bank
- Chambeshi Metals Plc
- Chibuluma Mines Plc
- Cyprus Amax Plc
- Konkola Copper Mines Plc
- Mopani Copper Mines Plc
- Copperbelt Energy Corporation Plc
- Bata Shoe Company Plc
- Arcades Development Plc

The exchange has been set up as a modern stock exchange based on the most current international standards and practices. These include use of a central depository system, trade for trade clearing and settlement process, rolling settlement three days after trade date (T+3), and meeting G30 recommendations for clearing and settlement system design and operation.

The LuSE offers several incentives to investors to promote

Zambia State Insurance Corporation has undergone drastic changes over the last years

rapid development of the capital market in Zambia. These include the absence of exchange controls, no restrictions on shareholding levels, no restrictions on foreign ownership, no capital gains tax, corporate income tax discounts, and no property transfer tax on listed securities.

LuSE has a unified market, comprising bonds and equities. The bond market consists of government bonds as well as corporate bonds. Government bonds are of 12, 18 and 24 months' duration and are issued by the Bank of Zambia (BoZ) on behalf of the Zambian government. After primary issue, sellers and buyers can trade the bonds on the LuSE. Participation in the government bond primary market is open to registered commercial banks and individuals with minimum bids of K30 million.

Several companies have issued corporate bonds. These include Farmers' House (US $1 million), Barclays Bank Zambia Plc (K30 billion), Lunsemfwa Hydro Power company (US $7 million) and Copperbelt Forestry (US $1 million). The LuSE operates as an order-driven market and consequently there are no official market makers in equity. However, under the Securities Act, the Zambian securities market permits dual capacity trading.

CAPITAL MARKET

LuSE market size grew by 11% in kwacha terms and 52% in US dollar terms to end the year at K8.6 trillion and US $2.5 billion. The growth in market capitalization is attributed to the performance of stock. Most shares recorded impressive capital gains which translated into a higher market cap.

The year 2005 was a more impressive year in terms of market returns than 2004. The US dollar return exceeded the 100% mark to close the year at 120% (2004: 75%). This is attributed to the impressive capital gains and the appreciation of the kwacha against the US dollar. However, due to the strengthening kwacha, returns in kwacha terms were 62% (2004: 77%).

Investors in equity earned better real returns on their investment in 2005 than 2004.
The number of trades in 2005 increased by 26% due to more investors coming to the market as a result of the awareness campaign by LuSE. The turnover increased by 123% in US dollar terms and by 104% in kwacha terms. This increase was underpinned by the higher prices of shares.

The number of shares transacted (volume) marginally increased, as there were no significant numbers of new shares offered into the LuSE Central Securities Depository (CSD) for active trading. Institutions also maintained their buy and hold strategy.

MAIN COMPANIES

AFRICAN BANKING CORPORATION

Mrs Zandile Shaba
Managing Director
4th Floor, National Credit and Savings Building, Cairo Road, North End
P O Box 39501, Lusaka
Tel: +260-1-234541/232991
Fax: +260-1-234542
Email: zshaba@africanbankingcorp.com

Activity: Bank
Date of Creation: 1984

In 1984, a group of experienced professional bankers, industrialists and prominent advocates decided to start a financial institution named Consolidated Finance Company. The company was established on 13th November 1984 with its registered office in Nairobi, Kenya.

The growth of Consolidated Finance Company was modest but progressive over the first nine years. In 1994, the results were so impressive that Consolidated Finance Company became one of the leading financial institutions in Kenya. In the same year when Central Bank of Kenya allowed financial institutions to convert into fully fledged commercial banks, Consolidated Finance Company became the first financial institution to become a commercial bank: the African Banking Corporation Limited (ABC Bank).

ABC Bank today has a very healthy liquidity position, in excess of Central Bank of Kenya's statutory requirement. ABC Bank has a wide network of seven branches, three in Nairobi and Mombassa and one branch each in Kisumu, Eldoret and Meru, and a team of over 120 qualified and professional bankers. The bank is fully geared up to meeting the changing financial needs of both local and international markets.

The bank has drawn up some realistic and achievable plans for future growth to see it become one of the largest private banks regionally, with a solid footing, adhering to banking practices and norms and with controls for consistent and continuous growth. The bank has put in place the appropriate infrastructure for providing a wide range of domestic and international financial services.

"ABC Bank offers a selection of financial solutions with innovative features and plenty of options to choose the banking that's right for you or your business. These include: deposits, advances, trade finance, money transfers, treasury, other products and services and future products."
Mrs Zandile Shaba, Managing Director

AON ZAMBIA LIMITED

Mr Vincent Witt
Managing Director
3rd Floor, Farmers' House, Central Park, Cairo Road
P O Box 35403, Lusaka
Tel: +260-1-236685/6
Fax: +260-1-236688
Email: vince_witt@aon.co.zm
Website: www.aon.co.zm

Activity: Insurance
Date of Creation: 1996
Employees: 30

Aon is a company that specializes in insurance broking and risk consultancy services. With over 600 offices in more than 125 countries, Aon is a leading global insurance brokerage company.

Aon has demonstrated its commitment to Africa, with an unrivalled network of subsidiaries in 16 countries and correspondent offices in a further 12.

Aon's presence in Zambia followed the acquisition of the Minet Group worldwide in 1997. Minet entered the Zambian market in 1996 following the liberalization of the insurance industry. Previously, Minet had been operating in Zambia from 1952 until 1976 when the insurance market was nationalized.

One of Aon's core business philosophies is that of interdependence through global networking, allowing Aon offices and their clients to access resources and expertise in any discipline from regional and international centres.

The company differentiates itself from its local competitors through its ability to provide a full range of insurance and risk consultancy services including retail insurance broking (all classes of non-life insurance), risk management services (loss control surveys), employee benefits consulting (group life assurance, funeral and medical schemes) and pension fund administration.

"Aon Zambia is the largest broker in the Zambian insurance market. The company conducts business with the highest professional and ethical standards and therefore counts many of Zambia's leading corporations among its clients."
Mr Vincent Witt, Managing Director

BANK OF ZAMBIA

Dr C. Fundanga
Governor
Bank Square, Cairo Road
P O Box 30080, Lusaka
Tel: +260-228888/228-903-20
Fax: +260-221722/237070
Email: pr@boz.zm
Website: www.boz.zm

Activity: Central Bank
Date of Creation: 1964
Employees: 1,400

National Pension Scheme Authority

The Bank of Zambia was established to take over from the Bank of Northern Rhodesia in 1964.

The Bank of Zambia is the regulatory financial institution in the country and aims at promoting monetary stability through sound financial structures and conducive credit and exchange conditions. The bank is also responsible for providing banking services to government and commercial banks and for providing a safe and efficient payment and settlement system for Zambia.

The Bank of Zambia has put emphasis on implementing appropriate monetary and prudent fiscal policies with a view to contributing to lowering inflation rates. In this regard, yield rates on composite Treasury bills and government bonds have declined from 31.7% and 41.4% in 2002 to 13.5% and 17.0% in January 2006.

Lowering inflation to a single digit number remains one of the crucial challenges since the liberalization of the economy. The implementation of an appropriate monetary policy, prudent fiscal policy and stable and competitive exchange rate is key to the attainment of low single-digit inflation. As at end-December 2005 inflation was 15.9% and has further reduced to 10.3% as at end-February 2006.

The Bank of Zambia has recently developed a broad-based inter-bank foreign exchange trading system as the new mechanism for determining the kwacha/dollar exchange rate in Zambia. Foreign exchange earners can now transact directly with any commercial bank of their choice as BOZ has ceased to auction foreign exchange markets on behalf of major foreign exchange earners.
BOZ is also in the process of implementing the Financial Sector Development Plan. The FSDP represents a comprehensive strategy addressing the weaknesses in the Zambian financial system (poor credit culture, weak regulatory framework, and inadequate provision of development finance, housing finance, rural banking and micro

finance). The Bank of Zambia is working with commercial banks and other stakeholders to help improve the credit culture in the economy through the establishment of a credit reference bureau. Guidelines for the licensing of credit reference agencies and consumer privacy data have been developed. This will enhance commercial banks' extension of credit to the productive sectors as they will have a screening mechanism that will eliminate potential bad debtors.

BDO CONSULTANTS

Mr W. P. Saunders
Showgrounds, Great East Road
P O Box 30333, Lusaka
Tel: +260-1-250222
Fax: +260-1-250631
Email: administrator@bdo.co.zm
Website: www.bdoglobal.com
Activity: Consultancy
Turnover: US $1.4 million

BDO Seidman LLP is a firm providing professional services such as assurance, tax, financial advisory and consulting services to private and publicly traded businesses. For 95 years BDO has provided quality service and leadership through the active involvement of the most experienced and committed professionals.

As a member firm of BDO International, BDO Seidman LLP serves multinational clients by leveraging a global network of resources comprised of more than 600 member firm offices in 105 countries. BDO International is a worldwide network of public accounting firms, called BDO member firms, serving international clients. Each BDO member firm is an independent legal entity in its own country.
BDO Zambia was established in 1999 as an international accountancy firm. Its activities include tax consultancy, audit and corporate finance and it also provides tailor-made consultancy services on setting up businesses in Zambia. BDO Zambia merged with the Mauritius firm De Chazel du Mee (DCDM) in December 2005.

The BOZ is implementing prudent monetary and fiscal policies to lower inflation rates

BDO's portfolio of clients is essentially made up of small foreign companies and NGO work. Its current turnover is estimated at US $1.4 million a year.

CAVMONT CAPITAL BANK

Mr Moses Malunda
Managing Director
Anchor House, Mezzanine Floor, Sapele Road
P O Box 38474, Lusaka
Tel: +260-1-221326/224286
Fax: +260-1-221326
Email: ann@cavmont.com.zm
Website: www.cavmont.com.zm

Activity: Bank
Employees: 125

Cavmont Capital Bank Ltd (CCBL) was created on 1st January 2004 as a merger between Cavmont Merchant Bank Ltd and New Capital Bank Plc.

Cavmont Capital provides a wide range of products and services that have been developed as a result of a deep understanding of the needs of the local market and its customers now and into the future. Its products and services are tailored to suit its clients' needs.

Cavmont Capital Bank's core business is to provide retail banking services, offering current, fixed deposit and foreign accounts. The bank also offers other kinds of services such as corporate, merchant, investment and community banking services. At the moment the company is developing an IT platform which will be revolutionary in the sector.

During 2005 the company had the difficult task of consolidating two different firms and developing a combined attitude towards the future. Since then, the bank has obtained more resources and has created synergies and expertise in the staff.

Cavmont Capital Bank's head office is situated in Lusaka and it has 10 branches, four in Lusaka and one each in Chingola, Ndola, Kitwe, Mbala, Mpulungu and Mansa.

CITIGROUP, CITIBANK ZAMBIA

Mr Rajaram Venkatraman
Managing Director
Chachacha Road
P O Box 30037, Lusaka 10101
Tel: +260-1-229025/8
Fax: +260-1-226264
Email: rajaram.venkatraman@citigroup.com
Website: www.citigroup.com

Activity: Banking
Date of Creation: 1979
Capital: US $25.5m
Turnover: US $14.6m
Employees: 57

Citibank Zambia was established in Zambia in 1979 where it opened its first office in Lusaka, the country's capital city. Citibank Zambia is a member of Citigroup. To date, Citibank Zambia has a physical presence in two of Zambia's nine provinces and a network of correspondent banking arrangements covering the other seven provinces.

The two branches are located in the provinces of Lusaka and the Copperbelt. The main branch is located in the heart of Lusaka. The other branch is located in Ndola in the Copperbelt province, which is the main mining province.

In addition to the above, Citibank also provides a daily travelling teller service for the UN agencies at the UN complex. Citibank has a wide local correspondent banking arrangement with three banks covering 16 centres.

Citibank Zambia has a well-defined target market that focuses on local and multinational top-tier corporations, non-governmental organizations, financial institutions, embassies and governmental institutions and public sector corporations.
Its broader product offering includes innovative cash management, trade finance, treasury, transaction banking and corporate finance solutions for its customers. It has dedicated and experienced staff, who are trained in

various Citibank training centres around the world.

Citibank is dedicated to helping build and improve the quality of life in the communities in which it operates and has created a social investment programme that provides support to micro-finance through Finca Zambia (Village Banking Project), and low-cost housing through Habitat for Humanity under the Work Build Project. Citigroup has in the past supported SOS Children's Village and has continued to support the two universities, namely University of Zambia and Copperbelt University, with a sponsored scholarship programme for deserving students.

DEVELOPMENT BANK OF ZAMBIA

Dr Bnalya Ng'anou
Managing Director
Corner of Katondo/Chachacha Roads, Lusaka
Tel: +260-1-221592
Fax: +260-1-222426
Email: bngandu@dbz.co.zm

Activity: Bank

The Development Bank of Zambia (DBZ) is a development finance institution (DFI) established in the early 1970s as a joint venture between the government of Zambia (GRZ) and public sector financial institutions on one hand, and local private sector and foreign bilateral and multilateral institutions on the other. At inception, the GRZ and public sector financial institutions constituted the class A shareholders and held 90% of the shares, while the balance of 10% was held by the class B shareholders.

DBZ has played a pivotal role in promoting Zambia's economic development. In its mandate to provide medium- and long-term development finance, the bank invested extensively in the agriculture, agro-business and mineral processing, forestry, quarrying, textile pulp and paper, fisheries and manufacturing sectors. Between the 1970s and early 1990s, DBZ held its place as the most significant financing institution providing medium- and long-term finance for fixed assets to medium- and large-scale enterprises in Zambia.

The bank has introduced a diversified portfolio of products and services in order to promote financial stability by spreading its risks across a variety of instruments, to expand its revenue base and to meet the financial needs of a wider market.

DBZ's strategic objectives for achieving its mission and playing an effective developmental role in Zambia are to effectively mobilize short-, medium- and long-term financial resources required for development and to provide on profitable and competitive terms short-, medium- and long-term financial resources. It also promotes economic activities in the export sector to enhance foreign exchange earnings.

"DBZ promotes environmentally friendly commercial and industrial activities and contributes to the development of Zambia's capital market."
Dr Bnalya Ng'anou, Managing Director

FINANCE BANK ZAMBIA LIMITED

Charles H. de B. Carey
Executive Director, Credit & Marketing
Chanik House, Cairo Road
P O Box 37102, Lusaka
Tel: +260-1-229733-40/221419
Fax: +260-1-227544/3359
Email: fbz@finanacebank.co.zm; ccarey@financebank.co.zm
Website: www.financebank.co.zm

Activity: Bank
Date of Creation: 1985
Capital: US $1.10m (shareholder equity: US $24m)
Turnover: US $36.140m (2005)
Employees: 600

Finance Bank Zambia Limited represents a unique key to the Zambian, COMESA and central African markets. As the leading and largest indigenous private bank, it has become a household name during its almost 20 years of service to the Zambian community.

Since inception, the bank has continued to register strong

performance and growth, from an initial single branch operation in Lusaka, to an impressive network of 33 branches and nine agencies located in all major commercial and agriculture centres of Zambia. Its network ranks second in the country and branches stretch to the Malawi, Congo, Angola, Namibia and Zimbabwe borders.

Finance Bank leverages a strong nationwide presence to deliver a broad range of core banking and tailored financial services, with specialized financing provided through the bank's head office, through which they have been able to contribute significantly towards Zambian business and economic development.

In project financing, the bank has been a leader through its creative financing and funding mechanisms. In the past four years, over US $40 million has been dispersed for small and medium-sized business development.

As part of its strategic growth plan, in 2003 Finance Bank entered into a long-term management services agreement with Loita Capital Partners International, a pan-African independent investment banking group with extensive and reputable bank management capacity throughout the continent. Loita Capital Partners International has seconded key personnel who, together with other Zambian colleagues, have ensured a quantum leap in performance, service delivery and professionalism.

"In Zambia, Finance Bank is a key to the Zambian market and the FBZ team is available to assist with any banking issues."
Charles H. de B. Carey, Executive Director, Credit & Marketing

GRANT THORNTON

Mr Hakainde Hichilema
Managing Director
Level 5, Mukuba Pension, Dedan Kimathi Road
P O Box 30885, Lusaka
Tel: +260-1-27722/226683
Fax: +260-1-223774

Grant Thornton International is one of the world's leading organizations of independently owned and managed accounting and consulting firms providing assurance, tax and specialist advice to independent businesses and their owners.

The firm operates in 111 countries in around 540 offices worldwide. Grant Thornton services international work through its local international business centre, drawing on international skills and local expertise and experience to help ensure clients receive outstanding service, wherever they are.

Many of the Grant Thornton international assignments are funded by the multilateral and bilateral development agencies, including the World Bank Group, the US Agency for International Development, the European Bank for Reconstruction and Development and the Asian Development Bank. Recently, the Millennium Challenge Corporation was added to the sources of US development assistance organizations.

The Grant Thornton member firm in Zambia managed a two-year World Bank urban local government capacity strengthening project. This project was funded by a credit from the International Development Agency (IDA) under the Ministry of Local Government and Housing.

It covered 10 local authorities and the four major cities in Zambia. The areas of capacity building covered by the study included financial systems and controls; revenue enhancement measures; introduction of a new broad-based flat tax by-law; and organizational restructuring. This was a complex, long-term project with a wide range of stakeholders. The Grant Thornton Zambia-led team was commended for an excellent job in delivering value-for-money service.

INDO-ZAMBIA BANK

Mr Hamainza
General Manager
Plot 6907, Cairo Road
P O Box 35411, Lusaka
Tel: +260-1-224979/224653
Fax: +260-1-225090
Email: izb@zamnet.zm; gmizb@zamnet.zm

Website: www.izb.co.zm

Activity: Bank
Employees: 200

The Indo-Zambia Bank is a unique institutional example of collaboration between Zambia and India; 40% of the ownership belongs to the Zambian government and the other 60% is divided between three important Indian banks.

Indo-Zambia Bank wants to act as a catalyst for the economic development of Zambia. As it celebrates 20 years of existence, Indo-Zambia Bank Ltd is setting new goals and challenges as it aims at reaching new horizons.

It has rededicated itself to the service of the nation and is committed to bringing good and efficient banking services to Zambian citizens. It is also emerging as the bank of choice for all retail and corporate needs.

The bank is a commercial bank specializing in retail banking. In the last few years it has increased the number of branches around the country, and now has nine. It wants to continue growing by opening new branches in key places.

Indo-Zambia Bank is proud of its use of new technologies and in 2006 wants to develop a complete new IT system which will connect all the different branches and enable e-banking.

"The Zambian economy is growing and, with all the potential it has and the good environment, I consider it is a good moment to invest in the country."
Mr Hamainza, General Manager

INVESTRUST BANK PLC

Mr Ndhlovu
Managing Director
Investrust House, Plot 4527/8, Freedom Way
P O Box 32344, Lusaka
Tel: +260-1-251311
Fax: +260-1-237060
Email: liz@investrustbank.co.zm
Website: www.investrustbank.com

Activity: Bank
Date of Creation: 1996

Investrust Bank Plc is a registered commercial bank in Zambia and has been in existence since 1996. The shareholders and directors of the bank are seasoned bankers with proven track records at the highest levels. The bank has branches in Lusaka, Kitwe and Chipata and agencies at Mulungushi House and Arcades Shopping Mall in Lusaka.

In domestic banking, its customers are able to maintain current, cheque savers and deposit accounts, each of which offers flexible investment opportunities. The bank offers competitive interest rates on various deposit accounts (in both kwacha and US dollars) and special customers enjoy negotiated rates and charges.

Investrust Bank offers a variety of treasury products and services to its clients and the public. The products offered are categorized into two groups, namely money market (treasury term deposits, government securities, fund transfers and payments) and foreign exchange-based products (foreign exchange transfers, deals, cash and drafts).

"We want to be the preferred and leading financial institution in our chosen markets, delivering customer-driven financial solutions and contributing to the growth of the Zambian economy, creating wealth for all stakeholders."
Mr Ndhlovu, Managing Director

LUSAKA STOCK EXCHANGE

Mr Joseph Chikolwa
General Manager
3rd Floor, Exchange Building, Central Park, Cairo Road
P O Box 34523, Lusaka
Tel: +260-1-225969/228391/228537
Fax: +260-1-225969
Email: info@luse.co.zm
Website: www.luse.co.zm

Activity: Security market, trading equities/bonds

Date of Creation: 21st February 1994
Capital: K9 trillion (US $260m)
Listed Companies: 13
Market return: 120% in US dollar terms (2005 figures)

The Lusaka Stock Exchange (LuSE) was established with preparatory technical assistance from the United Nations Development Programme (UNDP), the International Finance Corporation (IFC) and the World Bank in 1993.

In its first two years of operation the LuSE and the Securities and Exchange Commission (SEC) have been funded by the government as a project on financial and capital market development in Zambia under the multi-component private sector development programme. The number of listed companies has now increased to 13 and the number of companies quoted to 12.
The LuSE is made up of stockbroking corporate members and is incorporated as a non-profit limited liability company. The role of the exchange is part of the government's economic reform programme aimed at developing the financial and capital market in order to support and enhance private sector initiatives. Another important role of the exchange is to facilitate the divestiture of government ownership in parastatals and the realization of the objective of creating a broad and wide shareholding ownership by citizens via a fair and transparent process.

The LuSE expects to attract foreign portfolio investment through recognition of Zambia and the region as an emerging capital market with potentially high investment returns. There is no capital gains tax in Zambia and no restrictions on entering or exiting the market. The LuSE has been set up as a modern stock exchange based on the most current international standards and practices with a world-class system and custody services.

In the year 2004, LuSE was rated as the best-performing regional stock exchange by Standard and Poor's (S&P).

"This market offers one of the greatest opportunities amongst the emerging economies, and at the same time it is very safe and transparent."
Mr Joseph Chikolwa, General Manager

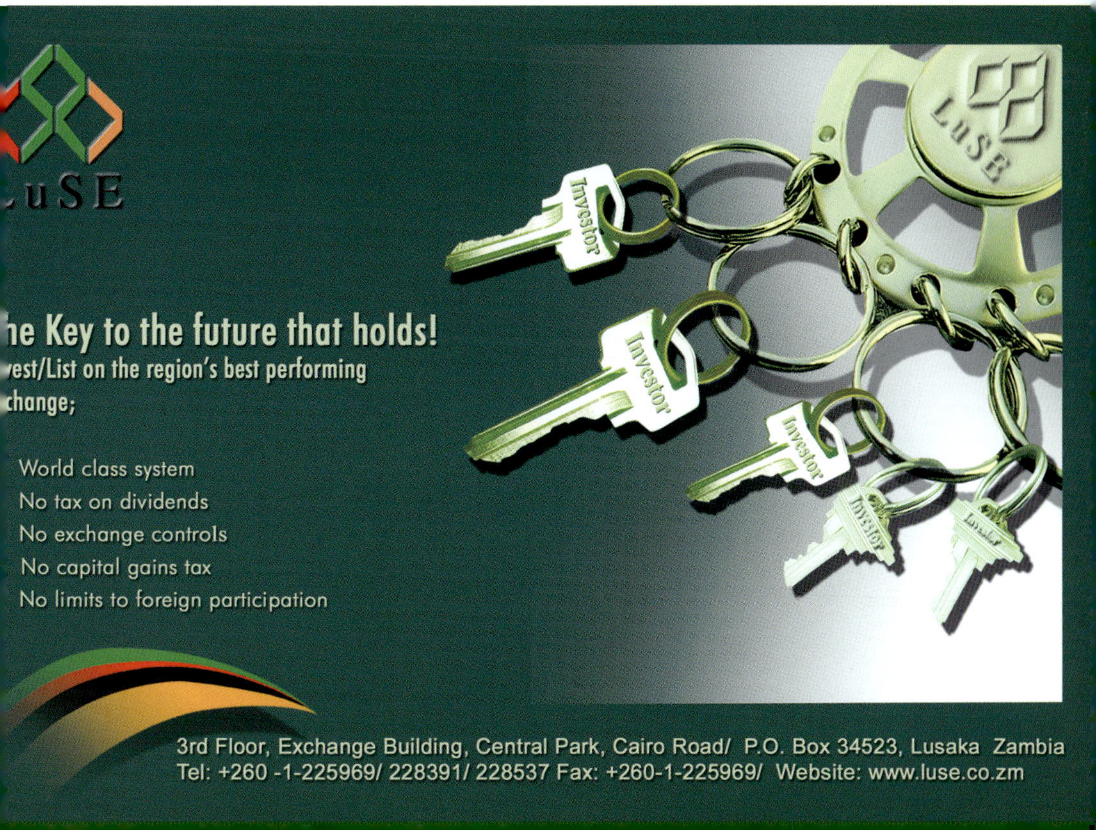

MADISON INSURANCE COMPANY ZAMBIA LTD

Mr Charles Sumbwe
Executive Director
Madison House, Plot 255, Keleya Road
P O Box 37013, Lusaka
Tel: +260-1-295311/295317
Fax: +260-1-295320
Email: charles@madison.co.zm
Website: www.madisonzambia.com

Activity: Insurance
Date of Creation: 1992

The Madison Insurance Group was the first to run a private insurance company in Zambia, commencing operations on 1st April 1992. The group comprises a general (short-term) company, a life (long-term) company, a health solutions company and an investment company. The holding company is Lawrence Sikutwa and Associates (LSA), owning the subsidiaries on a 100% basis. In addition to the foregoing, the group also manages a pension fund which is held separately under trust and, therefore, separate accounts are written for the Madison Pension Trust Fund (MPTF).

The life company underwrites group life assurance schemes, individual investment-linked products and personal pension plans. The life company also manages both the defined contribution and defined benefit group pension schemes. A funeral expense policy is also available for individuals and a group policy for employees of a company.

The health solutions company offers health insurance for local in-patient and out-patient treatment, whereas the general company underwrites all classes of general insurance business in respect of motor, marine, aviation, fire, engineering, liability and pecuniary types of general insurance.

The Madison Group has brought together excellent management and underwriting teams, which are well respected in the local insurance market. Their combined skills in insurance company management and insurance underwriting, coupled with the company's high standard of service and excellent reputation, have given the company a leading place in the Zambian insurance market.

It is a Madison policy to be prudent and conservative in underwriting all risks presented, bearing in mind the need to observe professional standards, good insurance practice and clients' needs. In order to personalize service each account is assigned a portfolio manager.

Madison maintains adequate liquidity within its investment programmes to meet day-to-day claim settlements, and the claims service is constantly being reviewed to achieve policyholder satisfaction. Claims are paid in the shortest possible time after receipt of all the required documentation.

NATIONAL PENSION SCHEME AUTHORITY

Mr Dann Musenge
Managing Director
P O Box RW51275, Lusaka 10101
Tel: +260-1-223772
Fax: +260-1-221195
Email: musengedk@napsa.co.zm
Website: www.napsa.co.zm

Employees: 500

The National Pension Scheme Authority was established following the reform of the Provident Fund started in 1995. The desire to strengthen pension provision in Zambia culminated in the enactment of legislation to establish a new national pension scheme to regulate both existing and new occupational pension schemes and to amend the civil service and local authority pension schemes to strengthen their administration and financing.

The Zambia National Provident Fund was a savings scheme where payment of a benefit was dependent on one contingency per member. The design of the Provident Fund failed to maintain the value of the members' contribution. Furthermore, the civil service pension fund and the local authority superannuation fund have had inadequate funding problems resulting in unfunded liabilities.

The design of the new National Pension Scheme Authority has taken into account protection against multiple contingencies. The benefits under NAPSA reflect a preservation of all financial elements in the pension's formula.

In 1996, the National Pension Scheme Act authorized the conversion of the Zambia National Provident Fund into a new national pension scheme under the National Pension Scheme Authority. The Pension Scheme Regulation Act 1996 established a regulatory framework for all pension schemes in Zambia except the new national pension scheme. NAPSA therefore applies to the civil service pension fund and local authorities superannuation fund as well as the numerous private pension schemes under one umbrella scheme.

NAPSA is currently the biggest pension house in Zambia with three million cumulative members and 450,000 current members. NAPSA has 12,000 employer companies registered, in both the private and public sectors. NAPSA has developed a large network of regional branches (23 points of contact) around the country, and is seeking to work more closely with institutions like National Savings and Credit Bank or the Zambia Revenue Authority to extend its regional reach. NAPSA is also currently developing an integrated IT system that will enable more efficient and faster delivery of service.

NATIONAL SAVINGS AND CREDIT BANK

Mr R. Mfula
Managing Director
Cairo Road, Plot 248B
P O Box 30067, Lusaka
Tel: +260-1-227534
Fax: +260-1-223296
Email: nscbmd@zamnet.zm

Activity: Bank
Date of Creation: 1972

The National Savings and Credit Bank (NSCB) is a government-owned financial institution and Zambia's oldest bank, established in 1972. The bank was created to promote saving, especially in rural areas.

The bank's efforts are focused on low and medium incomes. Initially the bank operated through the post office network countrywide. In 1992, the bank decided to establish its own branch network. In 2005, this network totalled 24 branches all over the country, and the bank is aiming at having 80 outlets by 2015, therefore being present in every district.

NSCB's main focus is to develop microcredit operations in outlying areas through community-based products. This unique feature was created to empower the people to control their financial activities.

NSCB provides its clients with a wide range of services, which include: savings accounts with low or no minimum balance required; loans for small and medium-sized enterprises (SMEs) and individuals; salary advances; payroll management, especially for the government; and making payments and collection of funds on behalf of institutions such as governments.

The bank has developed an institutional development plan (IDP) which spells out the future of the institution. This includes recapitalization of the bank and major activities will include computerization, branch expansion, staff training and improvements in infrastructure and transportation systems. The IDP will result in the bank becoming the biggest in the country in terms of its network. The IDP's main focus is on rural finance and wealth creation.

NICO INSURANCE

Mr Titus Kalenga
General Manager/CEO
1131 Parirenyatwa Road, Fairview
P O Box 32825, Lusaka
Tel: +260-1-222862/226456
Fax: +260-1-222863
Email: tkalenga@nicozambia.com

Activity: Insurance
Date of Creation: 1997

NICO Insurance Zambia Limited was incorporated in June

1997 and commenced operations in November 1997. The company offers the following insurance services to the Zambian public, among others: fire; consequential loss; house owner's/householder's policy; contractor's all risks cover; fidelity guarantees; professional indemnity; golfer's policy; marine; motor; and goods in transit. Although NICO is new on the Zambian market, the company has gained a significant market share and is already a household name.

The company is dedicated to the development, implementation and monitoring of cost-efficient and effective benefit programmes that can meet and exceed the needs and expectations of its clients. NICO is also totally committed to providing a level of service beyond what is typically available from larger, less personal insurance firms, plan administrators and internet-based companies.

PANGAEA HOLDINGS LIMITED

Mr C. Siwale
Executive Director
3rd Floor, Farmers' House, Central Park, Cairo Road
P O Box 30163, Lusaka
Tel: +260-1-220707/238709
Fax: +260-1-220925
Email: siwale@microlink.zm
Website: www.pangaeapartners.com/zamindex

Activity: Specialized financial services
Date of Creation: 1994

Pangaea Holdings is a subsidiary of the Pangaea Partners Group of Companies and the holding company of all Pangaea's interests in Zambia. Pangaea has offices in the US, UK, Turkey, South Africa, Kenya and Zambia, with its core business being in investment banking (securities brokerage), property investment, corporate finance, financial advisory services and asset management.

Pangaea played an important role in the creation of the Lusaka Stock Exchange, and as a licensed member and dealer of the exchange has conducted most of the brokerage/investment banking transactions in Zambia. Through the Zambian subsidiary, Pangaea/EMI Securities, Pangaea has been the market mover in listing/quoting most of the 20 companies on the exchange and served as advisor on the first rights issues, corporate bonds, debentures, delisting, share buy-backs and preference shares.

Pangaea has been involved in structuring the finance for a number of new property developments in Zambia. Currently, the group is involved in development of the Lilayi Housing Estate, a project with 5,000 fully serviced housing units to be acquired through a 15-year mortgage. In these transactions Pangaea's role involves structuring innovative security arrangements, repayment terms and other conditions that satisfy all parties to the transactions.

Pangaea provides financial advisory services to companies in Zambia as well as to those seeking to invest or otherwise establish a presence in the country. Such services include financial analysis, financial structuring and re-structuring, company valuations and due diligence reviews, detailed business and strategic planning, company formation and structuring, and other related financial advisory services.

Pangaea presently manages funds on behalf of third party investors making investments in corporate debt and equity securities (both listed and unlisted) and government securities. In addition, in conjunction with the corporate finance services it provides, the company also specializes in structuring financing transactions to meet the various requirements of both the lender/investor and the borrower/investor.

"Zambia has made significant strides in restructuring the macro-operations and policies of its economy and now is the time to invest in sectors that have scope for substantial growth."
Mr C. Siwale, Executive Director

RECOMMENDED PARTNER

STANDARD CHARTERED

Mr Tom Aaker
Managing Director
Standard Chartered House, Cairo Road
P O Box 32238, Lusaka
Tel: +260-1-229242/229259
Fax: +260-1-225148
Email: Thomas.aaker@standardchartered.com
Website: www.standardchartered.com

Activity: Bank
Date of Creation: March 1906
Capital: US $35.186m
Turnover: US $56.633m
Employees: 403

Standard Chartered has a history of over 150 years in banking and is in many of the world's fastest growing markets. It has an extensive global network of over 1,200 branches (including subsidiaries, associates and joint ventures) in 56 countries in the Asia Pacific Region, South Asia, the Middle East, Africa, the United Kingdom and the Americas. As one of the world's most international banks, Standard Chartered employs over 44,000 people, representing 89 nationalities, worldwide.

In Zambia, Standard Chartered Zambia was established in 1906 and employs 403 people, with 15 branches across the country. Standard Chartered Bank Zambia Plc is listed on the Lusaka Stock Exchange.

The bank serves both consumer and wholesale banking customers. Consumer banking offers a wide range of personal banking products and services including small and medium-sized enterprises banking, transactional current accounts, savings accounts, Visa Electron debit cards, personal loans and wealth management products through its 15-branch network countrywide, expert-driven banking, financial advice, cash management solutions, and world-class trade services.

Wholesale banking offers corporate and institutional customers flexible financial services including foreign exchange, cash management, web banking, trade services, premium service banking, global project plus, and one-stop banking solutions, encompassing the full spectrum of required products available to donor agencies and suppliers throughout Standard Chartered's global network. It has a solid position in the agricultural sector. The bank also provides quality advice and information on currencies, interest rates and risk management to customers.

"In 2005, Standard Chartered Bank Zambia was recognized as the best bank in Zambia by Euromoney, The Banker, The Financial Times and Global Finance."
Mr Tom Aaker, Managing Director

ZAMBIAN STATE INSURANCE CORPORATION

Mrs Irene Muyenga
Managing Director
Premium House, Independence Ave
P O Box 30894, Lusaka
Tel: +260-1-229343/57
Fax: +260-1-221758
Email: md@zsic.co.zm; zsic@zsic.co.zm
Website: www.zsic.co.zm

Activity: Insurance
Date of Creation: 1968

Zambia State Insurance Corporation Limited is Zambia's leading insurance company. It was established in 1968 and is engaged in providing all types of insurance, including life, pensions and general insurance. Other departments providing specialized services in the corporation are treasury and investments, real estate, finance, public relations, audit, administration, human resources, information technology, security and legal. Each department has independent financial management.

The result of the many changes in the Zambian economy in the last few years has been at times a flood of insurance services, and ZSIC has become the number one insurer. The corporation can be singled out as one of the major companies that have continued to support the growth of the capital markets in Zambia.

During the past year investments were made in different markets. As well as investments in government securities, the corporation also invested in a 12-year bond and further investments were made in commercial paper. All these investments not only assist in deepening the capital markets, but also yield good returns for the corporation.

The corporation's key strengths are a sound financial base and continued profitability, proficient management which is adaptable to change, and streamlined operations providing increased accountability and efficiency.

"The corporation has strengthened its financial discipline, especially with the formation of the Zambia State Insurance Corporation Pension Trust Fund. Due to careful management of funds, the company has surplus funds to invest in high-yielding low-risk investments, with its portfolio growing towards a more diversified and liquid portfolio."
Mrs Irene Muyenga, Managing Director

INDUSTRY & TRADE

"One who enters a forest does not listen to the breaking of the twigs in the brush"
Zambian proverb

OVERVIEW

Identified as one of the four strategic economic activities that will impact positively on poverty alleviation, the industry and manufacturing sector is expected to improve its contribution to GDP, export earnings and employment.

Growth in the sector continues to be driven by the agro-processing, textiles and leather subsectors. Other activities include the smelting and refining of copper and other metal products, and production of fertilizers, chemicals, construction materials and cement. The government promotes small and medium-sized enterprises in rural and urban areas so as to enhance labour-intensive light manufacturing. In order to achieve this objective, emphasis is placed on investment and export promotion, as well as the support of local products.

SECTOR PERFORMANCE

During 2004, manufacturing activities continued to be focused on food processing, with value added increasing to K327 billion – a growth of 5.1%. Some industries were revived in response to the reduction of import duties on raw materials. The good performance of the agricultural sector continues to support the manufacturing sector as a source of raw materials. Improved macroeconomic conditions and increased domestic demand partially explain the sector's growth.

Despite these positive achievements, the development of the sector faces a number of challenges. There is a need to strengthen the domestic market and broaden the country's export base as well as to heighten competitiveness in the manufacturing sector by reducing its cost base, improving coordination between producers and exporters, and facilitating access to affordable credit. Both vertical and horizontal integration is essential in order to create sustainable industrialization.

During 2005, the government increased its efforts to provide an enabling environment for growth. The focus was on making the sector more competitive by ensuring a responsive regulatory framework. Furthermore, the government has proposed to implement a principle that provides

Bottling line at Zambian Breweries

more relief on equipment than on raw materials, which should be produced locally, and the sector has been urged to manufacture some of the components of production required in both manufacturing and other sectors. For example, manufacturing should not just be a consumer of agricultural raw materials, but it should be a provider of equipment to the agricultural sector.

The Ministry of Commerce, Trade and Industry provides a legal and regulatory framework conducive for investment and the production of manufactured goods and for formulating enabling policies, programmes and incentives in the manufacturing sector. The government continues to focus on creating a business-friendly environment which is conducive to the growth of the manufacturing sector. Policies and programmes aim to stimulate investment, and laws such as the Investment Act are being amended so as to provide for special incentives and modalities that will encourage private sector participation.

SUBSECTORS

PROCESSED AND REFINED FOODS AND BEVERAGES

One of the most successful subsectors in the manufacturing industry, food processing and refining covers both large and small-scale industries. The premier export earner in this sector is the sugar industry, with other important industries involved in grain milling (both maize and wheat), carbonated soft drink production, clear and opaque beer brewing, and the production of cooking oil.

The growing and processing of oilseeds is becoming increasingly important. However, it is necessary for some constraints, such as limited processing capacity in rural areas, to be addressed. The downstream processing of livestock produce has potential, particularly in the beef and dairy subsectors. There are also indications that fish processing could gain momentum, provided refrigeration and storage facilities are expanded, or further processes, such as canning, developed to add value to the fish product. The processing of grocery items, such as cold meats, biscuits, tinned food, jam and cheese, is largely underexploited.

Paprika has been gaining prominence as a crop with export potential, and a great deal of its growth can be attributed to the development of privately managed extension and marketing services by investors seeking to trade this commodity. High-quality varieties are currently grown, for which it should be possible to obtain good prices. Although paprika has a lower return than other non-traditional agro-processed exports, it can be grown with less capital inputs than other crops in this category.

Small-scale agro-processing helps farmers increase the value of their produce by processing at the farm level. While large-scale processing facilities are usually limited to urban centres, creating employment only in those areas, small-scale industries are able to provide services and employment in rural areas. With small-scale processing, transaction costs are low as there is no need to transport crops to urban areas for processing and then back to rural areas for consumption. Additionally, since small-scale processing plants are less complex, they can be easily installed, allowing processing to be done at, or near, the point where the product is required.

TEXTILES AND CLOTHING

A market leader in the non-traditional export field, the textile industry in Zambia has long been one of the principal

Composition of Zambian Manufacturing

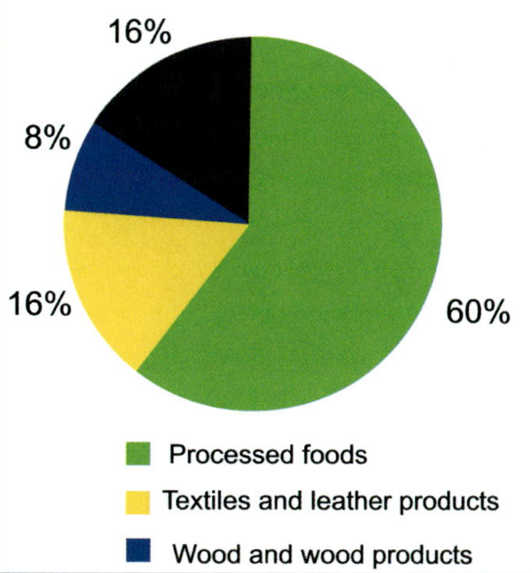

contributors to economic growth in the manufacturing sector, producing internationally competitive products from abundant raw material. Cotton is grown, ginned and spun in Zambia at industrial sites boasting state-of-the-art spinning, weaving and processing factories as well as warehouses. Products include cotton yarn and grey cloth of world-class quality, as well as garments. The industry has the potential to contribute greatly to the Zambian economy by way of employment creation (it is labour-intensive) and increased export earnings.

The EU is a major export market, with South Africa and Mauritius also recipients. Promising developments include the Africa Growth and Opportunity Act (AGOA), which has had the effect of substantially boosting clothing exports to the US. The main player in the industry is Swarp Spinning Mills Plc, which is one of southern Africa's foremost producers of spun cotton and polyester/cotton blended yarns, and is also one of Zambia's largest private sector employers.

Industry constraints, such as an oversupply of textiles internationally, high duty on imported inputs, and the undervaluation of imported fabrics, are being addressed by the Ministry of Commerce, Trade and Industry.

MINERAL PROCESSING

The secondary processing of minerals is gaining momentum within the manufacturing industry. Government incentives support new businesses that process copper rather than exporting raw copper bars. Copper wire and other copper products, such as copper plate and tubing, are an area of growth, with copper rod and cables making up a sizeable proportion of Zambia's non-traditional export earnings. The small-scale cutting and polishing of gemstones to be marketed abroad has great potential value, as does jewellery manufacture.

CHEMICAL PRODUCTS

The processing of minerals for the agro-industry is another area in which demand is fast growing. Zambia contains many agricultural minerals. Peat and limestone deposits are used to manufacture soil conditioners, while phosphates are used in the production of fertilizers. Fertilizer is produced at Nitrogen Chemicals of Zambia, which also operates a sulphuric acid plant and produces nitric acid, ammonium sulphate, liquid carbon dioxide and ammonium nitrate.

Minerals are used in the development of other chemical products, such as cement and adhesives, with industries including explosives plants, glass bottle factories and battery factories. Cement is produced at Chilanga Cement and glycerine at Refined Oil Products of Ndola.

Products manufactured for export include argon gas, sulphuric acid, detonators, automotive batteries, paints, cosmetics, soaps and detergents.

ENGINEERING

Engineering products have a ready local market and the subsector shows steady growth with considerable room for expansion. Supplying the copper mines with mining equipment, the manufacturing of engineering products also includes metal items such as window frames, doors and roofing materials, as well as nuts and bolts. Light engineering products include copper wire, cables and rods, alloys and ingots, cable carbon brushes, switchgears, pipes and rail sleepers etc.

LEATHER PRODUCTS

By-products of the livestock industry include large quantities of hides and skins, which find both regional and international markets, as well as finished leather products such as bags, footwear and leather garments. While predominantly cattle hides are tanned, the industry also utilizes hippopotamus and crocodile skins. This subsector has performed well and possesses potential for further expansion to meet a growing export demand.

HANDICRAFTS

Zambian handicrafts are crafted by local artisans and exported both regionally and abroad, where their quality has achieved widespread recognition. Comprising both decorative and utility items, products encompass carvings of soapstone, malachite and wood, clay pots, baskets and wooden furniture etc.

EXPORT DEVELOPMENT

The promotion of trade is in line with the United Nations Millennium Development Goals as well as the national agenda to reduce poverty and enhance economic development. There is a need for added value to be included in Zambia's exports. At present most items are exported in their raw or commodity form, with only yarn, cane sugar and cement having any degree of manufacture in them. Downstream processing is one of the best methods of increasing value.

Export development is promoted through the Export Board of Zambia (EBZ), which aims to broaden Zambia's export base, expand its share of the global market and increase foreign exchange earnings. In particular, the EBZ develops and promotes non-traditional exports (NTEs) from Zambia in the international market.

Further assisting the penetration of Zambian products abroad, two trade fairs are organized every year. The internationally recognized Zambia Agricultural and Commercial Show in Lusaka and the Zambia International Trade Fair in Ndola exhibit agricultural equipment, produce and manufactured goods and draw exhibitors from the region as well as abroad.

NON-TRADITIONAL EXPORTS

The significance of non-traditional exports (NTEs) to Zambia's economy cannot be overstated. Reducing the economy's reliance on traditional mineral exports such as raw copper and cobalt, NTEs are vital in increasing economic diversification and promoting growth.

Zambia's NTEs include sugar, cotton lint, floriculture, soybeans and other primary agricultural produce, with textiles, engineering products, cement and handicrafts also proving lucrative. Manufacturing exports have grown significantly, and there is room for further export production considering the great demand for the country's products in the international market. Zambia's top NTE producers include Zambia Sugar Company – which was named the country's largest non-traditional exporter during 2004 – as well as Swarp Spinning Mills, Agriflora Limited and ZAMEFA.

In a five-year period between 1999 and 2004, the contribution of NTEs to the GDP increased by 36.1%, mainly from the export of agricultural products, gemstones, horticulture, mining and engineering. Non-traditional exports registered strong growth in 2005, with earnings increasing by 18% to US $571 million. Accounting for this strong performance were burley tobacco, coffee, copper wire, electrical cables, fresh flowers, fresh vegetables, gemstones, scrap metal, cotton yarn, cotton lint and sugar exports.

Cost-effective ways of adding value to NTEs include shifting resources to higher-value products, improving market positioning by targeting higher-value segments and shortening the distribution chain.

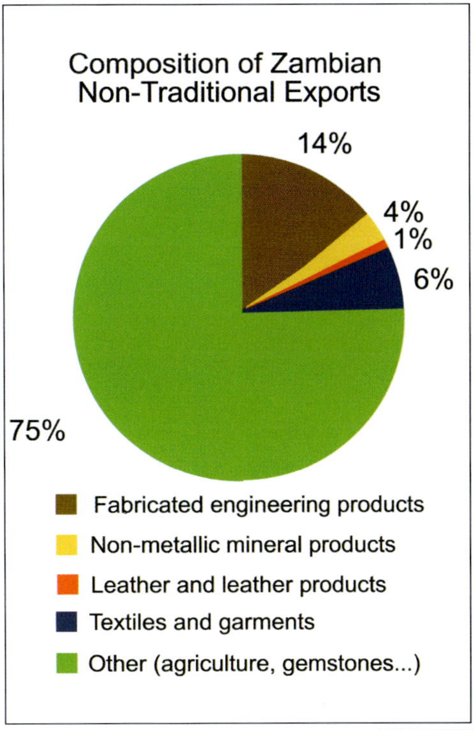

Mukuba Pension House

EXPORT DEVELOPMENT PROGRAMME II

Running from 2003 until 2007, the Export Development Programme (EDP II) is designed to support the implementation of economic diversification and promote the development of the private sector. Its forerunner, EDP I, ended in 1999 and extended assistance to producer associations in tobacco, horticulture, coffee and other high-value crops such as paprika. EDP II has allocated a total of 4.7 million euro for direct exporter support.

During 2004, K6 billion (1 million euros) in grants and loans was disbursed to six local producer associations under EDP II. Expected to create more than 2,000 jobs in the NTE sector by the end of 2006, funds are being used for export market research, participation in trade fairs, acquisition of small capital equipment and provision of working capital and pre-shipment finance.

THE ZAMBIA TRADE AND INVESTMENT ENHANCEMENT PROJECT

Funded by USAID, the Zambia Trade and Investment Enhancement Project (ZAMTIE) runs from 2002 to 2006. The programme involves the private sector and government on three components: the reduction of barriers to trade and investment through reduced non-tariff barriers; capacity building of public and private sector partners; and fostering linkages to optimize rural incomes, generating investment and trade opportunities between and among producers, suppliers, processors, traders, supporters and consumers within and outside of Zambia. Since 2002, ZAMTIE has contributed greatly to Zambia's export drive through close cooperation with the Export Board of Zambia (EBZ).

REGIONAL AND INTERNATIONAL TRADE

The South African market continues to be by far the largest for Zambia's NTEs. Principal export products to the EU, USA and Far East are cut flowers, fresh vegetables and fruits, cotton yarn, coffee, sugar, paprika, game trophies, tobacco, cotton lint and honey products. Markets within the SADC and COMESA region are supplied with sugar, cotton lint, electricity, cement, soybeans, animal feeds, tobacco, meat/poultry/dairy products, paprika, chemicals and petroleum products.

Trade liberalization is a pivotal element in Zambia's macroeconomic policy as part of its focus on an open, competitive market economy and adherence to the principles of multilateral trade. Trade barriers have been substantially reduced and customs duties are now the main trade policy instrument, with the highest tariff being 25% on finished products.

The promotion of trade is crucial to Zambia in its efforts to find additional regional and international markets for its products, and the country is a signatory to a number of bilateral, regional and multilateral trade arrangements.

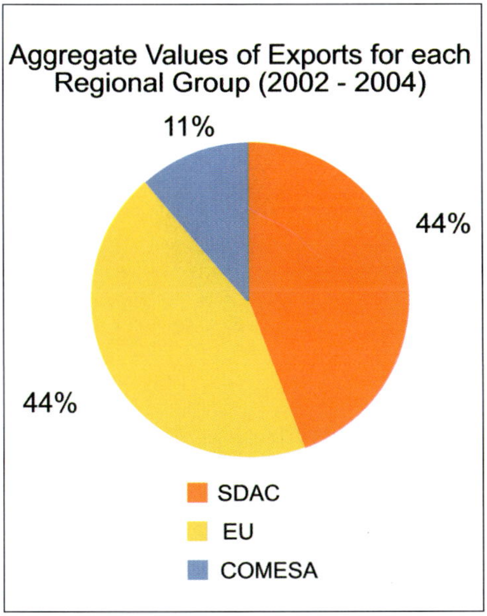

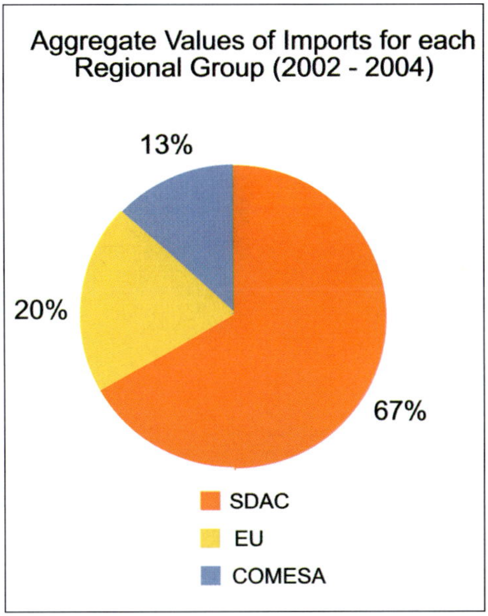

Trading partners within southern Africa include the Republic of South Africa, Malawi, Zimbabwe and the Democratic Republic of Congo (DRC), with reciprocal promotional and protection-of-investment protocols having been signed with most Common Market for Eastern and Southern Africa (COMESA) countries.

Important international trading partners are European Union (EU) countries such as Germany and the United Kingdom. In November 2001, COMESA signed a trade and investment framework agreement with the United States, in which Zambia is included. Zambia also has a bilateral investment treaty with Switzerland (1995). Zambia is a member of the World Trade Organization (WTO) and is therefore committed to the implementation of WTO agreements, including the progressive liberalization of trade.

COMESA was established in 1995, becoming a free trade area on 1st November 2000. Comprising 19 member states with a population of over 385 million and a gross domestic product of over US $388 billion, COMESA is a major market place for both internal and external trade.

The establishment of the COMESA Common Investment Area (CCIA) will enable the region to attract greater and sustainable levels of investment by harmonizing investment policies, laws and procedures. The CCIA investment framework agreement is expected to be submitted by the end of 2006.

Economic partnership agreements (EPAs) are being negotiated between the EU and the African Caribbean Pacific (ACP) countries in line with the Cotonou Agreement. Essentially reciprocal free trade arrangements, these new agreements will be compatible with the multilateral trade rules of the WTO and are scheduled to come into effect by January 2008 when the Cotonou Agreement expires. They involve the progressive phasing out of tariffs and non-tariff barriers to trade between the EU and ACP countries, as well as cooperation with respect to competition policy, protection of intellectual property rights, standardization and certification, trade and labour standards, and consumer protection policies.

Zambia is also a member of the Southern African Development Community (SADC), a grouping of 13 countries with a combined population of over 210 million people. SADC's other member states include South Africa, Zimbabwe, Lesotho, Malawi, Tanzania, Mauritius, Angola, DRC, Namibia, Botswana, Swaziland and Mozambique.

SADC's recent activities have focused on customs cooperation

Minister of Commerce and Chairman of COMESA shake hands at the second COMESA Business Summit

and trade facilitation. The SADC trade protocol, a legal framework within which the target of tariff reduction, as well as the elimination of non-tariff trade barriers in the region, is being pursued, underwent a mid-term review to assess progress on its implementation. The protocol aims to establish a free trade area by 2008 and a SADC customs union by 2010. Guidelines for the implementation of the customs union programme have been adopted. Furthermore, the protocol on finance and investment, which focuses on the establishment of a regional common market where there would be free movement of capital, labour and services, has been drafted.

The African Growth and Opportunity Act (AGOA) was promulgated in May 2000 to promote increased trade and investment between the US and sub-Saharan African countries by providing eligible countries with liberal access to the US market. AGOA was also created to promote increased access and opportunities for US investors and businesses in sub-Saharan Africa.

MAIN COMPANIES

AMANITA GROUP OF COMPANIES

Mr Diego Casilli
Managing Director
Mumbwa Road
P O Box 31412, Lusaka
Tel: +260-1-286445/286450/286460
Fax: +260-1-289283
Email: rambelo@amanita.com.zm

Activity: Manufacturing and commodity trading
Date of Creation: 1991
Employees: 300

The Amanita Group of Companies comprises several companies registered in Zambia, Mauritius and one in the British Virgin Islands, which operates as the direct holding company. Lusagen, a holding company incorporated in the British Virgin Islands, is the parent company of all the

Amanita Group companies. It is owned by DPF Holding SA. The acquisition of the Zambian companies was made in different phases. It started in 1991 with Amanita Zambia Limited. In 1997, the group decided to take advantage of the economic privatization programme by expanding the business through the acquisition of public companies from the Zambian government.

Over recent years, the Amanita Group has been conducting a complete restructuring and rationalization of its operations. It went into a major financial and operational restructuring process in order to reduce the group's external burden and rationalize operations.

This resulted in a concentration on maximization of trading in the cooking oil business with the development of derivative products. Amanita Premier Oils Limited is now the largest edible oil and cake meal production operation in Zambia. Due to its strategic location it not only has immediate access to the high consumer population of Lusaka, but has the advantage of accessing other consumer areas along the line of the railway. This location has also proved advantageous for Amanita Premier Oils' access to farming and other areas for the grains used in oil and cake meal production. Over the last three years it has been producing an annual average of 24,000 metric tonnes of oil and 12,500 metric tonnes of animal feed cake.

In 2005 Amanita started the production of table margarine, and Amanita Premier Oils saw an opportunity to produce the product locally, firstly for the local market and then for possible export to neighbouring countries. The current production consists of a foil-wrapped 250g pack and a 250g plastic tub.

"Amanita wants to maintain growth by focusing on its core business, improving its competitive activities such as commodities trading and oil processing, diversification and product development, and creating new alliances through joint ventures, with a view to increasing its market shares."
Mr Diego Casilli, Managing Director

ATLAS COPCO ZAMBIA LTD

Mr Alan Ferry
General Manager
210 Kabundi Road
P O Box 11291, Chingola
Tel: +260-2311281/313015
Fax: +260-2313877
Email: atlas.zam@atlascopco.com
Website: www.atlascopco.co.zm

Activity: Mining equipment supplier
Date of Creation: 1949

Atlas Copco Zambia Ltd is part of the Atlas Copco group, a global supplier of mining, construction and compressed air equipment, represented in 46 countries around the world and a leader in its field. Atlas Copco has been present in Zambia since 1949 and as such has been part of all major mining development in the Zambia Copperbelt.

Atlas Copco's main business in Zambia is concerned with construction and mining techniques. This business area develops, manufactures and markets rock drills, rock drilling tools, tunnelling and mining equipment, surface drilling equipment, construction tools, loading equipment and geo-technical drilling equipment.

This means that Atlas Copco has a complete line of drilling products which includes everything from production drilling rigs, to rock reinforcement bolts, to rock drills, all designed to help achieve high productivity with low maintenance costs. Through this business area, Atlas Copco is one of the world's leading producers of rock drilling and underground loading equipment. Besides drilling rigs, Atlas Copco also manufactures rock drilling tools, such as drill bits, rods, DTH hammers and cutters. Light rock drills, breakers, crushers and pulverizers are used for demolition.

Atlas Copco is a leading supplier to large infrastructure projects, including, in particular, power plant and transportation link construction projects, as well as global mining companies.

The company builds its business on its well-established reputation as a global supplier of state-of-the-art products. Atlas Copco Zambia aims to remain a leader in terms of quality, reliability, productivity, service, the environment and ergonomics.

Besides this, Atlas Copco does have a social responsibility to positively contribute to the community in which it operates. In 2002 Atlas Copco adopted Kapisha Basic School as its main community service project. Atlas Copco Zambia will continue with its community efforts in order to help and support the betterment of the community that it operates in.

BATA SHOE COMPANY ZAMBIA PLC

Mr Siwale
Manager Director
Mukwa Road, Stand No. 6437
P O Box 30479, Lusaka
Tel: +260-1-244397
Fax: +260-1-245663
Email: batashoe@zamnet.zm

Activity: Manufacturing shoes
Date of Creation: 1894
Employees: 40,000

Bata today manages a retail presence in over 50 countries, runs 40 production facilities across 26 countries, operates 4,600 retail stores and serves one million customers per day.

Bata has a worldwide reach, with operations across five continents managed by four regional meaningful business units (MBUs). Each unit benefits from synergies specific to its environment, such as product development, sourcing or marketing support. Each MBU is entrepreneurial in nature, and can quickly adapt to changes in the market place and seize potential growth opportunities.

Bata's four business units are: Bata Europe, Lausanne; Bata Asia Pacific/Africa, Singapore; Bata Latin America, Mexico; and Bata North America, Toronto.

Bata's strength lies in its worldwide presence. While local companies are self-governing, each one benefits from its link to the international organization for back-office systems, product innovations and sourcing. Bata is always ahead in new designs, new features and new products. A relentless search will continue for better quality and the pursuit of excellence.

Bata operates five shoe innovation centres (SICs). Research is conducted into the application of new technology, materials and design for shoe comfort features. Each SIC has a product focus to supply complete packages of services for the manufacturing and marketing of innovative shoes. In each SIC, international designers and technicians conduct advanced product research and establish strict quality control procedures.

In Zambia, Bata Shoe Company has been the leader in the shoe market during the last decades. It is dominant in the production of leather shoes. Meanwhile, Bata Zambia is importing ladies footwear from its sister companies to improve the range of shoes for its customers. Zambia Bata Shoe Company has started to export school shoes, gum and safety boots to new Common Market for Eastern and Southern Africa (COMESA) markets. Its exports business is steadily growing and Malawi accounts for all its export business within the COMESA region. Bata has plans to get into the mining market once it buys a new two-colour machine because then it will have the capacity to supply heat-resistant industrial boots.

COMMON MARKET FOR EASTERN AND SOUTHERN AFRICA (COMESA)

Mr J.E.O. Mwencha
Secretary General
Regional Headquarters
Ben Bella Road
P O Box 30051, Lusaka
Tel: +260-1-229725/229723/229724
Fax: +260-1-225107
Email: comesa@comesa.int
Website: www.comesa.int

Date of Creation: 1993

The COMESA Center hosts the regional headquarters of the COMESA

The Common Market for Eastern and Southern Africa (COMESA) was founded in 1981 as the Preferential Trade Area for Eastern and Southern Africa (PTA). It was changed to COMESA in 1994 following a new treaty. The change to COMESA was a fulfilment of the requirements of the PTA Treaty, which provided for the transformation of the PTA into a common market 10 years after the entry into force of the PTA Treaty.

In October 2000, COMESA established a free trade area and substantial progress has been made towards the eventual creation of a customs union scheduled for December 2008. The COMESA member states are: Burundi, Comoros, Democratic Republic of Congo, Djibouti, Egypt, Eritrea, Ethiopia, Kenya, Libya, Madagascar, Malawi, Mauritius, Rwanda, Seychelles, Sudan, Uganda, Swaziland, Zambia and Zimbabwe.

Within the framework of NEPAD and the African Union, COMESA is developing closer and more cooperative links with other regional organizations in Africa. For example, COMESA has good working relationships with other regional economic groupings (RECs) such as the East African Community (EAC), the Indian Ocean Commission (IOC), the Intergovernmental Authority on Development (IGAD) and the Southern Africa Development Community (SADC). The RECs are working towards harmonization of their trade regimes and programmes.

Over the years COMESA has created an independent family of institutions spread across the region, such as the COMESA Trade and Development Bank (PTA Bank) in

Burundi, the COMESA Reinsurance Company (ZEP-Re) based in Kenya, the COMESA clearing house in Zimbabwe, the Leather and Leather Products Institute (LLPI) based in Ethiopia, the Africa Trade Insurance Agency (ATI) based in Kenya and the COMESA Court of Justice based in Sudan.

The COMESA Treaty has two important innovations. In the first place, the concept of multiple speed, which provides for a group of countries to move faster in the regional economic integration process than some of the other countries. Secondly, sanctions can be imposed on countries that default in implementing agreed COMESA programmes.

COMESA aims at attaining sustainable growth of its member states by promoting trade and investment within the region. COMESA cooperates in the creation of an enabling environment for foreign, cross-border and domestic investment and in the joint promotion of research and adaptation of science and technology for development.

DISCOUNT STEEL

Mr David Gale
Manager Director
Lumumba Road
P O Box 38395, Lusaka
Tel: +260-1-231280/227426
Fax: +260-1-227368
Email: daveg@discountsteelzambia.co.zm
Website: http://zambia.discountsteel.co.za

Date of Creation: 1997
Employees: 100

Discount Steel was formed in May 1985, operating from a small town office in Pietermaritzburg (South Africa) with little or no cash reserves. Using a leased one-ton vehicle, Discount Steel traded primarily in reject tube to the Natal farmers and on a smaller scale to local industry. In 1988 the company moved from its interim base on a smallholding into a larger warehouse. Two additional new purpose-built warehouses and a new office block were then added. In November 1990 an additional company, Hodson and Rigby, was purchased and currently trades in the manufacture and distribution of borehole casing throughout southern Africa. Discount Steel has been exporting a wide range of steel products into southern Africa for a number of years and is currently one of the biggest movers of steel into the Zambian market. It is confident that through its buying power as a group it can continue to source both locally and internationally at competitive prices.

Discount Steel Zambia started in Lusaka in 1997, and one year later it expanded its operations to the Copperbelt. Nowadays the company has US $1 million in stock to be able to achieve its clients' needs in the smallest time possible.

This buying power and relationships with the mills enable it to procure material consistently and at competitive prices. The fleet of delivery vehicles enables it to provide one of the best services available in industry. Local and urban deliveries are made daily.

Discount Steel Zambia is the largest steel merchant operation in Zambia and stocks a large variety of plate, structural steel, angles, round bars, deformed bars, flat bars, window section, cold rolled sheet, galvanized sheet, roofing sheets, En8 and En19, stainless steel, piping, tubing and a large variety of other steel products.

EXPORT BOARD OF ZAMBIA

Mr Glyne Michelo
Executive Director
Kwacha House Annex, Cairo Road, 1st Floor
P O Box 30064, Lusaka
Tel: +260-1-228106/228107/232872
Fax: +260-1-222509
Email: ebztid@zammet.zm
Website: www.ebz.co.zm

Date of Creation: 1985

The Export Board of Zambia (EBZ) is a statutory body established by government under the 1985 Export Development Act. It was created solely to spearhead the development, promotion and encouragement of local products in foreign markets.

This was a consequence of the realization of the precarious nature of Zambia's foreign exchange earnings base and the need to diversify this base. Fluctuations in international commodity prices and the general vicissitudes of the international market in the 1970s and 1980s exposed Zambia's foreign exchange vulnerability.

The EBZ is involved in trade policy matters, to represent the interests of exporters to government and its agencies and to recommend policies in relation to trade promotion, development of export production and the regulation of export trade.

One important function it performs is to advise exporters, potential and existing, on export markets and trade information; on quality, supply and pricing of export products; and on existing export regulations, export incentives and available technical assistance.

The EBZ's role is to promote the development of exports in general and of specific products by liaising with missions and organizations in export markets, by trade fair participation, by undertaking trade missions and by other promotional activities. It helps to develop Zambia's human resource in export production and marketing through various training activities for officials, managers and technicians in the export sector.

The overall mission of the Export Board of Zambia is to broaden the foreign exchange earnings base and increase actual foreign exchange earnings through non-traditional exports (NTEs), i.e. all other products and services other than metals, and so reduce the country's dependence on metal exports.

"The strategy of the Export Board of Zambia is to ensure that the vast resources and economic potential in rural areas are put to good use for the economic emancipation of the communities."
Mr Glyne Michelo, Executive Director

METAL FABRICATORS OF ZAMBIA PLC

Mr Luis Corte
Managing Director
P O Box 90295, Luanshya
Tel: +260-2510479
Fax: +260-2511923
Email: lcorte@zamefa.co.zm

The manufacturing sector accounts only for 11% of the GDP

Website: www.pdic.com

Activity: Metal works
Date of Creation: 1968
Turnover: US $108m
Employees: 350

Metal Fabricators of Zambia (ZAMEFA) was incorporated in 1968. Located in Luanshya, the company supplies copper rods, bare copper wire, low voltage power cables, building wires, flexible cables and telecommunication cables.

ZAMEFA was privatized in 1996 and Phelps Dodges Corporation, the second largest producer of copper in the world, is the majority shareholder. The company was converted to a public listed company in 2004.

Since its privatization, ZAMEFA has invested substantially in capital expenditure in the form of plant modernization and capacity expansion. These investments and the recent acquisition of various casting machines have enabled the company to increase its production capacity by four since 1996.

Exports account for about 88% of the company's turnover, southern and eastern Africa and India being the most important export markets. In the forthcoming years, ZAMEFA is looking to develop new markets in west Africa, the Far East and the COMESA region. On the domestic market, ZAMEFA supplies cables to the electrical and telecommunications utilities and the mines, amongst others.

ZAMEFA is committed to health and safety in the workplace and protection of the environment. The company is ISO 9001:2000 and ISO 14000:2004 certified and has obtained certification marks for magnet

The growth of the manufacturing sector is a big challenge for the country

wires and low voltage cables from the South African Bureau of Standards. OHSAS 18001 accreditation is expected to be obtained in 2006.

NAMPAK ZAMBIA LIMITED

Mr Stewart Lamb
Managing Director
P O Box 30413
Lusaka 1010
Tel: +260-1-243615/243616
Fax: +260-1-247199
Email: stewart.lamb@nampakzambia.com.zm
Website: www.nampak.com

Activity: Manufacturing
Employees: 250

Nampak manufactures the most diverse range of packaging products in the world. Using a wide range of technologies in paper, plastic, metal and glass, Nampak is able to design and develop total packaging solutions. Nampak Zambia (ICP) produces a variety of metal packaging, conical cartons and corrugated board, and plastic containers, as well as paper-based labels and folding cartons.

Nampak has three main operations in Zambia: the metals division in Ndola, the paper and board division located in Lusaka and the liquid packaging division also located in Lusaka. The metals plant is situated in Ndola and is currently working towards ISO 9000 accreditation. The paper and board division has full lithographic and corrugated board manufacturing facilities. The liquid packaging division has a capacity to produce 120 million cartons a year.

As the only can, drum and crown manufacturer in Zambia, it has built up an enviable reputation as a supplier of high-quality metal products coupled with excellent service. Nampak is proud to supply to a number of multinationals and brands such as SAB Miller, Coca-Cola, Total and Exxon Mobil, as well as leading local brands.

It is the unique producer of fibreboard cartons for the sorghum beer industry, and offers a total packaging solution that includes quality packaging products, technical support and competitive filling and handling systems.

Nampak Zambia solutions are based on developing partnerships with customers by evaluating each product's requirements throughout the entire supply chain, using a unique approach, and incorporating both primary and secondary packaging materials.

"Nampak manufactures to exacting quality standards for the local market, backed by excellent service delivery. The company is developing new product lines to fulfil possible client needs."
Mr Stewart Lamb, Managing Director

PARMALAT

Mr Piet Theron
Managing Director
Mungwi Road
P O Box 34930, Lusaka
Tel: +260-1-286855/287745
Fax: +260-1-289388
Email: piet.theron@parmalat.co.zm
Website: www.parmalat.co.za

Activity: Dairy processing and marketing
Date of Creation: 1996
Employees: 173

Parmalat was founded in Italy in 1961. The company survived a 14 billion euro financial crisis in 2003, but was relisted on the Milan Stock Exchange near the end of 2005. Parmalat Africa continued with its business as usual and by good management established itself as a valuable asset for the group.

Parmalat entered the South African market in 1998 by acquiring two prominent SA dairies, Bonnita (owner of Zambia Dairy Produce Board) and Towerkop, and so became South Africa's second largest dairy company, with a national infrastructure and well-established brands.

The forerunners of Parmalat in Zambia had a staff complement of 106 employees. Many of these staff members had obtained their skills while previously working for the Zambia Dairy Produce Board. In 1998, Parmalat Zambia Ltd was established.
Since it established its dairy business in Zambia, Parmalat has grown in size by diversification of its product mix to become the largest processor of dairy and related products in the country. Whilst Parmalat does not have dairy farms of its own, it has entered into partnership arrangements with Zambian farmers whereby Parmalat purchases their milk production for processing in the company's factories within Zambia.

There are now 10 processing plants, 16 distribution centres and 6 agents operating around southern Africa, including Zambia, Botswana, Swaziland, Mozambique and South Africa. Parmalat is a dynamic leader in the local dairy industry.

SWARP SPINNING MILLS PLC

Mr Musho Shandavu
Managing Director
Mill Site, Plot 5258, Nakambala Crescent, Skyways Industrial Area
P O Box 71846, Ndola
Tel: +260-2-650821-5
Fax: +260-2-650172
Email: info@ssm.co.zm
Website: www.ssm.co.zm

Activity: Manufacturing (textile yarn spinners)
Date of Creation: 1981
Turnover: US $19m per annum
Employees: 1,100

Swarp Spinning Mills Plc, a Zambian company, is one of southern Africa's leading producers of 100% cotton yarns. The company is one of Zambia's largest private sector employers. The company has an installed capacity to produce over 12,000 tonnes of yarn per annum and the plant is situated on a landscaped 42 acres of land in the heart of Zambia's Copperbelt province. The company features among the largest exporters of yarn from sub-Saharan Africa to the European Union and attributes its success to state-of-the-art machinery, a high level of operator training, tight management controls and continuous attention to quality control and customer service. Around 97% of its products are exported, mainly to customers in Germany, UK, Switzerland, Italy, Spain, Portugal, France, Belgium, Greece and other European countries, as well as to South Africa, Zimbabwe, Malawi and Mauritius.

Swarp sees itself as a customized producer which is not bound by long production runs and can consequently tailor its production to meet customers' changing requirements. In other words – "the customer comes first". In the days of globalization and the emergence of powerful cartels dominating the market place, Swarp's old-fashioned attitude to its clients has resulted in the development of strong business relationships, which have carried the company through the recent world textile recession and have resulted in Swarp being one of southern Africa's leading exporters to the European Union.

Its comprehensive range of carded or combed, bleached or dyed, cotton or blended polyester/cotton yarns encompasses all counts required by the discerning textile producer whether in Africa, Europe or the USA.

"Swarp prides itself on its ability to meet customers' requirements in terms of both quality and delivery schedules. Swarp excels in a world where timely deliveries and minimal stock holding are of paramount importance."
Mr Musho Shandavu, Managing Director

TATA AFRICA

Mr Mutale
General Manager
Tel: +260-1-287160
Fax: +260-1-286081
Email: jhmutale@zamnet.zm

Activity: Holding
Date of Creation: 1970

The Tata Group is one of India's largest and most respected business conglomerates; it is a leading name in the engineering, agriculture, hotel and textile industries. The Tata Group made its first foray into Africa in the mid 1970s with Tata Zambia.

Tata Zambia has four business areas: the vehicles division looks after sales of vehicles (pick-ups, trucks and buses) and spare parts, workshops and the training centre; general trading deals with bicycles, steel, tyres, water-treatment chemicals, pipes, roofing, steel sheets, electrical supplies, school furniture and miscellaneous projects; the mining division provides products to the mining industry; and the investments and property division looks after the Taj Pamodzi and other properties.

From a single product in 1977, Tata Motors now sells trucks as well as buses. Over the years, its clientele has expanded to include the government, retail consumers as well as organizations in the trading, mining, transport, hotel and construction business. Today, Tata is the market leader in Zambia in the medium commercial vehicles segment.

Tata began operating Luangwa Industries, a bicycle manufacturing entity, from 1987 to 1997 before it was acquired in totality. This is now the bicycle division of Tata Zambia, manufacturing the 'Eagle' roadster and sports bicycles.

Another Tata Zambia enterprise is the Taj Pamodzi hotel, managed by the Taj Group from 1990 to 1996, when Tata Zambia bought a 70% stake in the hotel. It is now a public limited company with the 30% balance of shares held by the Zambian public and institutions.

Its textile division, Townap Textiles, is based in Livingstone and makes shirts, suits, bed-sheets, towels and other fabrics. The agricultural division, MATCO, distributes tractors from India and other agricultural and irrigation equipment.

An additional company, Tata Farms and Foods, was established in 1989. This grows field crops such as maize and wheat, vegetables and roses on a 500-hectare plot at Ngwerere, near Lusaka.

Mining is the mainstay of the Zambian economy and Tata Zambia serves this industry by supplying a number of mining products. These include valves, bearings, rubber linings, graphite electrodes (used in cobalt processing) and seals. Steel, mainly plates, is supplied to the local market and tyres are sourced from MRF in India.

ZAMBEEF PRODUCTS PLC

Mr Yusuf Koya
Group General Manager
Rhodes Park, Woodlands, Nkachibaya Road, Off Addis Ababa Drive
Private Bag 17, Lusaka
Tel: +260-1-252476/252657/252452
Fax: +260-1-252496
Email: yusufk@zambeef.co.zm

Activity: Manufacturing of agriculture products
Date of Creation: 1994
Capital: US $25m
Turnover: US $44m
Employees: 1,438

Established 11 years ago, Zambeef started out with an initial workforce of 60 employees and the company was slaughtering 180 cattle per month in a small rented abattoir. From these humble beginnings, Zambeef has grown to be one of the largest agribusinesses in Zambia and the region, involved in the production, processing, distribution and retailing of beef, chickens, milk, eggs and dairy products throughout Zambia. Zambeef Products has one of the largest retail distribution networks of any company in Zambia (82 outlets) and also operates three processing plants and five regional abattoirs.

Zambeef is the largest meat producer in Zambia, slaughtering over 60,000 head of cattle per year, and the largest feedlotter of quality beef cattle in Zambia, producing over 12,000 top-quality grain-fed animals per year. The company is also the largest chicken producer in the country, processing over 3.5 million chickens per annum and 20 million eggs per annum.

Zambeef Products is also the largest milk producer, milking 900 cows per day producing 8 million litres of milk per annum. The milk is processed, pasteurized, homogenized and packaged under the brand name Zam Milk. The new dairy plant produces natural yoghurt, drinking yogurt, butter and cheese.

The company produces 120 tonnes of stockfeed per day in its own stockfeed plant for the dairy, chicken and beef operations, making the company self-sufficient in stockfeed.

The company operates seven fast food outlets under the brand name of Zamchick Inn.

Through its own tannery, Zambeef Products processes 70,000 hides per annum, mainly for export to Europe, China and the Far East, and is the major shoe producer producing industrial footwear for the local and regional markets.

Zambeef Products also operates one of the largest cropping operations in Africa, growing wheat, maize, lucerne and soybeans with a total of 2,100 hectares of irrigated crops (34 centre pivots) and a further 1,500 hectares of dry land crops.

"Zambeef Products Plc is one of the most successful agribusinesses in Zambia and is a major player in the Zambian economy, with the aim to be the leading food provider in the region. The company has won numerous awards, including the "Best Performing Company of the Year – Domestic" for 2005, based on the Lusaka Stock Exchange performance records of all public companies."
Mr Yusuf Koya, Group General Manager

Zambia Bureau of Standards, setting high quality standards for Zambian products

ZAMBIA BUREAU OF STANDARDS

Zambia Bureau of Standards

Mr Mukelebai
Executive Director
Lechwe House, Freedom Way, South End
P O Box 50259, Lusaka
Tel: +260-1-231385/227182
Fax: +260-1-238483
Email: zabs@zamnet.zm

Activity: Standardization, quality assurance and metrology
Date of Creation: 1982
Employees: 55

The Zambia Bureau of Standards (ZABS) is a national standards body brought into being by an Act of Parliament in 1982. The Zambia Bureau of Standards administers the Standards Act of the laws of Zambia.

ZABS prepares Zambia standards and enforces their use. One of the main duties is to facilitate the examination and testing of commodities, materials and substances from which products may be manufactured processed and finished. Another important function ZABS has is to provide schemes of pre-export inspection of export products.

The Zambia Bureau of Standards formulates national standards which serve as minimum requirements in the country. The bureau sets different types of standards, most of which fall under basic standards, product standards or method standards. ZABS also implements standards through the certification mark scheme where, by good quality, products conforming to Zambia standards are given a mark which serves as an assurance to the buyer that the product has been produced under a strict quality control/quality assurance system approved by the bureau.

The ZABS Documentation and Information Centre has a large collection of standards and technical regulations issued by international, regional and national standards bodies. ZABS is a member of ISO and the selling agent in Zambia for foreign and international standards.

The Zambia Bureau of Standards Metrology Laboratory (ZABSML) provides calibration services linked to the national primary standards maintained by the Zambia Bureau of Standards, and thereby to the international measurement system. All measurements are thus traceable to the international standards.

ZAMBIA PRIVATIZATION AGENCY

Mr A. Chipwende
Chief Executive
Privatization House, Nasser Road
P O Box 30819, Lusaka
Tel: +260-1-223859/227735
Fax: +260-1-225270/225390
Email: zpa@zpa.org.zm
Website: www.zpa.org.zm

The Zambian Privatization Agency (ZPA) is an autonomous agency of the government of the Republic of Zambia, established in 1992 through the Privatization Act No. 21 1992. Its function is to plan, implement and control the privatization of state-owned enterprises in Zambia, in cooperation with the government, by selling them off to those who are more competent to run them and who have the required capital to do so.

The era of privatization was preceded by an era of rapid economic decline in Zambia. Many of the state-owned enterprises (SOEs) were eating into Zambia's resources by way of subsidies. The Zambian infrastructure was desperately in need of revival and investment, for example, the roads, schools and hospitals had become extremely dilapidated. Macroeconomic indicators had gone out of control with soaring inflation and the unchecked devaluation of the kwacha.

Nowadays the method used for offering shares depends on the type of company for sale. For example, smaller companies to be sold as a single entity will go under public tender, while larger complex organizations may be publicly floated. Other options include the management buy-out system (MBO), which gives the option of sale to management staff, who may or may not work with other partners to secure ownership of the establishment to own shares and invest in state-owned enterprises being privatized through the buying of shares on the stock exchange.

The ZPA's mission is to identify state-owned enterprises suitable for privatization in a transparent, efficient and effective manner. It contributes to the stimulation of economic growth, to the acceleration of development and to the generation of capital for the government and long-term potential for employment.

The ZPA has privatized more than 150 companies and units and is currently working on further important transactions. More companies under the Zambia Privatization Trust Fund (ZPTF) are yet to be floated to the public, while under some agreements privatized companies have made commitments to undertake public flotations.

ZAMBIAN BREWERIES GROUP

Mr Raymond Stark
Managing Director
Plot No. 6438 Mungwi Road, Heavy Industrial Area
P O Box 31293, Lusaka
Tel: +260-1-246555
Fax: +260-1-240642
Email: ray.stark@zambrew.co.zm

Activity: Brewery
Employees: 1,000

The Zambian Breweries Group (ZBG) is a producer and distributor of beer and soft drink beverages. These include four different beer brands, namely Castle, Mosi, Rhino and Eagle, the latest inclusion on the market.

The carbonated soft drink brands include Coca-Cola, Coca-Cola light, Fanta, Sprite and Schweppes mixers. Unlike its other brands, Eagle is produced 100% locally and using only Zambian natural resources.

This overall production is spread across three different production sites: one in Lusaka where beers and Coke are manufactured, one in Kitwe for soft drinks, and one in Ndola for beer products only. In order to market all this range of products, the company has opted to market each single brand independently.

Efforts are carried out daily to implement not only a more local production of its brands, but support for local sourcing of raw materials too, therefore generating indirect employment. Although the Zambian Breweries Group currently employs close to 1,000 people, the indirect employment of people benefiting from the spin-off of ZBG's activities is estimated at over 30,000.

"What singles out Zambian Breweries is its corporate social responsibility and investment within the wider community of Zambia. Not only is the company involved in helping to improve the health sector through its support of local and external interventions around HIV/AIDS and supporting local sports tournaments, but it is also trying to empower every one of its employees in their respective positions."
Mr Raymond Stark, Managing Director

ZAMBIA INVESTMENT CENTRE (ZIC)

Mr Chalimba Phiri
Acting Managing Director
6457 Los Angeles Boulevard

P O Box 34580, Lusaka
Tel: +260-1-254214
Fax: +260-1-252150
Email: invest@zamnet.zm; chalimba@zic.org.zm
Website: www.zic.org.zm

Activity: Promotion and facilitation of both foreign and local investment in the country
Date of Creation: 1991
Turnover: US $1m
Employees: 40

The Zambia Investment Centre (ZIC) is an autonomous statutory body which was formed by an Act of Parliament in 1991. It has a clear mandate to promote and facilitate both local and foreign investment in the country. The ZIC is also in charge of the coordination of policies on investment in Zambia.

The centre's primary functions include promoting of both local and foreign direct investment (FDI), facilitating the investment process and monitoring the implementation of projects.
The centre also issues the formal investment certificate that serves as the official recognition of investor status in the country. The ZIC monitors the performance of the enterprises holding investment certificates, establishes and maintains liaison arrangements, and assists investors in securing secondary licences, authorization and permits from any ministry department, local authority or relevant body. The Zambia Investment Centre records technology transfers and collects and disseminates information on relevant laws, regulations and technical matters.

The ZIC reports to the Investment Board, whose membership is drawn from both the public and private sectors. The Investment Board reports to the Minister of Commerce, Trade and Industry.

PUBLIC WORKS

"A tender bamboo cannot be eagerly desired for building"
Zambian proverb

OVERVIEW

Public expenditure has been directed at upgrading infrastructure that is essential for generating a positive investment climate as well as creating empowerment programmes for poverty reduction. The Department of Planning and Economic Management implements an economic development plan, which focuses on the efficient and effective allocation of resources, as policies and programmes must be developed within a framework of ongoing budgetary constraints and scarce public resources.

Strategic programmes have been put in place to implement reliable financial guidelines for public spending and build capacity within the sector. Integrated financial management information systems have been introduced, as well as a new code of conduct for the civil service. Zambia's public service reform programme involves the decentralization of the public service and devolution of power to district and local level in order to better target specific areas that will support development. District and local structures are being empowered to take responsibility for development decisions and activities.

CONSTRUCTION

Investment pledges in the construction sector totalled US $7.5 million in 2005.

The creation as well as rehabilitation of infrastructure is crucial to economic growth and investment, while requirements of this sector have provided employment for thousands of artisans, such as bricklayers, blacksmiths and plumbers.

Spurred on by public infrastructure works and the mushrooming private commercial and residential hou-

sing estates, the building and construction sector performed well during 2004, registering growth of 10%. Value added increased to K216 billion.

Of particular importance have been programmes directed at rural infrastructure, such as feeder roads, dam and irrigation schemes, as it is hoped that their rehabilitation will attract further investment to those areas. Construction in rural areas has also centred on the upgrading of educational and health facilities, with infrastructural rehabilitation programmes to continue under the Ministry of Education sector plan 2003–2007.

Funding for public works comes from the donor community (80%), with the balance being funded by government. During 2004, some K80 billion was set aside for non-poverty reduction programme road and infrastructure projects. The countrywide transport network – railways, airports and roads in particular – is receiving attention.

The Building Department of the Ministry of Works and Supply sets and monitors standards in the construction industry. A semi-autonomous organization formed with World Bank support, the National Council for Construction in Zambia formulates sectoral policy and also assists in monitoring the construction industry. Other functions of the council include consultancies and workshops addressed at improving standards and providing guidelines for the industry. The council also acts as a catalyst for economic growth, attracting capital from donors for infrastructure projects and hence creating employment opportunities in rural communities.

Private sector investment in the construction industry has taken off since the liberalization of the economy and the creation of an enabling business climate through privatization. Existing construction companies have expanded their operations, while new construction companies have also been established to cater for burgeoning private sector developments as well as the ongoing rehabilitation of public infrastructure. This subsector has seen the construction of houses, office complexes, commercial premises and the upgrading as well as construction of new accommodation facilities for the tourism industry – including top-quality hotels and game lodges.

Notable construction projects in the past few years have included Central Park, a K25-billion purpose-built business park designed to create a one-stop business and financial centre at the heart of Lusaka. Central Park consists of a three-storey circular tower and parking facilities for 250 vehicles, with two further blocks completing the development. Tenants include financial companies such as Pangaea, AON Minet Zambia Ltd, Industrial Credit Company, Intermarket Discount House, Lusaka Stock Exchange, Standard Chartered Bank, Barclays Bank and the Zambia Revenue Authority.

HOUSING

The National Housing Authority (NHA) and programmes such as the Presidential Housing Initiative have generated the construction of large numbers of housing units in district councils across Zambia. The government's national housing policy is aimed at providing affordable houses to citizens, and there have been some successes in various high- and low-cost housing schemes through the Presidential Housing Initiative. This has included the upgrading of unplanned settlements, creating employment for unskilled workers as well as additional skilled labour in the construction-related areas of engineering, architecture and surveying.

The Zambia National Building Society (ZNBS) in collaboration with Meanwood Housing Project has embarked on a five-year housing construction project to help empower Zambians. Being implemented near Kalikiliki compound in Lusaka, the project is aimed at giving those without shelter the opportunity to own a house. Some US $80 million was earmarked for the construction of schools, clinics, low-cost to executive houses and a shopping mall.

Despite the many ongoing construction programmes, local housing stocks urgently need to be increased. There exists a massive demand for housing development, in particular quality planned urban housing schemes in urban centres such as Lusaka, which have seen substantial population growth. It has been estimated that there is a need to construct approximately 110,000 houses a year in Lusaka alone in order to clear the backlog.

ROAD CONSTRUCTION

Policy on Zambia's road network is the responsibility of the Ministry of Communications and Transport. The Ministry of Works and Supply, through the Roads Department, is charged with the maintenance, rehabilitation and upgrading of the trunk, main and district road network. The Ministry of Local Government and Housing's Department of Infrastructure and Support Services is responsible for feeder and urban roads. The National Roads Board (NRB) was established in 1994 to administer the road fund. A new national transport policy was approved in 2002 and was followed by a consultancy on institutional reform.

Launched in 1997 with funding from government, road users and the cooperating partners, ROADSIP delivered the rehabilitation and maintenance of 50% of the road network at a cost of some US $500 million during the first phase of the programme from 1997 to 2002. This resulted in improvements in the condition of the paved road network from 20% good in 1994 to 60% good in 2002, surpassing the target set.

Specific objectives of ROADSIP include bringing a core road network into maintainable condition, strengthening technical and managerial capacity of road agencies, creating 30,000 new jobs, reducing road accidents by at least 20%, and providing an environment for improved road transport services. On a more general level, the programme's aim is to commercialize road maintenance, ensure the availability of sufficient resources from both private and public sectors, and establish a system of pricing to ensure reasonable return on investment.

Phase II of the ROADSIP project (2003–2007) was launched at a cost of US $800 million, with projects including the design of roads under World Bank and EU funding and Lusaka–Mongu road works under DANIDA funding. Phase II covers the rehabilitation of urban roads in provincial capitals, Copperbelt towns and other municipalities within Zambia, with the emphasis on employment creation and local construction industry development for poverty alleviation.

Financial reforms pertaining to the road sector have begun to be implemented in accordance with the approved national transport policy. Further, a fuel levy has now been budgeted under the Ministry of Finance and National Planning and is being channelled directly from the ministry to the road fund. The position of the government is that the fuel levy will be paid in full in order to ensure maintenance of the road network on a sustainable basis through performance contracts.

In the 2005/06 budget, some K112.3 billion went to the road fund as fuel levy collections, with the higher collections on account of higher fuel prices. All of the funds released to the former NRB were for road rehabilitation, while a total of K8.2 billion was released as counterpart

A new Protea Hotel is being built on Great East Road

Chilanga Cement from the Lafarge Group

funds towards donor-financed infrastructure projects.

MAIN COMPANIES

CHILANGA CEMENT (LAFARGE)

Mr Ian Coulter
Managing Director
Kafue Road, Chilanga
P O Box 32639, Lusaka
Tel: +260-1-279029
Fax: +260-1-278134
Email: ian.coulter@lafarge.com
Website: www.chilanga.co.zm

Activity: Cement
Date of Creation: 1949
Employees: 445

Chilanga Cement was founded in Lusaka in 1949 by the then government of Northern Rhodesia and the Colonial Office (now the Commonwealth Development Corporation (CDC)). Its core business is cement clinker and cement manufacture. During the early 1950s the company's shareholder base was broadened to include Anglo-American and Premier Portland Cement. In 1957 the company was fully privatized, but it was renationalized in 1973 when the government acquired a majority shareholding. In the 1960s, as the production started increasing strongly, the Ndola plant opened (1969), allowing the output to rise from 450,000 tonnes a year to 650,000 tonnes.

In 1994, Chilanga became the first large state-owned company to be privatized when the Commonwealth Development Corporation increased its shareholding to 50% and assumed management control. The residual government shares were sold in May 1995 to Zambians in

the country's first public offering and Chilanga became the first company to become listed on the Lusaka Stock Exchange in 1995. In 2001, the international group Lafarge bought a 51% majority shareholding in PanAfrican Cement (a holding company present in Malawi, Tanzania and Zambia through Chilanga) and therefore became the owner of Chilanga Cement. Currently, 84.6% of the capital is privately owned.

Chilanga Cement has an 88% market share and – taking advantage of Zambia's central geographical position in Africa – is exporting widely in the region to Malawi, Democratic Republic of Congo, Burundi and Angola.

The company is now focused on exploiting the potential given by the rise of new sectors such as agriculture and tourism to extend its activities in a still very young market. All employees of Chilanga Cement both locally and internationally receive extensive training.

Corporate social responsibility plans include construction of orphanages, schools and contributions to the health sector, especially in fighting the HIV/AIDS pandemic.

KNIGHT FRANK

Mr Tim Ware
Managing Director
Anglo American Building, 74 Independence Avenue, Lusaka
Tel: +260-1-286926
Fax: +260-1-287923
Email: tim.ware@knightfrank.com
Website: www.knightfrank.com

Activity: Real estate
Date of Creation: 1993

Knight Frank, through its strategic alliance with Grubb & Ellis and its partnerships and affiliates in more than 30 countries worldwide, has a network of 10,500 people in over 200 offices on five continents. It handles over £GB20 billion-worth of commercial, agricultural and residential property every year and advises the owners and users of land and property on every aspect of real estate.

The aim of the company is to give its commercial clients a competitive edge by providing world-class real estate and business support services around the globe. Residential

Workers in a construction site

WE HOPE YOU
HAVE ENJOYED
YOUR STAY
SPEED
LIMIT

clients are assured of the best advice from professionals who have a profound understanding of the market both locally and internationally.

Clients of Knight Frank have access to up-to-date national, regional and local intelligence on commercial and residential property markets. This, coupled with experience and expertise, helps the clients to capture, create and retain value in all of their property dealings.

Founded as Premier Property Consultants in 1993, the Knight Frank (Zambia) Ltd office is one of the newest offices in the Knight Frank Global Network.

Its team of nine staff covers valuations, agency, consultancy and management for both commercial and residential properties.

NATIONAL HOUSING AUTHORITY

Mr J.M. Kaoma
Chief Executive
Chiluya Mulenga Road, Long Acres
P O Box 50074, Lusaka
Tel: +260-1-251311
Fax: +260-1-253396
Email: kaomajoem@zamnet.zm; bmuzi@zamnet.zm
Website: www.nha.co.zm

Activity: Consultancy, construction and estate managers
Date of Creation: 1971

The National Housing Authority (NHA) was established in 1971 by an Act of Parliament to make better provision for the development and control of housing throughout Zambia.

A fully government-owned institution and the only major player in the country in the production of housing for sale as well as for rent, NHA has large tracts of land in the major cities of Zambia and acquiring extra land for housing is not a constraint. A large market exists for rented accommodation in all categories (i.e. executive, high-cost, medium-cost and low-cost houses) in the urban areas of

The road infrastructure is in an excellent state in the major urban centres

Lusaka, the Copperbelt and the provincial centres.
NHA is divided into five main business units: consultancy, town planning, construction division, finance division and personnel and administration division. The main functions of the institution are: to advise the government regarding the formulation and implementation of national policies on housing; to undertake, support and encourage research in all aspects of housing, with particular emphasis on low-cost housing development; to provide consultancy services in all fields associated with housing development; and to develop, manage and control housing estates.

In order to properly implement these different functions, the National Housing Authority provides its clients with different services ranging from town planning to land surveying, from architecture to engineering and quantity surveying services. The development of housing schemes by the National Housing Authority has spearheaded home ownership in various towns and cities where houses have been constructed and sold to the general public. In Lusaka, NHA is well known for the following schemes: Kabwata Estate, Woodlands Extension, Nyumba, Yanga etc.

At time of publication, the National Housing Authority offers different projects at different prices in the regions of Lusaka, Nyumba, Yanga, the Copperbelt and at Ibex Hill.

"NHA has large tracts of land in the major cities of Zambia and acquiring extra land for housing is not a constraint. Therefore the private sector and potential investors are invited to partner with NHA in the provision of housing in Zambia on a joint venture basis."

Mr J.M. Kaoma, Chief Executive

TAP (ZAMBIA) LTD

Mr E.T. Chawira
Chief Executive Officer
Off Kafue Road, Chilanga
P O Box 31522, Lusaka
Tel: +260-1-278315/278832/272783-87
Fax: +260-1-278206/278831
Email: tapzam@coppernet.zm
Website: www.tapzambia.com.zm

Date of Creation: 1943
Employees: 400

TAP (Zambia) Limited is a Zambian-domiciled company with its parentage in Zimbabwe. Prior to the change in shareholding in 1996, TAP operated as a subsidiary of Turnall and Newall of the UK (T&N). TAP has a history spanning 45 years in Zambia and has become part of Zambia's development process.

TAP exports to South Africa, Rwanda, Burundi, Tanzania, Malawi, Kenya, Angola and Democratic Republic of Congo and is making inroads into Europe and the Far East.
TAP is based in Zambia's capital city, Lusaka, and is close to its major source of raw material, cement. The company employs approximately 400 employees at peak demand periods and has a rated capacity of 55,000 tonnes of durable, trusted and affordable roofing, fluid delivery and garden decor solutions to all market segments in Zambia and in neighbouring countries.

TAP progressively supplies quality products that are of proven dependability, durability and are appropriate to our target markets. TAP's product range of roofing sheets, pressure pipes and accessories, sewer pipes and accessories as well as selected garden decor solutions are on display. TAP's main target market segments are low-cost housing, industrial structures, and irrigation and urban fresh water and effluent disposal.

TAP has not only invested in equipment but the total quality management concept adopted by management has warranted continued investment in human capital. Training and multiskilling is an ongoing practice at TAP.

"TAP's vision is to be the dominant stakeholder in Zambia and neighbouring countries in the supply chain and upgrade of infrastructure through manufactured fibre-cement roof cladding and fluid harnessing materials and ornaments."
Mr E.T. Chawira, Chief Executive Officer

UNION GOLD GROUP COMPANIES

Mr Mark O'Donnell
Manager Director
1663 Malambo Road
P O Box 51018, Lusaka
Tel: +260-226589/225542
Fax: +260-221175
Email: odonell@zamnet.zm

Activity: Holding company

Union Gold is an investment management holding company. During the constant changes Zambia has suffered in the last decade, Union Gold has expanded into different business areas when opportunities have arisen. Nowadays it is involved in a wide variety of business such as property business, construction and property developments, industrial companies and retail trading.

Union Gold intends to strengthen the boards of the subsidiaries and work with the subsidiaries to develop their businesses. The whole of the UG board is being reduced considerably to fall in line with the stated business objectives. Union Gold wants to reduce the Zambian board to three relevant members. Already Union Gold has specific boards in place for Arcades, Spar, PGE and Action Auto and the results show success, despite initial problems. It is now constituting specific boards in the following companies: Protea Hotels, Partsworld, Kazuma Plastics, Klaus Rygaard, Velos, Mr Price and Wildlife Shop.

Union Gold tries to empower management to accept responsibility and use that responsibility in the business in order for the business to develop to its maximum potential. Both management and staff are going to require further training to take this concept to the next level.

Union Gold has a vision for a strong hotel group. It wants to see Spar grow, is thinking of opening a new business in Mr Price, wants to see the plastics business grow, and is taking on a new agency at Partsworld.

Union Gold is also involved in the Lilayi Housing Development Project, a 5,000-unit housing development located on a 250-hectare site within the Lusaka city council boundaries and approximately 4 to 5 kilometres from Lusaka city centre. This project will see mortgages used in Zambia for the first time.

"We are continuously exploring new and exciting opportunities for further expansion. What we have to do is look after our investments and get our investments to perform to their full potential."
Mr Mark O'Donnell, Manager Director

TOURISM

"I am because we are, and we are because I am"
Zambian proverb

OVERVIEW

Investment in Zambia's tourism sector continues to grow, as evidenced by increased tourist arrivals and earnings, and investment in the country's tourism infrastructure. Given the country's immense tourism potential, this sector's contribution to foreign exchange earnings, economic growth and poverty reduction will continue to grow. In addition to a mild climate and long-standing political stability, Zambia boasts spectacular and varied natural resources, adventure tourism prospects, and opportunities to explore cultural and heritage sites.

In 2004 Zambia was named one of the top 10 world tourist destinations by the British Trends and Spends Survey. South Africa and Zambia were rated the two top tourist destinations on the African continent. The country's current prominence is largely due to a successful marketing strategy employed by the Zambia National Tourist Board. The government's investment in tourism is also evidenced by the fact that in February 2005 Zambia hosted the third International Institute for Peace Through Tourism conference. The country was chosen as host based on its political stability and the depth and variety of available tourism opportunities.

Zambia's tourism potential as a unique and authentic African destination has few parallels. Strategically located in southern and central Africa, the country's national parks and game management areas cover a third of the country.

Zambia boasts 19 national parks, 23 game management areas, 23 million hectares devoted to conservation of indigenous flora and fauna, and easy access to Victoria Falls, the largest waterfall in the world.

SECTOR PERFORMANCE

The industry's contribution to the economy in terms of foreign exchange earnings, balance of payments and tax revenue generation stands at 2.3% and is expected to rise to 10% by 2010 as a greater focus is put on the development of the sector.

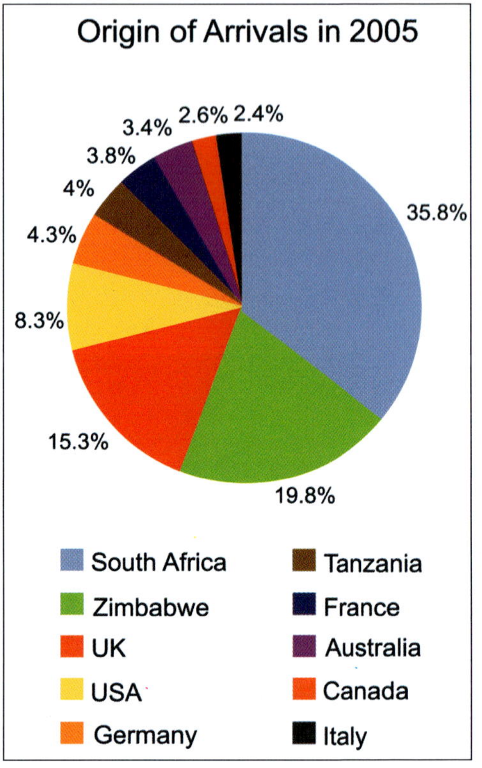

The tourism sector grew by 5.5% in 2004 from 6.8% in 2003. In the same period, the number of international visitors to Zambia's game parks increased by 9%.

International tourist arrivals have been on the increase in 2005, with a 7% further increase compared to 2004. Livingstone airport recorded a 39% increase in international arrivals for 2005. Mfuwe airport witnessed a 17% increase. These improvements have been attributed to the 'Visit Zambia' campaigns mounted by the Zambian government and tourism sector in 2005, and to a sustained increase in scheduled flights by existing airlines, with additional flights made possible by new operators.

TOURISM BODIES

The government is charged with regulating and monitoring the tourism industry. It does this through the Zambia National Tourist Board (ZNTB), an autonomous statutory body that implements all government policies on tourism. The board was created for the purpose of promoting

Zambia as an attractive tourist destination and also facilitating and coordinating all development activities of the industry at the national level.

Representing the various different tourism organizations that are part of the industry, the Tourism Council of Zambia (TCZ) has the goal of facilitating growth through the creation of an enabling environment. The council has worked in conjunction with the Zambia National Tourist Board to develop a tourism database, which is being made available to ZNTB's overseas offices as well as local and international travel agencies. TCZ also collaborates with the Ministry of Tourism, Environment and Natural Resources and the National Authorizing Officer to obtain further funding from the European Union.

DEVELOPMENT POLICIES AND PROGRAMMES

In recognition of the socioeconomic potential of the tourism industry, the Ministry of Tourism, Environment and Natural Resources has created a tourism policy based on the goal of sustainable growth and development. To enhance Zambia's already numerous attractions, the current policy focuses on improving infrastructure such as roads, airports and communications facilities, as well as security in tourism areas. Furthermore, community participation in the preservation of wildlife and natural resources continues to be encouraged. The tourism development master plan is an integral part of government initiatives.

In addition, under the ROADSIP II Project, the road from Kalomo to Itezhi-Tezhi and northwards up to the Kaoma–Mumbwa Road is being reconstructed. This will open up access to the spectacular beauty of the Kafue National Park and facilitate private sector investment in this vast area of high tourism potential. Further, additional investment will be made in the Luangwa and Lower Zambezi areas with a view to upgrading infrastructure.

Facilities at a number of lodges and camps have been improved, and there is emphasis on further development of tourist facilities by the government. Tourism develop-

Zambia, one of the last unspoilt paradises for wildlife

Stanley Safari Lodge, overlooking the spray of the Victoria Falls

ment programmes are focused on national parks and game management areas, with management plans being carried out and put to tender.

In 2004, the Zambian government sourced a loan from the World Bank for the Support of Economic Expansion and Diversification (SEED) programme. A key component of this loan was the improvement of infrastructure in areas targeted for tourism, such as Livingstone. Work commenced in 2005 on rehabilitation of roads, drainage systems and street lighting in the city. Finally, the Tourism and Hospitality Bill 2005 was enacted to facilitate reforms of bureaucratic and regulatory requirements surrounding tourism and to assist in building tourism infrastructure in the country.

The promotion of locally owned tourist facilities is also receiving further impetus, with K6 billion made available to local entrepreneurs in the tourism sector during 2004. Poverty reduction programmes are being focused on activities in the rural areas where the majority of poor Zambians are found. The 2004 national budget saw K5 billion released to the Tourism Development Credit Facility to facilitate the effective and meaningful participation of Zambians in tourism.

MARKETING CAMPAIGNS

In order to create awareness on both the local and international markets about Zambia's tourism products, the Zambia National Tourist Board embarked on an aggressive marketing campaign in 2005, the Visit Zambia 2005–2010 Campaign. The campaign, which is also aimed at branding Zambia as the home of the Victoria Falls, has been launched in South Africa, London, New York, Fort Lauderdale, Canada and Washington. The campaign has had remarkable results and a significant increase in the number of tourist arrivals has been recorded. The campaign has also opened up investment opportunities in the tourism sector. The new 2006 campaign was launched in February and promotes 'Zambia, home of magnificent waterfalls'.

On the international front, Zambia has continued to participate in a number of tourism fairs, conferences and exhibitions, all in an effort to market the country as a preferred destination. The Vakantiebeurs show in the Netherlands, the New York Expo in the USA, the Indaba in South Africa, the FITUR in Madrid, and the World Travel Market in London are some of the tourism fairs which Zambia has participated in. Zambia has also attended conferences such as the Africa Travel Association (ATA) conference in various parts of the world. Zambia also conducted a five-city roadshow in the USA and Canada.

Zambia has also been host to a number of conferences and exhibitions such as the ASATA Congress held in Livingstone, the IIPT conference in Lusaka as well as the Coffee Growers' Association exhibition held in Livingstone. Zambia is emerging as a popular conference destination.

On the domestic market, the Zambia National Tourist Board has continued with its activities to stimulate domestic tourism. This has resulted in the creation of awareness and generation of interest by the general public about Zambia's tourism products. This has been achieved through radio and television programmes, exhibitions conducted during local fairs and conferences, as well as through the use of the website. ZNTB has its own television programme aimed at stimulating domestic tourism, especially community-based tourism products.

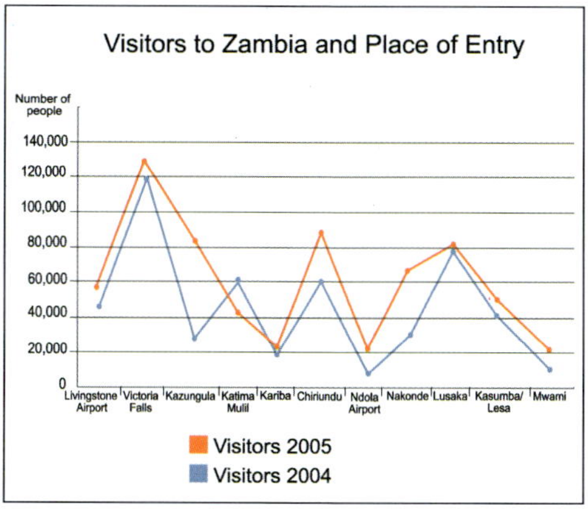

WILDLIFE CONSERVATION AND COMMUNITY EMPOWERMENT

Zambia's wetlands are becoming a focus for national development, with creation of wetland programmes the task of the Environmental Council of Zambia. While it is acknowledged that these areas have great potential, sustainable development is to be carried out according to the dictates of the Ramsar Convention.

The country's wildlife is managed by the Zambia Wildlife Authority, which encourages the appreciation and sustainable use of wildlife resources. The key to achieving this is involving local communities in the preservation and management of Zambia's wildlife and natural resources. Community-based natural resource management (CBNRM) is being employed in a number of conservation projects across various game management areas. This has the dual effect of empowering local communities while preserving the country's natural assets. For example, communities in the South Luangwa National Park will be able to recoup revenues generated by the area's wildlife through the Administrative Management Unit.

The luxurious tree houses of Sussi and Chuma Lodge, by the Zambezi River

CULTURAL TOURISM AND HERITAGE SITES

In the interests of promoting Zambia's national identity and protecting its diversity, the National Heritage Conservation Commission is charged with looking after objects and relics of archaeological, aesthetic or scientific interest. A wide range of heritage sites and structures is also managed. These comprise rock art sites, traditional shrines and burial sites, as well as over 600 historic or architectural sites such as buildings, monuments and ruins, and more than 60 recorded engineering heritage sites.

INVESTMENT OPPORTUNITIES

Facilitated by a comprehensive economic liberalization programme, Zambia's vast tourism potential has in recent years attracted viable investments and exploitation, especially around the Victoria Falls area. Investors with a keen interest in tourism ventures are emerging internationally, with funding from donor communities for the development of national parks – particularly with regard to infrastructure – also increasing significantly. The Zambia Investment Centre received pledges totalling US $18.6 million in 2005.

Currently, the bulk of the accommodation is found in tourist camps and lodges, with hotels of international standard in Lusaka and Livingstone. There is a healthy growth in seminars and workshops, which benefits local hotels, with Holiday Inn having experienced a substantial increase in occupancy rates following the opening of its conference centre.

The shortfall in all types of holiday accommodation, parti-

Sun International has established two hotels very close to the Falls/Zambezi Sun and Royal Livingstone

cularly good quality accommodation (though not necessarily five-star luxury) presents the biggest single opportunity for investment in the Zambian tourism industry. This investment can be profitably focused on upgrading existing establishments or in entirely new projects. Sites with attractive natural settings are readily available in national parks, game management areas and elsewhere. Nonetheless, Zambia has already begun to see change in this sector, with recent investment by Sun International Hotels in a hotel at Victoria Falls. This represents one of the largest investments ever in Zambian tourism infrastructure.

There are a number of tourist attractions that remain underdeveloped. At present, the Kafue National Park remains the largest potential tourism resource in the country. In recognition of this fact, during 2004 the government sponsored an investors' conference to attract credible investors to help develop this untapped asset.

With the tourist capital of Livingstone serving as a growth point for tourism in Zambia, there are many opportunities for productive investment in the industry. Potential investment areas include the following:

- Infrastructure and transport services, including luxury coaches, air charters and car hire operations. Organized tours, including day-trips and extended tours, to a variety of tourist attractions by car, plane, horseback or boat. Additionally, game fishing, photographic or hunting safaris may be organized in wildlife areas and national parks.
- Creation and upgrading of all types of accommodation and conference facilities, with attractive sites in natural settings readily available.
- Zambia's unique cultural heritage, including sites of scenic, cultural, artistic and historic interest offer abundant opportunities. Potential exists to develop museums, theme parks and galleries.
- Adventure tourism, particularly for the overseas market, including climbing, bungee jumping and hang-gliding.
- Water sports activities, with Zambia's abundance of lakes and rivers making it the perfect site for sailing, waterskiing, canoeing, white water rafting, boat charter services and cruises.
- Other sporting activities, such as horse-riding, golf and tennis, are well suited to local conditions, with the compilation of sports-based holiday packages a possibility.

MAIN COMPANIES

HOLIDAY INN

Mr Adrian Penny
General Manager
Cnr Church Road and Independence Avenue
P O Box 30666, Lusaka
Tel: +260-1-251666
Fax: +260-1-251501
Email: adrianp@holidayinn.co.zm
Website: www.holidayinn-zambia.com

Activity: Hotel

Holiday Inn Lusaka is located 4km from the city centre and only 27km from the airport. Specially built for business and leisure travellers, this hotel accommodates guests with the traditional warmth and hospitality for which Holiday Inn is renowned.

Holiday Inn Lusaka has 155 recently refurbished and decorated rooms, with air conditioning, en suite bathroom with bath and shower, electric razor plug, radio and telephone, colour TV with M-Net Movie Channel, BBC, CNN and SuperSport. Tea/coffee-making facilities are also available in the rooms. There are non-smoking rooms and rooms designed to suit disabled travellers.

Perfectly equipped to cater for the discerning business traveller, the hotel offers secretarial services and several conference rooms which can accommodate from 8 to 20 people. The banqueting room is suitable for workshops, seminars and functions and can accommodate up to 150.

Within the hotel is The Musuku Restaurant with a scenic view across the crocodile pond, and al fresco dining is a popular choice on the outside terrace. McGinty's Traditional Irish Pub is the perfect lively setting for a casual lunch or pre-dinner drink.

Every Wednesday a cocktail party is organized at 6pm as

a way to facilitate encounters between guests and these are often attended by the local business community.

INTERCONTINENTAL HOTEL

Mr C. Smith
General Manager
Haile Selassie Avenue
P O Box 32201, Lusaka
Tel: +260-1-250000
Fax: +260-1-250895
Website: www.ichotelsgroup.com

Activity: Hotel

The Intercontinental Lusaka sits in the heart of Lusaka's commercial and administrative district. Recently renovated, the hotel has 225 rooms of the highest standards, two restaurants, a swimming pool and a spa and health club. Self-catering apartments are soon to be opened within the premises.

The highest levels of information technology have been installed for the convenience of the guests with wireless high-speed Internet access in all the rooms and hotel facilities. Business travellers will find improved, extra-large workspaces, private meeting lounges and enhanced dining facilities on the executive Intercontinental Club floor.

The Intercontinental Lusaka also offers the best conferencing facilities, with nine meeting rooms hosting up to 700 persons for prestigious banquets, receptions and conferences.

In-house restaurants offer a wide choice of world cuisine including traditional local dishes and Spanish, Greek, Moroccan and Lebanese fare. The Savannah restaurant offers a casual and friendly ambience serving the very best of Zambian and international cuisine. A wide variety of buffets, barbecues and an à la carte menu are available. The Olive Grove restaurant offers a very special French/Mediterranean experience for the enjoyment of fine cuisine.
The Safari Bar is the meeting place in Lusaka for a Mosi (Zambian beer) with live entertainment by the famous Big Gold Six Tuesdays to Fridays and karaoke on Friday, Saturday and Sunday nights.

"The Intercontinental offers the best levels of service and attention to detail."
Mr C. Smith, General Manager

LILAYI LODGE

Mr Kevin Riddiford
General Manager
PO Box 30093, Lusaka
Tel: +260-1-279022-5
Fax: +260-1-279026
Email: lilayi@zamsaf.co.zm
Website: www.lilayi.com

Activity: Lodge
Date of Creation: 1991

Set in attractive parkland of 700 hectares, Lilayi Lodge is located only 20 minutes from Lusaka. 'Lilayi' means place of rest, and this lodge certainly lives up to its name. The lodge is built in traditional style, using burnt handmade bricks, thatched roofing and mukwa flooring. The 12 chalets and six deluxe chalets, recently refurbished, offer luxurious accommodation. The standard chalets, ideal for families, contain a shared lounge area and two bedrooms each with en suite bathrooms. The deluxe chalets have a double room, en suite bathroom and lounge.

Lilayi Lodge is also a private game reserve and visitors and residents will have the opportunity to see 14 species including antelopes, giraffes, zebras, warthogs, jackals, monkeys... Game drives, walking, biking and horse riding safaris can be arranged at the lodge.

Lilayi Lodge is ideal for business travellers seeking a quiet and peaceful environment very close to the city centre. Lilayi Lodge includes two top-rate conference facilities that can host up to 120 people, with a state-of-the-art multimedia and business centre. Conference services are provided on either a residential or non-residential basis. The lodge is also extremely popular for its Sunday lunch.

Just before the big fall...

The restaurant is open to the general public and renowned for its excellent cuisine.

"A bush experience, 20 minutes away from the city centre..."
Mr Kevin Riddiford, General Manager

MICHELANGELO

Mr Sergio Giorgi
Proprietor
126 Broadway
PO Box 70447, Ndola
Tel: +260-2-620325/620476
Fax: +260-2-620326
Email: vgstyle@zamnet.zm

Activity: Guest house

Conveniently and centrally situated in Ndola, the capital of the Copperbelt, Michelangelo is a top-of-the-range restaurant and deluxe guest house.

Michelangelo is well known in the region for its fine Italian cuisine and its unique deli with homemade cheeses and cakes.

Michelangelo has recently opened luxury accommodation of the very highest standard. On offer are 11 beautifully appointed en suite rooms with mini-bar and coffee-making facilities, DSTV, telephone, hair dryer and a safe. Set in a beautiful garden facing an inviting swimming pool, all rooms are air-conditioned and equipped with 24-hour high-speed Internet connection.

For longer stays, Michelangelo also offers 10 self-contained two- or three-bedroom apartments. The luxurious apartments are fully furnished and serviced with cleaning, security and laundry services.

Michelangelo is the preferred place for business travellers

and local business people; with wireless high-speed connection in all the common areas, and high-speed Internet connection in all the rooms, Michelangelo has become the place of choice for a short or long stay in the Copperbelt to mix business and pleasure.

NORMAN CARR SAFARIS

Mr Norman Carr
P O Box 100, Mfuwe
Tel: +260-6-246015/46025
Fax: +260-6-245025
Email: kapani@normancarrsafaris.com
Website: www.normancarrsafaris.com

Activity: Tourism and safaris

Norman Carr is a conservation legend in the Luangwa Valley. He pioneered walking safaris in the Zambian bush in the 1950s and is widely regarded as the father of walking safaris. He spent over 50 years devoting himself to the development of the South Luangwa National Park. He built Kapani Lodge in 1986 and lived there until his death in 1996. Now the business has five different lodges and camps in the Luangwa Valley.

Kapani is a beautiful permanent lodge situated on one of the many oxbow lagoons in the south of Luangwa. Accommodation consists of eight standard suites and two new lagoon houses, 20 beds in all. The brick chalets have thatched roofs, spacious living areas, luxurious interiors and walk-in mosquito nets. The lagoon houses offer more spacious rooms, private views and elegant furniture. It is the ideal place for people to spend their first night in Africa before moving on to the more rustic bush camps. There is a main chitenge with a bar and lounge area.

Nsolo Camp is a romantic, thatched camp situated on a waterhole in the shade of a large grove of trees.

Some lodges combine bush experience, adventure and luxury

Accommodation consists of four rooms built on raised wooden platforms under a thatched roof. Where possible, the natural features have been incorporated into the structure. At night, the canvas curtains can be drawn for added security. Rooms are open-fronted allowing extensive views. There is a small waterhole in front of the camp which attracts game.

Kakuli is a seasonal camp on the confluence of the Luwi and Luangwa Rivers. There are five spacious tents with en suite facilities under a shady thatched roof. All of the tents overlook the river and have modern en suite bathrooms in the shade of huge trees. There is a lovely chitenge overlooking the grazing lawn that leads down to the rivers. The camp is on a raised ridge allowing extensive views of the Luangwa for up to a mile. Several hundred hippo live in this stretch of the river.

Luwi is a seasonal camp nestled under huge mahogany trees on the banks of a permanent lagoon. Accommodation is in four huts that are made of grass and thatch with polished mud floors. All meals are served in the shade of the trees, with a view of the grassy plain that normally attracts lots of wildlife. Luwi is one of the camps situated deepest in the Luangwa wilderness, lending the camp a rustic appeal and providing a truly African bush experience.

Mchenja is a seasonal camp on the banks of the Luangwa River. Five wooden chalets have been built on raised platforms under thatch and nestle under a grove of ancient ebony trees. There is a main chitenge under thatch, which houses the bar and lounge area, although most meals are enjoyed under the canopy of the magnificent trees outside.

ROBIN POPE SAFARIS

Mr Robin Pope
P O Box 80, Mfuwe
Tel: +260-6-246090/91/92
Fax: +260-6-246094
Email: kim@robinpopesafaris.net
Website: www.robinpopesafaris.net
Activity: Tourism

Robin Pope Safaris is the most established and successful safari operator in the South Luangwa National Park. Its camps take, at most, a dozen pampered visitors, every one of whom is treated as a personal house guest and new best friend. The Popes have set a standard that has become Zambia's benchmark for excellence and their guides are astonishingly knowledgeable naturalists.

Africa House Safari is a safari combining the South and North Luangwa National Parks with a visit to the historical Shiwa House, an exceptional and unusual experience. In northern Zambia situated between rugged hills and a scenic lake lies Shiwa N'gandu, the former estate of Sir Stewart Gore Browne built in 1928. The house has recently been restored by grandson Charlie and wife Jo in keeping with the original style. The estate boasts a 1,000-hectare game farm with 22 mammal species, fishing and birding on the lake, walks around the estate, horse trails and a visit to the Kapishya hot springs.

Gem of Zambia Safari 14-night or 10-night safaris covering South Luangwa, Lower Zambezi and North Kafue, Zambia's three stunning premier parks, are all different. The camps are small, personal and owner run. This is a spectacular safari through Zambia within remote areas, with dedicated guides and excellent game.

For Zambia's Classic Safaris, Robin Pope Safaris has put together a 10-night itinerary incorporating everything from boating on the Zambezi to walking in the remote wilderness of South Luangwa.

The Two Rivers Safari is a week's safari in the areas of the two most scenic and dramatic rivers of Zambia, the Luangwa River and the Zambezi River. Staying at Tena and/or Nsefu in the South Luangwa for four nights and at Chiawa or Sausage Tree in the Lower Zambezi for three nights, this safari will include walking, drives and boating.

Due to overwhelming popularity and past success, Robin Pope Safaris is very excited to offer a wedding package designed for couples wanting a private ceremony for just themselves or for those desiring a more formal wedding with up to 60 guests.

SAFARI PAR EXCELLENCE

Mr Graham Nel
Managing Director
P O Box 60407, Livingstone
Tel: +260-3-320606/320597
Fax: +260-3-320609
Email: mdzam@safpar.com
Website: www.safpar.com

Activity: Tourism and safaris
Date of Creation: 1990
Employees: 200

Established as one of southern Africa's leading activity and safari outfits since 1990, Safari Par Excellence is a lodge owner on the Zambezi River, an adventure and activity specialist in Livingstone/Victoria Falls and lodge and canoe safari operator on the Lower Zambezi River.

Safari Par Excellence operates elephant-back safaris, tours and transfers, white water rafting, canoeing trails, river cruises and lion encounters from Thorntree River Lodge and The Waterfront in Livingstone. In the Lower Zambezi Valley, Safpar operates safaris from Kayila Lodge as well as Lower Zambezi canoeing safaris – The Great Zambezi Trail and The Island Trail. Safari Par Excellence is closely associated with other leading safari operators in Zambia, Zimbabwe and Botswana.

The Upper and Lower Zambezi regions offer some of Africa's finest traditional safaris – there's a full range of options for budget travellers, safari specialists, honeymoon couples and family groups. Combinations: a selection of easy-to-arrange and cost-effective safaris and activities from short break getaways to extended trips.

Currently Safari Par Excellence is constructing a new 144-bed four-star hotel. All 72 bedrooms and the central areas will face the River Zambezi. The hotel is to be named The David Livingstone Safari Lodge and will be managed by the Three Cities Group of hotels.

STAR OF AFRICA

Mrs Scotty Elliot
Marketing Director
P O Box 218, PB 891, Manda Hill, Lusaka
Tel: +260-1-271508/271509
Fax: +260-1-271398
Email: reservations@starofafrica.co.zm
Website: www.starofafrica.com

Activity: Tourism and safaris

Star of Africa Group is a Zambian-based luxury safari company. The company has established a series of stunning safari lodges and tented camps in four of Zambia's most prolific wildlife estates. Each property is unique in its concept and offers a diverse choice of environment and activities located in prime settings within national parks.

Sussi and Chuma Lodge is located in the Mosi-oa-Tunya National Park. This riverbank hideaway is located 10 minutes away from Livingstone, upstream of the Victoria Falls. The Sussi Lodge is composed of 10 luxury tree houses. The two Chuma houses are self-contained villas accommodating up to four guests, with their own private swimming pool and spacious outdoor veranda, kitchenette, lounge and dining area, with private guide, chef and housekeeper for the best of personalized service.

Lechwe Plains Tented Camp is located in the Lochinvar National Park and offers luxurious tented accommodation near the water's edge on the Chunga Lagoon, host to 428 bird species.

Kulefu Tented Camp is located in the rich Lower Zambezi National Park. Recently refurbished, Kulefu offers luxury accommodation in one of the most remote areas of the park, abundant with game and the 'big four'.

In the South Luangwa National Park, Star of Africa offers two luxurious options with the Puku Ridge Tented Camp, located on a ridge and overlooking spectacular game-rich floodplains.

Chichele Presidential Lodge is an elegant Victorian 'gentleman's lodge' initially constructed as a private residential retreat for the former president of Zambia Dr K. Kaunda. Guided walks, game drives, sunset cruises and canoe trips are organized for the guests.

As a safari company, Star of Africa has also developed a wide range of safari packages: Zambian Spice Trail, Zambian Explorer, Zambian Discoverer, Classic Zambezi, Zambian River Trail, Under the Zambian Stars Safari, and the Zambian Sun Walking Trail.

Star of Africa's newest and most exciting product is an exclusive walking safari in the South Luangwa National Park, with two mobile camps and highly experienced guides.

Star of Africa also offers air charter services for domestic and regional air transfers, with a fleet of five aircraft and experienced bush pilots ensuring maximum enjoyment from one wilderness area to the other.

SUN INTERNATIONAL

Mr Craig Storkey
Operations Manager
P O Box 60151, Livingstone
Tel: +260-1-321122
Fax: +260-1-322739
Email: sunint@coppernet.zm
Website: www.suninternational.com

Activity: Hotel

Sun International hotels, resorts and casinos allow you to immerse yourself in the full range of safari experiences.

The Royal Livingstone Hotel situated along the banks of the Zambezi River consists of a series of 17 colonial-style buildings. The main hotel is a sequence of thatched roof buildings, most African in their influence, and incorporates the lounge, restaurant and bar. A classic swimming pool visually links the waters of the river with the terraces of the hotel.

The resort offers an uninterrupted view of the Zambezi River and is the ideal place to curl up with a book discovered in the well-stocked library. The rooms are two-storey clusters and each cluster comprises approximately 10 en suite air-conditioned rooms, offering private balconies or terraces. Interior furnishings accentuate the influences of Africa translated into a cultured sumptuousness that reflects the essence of African bush life. Natural light invades the bathrooms.

The nearby three-star hotel, The Zambezi Sun, features adobe-style architecture. Simple finishes highlight bright mosaics and fabrics and the intoxicating environment is characterized by ethnic wall stencils, timber and plaster ceilings, Zambian artworks and accessories. It is constructed in a series of eight buildings, consisting of the guest rooms, a central pavilion of restaurants and a fabulous convention centre.

The Zambezi Sun is a 212-room hotel appealing primarily to families and conference delegates. The guest rooms acknowledge their African roots. During the early evening the dark outline of the hotel is set against iridescent curls of smoky vapour that dance above its roofline.

"Tourism in Zambia is still young; the groundwork has been done and now it offers many opportunities."
Craig Storkey, Operations Manager

TAJ PAMODZI HOTEL

Mr Anil Mohan
General Manager
Church Road
P O Box 35450, Lusaka
Tel: +260-1-254455
Fax: +260-1-250995/254005
Email: pamodzi.lusaka@tajhotels.com
Website: www.tajhotels.com

Activity: Hotel

Taj Pamodzi is the first and only hotel of the prestigious Taj Group of hotels in Africa.

Located in the heart of Lusaka's business and government district, just 22km from the airport and 5km from the city centre, Taj Pamodzi is a five-star luxurious hotel, recently renovated and refurbished, providing spacious comfort, modern amenities and the most comprehensive range of services.

The hotel has 200 rooms which are recently renovated, elegant and spacious, two luxurious deluxe suites and a presidential suite with private jacuzzi. All the rooms are equipped with broadband Internet connectivity, electronic key cards and safes.

The Taj Pamodzi Hotel also offers dedicated services to business travellers with special business executive rooms including all the standard amenities as well as valet service, complimentary ironing and complimentary cocktail hour every evening.

For its business clients, the Taj Pamodzi Hotel also has six modern conference halls, including a board room, comfortably seating up to 350 persons for conferences, cocktails and receptions. The hotel provides a fully equipped business centre with broadband Internet access, secretarial services and workstations.

The Taj Pamodzi prides itself on its fine cuisine restaurant, the Steaks & Grills, offering a wide variety of continental, Indian and Zambian specialities. The hotel is also famous for its coffee shop, the Jacaranda, which operates for breakfast, lunch and dinner. The Marula Bar serves international cocktails, wines and spirits and flows into the coffee shop.

For its health-conscious guests, the hotel offers a state-of-the-art gym, spa, salon and swimming pool.

Chaminuka Lodge is renowned for its large art collection

VOYAGERS

Mrs Molly Care
Manager
P O Box 37609, Lusaka
Tel: +260-1-253082/3/4
Fax: +260-1-253048
Email: travel@voyagers.com.zm
Website: www.voyagers.com.zm

Activity: Tour operator, travel agency and car hire company
Date of Creation: 1987
Turnover: US $20m a year
Employees: 100
Franchises: Europcar, Imperial Car Rental

Voyagers is a complete one-stop travel provider for the region. It organizes the ordinary to the extraordinary, from honeymoons to hotels, flights to fly fishing, tailor-made safaris, beach holidays and car hire to corporate travel, all with the advantage of extensive first-hand knowledge.

Zambia is its forte, a vast country in the very heart of the continent that is still wild and beautiful. This is the real Africa. Zambia has a rich cultural heritage and wonderful people, complemented by the breathtaking scenery of the Victoria Falls, one of the Seven Natural Wonders of the World, and the South Luangwa National Park, acclaimed as one of Africa's finest wildlife sanctuaries.

Voyagers is a proud member of the Carlson Wagonlit Travel Partners Network and offers you the convenience, service and security that only a local, Zambian-based company can provide.

"Relax and let us take care of everything, from the dream holiday of a lifetime to a successful business trip."
Mrs Molly Care, Manager

ZAMBIA NATIONAL TOURIST BOARD

Ms Charity C. Lumpa
Managing Director
P O Box 30017, Lusaka
Tel: +260-1-229087
Fax: +260-1-225174
Email: zntb@zamnet.zm; cclumpa.tourism@zamnet.zm
Website: www.zambiatourism.zm

Activity: Tourism marketing

The Zambia National Tourist Board (ZNTB) is a statutory body established under the Tourism Act 1979. Its key mandate is to market Zambia's tourism products in both international and domestic markets. Currently the board has five established offices in Lusaka (head office), Livingstone, Pretoria (South Africa), London (UK) and Washington DC (USA).

Zambia is an attractive destination, home to one of the Seven Natural Wonders of the World – the mighty Victoria Falls. It is a nation of friendly people with diverse cultures and colourful traditions. Surrounded by pristine wilderness with an abundance of wildlife, it is an oasis of peace, complemented by a beautiful climate. Its central location in southern Africa makes Zambia an ideal vacation and conferencing destination.

In its mission to promote and market Zambia's tourism products, the Zambia National Tourist Board has undertaken a number of different marketing activities, which include attending fairs in both the domestic and international markets.

In 2005, the Zambia National Tourist Board through its principal, the Ministry of Tourism, Environment and Natural Resources, launched a five-year awareness campaign called the Visit Zambia 2005–2010 campaign. The main theme of this campaign is branding Zambia as the home of the Victoria Falls.

In 2006 the theme Zambia – Home of the Victoria Falls and Land of Magnificent Waterfalls focuses on marketing other magnificent waterfalls that are found in different parts of Zambia, highlighting their tourism potential.

Tourists will also be taken off the beaten track to discover the new tourism delights of the waterfall circuit in the northern parts of Zambia, where they will also be exposed to the game-rich Luangwa Valley (North and South Luangwa) which boasts the largest concentration of wildlife and where the walking safari was first pioneered by Norman Carr over 50 years ago.

ZNTB invites the various service providers, ranging from transporters to hoteliers, to complement this campaign and consider extending their services to this area.

"Visit Zambia, the real Africa."
Ms Charity C. Lumpa, Managing Director

Just relax and enjoy...

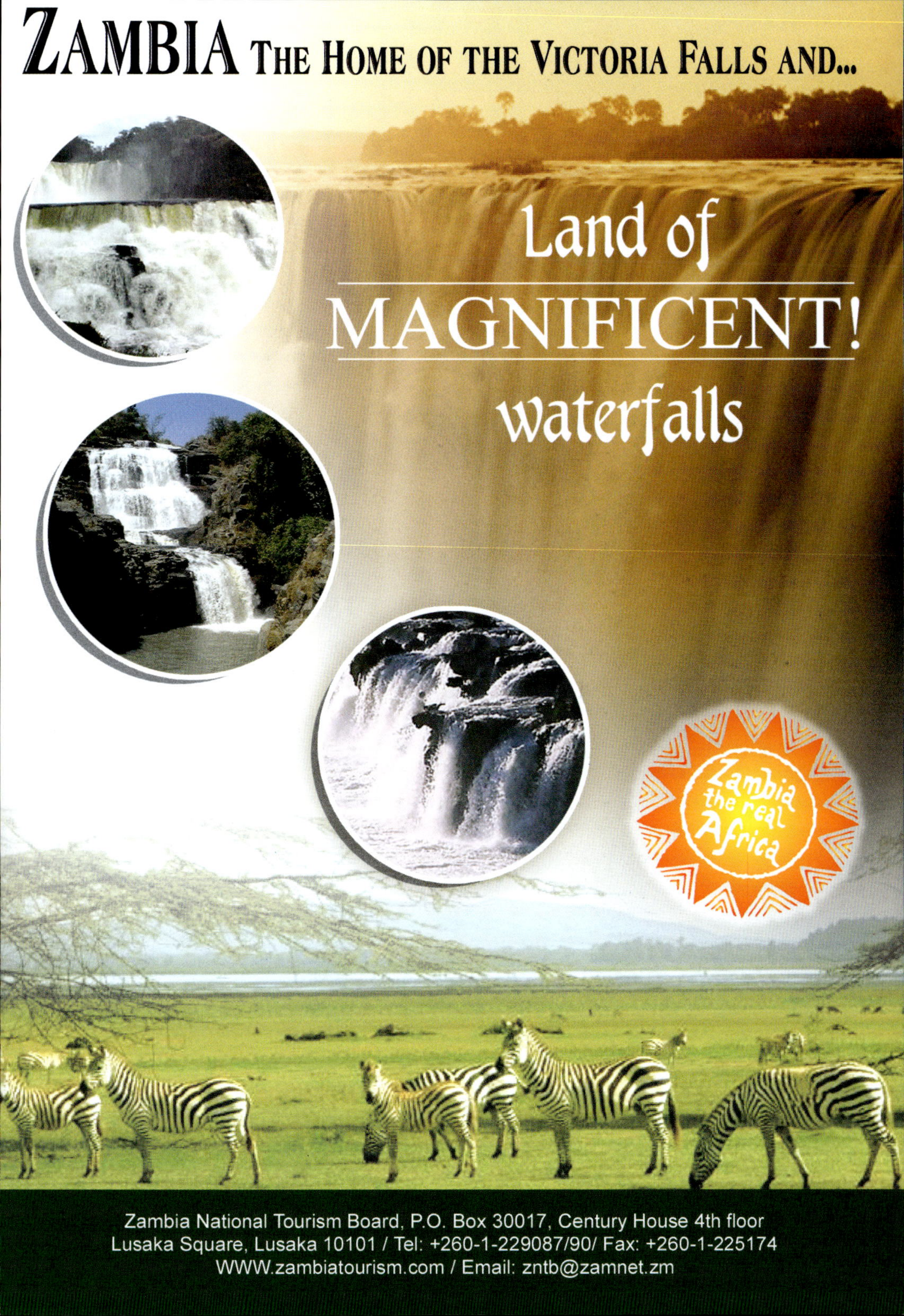
ZAMBIA THE HOME OF THE VICTORIA FALLS AND...
Land of
MAGNIFICENT!
waterfalls
Zambia the real Africa
Zambia National Tourism Board, P.O. Box 30017, Century House 4th floor
Lusaka Square, Lusaka 10101 / Tel: +260-1-229087/90/ Fax: +260-1-225174
WWW.zambiatourism.com / Email: zntb@zamnet.zm

TRANSPORT & COMMUNICATIONS

"A child that does not travel praises his mother as the best cook"
Zambian proverb

TRANSPORT

In view of its landlocked status, Zambia's road, rail and air transport networks are critical to the development of the country and the region. In addition to facilitating the influx of business travellers and leisure tourists, the transport infrastructure is pivotal to trade. Road and rail transport are traditionally the most suited to trade, particularly regional trade, although inland water transport is also used, with Mpulungu harbour on Lake Tanganyika seeing shipments of cement, sugar, steel, pharmaceuticals and many other products. Trans-shipping points for both imports and exports include the ports of Durban (South Africa), Dar es Salaam (Tanzania), Walvis Bay (Namibia) and Beira (Mozambique).

ROAD TRANSPORT

Increased passenger services have driven growth in the road transport subsector in recent years. With roads seen as being the most effective means of transporting goods, the subsector is expected to register further growth as the region's markets become better integrated and trade increases. Mechanisms are being put in place to harmonize the road transport subsector with regional transport networks.

Zambia has a road network of 37,000 kilometres of gazetted roads, of which about 6,300 kilometres comprise main roads, and about 30,000 kilometres of ungazetted roads, which include tracks, trails and footpaths. There are some 85,000 kilometres of gravel and 21,680 kilometres of earth roads. In 1991, when the present government came into power, 80% of the road network had deteriorated. Of the total road asset valued at US $2.3 billion, Zambia had lost US $400 million of road network due to neglected maintenance.

The four main arterial roads leading from Lusaka are:

- Great North Road to Kasama and via the Copperbelt to the north
- Great East Road to Chipata and the east
- Mumbwa Road to Mongu and the west
- Kafue Road to Chirundu, to Livingstone and to the south.

Zambia can be entered by road from the DRC, Zimbabwe, Malawi, Mozambique, Tanzania, Botswana and Namibia. All road borders are open 24 hours per day, except for Chembe, Kazungula, Kariba and Chirundu. Visiting drivers must hold an international driver's licence, and those wishing to bring a vehicle into Zambia must first obtain a temporary import permit. Bilateral road transport agreements exist with Namibia, Malawi, Zimbabwe and South Africa, which have had the effect of assisting cross-border trade and traffic.

Policy on Zambia's road network is the responsibility of the Ministry of Communications and Transport. The Ministry of Works and Supply, through the Roads Department, is charged with the maintenance, rehabilitation and upgrading of the trunk, main and district road network. The Ministry of Local Government and Housing's Department of Infrastructure and Support Services is responsible for feeder and urban roads. The National Roads Board (NRB) was established in 1994 to administer the road fund. A new national transport policy was approved in 2002 and was followed by a consultancy on institutional reform.

Launched in 1997 with funding from government, road users and the cooperating partners, ROADSIP delivered the rehabilitation and maintenance of 50% of the road network at a cost of some US $500 million during the first phase of the programme from 1997 to 2002. This resulted in improvements in the condition of the paved road network from 20% good in 1994 to 60% good in 2002, surpassing the target set.

Phase II of the ROADSIP project (2003–2007) was launched at a cost of US $800 million, with projects including the design of roads under World Bank and EU funding and Lusaka–Mongu road works under DANIDA funding. Phase II covers the rehabilitation of urban roads in provincial capitals, Copperbelt towns and other municipalities within Zambia, with the emphasis on employment creation and local construction industry development for poverty alleviation.

Financial reforms pertaining to the road sector have begun to be implemented in accordance with the approved national transport policy. Further, a fuel levy has now been budgeted under the Ministry of Finance and National Planning, and is being channelled directly from the ministry to the road fund. The position of the government is that the fuel levy will be paid in full in order to ensure maintenance of the road network on a sustainable basis through performance contracts.

In the 2005/06 budget, some K112.3 billion went to the road fund as fuel levy collections, with the higher collections on account of higher fuel prices. All of the funds released to the former NRB were for road rehabilitation, while a total of K8.2 billion was released as counterpart funds towards donor-financed infrastructure projects.

AIR TRANSPORT

Zambia has four international airports, namely Lusaka, Livingstone, Mfuwe and Ndola, with several secondary airfields and airstrips in Chipata, Kitwe, Kasama, Mongu, Solwezi and Mansa. Situated 24 kilometres from the centre of Lusaka, Lusaka International Airport is Zambia's main airport and connects the country with the rest of the world. The airports at Lusaka, Livingstone and Ndola have undergone rehabilitation work in order to boost the export and tourism trades.

As Zambia becomes more integrated into the global community, international flights are increasing. Although the liberalization of the air transport industry has resulted in the formation of private local airlines, growth in this sector has been slow due to factors such as high start-up costs, poor infrastructure and small passenger loads. Nevertheless, following the industry downturn in the wake of 9/11 and the SARS epidemic, passenger numbers are beginning to pick up once more as well as cargo volumes. With a significant proportion of travel to and from Zambia for business purposes, the substantial growth seen in both regional and international trade is expected to stimulate the airline subsector further.

The rebuilding of the national airline with private sector operators is being discussed. Zambia Airways was liquidated in 1994. The existence of a national airline is crucial when taking into account the Yamoussoukro declaration, which was aimed at creating a conducive environment for the development of intra-African and international air services.

Another key consideration in the decision to establish a national airline is the tourism industry, as scheduled domestic air services to provincial centres – many of which had great tourism potential – ceased with the demise of Zambia Airways. With tourism a significant earner of foreign exchange for Zambia, it follows that the establishment of a national flag carrier would help attract additional tourists to the country, as regional and international air travel is easier when a country has a national airline. A national carrier will also allow Zambia to promote its image abroad, helping to export Zambian culture to other countries.

RAIL TRANSPORT

Zambia's rail networks have for many years been controlled by Zambia Railways (ZR) and the jointly owned Tanzania–Zambia Railways (TAZARA). The network links Zambia to the Democratic Republic of Congo and Angola in the north and Zimbabwe and South Africa in the south, while the TAZARA network links into the line at Kapiri Mposhi and runs to the port of Dar es Salaam in Tanzania. Other promising rail routes are Zambia–Mozambique (Beira line), Zambia–Malawi (Muchinje line), Zambia–Namibia and Zambia–Angola.

As part of the government's privatization policy, Zambia Railways was concessioned during 2003 to a consortium comprising New Limpopo Project Investments (NLPI) and Spoornet, both of South Africa. The new firm, Railway Systems of Zambia, has been given a lease for a 20-year period, with an option to renew for a further 10 years.

Prior to the concessioning, a process of rehabilitation was begun on the rail network, with ZR also undergoing intense restructuring which saw the railway streamline operations to concentrate on major customers. While the mines are still among its top customers, others include Zambia Sugar Plc, Chilanga Cement, National Million, Maamba and Wankie Collieries and Nitrogen Chemicals of Zambia.

The construction of the Mchinji–Chipata rail line (abandoned in 1982) is to be revived through a private sector-driven project. The proposed 27-kilometre rail line from the border with Malawi to Chipata will connect Eastern province with part of Nacala in Mozambique. This is particularly important since Zambia's incorporation into the Nacala Corridor Development pact.

The jointly owned TAZARA is also undergoing commercialization, and Mulobezi Railways is to be commercialized and leased to the private sector.

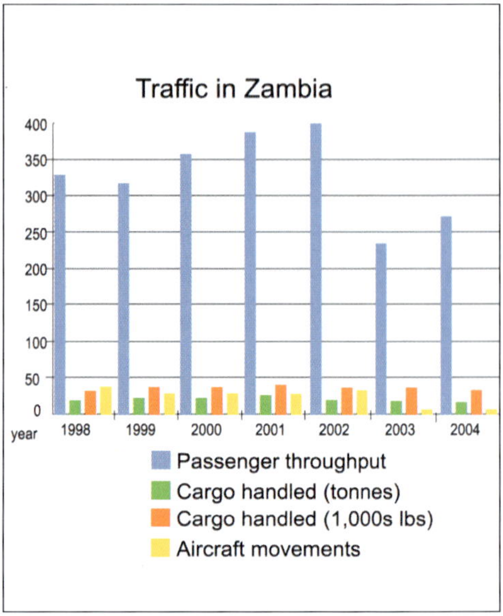

A railway connects Livingstone to the Copperbelt

Lusaka International Airport, modern and safe

COMMUNICATIONS

Characterized by a liberalized operating framework with healthy competition between a number of private investors, Zambia's communications sector comprises telephone systems as well as Internet, postal and courier services.

Supervised by the Ministry of Transport and Communications, the sector is regulated by the Communications Authority of Zambia, which was established in 1994. The Communications Authority is mandated to carry out the regulation and licensing of the provision of goods and services in the telecommunications sector in Zambia, including administration of the radio frequency spectrum on behalf of the government.

Its core activities include: awarding telecommunications licences; monitoring activities and compliance levels of service and goods providers; encouraging competition in the sector and the use of new technologies; encouraging investments by local and foreign entrepreneurs; protecting consumers of telecommunications goods and services; and managing telecommunications standards.

Zambia's telecommunications facilities are among the best in sub-Saharan Africa, with high-capacity microwave links connecting the majority of larger towns and cities. The country is a member of Intelsat and has an earth station in Lusaka providing direct telephone, telefax, email, Internet and television links with the rest of the world. A 24-core 520-kilometre optical fibre backbone in the Copperbelt covers all mining towns, and there is a 45-kilometre optical fibre cable between Lusaka and Kafue.

The Zambia Telecommunications Company Limited (ZAMTEL), the country's national telecommunications services provider, is the only licensed operator allowed to provide public switched telephone network (PSTN) services. ZAMTEL provides local, national, long distance and international fixed telephony, radio and mobile telephony, telex and leased line services, and its coverage includes all districts except Kaputa and Sesheke in the northern and western parts of the country, which are not connected to the network. ZAMTEL is being considered for future privatization.

By 2004 there were more than 96,000 main lines in operation and the telephone density was just under 1%. Home phones were predominantly fixed lines, with 98.4% being PSTN lines and 1.6% either radio or mobile phones.

GROWTH IN MOBILE TELEPHONY

A modern innovation in telecommunications, the provision of mobile telephone services is seeing remarkable growth, with improvements in extension of coverage and service quality, as well as a reduction of tariffs. Service providers include MTN, Celtel and Cell Z, ZAMTEL's cellular service. Celtel, the largest of them, boasted of 270,000 subscribers as at the end of 2004, while MTN and Cell Z had 83,000 and 60,000 subscribers respectively. The mobile phone subsector is expected to experience further growth, with its potential market estimated at 600,000 subscribers.

To enable more people to have access to the network and hence spur further growth in this area, the government reduced customs duty on cellular mobile telephone handsets from 15% to 5% during 2005.

There is the potential for further growth in the provision of Internet services, with around 45,000 Internet users in 2004 and penetration still low in the rural areas. Zambia's registered Internet service providers (ISPs) comprise Zamnet, which was established in 1994, as well as ZAMTEL Online, Coppernet, UUnet, Microlink and Celtel, which in 2004 had almost 12,000 subscribers combined. During 2005 AfriConnect announced the launch of its iConnect wireless broadband Internet service in Zambia, described as the country's first affordable, high-speed Internet solution.

A global phenomenon, the convergence of information and computing technology (ICT) is revolutionizing both developed and developing economies, where it is being used as a tool for both social and economic development. The success of the ICT industry is essential to the growth of the country, and Zambia is poised to exploit the changing dynamics of the marketplace through the utilization of state-of-the-art technologies. A comprehensive and effective national policy on ICT is being developed in order to help the ICT industry grow and, most importantly, establish a framework for achieving wider access to ICT for its citizens.

Zambia is the first country in the world to receive support from the International Institute for Communication Development's (IICD) Small Initiative Fund (SIF), aimed at enhancing livelihoods of disadvantaged communities through use of ICT.

There is room for investment in the telecommunications sector, with advanced telecommunications networks increasingly important to both the business world and tourists. Deregulation, privatization and new wireless technologies have opened up areas of potential, with Africa tipped to become one of the most promising ICT markets of the future.

MEDIA AND BROADCASTING

The liberalized media industry has experienced additional private sector participation and the emergence of new media institutions, with the electronic media now being dominated by the private sector. Three television and seven radio stations are owned and controlled by the private sector.

The state-owned Zambia National Broadcasting Corporation (ZNBC) offers one television service, ZNBC-TV, which broadcasts to major population centres. Private television broadcasters comprise Multi-Choice Zambia, Trinity Broadcasting Network and CASAT.

ZNBC has three radio services comprising Radio 1: 102.6 FM (seven languages), Radio 2: 95.8 FM (English) and Radio 4: 88.2 FM (English). Private radio stations include

CELTEL COMMUNITY
PAY PHONE
celtel
Making life better
COMMUNITY
PHONE
HERE

Satellite phone and Internet is the only way to communicate with some remote parts of the country

Radio Phoenix (Lusaka), Icengelo (Kitwe), Christian Voice (Lusaka), Radio Chikuni (Monze), Radio Mazabuka (Mazabuka), Radio Maria (Chipata) and Radio Yatsani (Lusaka).

Newspapers in Zambia include the state-owned *Zambia Daily Mail*, *Times of Zambia* and *Sunday Times of Zambia*, as well as *The Post*, *The Monitor* and *The People*, which are privately owned.

POSTAL SERVICES

Zambia is a member of the Pan-African Postal Union (PAPU). Postal services are operated by the Zambia Postal Services Corporation (ZAMPOST), which has a country-wide network of post offices, outlets and sub-post offices. It is essential that the postal services apply modern technology to improve the quality of services so as to meet growing and diversified customer needs. Effective deployment of strategically important new technology holds the key to untapped potential in the sector, with areas to be explored including the computerization of counter service operations to enhance security and tracking of mail as well as to provide value added services to customers, and services such as hybrid mail and e-post that combine electronic and hard copy delivery.

Private courier services providers are DHL and Fedex.

MAIN COMPANIES

AGS FRASERS INTERNATIONAL

Mr Lamiraux
Managing Director
Ukatasha Road, Plot 7242, Industrial Area
P O Box 37921, Lusaka
Tel: +260-1-286666/905
Fax: +260-1-286656
Email: ags@zamnet.zm
Website: www.ags-worldwide-movers.com

Activity: Transport

AGS Frasers International is an unrivalled leader in international relocation services in the world. The AGS group is the largest removal group on the African continent with 46 branches operating in 37 countries.

The group provides a professional solution for international removals between the northern and southern hemispheres, in particular between Europe and Africa. The group has focused on providing relocation solutions for developing countries in Eastern Europe and Africa, often some of the most difficult markets in the world.

Since its inception, AGS has focused mainly on international removals. For AGS, service does not end at the packaging of furniture, which itself remains an integral part of the removal. Services also include guidance and companionship: the company focuses on the client's individual needs and wishes.

Roads rehabilitation is a government priority

AGS services have been standardized, and all AGS branches have been ISO 9001:2000 certified. Established in Zambia for over 10 years, AGS Zambia offers a global solution to its clientele, with 100% coverage of the African continent and efficient and reliable deliveries.

"AGS Zambia prides itself on an excellent track record and superior quality of service."
Mr Lamiraux, Managing Director

CELTEL

Mr Venn
Managing Director
P O Box 32001, Lusaka
Tel: +260-1-250595
Fax: +260-1-250595
Email: beatricet@zm.celtel.com
Website: www.celtel.com

Activity: Telecommunications
Date of Creation: 1998

Celtel Zambia Limited was launched in 1998. The customer base has grown tremendously with its network covering all of the nine provinces in the country. Celtel was the earliest operator to provide a GSM service in the country, the first to introduce the roaming service and the first to introduce both per second and per minute billing. Besides the mobile phone business, it offers Internet connection, email services using mobile phone and prepaid and post-paid roaming. Celtel also offers value added services that come as a standard package on its network.

Celtel in Zambia continues being a success story. Celtel values customers greatly and strives to give second-to-none customer service. The company has customers right across the social spectrum from civil servants, business executives and artisans to housewives and students. The aim is to offer services that truly support the mix of social and economic groups and to offer services that are of value for people.

Celtel is committed to social responsibility. The company has partnered with the Ministry of Health to improve the health system in Zambia. It also promotes sports events, especially those considered minor sports: polo, motocross and motor rally. Celtel has partnered with a company called Lifeline, which operates a call centre open 24 hours a day for people to call in for counselling on HIV and AIDS.

"Celtel is Zambia's most innovative mobile phone operator and has been and continues to be a leader in innovation in the business."
Mr Venn, Managing Director

COPPERNET SOLUTIONS

Mr Philip Chitalu
Managing Director
Mukuba Pension House, Dedan Kimathi Road
P O Box 38671, Lusaka
Tel: +260-1-223333/224444
Fax: +260-1-226666
Email: phillip@coppernet.zm; milambo@coppernet.zm
Website: www.coppernet.zm

Activity: Internet service provider

CopperNET Solutions is an incorporated company which provides leading-edge technology in Zambia's information and technology industry. The company was incorporated in 1999 after a successful management buy-out by the conglomerate Zambia Consolidated Copper Mines (ZCCM). The buy-out resulted from the privatization exercise embarked upon by the Zambian government.

CopperNET Solutions has the largest commercial digital data network in the country. This backbone stretches from Chililabombwe in the Copperbelt to Livingstone in the southern part of the country. Over 10 towns along this stretch have wireless points of presence and play a pivotal role in its flagship product, VPN (virtual private network), in linking remote offices to their main office.

Areas not covered by its microwave network are serviced by small VSATs to make it possible for people in areas lacking good infrastructure to have services as good as those in well-serviced areas. This product has been received well on the market. CopperNET Solutions operates a telephone network in the Copperbelt and provides voice services to a number of customers who rely on the over 99.99% availability of this voice network.

The company provides a full web hosting service on Linux servers, including telnet access with your own home directory and full CGI scripting facilities. Web pages can be directly uploaded via FTP.

For CopperNET Solutions customer satisfaction comes first. To achieve this it runs network monitoring tools to keep an eye on customers' links and thus is able to react proactively to signs of network or connectivity problems on the links. Service level agreements (SLAs) are available to companies requiring more responsive reaction and added reliability for their network performance. All these abilities make CopperNET Solutions possibly the strongest IT firm in the country from a technological point of view.

"For CopperNET Solutions customer satisfaction comes first."
Mr Philip Chitalu, Managing Director

DHL EXPRESS

Mrs Carol White
Managing Director
Corner Parirenyatwa and Makishi Roads, Fairview Area, Lusaka
Tel: +260-1-229768/229771
Fax: +260-1-225529
Website: www.dhl.com

Date of Creation: 1985
Employees: 104

Following Deutsche Post World Net's acquisition of DHL in 2001, DHL is the world's leading express and logistics company, offering customized solutions from a single source. The move brought together DHL's traditional courier and express business, Euro Express's parcel business and Danzas' logistics business, making a one-stop shop for all movement of mail, documents, packages and shipments.

In Zambia DHL became fully operational in 1985. As the company grew, more and more products were introduced and launched, offering clients a breadth of products to suit their particular needs.

Today DHL Zambia offers a wide range of services including express delivery of documents and parcels worldwide, shipping of large, heavy and high-value goods, special services such as repair and return, time definite delivery and Saturday delivery, shipper's insurance and import express.

In recent years, a number of courier companies have opened offices and this has been welcome competition for DHL Zambia. Aside from being given impetus to improve the quality of service offered, DHL's strength has been proven. Its comprehensive global network that combines ground, air and ocean allows for optimal delivery performance. To most destinations in sub-Saharan Africa, delivery is possible overnight, with the latest pick-up times being offered.

With daily flights throughout central Africa DHL can collect and deliver anything. The focus of its business is to see how it can fit in with its customers' logistics. It finds out how it can help its customers with more power, more reach and more destinations. When DHL is contacted, the client is buying time; therefore it is important that the promise is delivered. When a courier picks up a parcel from a client, the whole focus of the company is to get the parcel on the DHL aircraft which leaves Lusaka each day. The parcel will then be delivered on or before the deadline – unless there is insufficient information on the airway bill. Clients can choose to receive reports on delivery progress across the globe on their cell phone or by email.

This efficiency is also experienced on the local scene. DHL Zambia has five service centres in Lusaka, Ndola, Kitwe, Chingola and Solwezi and 12 agencies countrywide. Service is offered to all nine provinces.

KUEHNE + NAGEL

Ms Juwayhir
Operations Director/General Manager
National Head Office Zambia

DHL offers door to door delivery even in the remotest parts of the country

Tel: +260-1-287872
Fax: +260-1-287871
Email: info.lusaka@kuehne-nagel.com
Website: www.kuehne-nagel.com

Activity: Transport and logistics
Employees: 26

Kuehne + Nagel operates across a global network of 750 offices staffed by over 40,000 logistics specialists. The company provides integrated, value-creating solutions to the world's major industries. With proven end-to-end supply chain expertise and dedicated industry specialists, the company fully understands what drives the various sectors, anticipating their respective logistics requirements.
Kuehne + Nagel combines its entire suite of services from across its business fields and develops and implements customized logistics solutions throughout the supply chain, from logistics consulting and planning right through to after-market services.

Today, the company's activities are in the global seafreight, airfreight, overland and contract logistics businesses with a focus on providing IT-based supply chain management services. Kuehne + Nagel's globally standardized, leading-edge information technology facilitates the synchronized display and control of each transport movement across the supply chain. Innovative lead logistics capabilities and a comprehensive range of niche and industry solutions complement its portfolio.

Kuehne + Nagel focuses on getting goods to the customer faster, better controlled and more economically. Kuehne + Nagel has developed from a traditional international freight forwarder to become a leading global provider of integrated logistics and supply chain solutions. By transferring best practices, experience and technology developed in one sector to another, the company ensures continuous service improvement for every customer.

Kuehne + Nagel has four strategically located offices in Zambia, namely Lusaka, Lusaka International Airport, Livingstone and Chirundu. In Zambia it has its own warehousing facilities (bonded and free store) at all offices except Chirundu, consisting of a total of 6,250 square metres. All the offices are fully computerized, with detailed stock control systems, allowing efficient processing/warehousing of all consignments. The company imports and exports cargoes from/to various destinations in Africa and across the rest of the world, applying all modes of transport. Furthermore, it has regular sea-freight shipments from all over the world.

"Kuehne + Nagel meet companies' global business requirements in each of the local markets and underpins these solutions with strong visibility and monitoring capabilities across its network."
Ms Juwayhir, Operations Director/General Manager

MTN

Mr Mike Blackburn
Managing Director
5033 Longolongo Road, Rhodespark
P O Box 35464, Lusaka
Tel: +260-1-220006/096-750750
Email: mtn@mtnzambia.co.zm

Activity: Telecommunications

As a major communications company, MTN is focused on the African continent. It believes that through access to communication comes economic empowerment. The MTN Group operates three business divisions: MTN-SA (South Africa), MTN International, and Strategic Investments. MTN is listed on the Johannesburg Stock Exchange under the telecommunications service sector (which falls under the industrial non-cyclical services).

As at 31st March 2005, the group generated R29 billion in revenue and had 14.3 million subscribers across its cellular network operations. To date, MTN Group has invested approximately R23.4 billion in telecommunications infrastructure across the African continent. As at 30th June 2005, MTN Group had over 17 million subscribers across its cellular network operations.

On 1st July 2005, MTN acquired a controlling stake (51%) in Loteny Telecom, operating under the name Telecel Côte d'Ivoire, in Côte d'Ivoire. The group has also entered into an agreement to acquire 100% of Telecel Zambia, the conclusion of which is subject to approval of the Zambian regulatory authority. The group has also acquired the remaining 40% in MTN Network Solutions (Pty) Ltd to take full ownership of this company, which has been fully integrated into MTN South Africa.

MTN bought Telecel Zambia in June 2006 and vowed to invest US $70 million (R423.5 million) to expand its network and win more subscribers. The company plans at reach 70% of the country's 10 million population.

Strategic Investments is responsible for identifying and exploiting new growth opportunities on behalf of the group, both in South Africa and internationally. The division also manages the group's investments in non-mobile ventures, including MTN's research and development unit responsible for exploitation of innovation and intellectual property and the group's electronic funds transfer operation in Nigeria. MTN snapped up stakes in a string of African operators in 2005, including in Zambia and Botswana, and secured a major acquisition in Iran as part of its quest to become the leading operator in developing markets.

MULTICHOICE ZAMBIA

Mr Alex Mayeya
General Manager
Plot D18 Bishop Road, Kabulonga
P O Box 320011, Lusaka
Tel: +260-1-261616
Fax: +260-1-261533
Email: amayeya@zambia.multichoice.co.za
Website: www.dstv.com

Activity: TV provider
Date of Creation: 1995

MultiChoice Zambia, the official agent of MultiChoice Africa in Zambia, was established in 1995 to provide subscriber management services for DStv subscribers in Zambia.

MultiChoice Zambia is part of the DStv offering, which has improved the standard and scope of African television entertainment by providing subscribers with a choice of over 50 world-class television channels and over 20 audio channels to satisfy the different language, cultural, informational and entertainment needs of African subscribers.

The company has grown rapidly to reach over 21,000 active viewers and plans to double the subscriber base in the next five years. With two branches in Lusaka and Ndola and over 50 installers across the country, MultiChoice is able to install DStv everywhere around the country. To facilitate payment in rural areas, the company has established strategic alliances with banks across Zambia.

MultiChoice is very active in the local community: the company provides free DStv to a number of schools to support education and participates in a number of development programmes.

"MultiChoice prides itself on an excellent level of customer service. The company is strongly investing in training for all its employees to provide the best service for the customers."
Mr Alex Mayeya, General Manager

NATIONAL AIRPORTS CORPORATION LTD

Miss Chileshe Kapwepwe
Managing Director
P O Box 30175, Lusaka
Tel: +260-1-271313/271281/271372
Fax: +260-1-224777
Email: naclmd@zamnet.zm; nacl@zamnet.zm
Website: www.lun.aero; www.nacl.co.zm

National Airports Corporation (NACL) has four international airports under its management, namely Lusaka, Ndola, Livingstone and Mfuwe. These offer competitive services to both passengers and aircraft operators alike.

Lusaka International Airport is the main gateway into Zambia. It is situated only 26 kilometres from the centre of Lusaka. It has modern terminal and passenger facilities.

The Lusaka Airport has the biggest capacity and circulation in the country. It has an annual capacity of 390,500 passengers. Within the passenger facilities it offers: 10 check-in desks, two gates, two baggage claim belts, 1,000 short-term parking spaces, 100 long-term parking spaces, post office, bank, bureau de change, restaurants, cafeterias, bars, VIP lounge, duty free shop, newsagent/tobacconist, chemist shop, gift shop, travel agent, tourist help desk, car rental, taxi service/rank, first aid, disabled access/facilities and a business centre.

In the Copperbelt, Ndola International Airport is a vital component in the development of the mining industry as well as a refuelling point for northbound aircraft. The airport offers direct flights to Johannesburg and Lubumbashi.

Livingstone International Airport services the tourist capital of Zambia with direct flights to and from Johannesburg and Lusaka.

Mfuwe International Airport is located in the deep heart of the Luangwa National Park. The airport has easy connections to Lusaka and Lilongwe in Malawi.

NACL has recently acquired new aircraft and passenger handling equipment. This has greatly improved the ground handling services it is providing to the airlines operating into and out of Lusaka International Airport.

Its cargo facilities have a capacity of 14,735 tonnes (32,484,000lb), a 9,000-square metre warehouse (96,875 sq. ft), and three 747 freighter docks. NACL is able to offer the following services: bonded warehouse, transit zone, domestic cargo, mechanical handling, air-conditioned storage, refrigerated storage, deep-freeze storage, mortuary, fresh meat inspection, health officials, X-ray equipment, security for valuables, dangerous goods, very large/heavy cargo, express/courier centre and handling equipment.

PROFLIGHT COMMUTER SERVICES LTD

Mr Richard Franklin
General Manager
Stand 15b, Private Hangars, Lusaka International Airport
P O Box 30536, Lusaka
Tel: +260-1-271035/2
Fax: +260-1-271139
Email: proflight@iconnect.zm
Website: www.proflight-zambia.com

Activity: Transport
Date of Creation: 1st November 2004

Proflight Air Services was founded over 10 years ago by ex-Zambian Airways pilot Tony Irwin. In 10 years, the company has grown from a small charter flight company to one of the fastest growing charter and scheduled flight companies in Zambia. In November 2004, two new investors joined Tony and Proflight Commuter Services Ltd was formed.

With the largest fleet of aircraft in Zambia, Proflight operates a fleet of nine aircraft (3-seaters up to 18-seaters) offering both scheduled and charter services. The company is currently in the process of acquiring a tenth aircraft. With two aircraft operating schedule flights and seven aircraft for charter services, Proflight will run an average of 12 flights a day (4,000 a year) in 2006.

Scheduled operations include flights from Lusaka to Livingstone, Lusaka to Mfuwe, Livingstone to Mfuwe, and shuttles twice daily to the Lower Zambezi.

In 2006, the company will open a new route to Ndola, Solwezi and will also open a Proflight Livingstone office, operating direct routes from Livingstone to Lower Zambezi, and Livingstone to Kruger National Park, South Africa and Maun, Botswana.

Proflight Commuter Services is the only locally operated airline company to be part of the international IATA booking system.

Proflight Commuter Services prides itself on an excellent level of customer service. The company offers a meet and greet service to all passengers travelling on Proflight scheduled or charter flights. All passengers are met off domestic and international flights no matter what time they arrive. Proflight has an executive air-conditioned minibus available to transfer passengers from the main terminal to the private lounge at the hangar. All staff, from the baggage handlers to the pilots and general manager, have undergone a PR training course on the importance of service and the customer.

RAILWAY SYSTEMS OF ZAMBIA

Mr Avishay Dvir
Chief Executive Officer
Head Office, Corner of Butungwa and Ghana Avenue, Kabwe
Tel: +260-5-223074/290847
Fax: +260-5-223074
Email: advir@rsz.com.zm

Activity: Railway
Date of Creation: 2003
Employees: 2,500

Since commencement of operations in December 2003, RSZ has continued to play some meaningful role in contributing to the Zambian economic development. RSZ has a main role in both passenger and goods transport in Zambia. RSZ has been undergoing a rehabilitation programme to achieve high standards in its services.

The first phase of the track rehabilitation project started in November 2004 and was completed in March 2006. This covered a total of 150km on the branch lines (lines beyond Ndola) and 400km on the main lines (lines south of Ndola) with the primary objective of reducing the risk of derailments and to improve the general condition of the track.

RSZ has ordered eight fully reconditioned locomotive engines from the USA, of which four are from General Motors and four are from General Electric. So far three GM locomotives have been fully rehabilitated using these engines while the rest of the works are in progress. The remaining two are still under rehabilitation in the USA and will be ready soon.

The wagon maintenance and rehabilitation programme started in earnest during the first half of 2005. This has continued and to date over 1,340 wagons have passed through the workshops under this programme. A full programme of telecommunications systems rehabilitation is now in full swing. RSZ has ordered the required equipment, of which some has already arrived in Zambia.

The issues of safety and environmental management are important in ensuring that while improving on the business performance of the company through safe operations, the waste that is generated is appropriately managed in line with established environmental management standards.

Right now RSZ is working on many special projects with different companies and organizations, including: EU sugar movement, Nampundwe pyrites, Maamba collieries, coal movement from Wankie colleries, clinker for Chilanga Cement and maize and wheat imports.

A number of challenges have presented themselves since commencement of operations in December 2003. The investments that are being undertaken in locomotives, wagons and track rehabilitation bear testimony that the company is in Zambia to stay. RSZ works in partnership with the Zambian government for the future development of Zambia.

"We are fully committed to continue with our investment programme in accordance with the signed agreement between us and the GRZ."
Avishay Dvir, Chief Executive Officer

SDV-DELMAS

Mr Bernard Guillot
Managing Director
Corner Lumumba and Malambo Roads
P O Box 30131, Lusaka
Tel: +260-1-243351/246061/246191
Fax: +260-1-246106
Email: sdvho@sdv.com.zm
Website: www.delmas.com

Activity: Cargo and shipping
Turnover: 850m euros
Employees: 12,000

Founded in 1867, Delmas is the premier French liner company on the north–south trade route.

From Morocco to Kenya and the Indian Ocean islands, Delmas, with its seven regular lines to and from Europe and Asia, offers customers the most comprehensive coverage of African ports combined with the ability to on-carry cargo to any inland destination. With its cross-trade services, Delmas also connects Africa to any part of the world.

With its control over land operations in Africa, Delmas can handle the shipment of any type of cargo, both on sea and on land, whilst keeping customers informed of its status via the website.

Delmas operates 60 modern vessels, fully geared and with their own fleet of cargo handlers. The combination of fully cellular, conbulker and ro-ro vessels allows Delmas to meet all the logistics expectations and to carry all types of cargo, containerized or conventional, hazardous or controlled atmosphere cargoes, heavy lifts or out-of-gauge, project cargo, logs, rolling stock etc.

All the containers conform to ISO standards and also meet rail and other specifications. The ISO standard includes an international container identification system.

ZAMBIAN AIRWAYS – AIRWAVES

Mr Don MacDonald
Chief Executive Officer
Lusaka International Airport
P O Box 310277, Lusaka
Tel: +260-1-271230/1342
Fax: +260-1-271054
Email: info@zambianairways.com
Website: www.zambianairways.com

Activity: Postal services
Turnover: US $16m

Zambian Airways is a Zambian-owned airline established in 1948 and privatized by MBO in 1998 offering regular scheduled flights to Livingstone, Ndola and Mfuwe in Zambia, Johannesburg in South Africa, Harare in Zimbabwe, Lumbumbashi in DRC, and Lilongwe in Malawi.

In 2005, Zambian Airways entered into a close strategic alliance with Airwaves, flying under the banner of Freedom of Africa as an operationally combined airline. Fleet, maintenance, technical services and operations are now pooled, and both companies fly one schedule. The new alliance has provided extra strength to the company enabling synergies and cost cuttings. Zambian Airways prides itself on its track record in the domestic, regional and business markets and has an important national dimension, and Airwaves brings its expertise and strong brand name in the tourism industry. Zambian Airways has recently signed a partnership with kulula.com and has opened a new route to Johannesburg, positioning itself as the pioneer of low-cost flying in Zambia. In the coming years, Zambian Airways plans to open new routes to all regional capitals (Maputo, Luanda, Windhoek etc) and routes to major international hubs such as Nairobi and Lagos, positioning Lusaka as a secondary regional hub.

Zambian Airways has recently launched e-ticketing and e-booking and should provide e-payment facilities by the end of 2006.

Following its partnership with Airwaves, Zambian Airways has developed holiday package products.

"Zambian Airways has become the first and only airline that can fly you directly from a major international hub like Johannesburg to a local airstrip in the bush for your safari."
Mr Don MacDonald, Chief Executive Officer

Zambian Airways, the largest and most reliable domestic carrier has opened a route to Johannesburg

ZAMNET COMMUNICATION SYSTEMS LTD

Mr Raphael Maseko
Acting Managing Director
Comesa Centre
P O Box 38299, Lusaka
Tel: +260-1-224665
Fax: +260-1-224775
Email: ralph@zamnet.zm
Website: www.zamnet.zm

Activity: Telecommunications (Internet and communication solutions)
Date of Creation: 1994
Employees: 35

ZAMNET Communication Systems was established in 1994 as Zambia's first fully featured Internet service provider. In 11 years, the company has become the one-stop shop for Internet solutions, leading the market with a high market share.

The company has been in the forefront of designing and deploying high-quality Internet solutions, and prides itself on providing the fastest Internet access. ZAMNET offers solutions tailored to the specific needs of individuals and corporate organizations, adapting to the size of the organization and the budget.

ZAMNET offers a wide range of products and services including dial-up, wireless connection, DSL, satellite Internet access, virtual private network (VPN), intranet, domain name registration, network design and installation, SMS solutions, email to fax services, web design, and web hosting.
The company also offers consultancy services and training programmes that prepare IT professionals for management of Windows- and UNIX/LINUX-based platforms, as well as other tailored courses.

As an authorized prometric testing centre, ZAMNET is a testing centre for IT professional and certification courses. The company provides testing for CISCO, Microsoft (including MCSE), A+ and N+, etc.

ZAMBIA TELECOMMUNICATIONS COMPANY LTD (ZAMTEL)

Mr Simon Tembo
Managing Director
Provident House, 7th Floor
P O Box 71630, Ndola
Tel: +260-2-612399
Fax: +260-2-615855
Email: md@zamtel.zm
Website: www.zamtel.zm

Activity: Telecommunications
Date of Creation: 1913
Employees: 2,800

The history of Zambia Telecommunications Company dates back to 1913 when the first telephone exchange was installed in Livingstone. Since then, the company has grown to be a pioneer of the telecommunications industry in Zambia by providing cost-effective, comprehensive and high-quality telecommunications facilities and services to its customers.

ZAMTEL offers a wide range of services on its fixed line network. In addition, ZAMTEL offers mobile phone services and Internet services under the well-known brands of Cell Z and ZAMTEL Online. ZAMTEL has been able to keep up with the competition by providing cost-effective solutions and value-for-money services to its customers, while keeping up with the latest technologies and highest levels of services. Latest innovations include the recently introduced prepaid services and prepaid calling cards for the fixed line network. Online web-based billing will be implemented before the end of 2006. Cell Z emerged as the first mobile service to offer per second billing and recharge units in local currency. Cell Z is also the only operator to offer equal tariffs for calls within the network and to other networks. For its business clients, Cell Z has developed a highly competitive virtual private network (VPN) solution with cost-effective intra-company tariffs.

In 2003, Cell Z was awarded Best Marketing Campaign of the year, Best Consistent Electronic Advert and Best Product Launch by the Zambia Institute of Marketing.

ur ONE STOP Communications Solutions provider
Connecting
you!
Connecting
your business!
onnecting you to
the World!
FCB Zambia
tact any of our sales outlets countrywide.
Zamtel
Connecting the Nation

ZAMTEL Online is the leading Internet service provider in Zambia offering a full range of both dial-up and high-speed services.

ZAMTEL has over 93,000 fixed lines and over 130,000 GSM mobile customers. The company has embarked on an ambitious expansion programme to provide all provinces and districts of Zambia with fixed lines, cellular and satellite services. The microwave links and VSAT equipment are being upgraded to cater for the increased bandwidth demand for fixed lines, mobile and Internet services.

By the year 2007, ZAMTEL aims to provide a nationwide fibre optic network to make available broadband backbone connectivity. The company is participating in the East African submarine cable system (EASSY) that together with the nationwide fibre optic network will lead to lower local and international tariffs.

LEISURE

"When weeds invade the land, it means the owner is absent"
Zambian proverb

OVERVIEW

Zambia is well known for being the land of the earth's biggest waterfall, the legendary Victoria Falls, but Zambia houses numerous other treasures... The wild Zambezi River, more than 17 other waterfalls, breathtaking lakes and wetlands, abundant wildlife, the big five and a profusion of birds. Zambia is fed and shaped by three great rivers and bordered by three massive lakes. Zambia offers holidays filled with adventure and scenic beauty and beckons to the intrepid and the adventurous... Zambia is raw, pulsating wilderness, all in one friendly and very safe, unspoilt country.

Zambia has emerged after many years of uncertainty as one of the finest providers of safaris and activities. It is a large country offering a wide range of hi-action activities: from the legendary walking safari, deep in the wilderness, to world-class river rafting, bungi jumping into the deep gorge below the Victoria Falls, abseiling, canoeing safaris down the Zambezi, river surfing, elephant-ride safaris, and sunset cruises. These are just a few of the numerous activities on offer in Zambia.

After promoting Zambia as 'The Real Africa', 'Zambia – the land of magnificent waterfalls' will be the theme for the 2006 campaign launched by the Zambia National Tourist Board. Zambia has long been underestimated as a tourism destination, overshadowed by its big brothers like Tanzania, Kenya and, to a certain extent, Zimbabwe and Botswana; unlike those countries, whose national parks are suffering from mass tourism and overexploitation, Zambia is one of the last hidden pieces of paradise, offering unspoilt wilderness,

Beautiful faces of Zambian children

NSHIMA RECIPE
(4 PEOPLE)

4 cups water
2 cups plain corn meal

Pour 4 cups of water into a medium-sized cooking pot. Heat the water for 3 to 4 minutes or until lukewarm. Using one tablespoonful at a time, slowly sprinkle 3/4 cup of the corn meal into the pot while stirring continuously with a cooking stick. Keep stirring slowly until the mixture begins to thicken and boil. Turn the heat to medium, cover the pot, and let simmer for 3 to 5 minutes.

Cautiously remove the top. Slowly, a little at a time, pour into the pot 1 and a quarter cups of corn meal and briskly stir with the cooking stick until smooth and thick. Stir vigorously. Sprinkle a little more corn meal and stir if you desire the nshima to be thicker, or less if you want softer nshima. Cover, turn the heat off, and let the nshima sit on the stove for another 2 to 3 minutes.

Serves 4 people. Must always be served hot with a vegetable, bean, meat or fish dish or ndiwo.

THE NDIWO DISH
(4 PEOPLE)

Collard Green Leaves with Peanut Powder
7 cups or 1lb chopped collard greens or spring greens
1 large chopped tomato
1 1/2 cups raw peanut powder
2 cups water
1/2 teaspoonful baking soda
1/4 teaspoonful salt

Pour 1 cup of water into a medium-sized cooking pot. Add half a teaspoon of pure baking soda and stir until thoroughly dissolved. Place pot on burner on medium heat. Add 7 cups of chopped collard greens and the 1 chopped tomato. Cook on medium to high heat for 5 to 8 minutes. Add 1 1/2 cups raw peanut powder, 1/4 teaspoon salt and 1 cup of water. Stir thoroughly and lower the heat to below medium. Cover and simmer for 15 to 20 minutes stirring every 2 to 3 minutes to prevent bottom from burning. Serve hot with nshima.

breathtaking scenery, with luxurious accommodation possibilities.

CULTURE

Zambia's contemporary culture is a blend of the values, norms, material and spiritual traditions of more than 70 ethnically diverse peoples. During the colonial period, the process of industrialization and urbanization saw ethnically different people brought together by economic interests. This, as well as the very definite influence of western standards, generated a new culture without conscious effort of politically determined guidelines. Many of the rural inhabitants, however, have retained their indigenous and traditional customs and values. After independence in 1964, the government recognized the role culture was to play in the overall development of a new nation and began to explore the question of a national identity. As a result, private and public museums and cultural villages were established to promote the expression of artistic talents.

FOOD AND DRINKS

TRADITIONAL ZAMBIAN FOOD

Nshima

The Zambian staple meal of nshima is cooked from plain maize or corn meal or maize flour known as mealie-meal among Zambians.

Nshima is eaten in all homes twice per day, for lunch and dinner. The nshima is served with a second smaller dish, the 'relish' (ndiwo, ndiyo or umumunani). The ndiwo can be fish, beans, chicken, beef or vegetables.

Eating is always with only the right hand. Both hands are never used when eating nshima. The right hand will get a lump of nshima, gently mould it into a beautiful ball, and dip it into the ndiwo or relish before eating it.

Zambians usually consider that only nshima constitutes a full and complete meal. Any other foods eaten in between are regarded either as snacks or a temporary less filling or inadequate substitute or a mere appetizer.

Nshima is such a key factor in the diet and loaded with such emotional investment that many rituals, expectations, expressions, customs, beliefs and songs have developed in the culture around working for, cooking and eating of nshima.

The Ndiwo Dish

One of the most significant aspects of the Zambian staple meal by which the nshima is ultimately identified is the 'relish'. The relish is a second dish that is always and without exception served with the nshima. The ndiwo is often cooked from domestic and wild meats including beef, goat, mutton, deer, chicken or wild pig, or vegetables like beans, rape, cabbage, squash, pea leaves, cassava leaves, bean leaves, kabata leaves etc...

This is the most basic and popular recipe in Zambian traditional cooking as it is used for cooking the majority of the many green leaf vegetables including squash or pumpkin leaves, bean and pea leaves, cassava leaves and wild mushrooms.

The peanut powder has multiple uses in the cooking of many traditional Zambian foods. Bala lotendela is porridge cooked with peanut powder. Mpunga wotendela is rice cooked with peanut powder.

Once the woman has finished cooking the nshima, she serves it according to the number, ages and types of people partaking in the meal. The diners sit around the meal making a circle. The oldest person washes their hands first and the youngest last.

Fried Termites

At the beginning of the rainy season (in November), the first rain brings termites out of their nest to mate. The termites are attracted to light and only live a few hours and then lose their wings. Termites are collected, the wings removed, and they are fried with cooking oil and salt. The termites are cooked until they are crisp and golden brown (about 1 minute). A Zambian delicacy!!

LOCAL DRINKS

Most spirits and South African wines are available in the cities. Major brand soft drinks and juices are found everywhere.

There are several types of beer or mooba (in Nyanja) produced in Zambia. Mosi lager is a bottled beer reflecting the local name for Victoria Falls (Mosi-Oa-Tunya – the smoke that thunders). It is one of the most popular beers in Zambia. Rhino is another bottled lager produced and distributed in Zambia.

The local beers, made of fermented maize meal with a thick consistency, can be found in all markets and township bars, but be warned that it is an acquired taste!

Shake-Shake, a more opaque beer, is a favourite amongst the less affluent Zambians.

Zambia has a long tradition of homemade brew and distilled beverages. The most popular and strongest local alcohol is kachasu, a distilled spirit made of sorghum, maize, sour beer, sugar and yeast. This highly alcoholic drink is brewed in villages or at shebeens and is illegal and can damage your liver and kidneys.

Kachasu is fondly described as 'catch us all' or 'bomb' because of its potency (about 20% to 30% alcohol).

CUSTOMS AND TRADITIONS

CEREMONIES

There are more than 20 annual traditional ceremonies in Zambia, manifesting customs, social life, rituals, oral history, material and spiritual culture. They provide a valuable insight into a traditional culture that has been passed down from generation to generation.

Most ceremonies have a deep meaning, in many cases designed to invoke memories of the transformation from childhood to adulthood.

The open ceremonies that visitors can watch are those that signify ancient times, when new kingdoms were being founded by ancient chiefs and are usually splendid, colourful affairs with much symbolism in their dancing and drumming.

The decline of traditional customs and culture has been brought about by the infiltration of the West and Western ways and the melting pot of various tribes living in the same areas. There has recently been a realization of the value of traditions and a conscious effort is being made to preserve them

The Kuomboka

The name means 'to get out of the water onto dry ground'. Every year towards the end of the rainy season as the floodplain of the Upper Zambezi Valley rises, the Lozi people make a ceremonial move to higher ground. When the chief decides that it's time to leave (anytime from February to May), the drums signal to all the people. They pack their belongings into canoes and the whole tribe leaves en masse, the chief in his barge with his family and a troop of traditionally dressed paddlers in the lead. It takes about six hours to cover the distance between the dry season capital Lealui and the wet season capital Limulunga. There the successful move is celebrated with traditional singing and dancing. This ceremony dates back more than 300 years when the Lozi people broke away from the great Lunda empire to come

Little girl carrying a baby

and settle in the upper regions of the Zambezi. The vast plain with abundant fish was ideal for settlement but the annual floods could not be checked, so every year they moved to higher ground until the rainy season passed.

This ceremony takes place in Western province during February or March just before the full moon.

The Umutomboko

The celebration is an annual reminder of the victories of chief Mwata Kazembe, when his great kingdom migrated en masse into Luapula from the Congo earlier this century. Legend has it the dispersal began when the kingdom's paramount chief, Mwata Yamva ordered his people to build a tower which would reach the sky so that they could bring him the sun and the moon. The tower collapsed during vain attempts to build it, killing many of the builders and causing many of the families to flee in terror. Under the leadership of Kazembe, they travelled away across the river and into the east, conquering nearly all the tribes they encountered. Each time they conquered a people, they celebrated the victory, which they called Umutomboko.

The two-day ceremony is a grand affair, mixed with ritual, semi-mystic performance, pounding drum beats and long speeches. Tributes of beer and food are brought to the chief by the women and the chief, smeared with white powder, then goes to pay homage to his ancestral spirits and is carried back to his palace to the beating of drums. On the second day, a goat is slaughtered before the Mutomboko dance, led by the chief. At the climax of the ceremony, the chief takes his sword in his hand and points it in all directions, implying that there is nobody who can conquer him except God, as he points upwards. He then points down to indicate his place of rest when he dies. The brightly coloured cotton skirts worn by the chiefs and senior council are in memory of an early king who received gifts of cloth from Portuguese ambassadors.

It takes place in a specially prepared arena on the banks of the Ng'ona River in Luapula province on 29th July or the nearest weekend.

The Shimunenga

Shimunenga is a traditional ceremony held during the weekend of a full moon in either September or October. The Ba-ila tribe at Maala on the Kafue Flats express their devotion to their divine ancestors

Shimunenga is considered by the Ba-ila people of Maala to be a divine being to be approached when the crops need blessing, the cattle are to be taken to the plains or when a murder is committed. The Shimunenga ceremony is the time for the people to thank their god for providing for them over the period which has just passed. The ceremony takes place once a year between September and November at the close of the old year and the beginning of the new. It lasts for three days and takes place at the home of the Ba-ila of Maala.

The N'cwala

The N'cwala is a religious ceremony performed by the Ngoni people of eastern Zambia giving thanks for the harvest. Taking place at Mutenguleni Village on 24th February, the ceremony involves tasting the first fresh produce of the year, which is accompanied by the consumption of vast quantities of beer and traditional dancing.

Likumbi Lya Mize

Likumbi Lya Mize takes place at Mize, the official palace of senior chief Ndungu in North-Western province. People of the Luvale tribe gather to celebrate their cultural heritage, bringing displays of all types of handicrafts and engaging in traditional singing and dancing.

MUSIC AND DANCE

Many traditional instruments are still played throughout the country. The more common ones are the hand piano, a small instrument with iron keys mounted on a rectangular box and plucked by both thumbs, and the silimba, a xylophone-type instrument with a range of flat wooden keys mounted over gourds. The most common, of course, is the drum and drumming plays an important part in rituals, ceremonies, celebrations and community communication.

Dance is an important part of musical expression among Africans and, along with the ideas the dances express, serves as a reflector of life and thought over the centuries – of times of turmoil and peace, tension and confidence, retreat and advance, conquest and defeat.

The influence of the West and the rest of Africa is well entrenched in music tastes of the current generation in Zambia. In the big towns, nightclubs and shebeens belt out the sounds of kwela and rumba and many local bands play to the increasingly westernized youth.

ARTS AND CRAFTS

Zambia's diverse cultures bring with them a wide variety of traditional skills. Crafts can be found in great variety if not in abundance and among them is some of the finest basketry in Africa.

The economy of most of the craftspeople is based on fishing, cattle or the cultivation of crops. Craftwork is often done seasonally to supplement the incomes of many families.

Traditionally-made pots and baskets in the more populated areas, however, are being replaced by commercially manufactured utility items made of plastic or tin.

Basketry, practised by both the men and the women, is widespread. The many forms and raw materials used reflect the environment in which they are made: bamboo, liana vines, roots, reeds, grasses, rushes, papyrus palm leaves, bark and sisal. They are decorated with symbolic designs using traditional dyes made from different coloured soils, roots, bark and leaves. The variety of uses for basketry is wide: carrying and storage, fishing traps, beer strainers, flour sieves, sleeping and eating mats and a variety of tableware. The Lozi and Mbunda peoples in the Western province are particularly skilled in this field.

CONTEMPORARY CULTURE

Zambia's contemporary culture is a blend of the values, norms, material and spiritual traditions of more than 70 ethnically diverse peoples. Most of the tribes of Zambia moved into the area in a series of migratory waves a few centuries ago. They grew in numbers and many travelled in search of farming land and pastures to establish new kingdoms.

During the colonial period, the process of industrialization and urbanization saw ethnically different people brought together by economic interests. This, as well as the very definite influence of Western standards, generated a new culture without conscious effort of politically determined guidelines.

Many of the rural inhabitants, however, have retained

Zambians are very gifted craftsmen

their indigenous and traditional customs and values. After independence in 1964, the government recognized the role culture was to play in the overall development of a new nation and began to explore the question of a national identity.

Institutions to protect and promote Zambia's culture were created, including the National Heritage Conservation Commission. Private museums were also founded and cultural villages were established to promote the expression of artistic talents.

URBAN LIFE – RURAL LIFE

The principal urban centres, Lusaka, Livingstone and the towns in the Copperbelt, are where most of the rural people head when they make the decision to leave their villages. The impact on the cities has been immense. A ring of shanty towns around the peripheries, with no electricity or adequate sanitation, increases both disease and crime. But the shanties are filled with people who have made a fine art out of surviving with very little. Home industries spring up everywhere from tailors, cobblers, vegetable sellers, money exchangers, to hundreds of walking salesmen selling anything from frying pans, electric plugs and batteries to fruit, vegetables and nuts. The unemployment figure is currently about 60%.

The impact on rural villages will have long-term detrimental effects as it is mostly young men under 25 who leave, leaving the women to raise children, tend to the fields and make a living by themselves, since little money is made in the cities so little is ever sent back. Fewer traditional farmers are making a living by agriculture and crop output for the nation is reducing as a consequence. Zambia faces an enormous challenge to cope with this trend, not only to lure people back to the country to cultivate the land, but to ensure the people who won't leave the cities are gainfully employed.

However, Zambia also has a growing number of well-educated middle and wealthy class white collar workers and entrepreneurs. Many women are in management positions or have their own companies and several are in government.

THE CAPITAL AND ENVIRONS

Compared to most African capitals, Lusaka appears quiet, clean and peaceful. The city lies at the junction of the main highways to the north, east, south and west at an altitude of 1,300m above sea level. The capital covers an area of over 70 square kilometres and is one of the fastest-growing cities in central Africa. Lusaka is a sprawling, unplanned metropolis mixing multi-storey buildings and busy shanty towns. Fast-growing industrial development has brought together people of many nationalities, making it a bustling centre for economic, political and cultural activities.

The tourists passing through the capital may not see any reason to stay, but Lusaka is the product of a country battling to find its way in a new world, caught between colonial beginnings, years of socialist independence and now democracy. Lusaka is as much a part of 'the real Africa' as the rich national parks and stunning scenery.

The markets are a hive of activity, with the thousands of stalls, street sellers, restaurants, hairdressers, fishmongers, fruit sellers and rows and rows of 'salaula' – discarded clothing from the West sold to Africa by the bale. Over 60% of its two million inhabitants are unemployed, but there are surprisingly few beggars.

Lusaka has changed a lot over the past five years: a walk around the city will reveal new shops,including two new multi-million-dollar shopping malls, smart fast food outlets, double carriageway roads, old buildings being refurbished and the transformation of the city's parks.

For many, this is the perfect example of what economic liberalization has done for the country. And viewed from the villages, Lusaka is the glittering capital, which still persuades rural Zambians to take the bus there in search of jobs and dreams.

Cairo Road, Lusaka's busiest street

WHERE TO STAY

Choice of luxury accommodation in Lusaka is limited and you should book your hotel in advance. There are choices to suit all tastes and budgets, from five-star hotels and game lodges on private game reserves, to quieter guest houses in the suburbs.

RECOMMENDED

Chaminuka Lodge
P O Box 35370, Lusaka
Tel: +260-1-213303/4/5/225432
Fax: +260-1-222815
Email: ronald@chaminuka.com.zm
Website: www.chaminuka.com
Luxury lodge located on a hill overlooking Chitoka Lake. Only 45 minutes outside Lusaka, Chaminuka is a perfect safari retreat for the weekend. Famous for its impressive art collection scattered around the lodges, restaurant and even the garden.

Chaminuka is also the biggest private game reserve with elephants, giraffes, lions, antelopes... Walking, driving and horse riding safaris available. Don't miss the heated swimming pool and jacuzzi in the garden!

Chrismar Hotel
Los Angeles Boulevard
P O Box 36043, Lusaka
Tel: +260-1-253036/253605
Fax: +260-1-252569
Email: chrismar@zamnet.zm
Website: www.chrismar.co.zm
Middle-range hotel in the heart of Lusaka. Clean and comfortable.

Cresta Golfview Hotel
Great East Road, Munali
P O Box 38929, Lusaka
Tel: +260-1-290718/290770/291858/96
Fax: +260-1-292049
Email: reservations@cresta.co.zm
Website: www.cresta-hospitality.com

Fairview Hotel
Church Road, Lusaka
Tel: +260-1-222604/5

Fax: +260-1-237222

Email: Fairview@zamnet.zm

Mid-range hotel, cheaper than the Chrismar. Old-fashioned rooms but clean.

Holiday Inn

Church Road

P O Box 30666, Lusaka

Tel: +260-1-251666

Fax: +260-1-253529

Email: holinn@zamnet.zm

Website: www.holiday-inn.com/lusakaridgeway

In the heart of Lusaka, Holliday Inn offers probably the best value for money with good accommodation standards. Two main restaurants including an Irish pub offer good dinner options.

Intercontinental Hotel

Haile Selassie Avenue

P O Box 32201, Lusaka

Tel: +260-1-250000/250600

Email: Lusaka@interconti.com

Website: www.intercontinental.com

One of the two five-star hotels of Lusaka. Spacious and top-of-the-range rooms with a nice pool area. Food at the Savannah Grill can be disappointing but the Olive Grove makes up for it with its fine cuisine.

Lusaka Hotel

Cairo Road

P O Box 30044, Lusaka

Tel: +260-1-229049-52

Fax: +260-1-225726

Email: lushotel@zamnet.zm

Mid-range hotel located on busy Cairo Road.

RECOMMENDED

Lilayi Lodge

P O Box 30093, Lusaka

Tel: +260-1-279022/5

Fax: +260-1-279026

Email: lilayi@zamsaf.com.zm

Lilayi Lodge entrance

Website: www.lilayi.com

A real bush experience, only 20 minutes out of Lusaka. Of all the safari/private game reserve lodges outside Lusaka, Lilayi is the most accessible and can be a good accommodation option to avoid busy Lusaka but close enough to go into town in 20 minutes. Offers game drives, walking and horse riding safaris. Famous for its Sunday lunch.

Mulungushi Village Complex (long-term stay)

Opp. UNZA Plot 10968, Lusemfwa Road, Kalundu, off Great East Road

P O Box 37157, Lusaka 10101

Tel: +260-1-292629/291416

Fax: +260-1-290830

Email: mvc@zamnet.zm

Website: www.mulungushi.com

Located in the quiet residential suburb of Kalundu, this nice and safe village offers 89 four-bedroom fully furnished villas, swimming pool, restaurant, squash and tennis courts. Perfect location for mid- to long-term stays.

Protea Safari Lodge

P O Box 51018

Chisamba, Lusaka

Tel: +260-1-212843

Located 60km outside Lusaka on a private game reserve. Good retreat for the weekend.

Protea Hotel Lusaka

Opposite Arcades Shopping Centre, off Great East Road

This new three-star hotel is still in construction but should be opened in 2007.

Taj Pamodzi Hotel

Church Road

P O Box 35450, Lusaka

Tel: +260-1-250995/254455

Fax: +260-1-254005

Website: www.tajhotels.com

The other five-star hotel in Lusaka, but definitely more pleasant than the Intercontinental. Recently refurbished to high standards. Enjoy the African ethnic decor and the warm atmosphere. Famous for its 'Indian nights' and 'Chinese nights'.

WHERE TO EAT

Top of the Range

Arabian Nights Restaurant
Arcades Shopping Centre, Great East Road
Tel: +260-1-257085

Arabian Nights Restaurant and Lodge
11789 Kabompo Close, Kalundu
Tel: +260-1-295613
Although not as good as Arabian Nights in Kitwe, the two Arabian Nights in Lusaka offer a good selection of Indian and Pakistani food in a nice decor.

Dil Restaurant
Ibex Hill
Tel: +260-1-262391/2691
One of the best Indian restaurants in Lusaka. A must.

Marlin Restaurant
Lusaka Club, Los Angeles Boulevard
Tel: +260-1-252206/96-765462
A local favourite in Lusaka. The menu is extensive (Indian, Creole, Chinese...) but people come for the famous pepper steak.

Rhapsody's
Arcades Shopping Centre, Great East Road
Tel: +260-1-255555/256705/6
Email: rhapsodys@zamtel.zm
Combination of restaurant, wine bar and bar. Excellent original African fusion food; don't miss the beef espetada!! Also a great place to have a drink at the weekend.

Olive Grove
Intercontinental Hotel, Haile Selassie Avenue
Tel: +260-1-250000/250149
Fine cuisine with Mediterranean specialties; treat yourself...

Lilayi Lodge
15km outside Lusaka, off Kafue Road
Tel: +260-1-279022
Famous for the Sunday 4-course lunch. Enjoy a drink by the pool in a beautiful setting.

Middle Range

Danny's/Memories of China
Haile Selassie Avenue, Longacres
Tel: +260-97-585746
An extensive menu of Indian dishes, as well as good steaks.

Gerritz Restaurant
26 Chaholi Road, off Addis Ababa Drive
Tel: +260-1-253639
Fusion food (lunch only).

Green Ethiopian Restaurant
Plot Number 6756, Chainama Road, Olympia Ext, off Katima Mulilo Road
Tel: +260-1-291578
Cell: 096-764426/96-752065/97-809632
Serving can take a long time, but it's a worthwhile experience.

McGinty's
Holiday Inn Hotel, Church Rd, Ridgeway
Tel: +260-1-251666
Pub meals, good Sunday brunch and atmosphere in the Irish tradition.

Savannah Grill
Intercontinental Hotel, Haile Selassie Avenue
Tel: +260-1-250000/250149
International cuisine. Good for lunch; not the best value for money.

Makubi
Haile Selassie Avenue
Tel: +260-1-250000/250149
Resident band. Speciality nights Monday – Italian, Friday – African drums.

Johnny's Bar and Restaurant
Lagos Road
Tel: +260-1-252152/97-771212
Traditional Chinese fare; better as a nightclub than a restaurant.

Muskaan Restaurant
Plot 10C, off Chindo Road, Kabulonga
Tel: +260-1-265976/97-768779
Indian cuisine.

Ocean Basket
Arcades Shopping Centre, Great East Road
Tel: +260-1-256832/97-752673
Website: www.oceanbasket.com
Despite being a landlocked country, Zambia can offer some very good seafood!!

Chang Shun
Independence Avenue
Tel: +260-1-252654
Good traditional Chinese food.

La Gondola
Arcades Shopping Centre
Tel: +260-1-250280
Quiet and casual Italian food; good pizzas.

Le Triumph Dolphin
Northmead
Tel: 097-774954/+260-1-293133
Email: letriumph@zamnet.zm

Spice Paradise
Kabulonga Road
Tel: +260-1-262078
Indian cuisine.

Chit Chat
Omela Mumba Road
Tel: +260-1-234324
Popular lunchtime hang out. Great fusion food menu; good food, great outdoor setting.

Cattleman's Grill
Chrismar Hotel, Longacres
Te: +260-1-253036/253605
Breakfast bar and restaurant. Good Sunday lunch but the tacky decor is a deterrent.

O'Hagan's
Manda Hill Shopping Centre, Great East Road
Tel: +260-1-264298
Traditional Irish food. Good for Sunday brunch.

Oriental Gardens
United Nations Avenue
Tel: +260-1-224209
Good Indian/Chinese restaurant.

Jacaranda
Pamodzi Hotel, Addis Ababa Drive
Tel: +260-1-254455
Coffee shop and grill/Indian night every Friday and Chinese dinner every Wednesday.

Zhong Guo
Zambezi Rd
Tel: +260-1-290278
Traditional Chinese food.

Polo Grill
Nangwenya Road, near Showgrounds
Tel: +260-1-255200
The food is not great but you can enjoy watching the polo games from the big open bay window.

Piccolo Restaurant
12 Serval Road, Twin Palms
Tel: +26-1-261316/22/96-772445
Mixed continental cuisine. Nice setting by a swimming pool in this quiet lodge.

Whispers Restaurant
Showgrounds
Tel: +260-1-250111/96-748622
Indian and Chinese.

Lunch and Coffee Shops

The Garden Café

Off Addis Ababa Road

The food is not great. Come for an afternoon coffee in the beautiful quiet garden.

La Mimosa Coffee Shop

Arcades Shopping Centre, Great East Road

Tel: +260-1-257264

Coffee shop and light meals. Good for lunch or for an ice cream after going to the cinema. Don't miss the crepes!

Café d'Afrique

Lufubu Road, Kalundu

Tel: +260-1-237745

Good for lunch. Great cultural entertainment.

Le Soleil

Zambezi Road, Roma Extension

Tel: +260-1-212437

Cell: +260-97-802533

The food is not great but the garden/swimming pool setting is nice. Come for an afternoon of beauty treatment, massage, yoga and pilates classes.

Le Bistro – Alliance Française

Alick Nkhata Avenue

Tel: +260-1-253467

Snacks or full buffet; excellent food and atmosphere for a nice lunch in the garden of the Alliance Française.

Coffee Talk

Farmers' House, Central Park, Cairo Rd

Tel: +260-1-235276/78

Cappuccino, espresso, fresh cakes, bread and savouries and sandwiches.

The Bakery

Kabulonga Arcade

Tel: +260-1-264253

Cakes, teas, coffee and light lunches.

Le Bistro, Alliance Française

Fast Food and Takeaway

Steers
Manda Hill and Kabulonga Shopping Centre
Tel: +260-1-255557
Pizza/Burgers Takeaway

L.A. Ranch Fast Food
Haile Selassie Avenue, Longacres
Tel: +260-1-254703
Chinese, ice cream, burgers.

Nando's
Manda Hill Shopping Centre and Cairo Road
Tel: +260-1-252773
Chicken the Portuguese way, chicken burgers, pitta breads, salads.

Debonair's Pizza
Manda Hill Shopping Centre, Great East Road
Tel: +260-1-255578/9
Cell: +260-97-790567/6
Kabulonga Shopping Centre
Tel: +260-1-264069/264054
Takeaway and deliveries.

El Toro
Sable Road, Kabulonga
Tel: +260-1-263272/96-758595
Full meals, burgers and samosas; also good for lunches and gateaux. Eat in or take away.

A DRINK OR TWO IN LUSAKA

Alpha Bar
Northmead
Quite an experience...

Brown Frog
Kabulonga Road
Tel: +260-1-225756
Spacious pub with music and live bands on occasion. Casual, friendly atmosphere.

Chez n' Temba
Town centre and Downtown Shopping Centre
Very popular rumba club.

Chit Chat
Omela Mumba Road
Tel: +260-1-234324
Good outdoor setting for an evening drink. Particularly good for special monthly venues and parties (check The Lowdown).

Danny's
Haile Selassie Avenue
Longacres
Tel: +260-97-585746
Most of the time it's only a restaurant. Once a month, it organizes a special party (check The Lowdown).

Johnny's Bar and Restaurant
Lagos Road
Tel: +260-1-252152/97-771212
Good nightclub with an indoor swimming pool and mezzanine floor. House music.

Rhapsody's
Arcades Shopping Centre, Great East Road
Tel: +260-1-255555/256705/6
Everybody's favourite to start the night and meet up with friends. Restaurant, wine bar; always busy, friendly atmosphere.

Safari Bar
Intercontinental Hotel
Haile Selassie Avenue
Tel: +260-1-250000/250149
Cosy meeting place for drinks and cocktails.

Times Café
Arcades Shopping Centre, Great East Road
Tel: +260-1-256811
A Zambian favourite. Always busy and crowded. Nice friendly atmosphere with good music.

Zenon Infinity Nite Club
Northmead

The latest trendy nightclub/bar. Good place to keep the night going.

WHAT TO SEE AND DO

Shopping

Lusaka has three modern shopping malls with an excellent range of shops and boutiques:

Manda Hills: Located on the Great East Road, Manda Hills has a big Shoprite supermarket and offers cafés, fast food, an Irish pub and a variety of small shops (several clothing stores, banks, forex bureaux, a craft shop etc).

Arcades: Located further down Great East Road, Arcades Shopping Centre complements Manda Hills with another supermarket (Spar) and a large range of clothing stores, banks and boutiques. Arcades also has a high-speed wireless cyber café, a very modern cinema and a bowling alley.

The Castle: Located on the Kafue Road, less modern than Arcades or Manda Hill, the Castle Chopping Centre has a Shoprite supermarket and several other stores and boutiques.

Other supermarkets can be found on Cairo Road (Shoprite), Kabulonga (Melissa Supermarket), and Northmead; supermarkets usually supply anything you need, mostly imported from Zimbabwe or South Africa and therefore a little pricey.

Markets

If not for shopping, it's an interesting experience and well worth a visit, if just for the colourful and lively atmosphere. The Soweto Market is two roads west of Cairo Road, and the other main market is opposite the Tazara building in Independence Avenue. A new smarter roofed market has just been built along Freedom Way.

Curios and Crafts

There are several craft and curio markets in Lusaka. Certainly one of the most interesting is the Kabwata Cultural Centre on Burna Road. You will see the rondavels from the road. These are the remains of 300 huts built in the 1930s. You will find all the best of Zambian art including masks, wooden animal carvings, batiks, copper and malachite jewellery etc.

Moore Pottery on Kabulonga Road has an excellent range of ceramics.

Zintu Za Nyimba at the bottom end of Panganani Road sells a wide range of locally made wooden furniture, batiks, candleholders, lampshades, hand-dyed cloths and carvings. Definitely worth a visit.

Every last Saturday of the month there is an excellent craft market in Kabulonga suburb at the Dutch Reform Church grounds.

Gemstones and Jewellery

Jagoda Gems
1 Luano Road, Fairview
Tel: +260-1-223131

The Taj Pamodzi and Intercontinental Hotels each have a fine jewellery boutique with a large range of local gemstones and settings.

EXCURSIONS AND VISITS IN LUSAKA

Munda Wanga Environmental Park
Tel: +260-1-278456/529
Email: biopark@zamnet.zm
A functional educational and recreational centre including the wildlife park and sanctuary: a zoo with lions, tigers, elephants, painted dogs and primates. Feeding time at 14h00 is very popular at the weekends.

The Environmental Park also has a Botanical Garden offering tranquillity, calm and beauty.

The terrace bar and café, braai stands, jungle gyms and playground, swimming pool and recreational area pro-

Arcades, very modern shopping mall with cinema, restaurants, bowling...

vide additional fun for the whole family.

About 20 minutes' drive from Lusaka, on the Kafue Road, near Chilanga.

Open 365 days of the year, 09h00 until 17h00.

Kalimba Reptile Park

Tel: +260-1-233272

The park has an impressive collection of snakes, all found in the surrounding area, crocodiles, tortoises and some of the most unusual chameleons found in Africa. The park is set in a lush garden with a kids' playground, putt-putt course and a verandah where refreshments are served.

Head out of town on the Great East Road towards the airport and turn left at the last Caltex garage before the airport turnoff. Follow the signs for about 11km. The park, which is part of a fish farm, also sells fresh frozen fish and crocodile tails, as well as a range of crocodile bags, purses, belts etc.

The Lusaka National Museum

Tel: +260-1-228806

Located on Independence Avenue, the National Museum is undoubtedly one of the most attractive public buildings in the city. The museum was opened in 1996 and the collection is still too small to fill up the large modern building. The museum hosts four collections: history of Zambia, traditional cultures and witchcraft, urban culture and children's corner. The upper floor houses historical and cultural artefacts. The large hall on the ground floor houses an exhibition of modern paintings and sculptures by Zambian artists. The museum is currently undergoing major changes in line with a new exhibition design plan. The Lusaka National Museum has a partnership with the Royal Tropical Institute in the Netherlands.

The museum has a small library, a small conference room and a snack shop.

Opening hours: 09h00 to 16h30 daily; closed public holidays.

Admission: US $2 adults, US $1 children.

Guided tours possible.

Adventure City

Tel: +260-1-287751/4/233888

The park offers three different types of attraction: Botanical World, featuring desert, tropical and indigenous plants, picnic spots, braai areas and green lawns for fun and games; Water World consists of curved swimming pools for all ages, one of which has a water volleyball court; and Jungle Monkey.

Located 2km off Leopard's Hill Road near the American International School.

Nembo Scenic Park

Tel: +260-1-250152

Located 11km from the city centre at Ngwerere. This scenic park is designed to scale over a 47,000-square-metre area depicting a model of the map of Zambia, featuring the waterfalls and lakes of the country.

Open from 10h00 to 17h00.

The Henry Tayali Visual Arts Centre

Tel: +260-1-254541

Located in the Showgrounds, the Arts Centre has a fine selection of works by Zambian artists. Permanent collections as well as changing exhibitions. Single exhibitor and group shows are held every month.

Open daily from 10h00 to 12h00, 14h00 to 16h00.

Zambili Crafts and Café D'Afrique

Near the craft centre, situated in Kalundu, the café is a great place to stop over for lunch. Traditional foods and cultural performances.

Lusaka National Museum on Independence Avenue

JLazyJ Farm

A 1,500-hectare bird sanctuary 20 minutes from town. The owner will take you horseback riding through the pristine miombo woodland or you can simply do walks and birdwatching on your own.

Trotover Equestrian Centre

Offers horseback hacks through indigenous forest with natural obstacles, or birdwatching walks. This is a great spot for a family picnic, with a pool and a few streams.

EXCURSIONS: LODGES AND PRIVATE GAME PARKS OUTSIDE LUSAKA

Lilayi Lodge

Tel: +260-1-279022/5

Fax: +260-1-279026

Email: lilayi@zamsaf.co.zm

Website: www.lilayi.com

Located only 20km out on the Kafue Road on a private game ranch of 700 hectares. Lilayi Lodge offers luxury accommodation as well as daily excursions for day visitors including game drives, bicycle rides, walking and horse riding safaris on the ranch.

This private reserve has elephants, giraffes, 14 species of antelope, warthogs, zebras, monkeys...

Kyindu Private Game Reserve/The Lion House

Out on the Leopard's Hill Road, northeast of Lusaka, you'll find the Kyindu Private Game Reserve featuring the luxurious Lion Lodge (a large male lion lives at the lodge), and Elandsong Bushcamp, a more rustic camp deep in the heart of this private reserve.

Protea Safari Lodge

Tel: +260-1-226589

Fax: +260-1-221175

Email: chisamba@zamnet.zm

Located about 35 minutes out on the Great North Road. Set in a well-stocked private game ranch, the Safari Lodge offers accommodation and an excellent restaurant. Well known for its superb Sunday lunches. The ranch stocks most of the antelopes found in the country and has game drives and walking trails through the bush.

Chaminuka Private Game Reserve

Tel: +260-1-213303/4/5/225432

Fax: +260-1-228115

Email: information@chaminuka.com

Website: www.chaminuka.com

Located about 45 minutes north of Lusaka is the extensive Chaminuka Private Game Reserve. The biggest private game reserve of Zambia it has a large variety of game, including lions, elephants, giraffes, zebra and antelopes, in untouched wilderness. The well-appointed lodge also has an extensive collection of African art, with more than 1,000 pieces of art, ranging from traditional artefacts collected in over 35 countries in Africa to contemporary sculpture and painting collections.

Walking, driving and horse riding safaris can be arranged at the lodge. You can also enjoy a swim, play tennis and relax in the outdoor jacuzzi, heated swimming pool and sauna.

Drive towards the Lusaka Airport and turn left at the airport junction. Follow the signposts. Four-wheel drive necessary.

Lechwe Game and Fish Farm

Tel: +260-1-222083/84/73

Fax: +260-1-222684

Email: kflechwe@zamnet.zm

A one-hour drive from Lusaka is the Lechwe Lodge, on the banks of the Kafue River. The river's proximity attracts many waterbirds. Sixteen different antelope species can be seen in the woodlands and floodplains of the area. On offer are horse trails and boat rides down the river.

Blue Lagoon National Park

Until recently, this park was not open to the public as it fell under the preserve of the Ministry of Defence. It was established some years back by the Critchleys, an environmentally oriented farming family who then sold it to the National Parks Department.

Blue Lagoon lies west of Lusaka on the Kafue Flats and

Chamunuka Lodge, well known for its large art collection

the vast floodplain attracts thousands of Kafue lechwe, some buffalo and numerous waterbirds. The plains are fringed with acacia woodland. This park is a birdwatcher's dream.

Take the Mumbwa road from Lusaka then turn left at a faded blue ZCCM sign about 27km from Lusaka opposite a store called the Bancroft Supermarket. This road eventually leads to the park gate.

SPORTS

There are several sports clubs in Lusaka which offer facilities for golf, tennis, swimming and squash. You can find good gyms and swimming pools at the Holiday Inn, Intercontinental and Taj Pamodzi Hotels. Also:

Active Bodies
Great East Road
Tel: +260-1-290285
Small health club.

Bowling Alley
Arcades Shopping Centre, Great East Road
Tel: +260-1-256601/2

Chainama Hills Golf Club
Kamloops Road
Tel: +260-1-290073
Quieter golf course, off Great East Road on the way to the airport. Beginners will prefer it to the Lusaka club.

Lusaka City Council Swimming Pool
Off Lubu Road
Tel: +260-1-251071
Email: lowdown@zamnet.zm
Website: www.lowdown.co.zm
Open every day except Mondays from 10h00 to 18h00.

Lusaka Golf Club

Los Angeles Boulevard

Tel: +260-1-250697

The favourite course in Lusaka. It gets very busy during the weekend. You can take lessons.

Millennium Village Complex

Birdcage Walk, Longacres

Tel: +260-1-228842

Good gym and Olympic-sized swimming pool.

Mulungushi Village

Off Great East Road, Kalundu

Tel: +260-1-292629

Swimming pool, squash and tennis courts.

Polo Club

Nangwenya Road

Near the Showgrounds

Tel: +260-1-255200

The polo season starts in April. Games at the weekends.

The Lusaka Club

Los Angeles Boulevard

Tel: +260-1-252441

Bowls, tennis and squash.

To know what is happening in Lusaka (social events, parties, going out etc.) consult The Lowdown, published once a month.

Lusaka Golf Club

LIVINGSTONE & THE VICTORIA FALLS

Livingstone was named after the famous Victorian missionary explorer Dr David Livingstone. The town was established in 1905 and was made the capital of Northern Rhodesia in 1911. It remained the capital of Zambia until 1935. As the capital, it enjoyed excellent facilities far superior to anything in the country, as can be seen from the surviving Edwardian colonial buildings that line the city's main road.

The proximity to the Zambezi River and the spectacular Victoria Falls has led it to become a base for travellers from all over the world wanting to explore this Seventh Natural Wonder of the World.

LIVINGSTONE

GETTING THERE

By Air

Proflight and Zambian Airways have daily scheduled flights to Livingstone from Lusaka. British Airways/Comair fly three times a week from Johannesburg. Nationwide Airlines has several flights a day directly from Johannesburg.

Cultural dancing

By Road

Livingstone is 470km from Lusaka. Take the southbound Kafue Road out of Lusaka and just after the Kafue River Bridge, turn right towards Mazabuka. This road leads straight to Livingstone.

Livingstone can also be approached from Zimbabwe (cross the border at the town of Victoria Falls over the famous Victoria Falls Bridge), and from Botswana (cross the border at Kazungula by ferry).

WHERE TO STAY

Most of the nice hotels and lodges are located outside the town, closer to the Falls, or in remote areas upstream (see listings in Victoria Falls section). In Livingstone town, the lodging options are limited to low-budget guest houses.

New Fairmount Hotel
Mosi-Oa-Tunya Road
Town Centre
Tel: +260-3-320723/320075
Email: nfjc@zamnet.zm
Newly refurbished, with 73 rooms.

WHAT TO SEE AND DO

The Livingstone Museum
Tel: +260-3-321820
It is the country's biggest and oldest museum, dating back to the 1930s. It has five sections. The Archaeology Gallery describes human evolution and cultural development in Zambia from the Stone Age to the Iron Age. The Ethnography and Art Gallery shows objects relating to the different cultures of the country including handicrafts and musical instruments. The History Gallery includes the origins of the Bantu people, the development of British colonial rule and the attainment of independence. It also houses a large collection of David Livingstone memorabilia, donated by the Livingstone family. The Natural History Section shows various indigenous animals in their

Magnificent Victoria Falls...

natural habitat. There is also an extensive library with books ranging from archaeology to wildlife and also some of Livingstone's journals.

The museum is open every day from 09h00 to 16h30 and is on the main road through the centre of town. Entry fee: US $3.

The Railway Museum

Tel: +260-3-323452

The museum holds some fine examples of Zambia's railway heritage including old steam locomotives and vintage coaches, to the tiniest railway memorabilia and old photographs illustrating life in the pioneer days of the town.

THE VICTORIA FALLS

Described by the Kololo tribe living in the area in the 1800s as 'Mosi-oa-Tunya' – 'the Smoke that Thunders' – and in more modern times as 'the greatest known curtain of falling water', Victoria Falls are a spectacular sight of awe-inspiring beauty and grandeur on the Zambezi River, bordering Zambia and Zimbabwe.

FORMATION

The basalt, through which the Zambezi runs for 209km in the Livingstone area, is characterized by very marked joints or cracks, which may have developed as the molten lava cooled after an earth movement. One dominant series of joints running in an east–west direction is associated with zones of soft material within the basalt.

Since the Zambezi is flowing due south in the Livingstone area, these softer materials are very easily eroded to form the great east–west gorges. Upstream retreat of the Falls is due to a second major series of joints running north–south. Gradual erosion of small joints that run north–south caused the river to be concentrated into a narrow fissure and the broad fall line was abandoned. Once this happened, it was only a question of time before the narrow gorges cut back into another transverse fracture zone of soft material. This gouging out of the soft zone again established a broad fall. This process has been repeated over many years and the zigzag gorges represent seven previous lines of falls.

The Devil's Cataract, on the Zimbabwe side, which is 21m to 37m lower than the rest of the present Falls, shows how the force of water is starting to cut back along such a line of weakness. It will probably erode its way back to another east–west joint where a future line of the Falls will eventually become established.

LIVINGSTONE'S FIRST SIGHTING

In 1851, Livingstone first heard of the great waterfall, but it was only in 1855 that he set out to visit it. He spent the night on Kalai Island a few kilometres upstream of the Falls, having come down river by foot, and the next morning set off in a small canoe to approach the thundering smoke. He landed on the biggest island on the lip of the falls, now called Livingstone Island, and from there obtained his first view of the Falls.

The falls are almost empty at the end of the dry season in October

WHERE TO STAY

There are several hotels and lodges in the Victoria Falls area providing a wide range of accommodation.

Islands of Siankaba

Tel/Fax: +260-3-324490

Cell: +260-97-791241

Email: siankaba@zamnet.zm

An exclusive luxurious tented camp sleeping only 12 guests with an haute cuisine restaurant, all on two densely forested islands in the mighty Zambezi River. The lodge is located 24 miles upstream from the Victoria Falls and just 30 miles from Chobe Game Park.

Jungle Junction

A magical jungle island right in the middle of the Zambezi. They'll take you over to the island in a traditional makoro and give you a secluded and comfortable bed to camp down for the night. Wander around the lush island and find one of the many isolated hammocks to kick back and soak up the therapeutic rhythm of this great river.

Maramba River Lodge

Tel: +260-3-324189

Email: maramba@zamnet.zm

Located only 4km from the Victoria Falls, Maramba River Lodge offers chalets with en suite bathrooms, safari tents under thatch, and spacious lawned camping areas nestled under a shaded canopy of indigenous riverine forest.

RECOMMENDED

Stanley Safari Lodge

Email: reservations@stanleysafaris.com

A very exclusive lodge erected on a hill overlooking the spray of the Victoria Falls and the Zambezi River. The seven luxury cottages are completely open to the exterior and offer a fabulous view and stunning sunsets. The four suites have a private plunge pool. A private butler is assigned to each cottage for a service of the highest standard.

Sun International Resort

The Zambezi Sun Hotel (three-star plus hotel)

Mosi-oa-Tunya Road

P O Box 50151, Livingstone

Sussi and Chuma Lodge... luxurious hideway on the upper Zambezi

Zebras wander freely around Zambezi Sun Hotel

Tel: +260-3-321122

Fax: +260-3-322225

Email: sunint@coppernet.zm; zamres1@sunint.co.za

Located next to the Royal Livingstone, along the banks of the river, the Zambezi Sun is decorated as a fun paradise with ethnic fusion architecture and earthly colours. Perfect for families.

RECOMMENDED

Sussi & Chuma

Tel: +260-1-271366/271508/271509

Fax: +260-1-271398

Email: reservations@starofafrica.co.zm; res2@starofafrica.co.zm

An enchanting riverbank hideaway just 10 minutes upstream of the Victoria Falls. The lodges are private luxury treehouses, built among the branches of a huge ebony tree. It is not uncommon to see elephant, buffalo or rhinoceros passing below the walkways. An elegant central thatched building with dining area, swimming pool, bar and lounge services the 10 luxury treehouses, each with a river view. The Chuma house (two bedrooms and three bathrooms) offers a luxury hideaway with its own private garden, plunge pool and butler service.

Taita Falcon Lodge

Tel/Fax: +260-3-321850 (office)

Cell: +263-11-208387 (lodge)

Email: taita-falcon@zamnet.zm

The lodge nestles high up on the cliffs of Batoka Gorge and has spectacular views of the Zambezi winding its way through the gorge. Watch the rafters surf the rapids.

Perched above Rapid 17 on the very edge of the Batoka Gorge, Taita Falcon offers superb views of the raging Zambezi waters 200m below.

The Royal Livingstone (five-star hotel)
Royal Livingstone
P O Box 50151
Livingstone
Tel: +260-3-321122
Fax: +260-3-322225
Email: sunint@coppernet.zm; zamres1@sunint.co.za
Located next to the Zambezi Sun, this impressive five-star complex offers 173 luxurious rooms overlooking the Zambezi River at a walking distance from the Falls. The sumptuous and classy colonial-style decor and tastefully decorated rooms and restaurants offer a serene refuge.

Thorntree
Bookings through Safari Par Excellence
With six twin rooms and two honeymoon suites, Thorntree River Lodge offers its guests a unique view of the Zambezi River. Each accommodation unit has its own en suite facilities and all are beautifully appointed. The elephant ride starts from this lodge.

Tongabezi
Tel: +260-3-324450/323235
Lodge Tel: +260-3-324450/68
Fax: + 260-3-324483
Cell: 097-771488
Email: reservations@tongabezi.com
An exclusive and romantic lodge beautifully positioned on the banks of the river, with stunning views across the Zambezi. It is home to just 22 guests in five river cottages along the river bank and four houses. A special feature is the huge open-air sunken bath with a beautiful view of the river. Personal valets and attention to detail complete an African dream, with emphasis on style, service and atmosphere.

Zambezi Royal Chundu Fishing and Safari Lodge
Tel/Fax: +27-11-9533224
Email: chundu@icon.co.za
This luxury lodge is located further upriver and offers riverfront chalets and three treehouses. The Zambezi Royal Chundu offers specialized fishing facilities and caters for all angling requirements, from fly fishing to bait casting.

WHERE TO EAT

Most of the lodges have restaurants and rates are on a full-board basis. The Sun International, with its two hotels, offers nice restaurant options.

WHAT TO SEE AND DO

Falls Sightseeing

Columns of spray can be seen from miles away as 546 million cubic metres of water per minute plummet over the edge (at the height of the flood season) over a width of nearly 2km into a deep gorge over 100m below. The wide basalt cliff over which the Falls thunder transforms the Zambezi from a wide placid river to a ferocious torrent cutting through a series of dramatic gorges.

From the Zambezi Sun Hotel or the Royal Livingstone, the Falls are at a walking distance (and the price of the room includes the entrance fee to the Falls). If you stay in another lodge, you will probably need a transfer service from your lodge.

A path along the edge of the forest provides the visitor who is prepared to brave the tremendous spray with an unparalleled series of views of the Falls. The well-marked and paved path will take you through the rain forests. Every so often the path will open out into a clearing for a view of the Falls.

Further along this path is the Knife Edge Bridge which offers an impressive panorama depending on the time of year. Although less can be seen of the width of the Falls during the wet season, the intense spray is an amazing experience and will create beautiful rainbows. Don't carry anything you don't want to get wet!

Another path leads the visitor to the point upstream just at the point where the water falls into the gorge.

Boiling Pot

Another interesting perspective is deep within the gorge into which the Falls descend. From the car park, look for the signs pointing to The Boiling Pot. It's quite a steep climb, but well-worn steps make it a fairly easy descent. Coming up is, of course, a little more strenuous, but the view from below of the wide Zambezi thundering over the cliff, then compressed into the deep thin crevice turning into the Batoka Gorge, crashing and swirling over rapids, is quite spectacular. From this vantage point you can also see up to the impressive Victoria Falls Bridge, spanning the gorge over 100m above.

The Victoria Falls Bridge

Commissioned by Cecil John Rhodes in 1900, the bridge offers a magnificent view both down the gorge on the one side and through to the Falls on the other. The immense depth of the gorge can be fully appreciated from this perspective and, combined with the sea-green river below, the shiny black rock face and lush green foliage, the 360-degree view from the bridge is breathtaking.

Aerial View of the Falls

To fully appreciate the incredible size of the Falls, and the awesome power of the water as it carves into the deep zig-zagging gorges for 8km, you must see it from the air.

The pilot will take you along the wide tranquil Upper Zambezi, and over the huge 2km rent in the earth. The breathtaking sight of this magnificent natural phenomenon, seen in all its glory from the air, is unforgettable.

All arrangements can be made through the hotel or lodge where you are staying.

Microlight Flights

Fly like a bird over the Falls. With the microlight you are completely exposed to the wind. You are not able to take your camera with you for safety reasons

US $100 per person for 35 minutes, US $150 for 55 minutes.

Victoria Falls bridge offers a beautiful perspective of the Falls

Helicopter Flights

A 15-minute flight takes you into the Falls and the national park. For 30 minutes you will also fly over the gorges.

US $85 for 15 minutes, US $170 for 30 minutes. Price includes transfer from the hotels.

Tiger Moth Flights

Flying over the Falls is amazing, but doing it in a 1941 two-seater Tiger Moth bi-plane makes you feel like Robert Redford in Out of Africa, with your leather flying helmet and goggles. The flight offers amazing views of the Falls and takes you upstream over the national park and the gorges.

US $120 for 20 minutes, US $170 for 30 minutes, including transfer from lodge.

Livingstone Island

During the dry season, be sure to take a walk along the lip of the Falls themselves. Sometimes the water is low enough to walk all the way across to Livingstone Island, the place where David Livingstone had his first glimpse of the Falls. This is surely one of the most magnificent views in the area.

During the month of October, when the water is almost absent from the Falls, visitors can enjoy a swim at the very edge of the Falls.

Hotels and lodges organize half-day trips including a sumptuous lunch on the bank of the river and a guided swim in the 'Devil's pool'.

Mukuni Victoria Falls Craft Village

The curio market is located in the parking area just above the Falls where most of the walks begin. Includes intricate animal carvings in stone, wood or the beautiful green malachite, masks, drums, marimbas, spoons, book ends, walking sticks, jewellery and much more.

Victoria Falls Field Museum

This little museum attempts to explain how the Falls were formed over the millennia. It is built over an actual excavation site that has uncovered evidence of early hominids who lived in the area as far back as 2.5 million years ago.

Mosi-Oa-Tunya National Park

Situated along the Upper Zambezi stretching from and including the Falls for about 12km upriver. It is only 66 square kilometres but provides a home for numerous elephants, antelope species, zebras, giraffes and the recently acquired white rhinos. These are the only rhinos to be seen in Zambia as its previously large population has been completely eliminated through poaching. You can take a pleasant drive around the park in a couple of hours and almost all the species there should be seen at close range. Since there are no predators, they are very relaxed and afford some excellent photo opportunities.
It is also very interesting to discover the park through a river cruise, as you are very likely to witness elephants crossing the river between Zambia and Zimbabwe.

Chief Mukuni's Village

This village is home to the Leya people and has been in existence since the 11th century. Livingstone visited the village on several occasions to meet with the chief. The descendant of the chief still lives there with 7,000 inha-

Breathtaking aerial view of the Falls from a tigger moth plane

bitants. Mukuni is an authentic tribal village where thousands of people live and work. In July of each year the Leya people partake in the colourful Lwiindi ceremony. The local people believe the spirits of their ancestors still dwell in the gorges of the Falls and during the Lwiindi, they offer sacrifices to them for rain.

Many lodges organize guided tours of the village.

ADVENTURE ACTIVITIES

The Victoria Falls area is rapidly becoming known as the 'Adventure Centre' of southern Africa, with various adrenaline sports, unmatched scenery of breathtaking proportions and many other leisure options for outdoor lovers.

White Water Rafting

Considered one of the best stretches of commercially run river in the world, Batoka Gorge provides one of the most intense white water rafting experiences. Its 23 rapids offer the adrenaline junkie a wild roller coaster ride along a route carved out by the great Zambezi.

The rapids are run in large rubber rafts, launched from just below the Falls. You can do a half-day trip, full day or two days.

When the river is high (March to July) only the last 13 rapids can be done. As the water subsides (from June to February) all 23 are navigable. Most of the rapids are graded category IV and V (out of a maximum of VI), but fortunately, the vast majority are not 'technical' to run. However, be prepared to flip over and find yourself in the water very often!

The river guides will shout safety instructions and commands to tell you what to do. You are an active participant and therefore responsible for how successfully you run the rapids. Guides handle flip-over very well, and will always bring you back safely into the boat. The boat is always accompanied by a professional white water kayaker who helps pick up the 'swimmers'.

The climb down and out of the gorge to begin and at the end of the rafting is probably the more strenuous part of the day. You can opt for a 'fly out' in a helicopter, at an extra cost, and combine a beautiful aerial view of the gorges after a day in the gorges...

The thrill of swimming at the edge of the Falls...

White water rafting, an exciting experience

NOTICE! See listing of specialized tour operators at the end of this chapter.

River Boarding/Wave Surfing

Armed with a body board, a wetsuit, a life jacket, a helmet and fins, you will embark on a river journey, playing in the currents, charging the rapids and surfing some of the world's biggest fresh water standing waves.

The main difference between river surfing and rafting is that you are in charge of your own vessel on the river. Although instructors teach and guide you, you are the one taking on the rapids.

No previous body boarding experience is necessary. Confidence in the water is however a requisite! Wave surfing is also possible on the sensational standing waves.

NOTICE! See listing of specialized tour operators at the end of this chapter.

White Water Kayaking

Another way to experience the incredible power of the Zambezi below the Falls is to paddle the rapids with seasoned white water kayakers.

After taking receipt of your paddle, life jacket and helmet at the top of the gorge, and an easy walk down to the Boiling Pot, you will receive a comprehensive safety briefing and a practice session prior to commencing your trip.

An experienced white water kayaker will steer the boat through the rapids, with you adding your support.

The trip is run in conjunction with a rafting trip for added safety and it will be up to you, and your personal guide, to ensure that you stay in the kayak or you could end up swimming the rest of the rapid!! No previous experience required.

NOTICE! See listing of specialized tour operators at the end of this chapter.

Jet Boards

30-minute jet trips between Rapid 23 and Rapid 27 offer a thrilling ride.

Canoeing

A canoeing safari on the Upper Zambezi River is a wonderfully relaxing way to enjoy the astonishingly beautiful scenery that lines the river before it takes its plunge over the Falls.

This part of the river is dotted with many islands of varying size and is home to many birds and small animals.

This is the route David Livingstone took on his way in search of the rising clouds of mist. It was in fact along these banks that he remarked, "Scenes so lovely must have been gazed upon by angels in their flight."

The silence of the canoes makes them ideal to witness elephants, hippos and crocodiles!

NOTICE! See listing of specialized tour operators at the end of this chapter.

Bunji Jumping

The second highest jump and the highest commercial bridge jump (111m) in the world in the most spectacular setting!

This is the ultimate adrenaline rush, as you leap into space, free as a bird, saved from the swirling water below by the rebound of the cord, then hurtle upwards again at great speed. Four seconds of free fall, 140km per hour speed. It's an indescribable feeling that will probably change your life! Five.... four.... three... two.... one... bungi!!!!!!!

No booking is necessary, just take a stroll down to the bridge. You'll have to go through the border post as the bridge is in no-man's-land between Zambia and Zimababwe, 111m high, spanning the magnificent Batoka Gorge.

High Wiring, Gorge Swinging and Rap Jumping

This is the world's first commercial high wire. A cable is spanned across the gorge 135m long and 75m above the ground. A full body harness is attached securely from your back to the cable and you take a running dive off the edge of the cliff. Soar across the deep gorge like a bird in flight. US $30 for three tries.

The gorge swing offers another thrilling experience: the swing is a fixed 135-metre cable spanning the gorge. Participants are harnessed to a rope attached to the middle of the cable and experience a heart-stopping 53-metre, three-second free fall, followed by a pendulum-like swing across the gorge for two minutes before being lowered down to the ground. It's even possible to try it in tandem.

Be prepared to hike for 30 minutes out of the gorge...
It is possible to do each activity on its own or opt for a package that will give you as many rides as you dare to try!

Abseiling

You will be attached to the main rope and safety rope from a harness, then gently lowered over the platform. Slowly the rope is let out as you make your way down the rock face. You will improve with each attempt and can go down as often as time allows.

On reaching the base of the gorge you have the choice of walking out or being hauled back up. The walk up has been designed as an integral part of the day's activities. A gentle slope with plenty of rest stops has been chosen. It is a pretty walk, especially when all the trees are in leaf.

5, 4, 3, 2, 1... bunjiiiiii !!

Elephant Riding

Organized through Safari Par Excellence – see listing at the end of this chapter.

Safari Par Excellence offers the only elephant-back safari in Africa. Based at Thorntree River Lodge, you will experience a one-hour ride on a majestic African elephant through the bush of the national park and along the river.

All the elephants were orphans and were raised on farms and trained to be around people. In their 'free time', these 'domesticated' elephants roam freely in the park and interact with wild elephants. Some elephants have even given birth to babies with wild elephants.

You will be offered the chance to feed them and interact with them, or even sit on their 'laps' at the end of the ride! The elephants even understand a few words and you can request them to 'talk', move their trunk up or stop... An unforgettable and moving experience.

Breakfast/lunch and transfers included.

As there are only six elephants, it is highly recommended to book a long time in advance.

Sunset Cruise

Bookings through Safari Par excellence or directly contact African Queen.

Sunsets on the Upper Zambezi to enjoy wildlife with a glass of wine can be a lot of fun! You can choose from breakfast, lunch, sunset or dinner cruises. The African Queen is an old-style double-decker; it was on this boat that George VI cruised the river during his visit in 1947. Guests can enjoy drinks and appetizers to the sound of soft African music. A unique dining experience amongst rhinos, hippos and elephants crossing the river...

US $44 per person for a two-hour lunch or sunset cruise including drinks and canapés.

Elephant riding is an unforgettable moving experience...

African Queen
P O Box 60733
Livingstone
Tel: +260-3-321513
Fax: +260-3-324070
Email: African.queen@thevictoriafalls.co.zm
Website: www.theafricanqueen.co.zm

TOUR OPERATORS FOR ACTIVITIES

Batoka Sky
Maramba Aerodrome, off Sichango Road
P O Box 60971
Livingstone
Tel: +260-3-320058
Fax: +260-3-324071
Email: freedom@zamnet.zm
Website: www.batokasky.com

Bushtracks Africa
P O Box 60719
Livingstone
Tel: +260-3-323232
Fax: +260-3-324434
Email: victoriafalls@bushtracksafrica.com
Website: www.bushtracksafrica.com

Bundu Adventures
699 Industrial Road
P O Box 60773
Livingstone

Sunset cruise on the Zambezi River

Tel: +260-3-324407
Fax: +260-3-324406
Email: zambezi@zamnet.zm
Website: www.bundu-adventures.com

Kayak-the-Zambezi
Livingstone Adventure Centre
P O Box 60947
Livingstone
Tel: +260-3-322089
Email: kayak@thezambezi.com;
sventhunderlord@yahoo.com

Safari Par Excellence
P O Box 60407
Livingstone
Tel: +260-3-321629
Fax: +260-3-326629
Email: safpar@zamnet.zm
Website: www.safpar.com; www.zambezisafari.com

United Air Charters
P O Box 60428
Livingstone
Tel: +260-3-323095
Fax: +260-3-323095
Email: uac@zamnet.zm
Website: www.uaczam.com

LOWER ZAMBEZI

The Zambezi River rises in northwestern Zambia and its catchment area covers 1,352,000 square kilometres and eight countries, namely Angola, Botswana, Malawi, Mozambique, Namibia, Tanzania, Zambia and Zimbabwe. It enters the Indian Ocean in Mozambique.

It flows for some 2,650km from its source to the Indian Ocean. It is the fourth largest river in Africa.

Lower Zambezi National Park is Zambia's newest park and as such is still relatively undeveloped. The diversity of animals is not as wide as in the other big parks, but the opportunities to get close to game wandering in and out of the Zambezi channels are spectacular.

The Lower Zambezi National Park covers an area of 4,092 square kilometres, but most of the game is concentrated along the valley floor. Enormous herds of elephants are often seen at the river's edge. 'Island hopping' buffalo and waterbuck are common. The park also hosts some lions and leopards. Lower Zambezi is also a birdwatcher's paradise, with over 350 species of bird including the famous fish eagle.

HOW TO GET THERE

You can drive into the national park on your own but it is very underdeveloped and not really structured for vehicle visitors yet. The existing lodges and canoeing operators provide the best access to the park. They all offer pick-ups from either Lusaka or Chirundu, or Kariba in Zimbabwe.

The Chongwe River demarcates the western boundary of the park and can be accessed from Chirundu along a rough road, crossing the Kafue River by pontoon just beyond Gwabi Lodge.

There is a pontoon that crosses the Zambezi from Luangwa town to Kanyemba in Zimbabwe and to Zumbo in Mozambique.

Fly a 1941 Tiger moth..

WHERE TO STAY

The following listing of the lodges is arranged according to their location (east to west) and indicates which ones are inside and outside the national park.

Kanyemba Lodge
(located outside the national park)
Tel: +260-97-755720/96-784516
Email: info@kanyemba.com
Website: www.kanyemba.com
The newest lodge in this area. Five bungalows and the romantic honeymoon suite forming the lodge are discreetly located on the river bank under the shadow of wild mangoes and huge trees. Expert guides will be at your disposal to take you on daytime photographic safaris or night excursions to observe animals while feeding, drinking or hunting.

Kiambi Lodge
(located outside the national park)
Kiambi Safari Limited
Tel: + 260-96-655878
Email: kiambi@coppernet.zm
Kiambi Lodge offers superb views over the Zambezi and Kafue Rivers and is only 20km from the Chirundu border, so easier to reach than any of the other lodges. Good to go for the weekend from Lusaka.

Kayila Lodge
(located outside the national park)
Bookings organized through Safari Par Excellence
Small and exclusive safari lodge in a private wildlife sanctuary overlooking Mana Pools National Park on the Lower Zambezi. Six beautifully appointed twin en suite thatched lodges, a honeymoon suite with its sunken bath, a famous Kayila treehouse suite, a double lodge built 9m up an African sausage tree (Kigelia africana) and a duplex chalet with two separate en suite twin rooms as well as a family room with a double and two singles.

Mvuu Tented Lodge
Tel: +27-16-9871837
Fax: +27-16-9872655
Email: info@mvuulodge.com
Located in an attractive setting on the banks of the Zambezi is a fully catered camp with the option of self-catering. There is also a campsite for those on a budget. Activities available are canoeing, game viewing, birding, fishing and soaking up the wonderful sunsets.

Kasaka River Lodge
(located outside the national park)
Nyamangwe Safaris Limited
Tel: +260-1-26583/260012
Fax: +260-1-260012
Email: bookings@kasakariverlodge.com
A beautifully situated lodge on a raised section of the Zambezi River bank with excellent views. Wooden walkways link the chalets and elephants often walk right underneath them.

Royal Zambezi Lodge
(located outside the national park)
Tel: +260-1-278248/9
Fax: +260-1-278249
Cell: +260-96-861020/1030
Email: rzl@iconnect.zm
This lodge has its own 3.5 kilometres of unspoiled river frontage with a beautiful view of the mountains. Fly in to the Royal Zambezi's private airstrip in the comfort of a chartered aircraft only half an hour's flight from Lusaka.

Chongwe River Camp
(located at the western border of the national park)
Tel/Fax: +260-1-286808
Cell: +260-97-772905/97-801810
Email: info@chongwe.com
Situated at the Chongwe River and Zambezi River confluence, opposite Mana Pools. It has six chalets under the canopy of huge acacia trees. Unparalleled tiger fishing area, with great game and bird viewing opportunities.

Chiawa Camp
(located inside the national park)
Tel: + 260-1-261588
Fax: +260-1-262683
Email: info@chiawa.com
Chiawa Camp offers luxury tented en suite accommoda-

Fisherman on the Zambezi River

Even the simplest "tented lodges" offer a lot of comfort

tion for 14 guests. Its specialities are game viewing by motorboat, by open vehicle in the park, night drives, bush walks, canoeing, river cruises and angling safaris. Operating season is from May to October.

RECOMMENDED

Sausage Tree Camp

(located inside the national park)

Tel: + 260-1-212597

Fax: + 260-1-272456

Email: info@sausagetreecamp.com

Website: www.sausagetreecamp.com

Offers superb comfort in a rustic setting on the banks of the river. Canoeing safaris as well as game drives and night drives, walks in the bush, birding trails and often you can just sit in your tent and watch the action! A must!

Mwambashi River Lodge

(located inside the national park)

Tel: +260-3-320606/7/8

Fax: +260-3-320609

Email: safpar@zamnet.zm

East-African style tented safari camp deep in the relatively unexplored Lower Zambezi National Park. This lodge is remote and highly recommended as a walking safari destination – safari enthusiasts usually stay a minimum of three nights at Mwambashi.

RECOMMENDED

Kulefu Tented Camp

(located inside the national park)

Star of Africa

Tel: +260-1-271366/271508/271509

Fax: +260-1-271398

Email: reservations@starofafrica.co.zm
Website: www.starofafrica.com
Deep in the game-rich Lower Zambezi National Park, there is a secluded intimate safari camp settled comfortably in the deep shade of tall riverine trees. Profoundly peaceful, eco-friendly and well appointed, the camp overlooks one of the permanent channels of the Zambezi River. Eight spacious luxurious tents are set on platforms at the river's edge geared for boat and land-based wildlife viewing, in a prolific wildlife area. Access by air only.

Ana Tree Lodge
(located inside the national park)
Tel: +260-1-287508/250730
Email: anatreelodge@zamnet.zm
Website: www.anatreelodge.com
This lodge is located within the national park and has five raised en suite safari tents with private balconies. Game often walks right through the camp and can be enjoyed from the comfort of the lodge, on game drives or walks. Good fishing spot too.

Redcliff Zambezi Lodge
Tel: +27-12-6532664
Fax: +27-12-6544015
Cell: +27-83-2289755
info@redcliff-lodge.com
Sited on the banks of the Lower Zambezi much further down the river to the east, beyond the eastern edge of the park, this lodge provides an exciting fishing point for the traveller seeking a true African adventure at an affordable price.

WHAT TO DO

Sightseeing

The escarpment and plateau regions are largely inaccessible and have not been formally surveyed. The valley floor, although a small area, is host to many of the bigger mammals including elephant, buffalo, hippo, waterbuck, kudu and zebra and crocodiles, impala and warthog.
Occasionally, roan, eland, Samango monkey, and nocturnal animals like hyaena, porcupine, civet, genet and honeybadger can be seen.

The birdlife along the riverbanks is exceptional. Many fish eagles can be seen and heard for miles around. Nesting along the cliffs are white-fronted and carmine bee-eaters. Amongst others are the red-winged pratincole, crested guinea fowl, black eagle, vast swarms of quelea, trumpeter hornbill, Meyer's parrot and Lilian's lovebird.

Fishing

Fishing possibilities are excellent along the river, and all three lodges offer fishing with rods and simple tackle provided. Healthy tiger fish and bream catches are common as well as vundu, a member of the catfish family, weighing up to 50kg. Strangely, cheap strong-smelling soap is an excellent bait.

Canoeing

Canoeing is a must. The lodges will provide day-long canoeing trips. Float down the river at your leisure and they'll pick you up in a speedboat at the end of the day to bring you back. The river has a strong enough current to take you easily down the river with little effort.

Several operators run three- to five-day trips, overnighting at very comfortable bush camps on the banks of the river. These trips are highly recommended if you are looking for off the beaten track adventure. The river guides will take you down remote channels between the islands where your opportunities to get close to game are very high. Hippos are always in sight, and elephant, zebra, crocodiles, puku, impala, buffalo, kudu and baboons can be seen browsing on the banks from the laid-back comfort of your canoe.

Canoeing safaris that extend over four days are re-supplied by vehicle and uplifted at the end of the safari by 4x4 vehicles.

Safari Par Excellence offers 'participatory' canoeing trips of any duration. All gear is carried in the canoes and camps are erected on islands in the river along the way. Everyone gets involved in setting up camp and cooking. These trips are obviously cheaper and a touch less comfortable, but the thrill of the wilderness is that much more intense.

Karibu Safaris organizes canoeing safaris with 'limited participation' camping (no equipment carried in the canoes, excellent meals prepared by crew). Guests are met at Kariba and are transferred to exclusive campsites on the banks of the Zambezi. Guests canoe their way down the river with their experienced and knowledgeable river guides, staying at a different campsite each night. Six-day and four-day packages are offered.

Karibu Safaris
Tel: +27-31-5639774/5631957
Email: karibu@karibu.co.za

River Horse Safaris
Tel: +263-61-2447/2944/2442/+260-1-511107
Cell: +263-91-235340/235311
Email: enquiries@riverhorsesafaris.com
Website: www.riverhorsesafaris.com

LAKE KARIBA

Although the building of the Kariba Dam was surrounded by controversy, both environmentally and socially, it is an impressive monument to engineering expertise. The massive valley which now forms Lake Kariba has survived, with most plant and animal species having adapted to the changed conditions.

HISTORY

Kariba Dam is located approximately halfway down the Zambezi River. The dam was an initiative of the federation existing at the time between British-ruled Northern and Southern Rhodesia and Malawi. To dam the great Zambezi floodplain, vast areas of forest and scrub were inundated.

The vegetation was strip-cleared and burnt, making the lake rich in chemicals from the fired wood and the considerable number of remaining trees provided an essential habitat for many creatures that found their way into the lake.

Building of the dam wall began in the late 1950s. Well over a million cubic metres of concrete was poured into the 36.6-metre-high wall with a thickness of over 24m to sustain the pressure of nearly 10 million litres of water passing through the spillway each second. At the end of 1958, the sluice gates were closed and in 1963 the maximum level was reached.

A river gauging station was set up at Chirundu to provide hydroelectric power.

Canoe safaris on the Zambezi River

The Displaced Tribe

Within the area lived over 50,000 people, mostly of the Batonga tribe. Although land was set aside for them further up the valley, they were reluctant to leave their tribal lands. Eventually, when the trucks moved in to relocate them, they conceded, having little choice. Ceremonies were held to honour their gods and the journey to new lands began. Schools and clinics were built in some of the new areas and wells installed for their arrival. Some new villages that were relocated close to the water's edge have prospered with the new fishing opportunities on the lake. But many mourn the loss of the rich alluvial river soil and battle to produce crops in the higher sandier areas. For the most part, the move was a severe disruption of their way of life and compensation minimal.

Operation Noah

As the dam began to fill, it became evident that thousands of animals stranded on islands were going to drown. Appeals were made and money raised to buy boats and equipment for their rescue and relocation. This project became known as Operation Noah. It was a mammoth task. Submerged trees and stumps threatened the hulls of the boats and on the islands there were huge concentrations of snakes including the deadly black mamba. Even so, thousands of animals were successfully rescued thanks to the efforts of a few.

Fishing

The conditions that had made life difficult for animals and people also conspired to produce an instant paradise for the fish. The rich fertilizing effect of the chemicals from the strip clearance gave a spurt to the growth of the lake fauna. The introduction to Kariba of kapenta, tiny sardine-like fish, has proved very successful. Shoals were airlifted from Lake Tanganyika to Lake Kariba in 1967.

HOW TO GET THERE

From Lusaka, it's a two-and-a-half-hour drive to Siavonga through the scenic Zambezi Rift Valley on one of Zambia's best roads. In Lusaka, take the Kafue Road to Chirundu and turn right onto the M15, 18km before the

Sunset on Lake Kariba

The Kariba dam wall is 36 metres high

Zimbabwe border. From Harare, take the turnoff to Kariba and cross over the dam wall to Siavonga. An airport is due to open in Siavonga in the near future.

WHERE TO STAY

On the Zambian side of Lake Kariba the tourist industry is in its infancy but you can find very comfortable hotel accommodation all around Siavonga, which is about 7km from the dam wall.

Eagles Rest Resort

Tel: +260-1-511168

Cell: 095-755291

Email: reservations@eaglesrestresort.com

Website: www.eaglesrestresort.com

Situated right on the shores of the lake, just 8km from the dam wall, the resort offers several possibilities of accommodation including bed and breakfast, full board, self-catering, camping and houseboating. The lodge is mainly geared towards the conference market and is a popular workshop venue for Lusaka companies.

The hotel organizes trips into the control room and turbine hall of the dam wall. Canoeing safaris through the Zambezi gorges and on the Lower Zambezi can be arranged. The Bateleur Houseboat is moored here.

Lake Kariba Inns

Tel: +260-1-253768

Fax: +260-1-252518

Cell: 097-796958

Email: info@karibainns.com

Also located on the banks of the lake at Siavonga, this hotel is a popular conference venue. There are 36 rooms, a pool, gym, houseboat, and the restaurant is excellent.

Lake Safari Lodge

Email: info@lake-safari.com

On the banks of the lake at Siavonga is a popular weekend

getaway and conference venue with 50 air-conditioned en suite rooms, good food and a great bar. It offers a range of activities such as boating, water sports and visits to the dam wall.

Manchinchi Bay Lodge

Located in Siavonga, this hotel offers 30 air-conditioned, en suite rooms with a balcony overlooking the lake. Conference and banqueting facilities are available. It has a large launch offering sundowner cruises.

Houseboating on the lake has been popular for a long time in Zimbabwe, and Zambia is progressively catching up:

Bateleur Houseboat

Tel: +260-1-511168

Cell: +260-95-755291

Email: reservations@eaglesrestresort.com

This houseboat is moored at Eagles Rest Resort in Siavonga. Bateleur offers charter cruises on the lake from one to 10 nights. The boat sleeps 14 passengers and has four crew members. On the lower deck are three cabins accommodating six passengers, two public toilets/showers, a lounge and a fully equipped kitchen. There is also a large pool/sun deck with a fully operational jacuzzi to cool off from the heat of the day. On the upper deck is the Captain's Bar and a large comfortable lounge area. Day seating on the upper deck converts to sleeping accommodation at night, and each bed is fully mosquito proofed. Two tender boats are normally towed behind the houseboat for fishing and/or sightseeing.

Matusadona Houseboat

This houseboat offers three-day to five-day fishing/cruising trips with a crew of three and accommodates up to six guests in style. The tariff includes all meals and an ample bar. Included in the itinerary is a stopover at Kota Kota Game Reserve for lunch and a game drive. A tender boat is towed behind for forays to the shore.

Cipembere Camping Boat

Available for groups of up to 10, sleeping casually on deck on mattresses and hammocks. It has a built-in barbecue, toilets and shower. A smaller boat is towed behind. Self-catering and full catering tariffs available. Great fun.

There is also good accommodation in the town of Sinazongwe, 120km uplake from Siavonga.

Gwembe Safaris

Tel: +260-32-20169/20021

Fax: +260-32-20054

Cell: 097-803292/777719

Email: info@gwembesafaris.com

Website: www.gwembesafaris.com

Located further up the lake near Sinazongwe, this privately owned 600-acre island on the lake is stocked with a variety of antelope and abundant birdlife. This is a perfect getaway for the bush lover, fishing enthusiast and bird-watcher.

Chete Island Deluxe Tented Safari Lodge

Tel: +260-1-483144

Fax: +260-1-483045

Email: info@cheteisland.com

Website: www.cheteisland.com

Situated on an island in the middle of the lake, this lodge is the only lodge on the island. Chete Island is a wild water wilderness, where the Zambezi Valley game and birds flourish, unmolested and protected by the status of Chete National Park. The lodge is peaceful, far from the 'madding crowds' of houseboats, power boats and game drive vehicles. It nestles in amongst a beautiful archipelago of remote islands hitherto virtually unvisited by the tourist world, scattered with floodplain shorelines, craggy cliffs, spectacular gorges and African lowveld woodlands.

WHAT TO DO

The Dam Wall

Any time spent in the Kariba or Siavonga area should include a visit to the dam wall to witness the size of this awesome structure. There is a display at the entrance to the bridge describing the building of the wall and the statistics involved. The wide bridge offers ample room for walking on either side. The contrasting views – the vast lake stretching to infinity on the one side and the sheer drop to the gorge on the other side – are breathtaking.

Chirundu Fossil Forest

21km from Chirundu, on the road to Lusaka, lies a fossil forest with remnants of trees over 150 million years old. Sections of tree trunks up to 3m long are exposed as a result of erosion of the surrounding soft red sandstone.

Fishing

Sport fishing in the Siavonga area is not as good as it used to be but further down the lake shore at Sinazongwe, the annual tiger fishing competition attracts anglers from all over the subcontinent and is held in May.

Water Sports

The lake is a superb playground for all kinds of water sports including windsurfing, paragliding and waterskiing. Most of these activities can be arranged through the hotels and resorts.
A trip on a houseboat is highly recommended, especially at full moon. The tranquillity of watching the deep orange sun sink on one side of the lake and the moon rise over the shimmering waters on the other is very special.

Most hotels in the area have a range of boats for hire and organize dinner cruises and champagne breakfasts.

Plans for a marina are in the pipeline, but try Lake Kariba Inns lodge if you need to launch a boat at Siavonga.

THE LUANGWA VALLEY

The Luangwa Valley is one of Africa's prime wildlife sanctuaries, with concentrations and varieties of game and birdlife that have made it world famous.

The valley lies at the tail end of the Great Rift Valley, which runs from the Red Sea down the length of East Africa. This accounts for the spectacular escarpment scenery in east Africa as well as the African lakes.

Down the centre of the valley flows the Luangwa River, fed by dozens of sand rivers that come down during the rainy season.

The countryside is spectacular in its rugged beauty, the vegetation thick and near the Luangwa River and its many tributaries a lush riverine forest occurs that is green all year round.

The development of game protection in the area began in the late 19th century when the British South Africa Company was administering the territory. It imposed a total ban on the hunting of hippo and elephant due to massive exploitation by the Chikunda tribe from Mozambique and the Arab traders from Malawi. Today there is an over-abundance of hippos along the Luangwa River.

The BSAC established the first game reserve in the Luamfwa region in 1904. An in-depth survey was completed in 1932 recommending the proclamation of game reserves and the appointment of an elephant control department.

Norman Carr and Bert Schultz were appointed as game rangers in 1939. Villages within the reserves were moved to the periphery.

In 1973 the elephant population was estimated to be 100,000 and found to be causing a major impact on the surrounding areas, but poaching was rampant too and numbers of elephant and the endangered rhino began to decline steadily.

The privately funded Save the Rhino Trust was established in 1980 and extensive anti-poaching patrols were carried out. Elephant poaching was curbed to some extent but rhinos unfortunately could not be saved and today they are entirely absent from the area.

Today there are about 20 operators in the valley, spread out along 150km of the Luangwa River. They range from budget camps to sophisticated lodges and offer walking safaris, game drives, night drives and photographic safaris.

NORTH LUANGWA NATIONAL PARK

This remote tract of land covering 4,636 square kilometres offers one of the finest wilderness experiences in Zambia. It is not open to the public and there are no permanent lodges there. Access is with one of the few safari operators granted permission to conduct walking safaris there.

Like the South Park, it lies on the western bank of the Luangwa River, bordered on the other side by the dramatic Muchinga escarpment which rises over 1,000m from the valley floor.

There are a number of tributary rivers running through the park and into the Luangwa. The crystal-clear Mwaleshi River trickles down the escarpment in a series of small waterfalls. It recedes in the dry season, leaving many pools along the way, drawing the animals from the bush to its banks in search of water. No game drives are permitted in the Mwaleshi area; access is by organized walking safaris only.

GETTING THERE

Although this park was officially opened to the public in 1984, the infrastructure in and to the park is not sufficiently developed to cater for the independent traveller. Special permission to enter it must be obtained from the Department of National Parks and Wildlife Services. The best way to experience this park is with one of the operators running safaris here. You can fly in to either Mfuwe International Airport, about four hours away, and be picked up, or be brought in from the Mpika side of the escarpment. There are two airstrips that are open for charter traffic.

WHAT TO SEE AND DO

The park is noted for its massive herds of buffalo, a spectacular sight if they're seen on the run, kicking up dust for miles behind them. Large prides of lion inhabit the territory and it is not uncommon to witness a kill. Other common mammals are hyaena, Cookson's wildebeest, bushbuck, zebra, warthog, baboon, vervet monkey, puku and impala. Elephant and leopard are also seen, but not as frequently as in the South Park. All the birds in the South Park have been recorded here as well.

WHERE TO STAY

There are no lodges open to the public in the North Park but several operators run pre-booked, organized safaris and removable bush camps there.

Shiwa Safaris

Tel +260-1-229261

Website: www.shiwasafaris.com

This is a seasonal bush camp based in North Luangwa. Normally the camp is open from 1st June to the first week of November. There are two bush camps and safaris begin at the Shiwa Ngandu estate over the western side of the escarpment, 100km off the Great North Road.

Big herds of Elephant can be witnessed in South Luangwa

The camp consists of four chalets, all en suite, plus one guide's chalet. Two of the chalets are built up on stilts overlooking the Mwaleshi River. A maximum of eight clients can be accommodated at a time. The area is predominantly for walking safaris but will do limited game/night drives.

Kutandala Camp

Email: info@kutandala.com

Website: www.kutandala.com

This is Zambia's smallest owner-operated camp, catering for only six guests on each safari. All the rooms have an unrestricted view of the Mwaleshi River and its floodplain throughout the day. It specializes in walking safaris.

Mwaleshi Camp

Tel: +264-61-240561

Email: tafika@remoteafrica.com

Website: www.remoteafrica.com

Situated on a scenic bend of the Mwaleshi River, it comprises three attractive reed chalets, each with stunning views over the river. Game viewing is on foot, in a remote area renowned for its lion, huge herds of buffalo and endemic Cookson's wildebeest.

The accommodation is in a grass pole bush camp with four double chalets with en suite facilities.

Kingdom of the mighty lion

SOUTH LUANGWA NATIONAL PARK

Experts have dubbed South Luangwa as one of the greatest wildlife sanctuaries in the world. The concentration of game around the Luangwa River and its oxbow lagoons is among the most intense in Africa.

The Luangwa River is the most intact major river system in Africa and is the lifeblood of the park. The park hosts a wide variety of wildlife, birds and vegetation. The now famous walking safari originated in this park and is still one of the finest ways to experience this pristine wilderness first-hand. There are 60 different animal species and over 400 different bird species. The only notable exception is the rhino, sadly poached to extinction.

If you're in your own vehicle, be sure to get a map of the park from the Crocodile Farm at the park entrance and follow the loop roads graded in the park, past dambos bursting with hippos, crowned cranes, grazing antelope and scurrying baboons. Further out on the plains you're bound to see the large elephant herds, reaching up to 70 in number. Buffalo are abundant and spread throughout the valley.

GETTING THERE

Mfuwe Airport recently achieved international status and various airlines are looking at scheduled flights from abroad.

Domestic flights operate about 10 times a week in peak season (June–Oct) from Lusaka. Check with any travel agent for schedules.

Charter planes from outside the country can now fly direct without clearing customs at Lusaka and there are a number of charter companies in Zambia which can fly to and from Zambia's top destinations. All lodges do transfers to and from the airport. Zambian Airways has scheduled flights from Lusaka to Mfuwe. Air Malawi has scheduled flights from Lilongwe to Mfuwe.

Driving, the usual route is from Chipata. This is a decent road and the 123km-drive takes about two hours to Mfuwe, just outside the park. If travelling in a robust 4x4 from Lusaka, it is possible to take a shortcut from the Great East Road at Petauke, up alongside the Luangwa River to Mfuwe. Only to be attempted well into the dry season. A good overnight stop along the way is at the Luangwa River Bridge at Bridge Camp.

WHEN TO GO

Seasonal changes are very pronounced in Luangwa. The dry season begins in April and intensifies through to October, the hottest month, when game concentrations are at their height. Warm, sunny days and chilly nights typify the dry winter months of May to August. The wet season begins in November as the leaves turn green, and the dry bleak terrain becomes a lush jungle. The rainy season lasts until the end of March and the migrant birds arrive in droves. Each lodge stays open for as long as access is possible, depending on its location in the area.

WHAT TO SEE AND DO

Wildlife

The hippopotamus is one animal you won't miss. There is estimated to be at least 50 hippos per kilometre of the Luangwa River!

Zebra can be seen running in small herds of about a dozen. Thornicroft's giraffe, unique to Luangwa Valley, should be easily spotted. The park has many different antelope species: bushbuck, duiker, eland, impala, puku, the famous kudu, reedbuck, roan, sable, hartebeest, grysbok, klipspringer and oribi.

Of the primates, baboons and vervet monkeys are prolific. More scarce is Maloney's monkey. Present, but unlikely to be seen except on night drives, are the night ape and the nocturnal bushbaby. Hyaenas are fairly common throughout the valley.

South Luangwa has a good population of leopard but they are not that easy to spot and tend to retreat when they hear vehicles. Many of the lodges' game trackers are skilled in finding leopards on night drives, however, and often visitors are rewarded with a full view of a kill.

Lions are as plentiful as in the Luangwa. Very often they roam in prides of up to 30. Of the other carnivores, present but not often seen are the caracal, wild dog, serval and side-striped jackal.

The Luangwa River also has an extraordinarily high number of crocodiles.

Birdlife

Birdwatching is superb in the valley. Near the end of the dry season, hundreds of large waterbirds can be seen wading through the shallows. These include the red-faced yellow-billed stork, pelican, saddle-billed stork, marabou stork, great white egret, black-headed heron, open-billed stork and the stately goliath heron that can stand in the same position for hours before pouncing. Of the most beautiful are the elegant crowned cranes, with their golden tufts, congregating in large flocks at the salt pans. Just before the rains set in in November, the migrants from Northern Europe and the intra-African migrants arrive to exploit the feeding opportunities. These include the red-chested cuckoo, white stork and European swallow, swift, hobby and bee-eater, as well as birds of prey such as the Steppe eagle and Steppe buzzard that come all the way from Russia. A special sight is the hundreds of brightly coloured carmine bee-eaters nesting in the steep sandy banks of the river.

With about 400 of Zambia's 732 species of bird appearing in the valley, including 39 birds of prey and 47 migrant species, there is plenty for the birdwatcher to spot, whatever the season.

Buffalos and Elephants coexist peacefully

WHERE TO STAY

There are many varied places to stay in the valley ranging from luxurious safari camps to budget chalets and camping. Most of the lodges are spread along the east bank of the Luangwa River, in the adjoining game management area, and they conduct game drives and walking safaris along the west bank in the park itself. Some of the lodges have bush camps deep in the park for remote walking safaris.

Kaingo/Mwamba Bush Camp

Tel: +260-0-6245064 (20 May–31 Oct)
Email: info@kaingo.com
Website: www.kaingo.com

Kaingo is a small, very comfortable lodge, one of the few inside the park itself, with an emphasis on personalized walking safaris and game drives. Mwamba Bush Camp is three hours' walk north of Kaingo, set under shady ebony trees along the Mwamba River; it is an excellent game area. An ideal safari includes three nights at Kaingo and three at Mwamba Camp.

Kapani

Tel: + 260-6-246015/246025
Email: kapani@normancarrsafaris.com

One of the most well-known and established lodges, built by Norman Carr, the 'father' of conservation in Zambia. It has comfortable, well-appointed brick and tile chalets and top-quality catering. Kapani is a permanent camp that runs all year. Accommodation consists of eight standard suites and two new Lagoon Houses, 20 beds in all.

Kapani also runs three bush camps in the park during the dry season, Luwi, Kakuli and Nsolo, with the emphasis on walking safaris. (June to October)

Chichele Presidential Lodge

Star of Africa
Tel: +260-1-271366/271508/271509
Fax: +260-1-271398
Email: reservations@starofafrica.co.zm
Website: www.starofafrica.com

An elegant Victorian 'gentleman's lodge' initially constructed as a private residential retreat for the former President of Zambia Dr Kenneth Kaunda. Chichele occupies one of the most breathtaking sites in the entire South Luangwa National Park, home to elephants, lions, leopards etc. With its magnificent hilltop position inside one of Africa's most prolific game-viewing areas, Chichele is set to become one of the greatest safari lodges in Africa.

Puku Ridge Tented Camp

Star of Africa
Tel: +260-1-271366/271508/271509
Fax: +260-1-271398
Email: reservations@starofafrica.co.zm
Website: www.starofafrica.com

This superb property with attention to luxury is located on a ridge overlooking spectacular game-rich floodplains. Guided walks, game drives and night drives are conducted by armed professional safari guides.

Mfuwe Lodge

Tel/Fax: +260-6-245041
Tel (satellite): +871-76-2280123
Website: www.mfuelodge.com

A fine luxury lodge in one of South Luangwa's prime locations, built between busy lagoons within the park itself. It has two trail camps for walking safaris operating from July to October. The main lodge has 18 en suite luxury thatched chalets, each with a private decking area overlooking the lagoon. The main lodge is open all year round.

Robin Pope Safaris

Robin Pope, a well-known safari expert, runs three camps in the Luangwa area:

1) Tena Tena

A luxurious tented camp under a shady mahogany grove in the northern section; the lodge can accommodate up to 10 guests in a luxurious tented camp along the river. (June to October)

2) Nkwali

The picturesque Nkwali Camp further south boasts the 'best bar in the valley'. The chalets are cool and spacious, overlooking the river. Access to the park is by boat or nearby pontoon. The area is famous for leopard and giraffe sightings. (April to December)

3) Nsefu

Tel: + 260-6-246090/91/92

Fax: +260-6-246090/91/94

Website: www.robinpopesafaris.net

Located 12km north of Tena Tena. It's the oldest camp in Luangwa, dating back to the early 1950s. The original rondavels have been extended, with a spacious bathroom added. Each room has a clear view of the river through large windows and from the new wooden verandah. The camp offers a spectacular view across the Luangwa River.

The Bush Camp Company

Tel: +260-6245041

Tel (satellite): +871-76-2280123

Email: Alison@bushcampcompany.com

Website: www.bushcampcompany.com

The Bush Camp Company operates four very comfortable bush camps along the Luangwa.

Kafunta

Tel: +260-6-246046

Tel (satellite): +871-76-2068427

Email: kafunta@luangwa.com

Website: www.luangwa.com

Each spacious log cabin is made from natural material with a splendid view over the winding Luangwa River. This small, personalized camp lies under a grove of mahogany trees on the only habitable island in the Luangwa River. The Island Bush Camp offers rustic accommodation in grass/reed huts. Each chalet has a private verandah overlooking the Luangwa River.

Luamfwa

Tel: +260-1-261683/261732/214032/214029

Fax: +260-1-262438

Cell: +260-97-802524/882210

Email: info@luamfwa.com

Website: www.luamfwa.com

Another of the valley's oldest lodges, deep in the south end of the park, recently refurbished and nestling in a very remote section of the park itself. Its wooden chalets overlook a busy lagoon. (June to October)

Tafika

Tel: +264-61-240561

Email: tafika@remoteafrica.com

Website: www.remoteafrica.com

Offers unique, quality game viewing in Zambia's pristine Luangwa Valley. Five chalets built from local materials, offering excellent cuisine, personalized attention and respected and dedicated guides in a relaxed family atmosphere. Tafika offers microlighting as an optional extra to the excellent drives and walking safaris.

LAKE TANGANYIKA

Tanganyika's waters lap Tanzania, Burundi, DRC and Zambia. It is the longest fresh water lake in the world and the second deepest after Lake Baikal in Russia. The immense depth is because it lies in the Great Rift Valley, which also has created its steep shoreline. It reaches a depth of 1,433m, which is 642m below sea level.

The bottom 1,200m of the lake remain 'dead' – either too high in hydrogen sulphide or too low in oxygen to support life. This 'fossil water' may be as old as 20 million years.

It is essentially a landlocked sea but in years of heavy rain the lake overflows into the Lukuga River, which in turn feeds DRC's Lualaba River.

Although Zambia can only claim 7% of its surface area, it stretches north to south a distance of 677km (420 miles) and averages about 50km wide. The clear waters host more than 350 different species of fish and are well known for angling.

Like Lake Malawi, Lake Tanganyika is extremely old, and the combination of its age and ecological isolation has led to the evolution of unique fish populations. Sport fishing is very popular here and catches include the goliath tiger fish and Nile perch. Crocodiles inhabit most of the shoreline, except around Mpulungu, probably due to the noise of people and motorboats.

Swimming in the lake (in the Mpulungu area only!) is an absolute treat: warm, clear, salt-free water that changes from silky stillness to high waves for a great body surf (ferocious surface storms can provoke driving waves up to 6m high).

GETTING THERE

You can go straight to the port of Mpulungu on the Great North Road via Mpika and Kasama. Or drive to Nsumbu National Park, which borders the lake, via Mporokoso. Kasaba Bay cannot be reached from Mpulungu as there are mountains and a river in the way, but it is possible to take a boat, a distance of about 60km. There is an airstrip at Kasaba Bay for chartered flights, but no scheduled flights go there at present. This may change with the imminent re-opening of the three lodges there.

WHERE TO STAY

Kasakalawe Lodge

Situated 3km from Mpulungu on Lake Tanganyika's shore. Four en suite chalets (sleeping 10 people). Camping is possible. The lodge offers fishing, boat trips, trips and hikes to Kalambo Falls and snorkelling.

Tanganyika Lodge

A few kilometres west of town on a beautiful stretch of rocky lakeshore. It has three twin chalets, two en suite family chalets and camping facilities. Fresh fish is available every day and it offers both catering and self-catering rates. Boats can be arranged for fishing and trips to Kalambo Falls.

Mishembe

Tel: +260-4-221615

This is a small private secluded beach at the base of Kalambo Falls owned by Luke Powell. The only way to access the bay is by boat, which makes the place even

Puku Ridge Tented Camp

Lake Tanganika is one of the oldest and deepest lakes in the world

more peaceful and remote. The beach is made up of fine white sand which leads into the clearest blue water where tropical fish can be seen. At present only tented accommodation is available, either catering or self-catering. Luke offers guided walks up to the Falls, boat trips up the river mouth and fishing.

WHAT TO DO

Lake Tanganyika Ferry

The MV Liemba, a large ex-German warship that has been converted into a passenger ferry, arrives at the port of Mpulungu every Friday morning and leaves in the afternoon for Kigoma in Tanzania and Bujumbura in Burundi.

If you have time to do the week-long trip there and back, or if en route further up Africa, this is an experience not to be missed. It's not luxurious but the trip itself offers a spectacular experience of this vast lake in the heart of the continent. There are 'first class' cabins with double bunks and one family cabin with en suite facilities. The toilets seldom work properly so be prepared. It has a carrying capacity of 500 passengers and by the time it has left Kigoma, it is usually full.

Niamkolo Church

Located 2km east of Mpulungu town, this church was built in 1895 by the London Missionary Society; it is the oldest surviving stone-built church in Zambia. The 15-metre tower was a landmark for boats using the port of Mpulungu.

Kalambo Falls

Located on the Kalambo River bordering Zambia and Tanzania. They are the second highest waterfalls in Africa plunging a breathtaking 221m in one uninterrupted drop – over twice the height of the Victoria Falls! The width of the falls varies from 2m in the dry season expanding to an impressive 15m after heavy rains, cascading down a sheer cliff into a deep green pool below, through the gorge and on about 3km more into Lake Tanganyika.

There are two access options. You can drive via Mbala, then take the northerly road to the border of Tanzania, bearing left at road junctions.
The other way is to hire a boat from Mpulungu across the lake, taking about an hour. Then climb up to the summit where the Falls begin. This is about a two-hour hard walk.

There is a cliff path along the southern side of the gorge leading to a viewpoint directly opposite the Falls and another further along overlooking Lake Tanganyika.

Sumbu National Park

The park lies on the edge of Lake Tanganyika about 60km west of Mpulungu. This area used to be an active slaving point. Up until the middle of the 1800s, Nsumbu was often the area from which slaves were shipped across the lake to the Tanzanian mainland before being sent onwards to the slave market in Zanzibar.

Nsumbu National Park

Lying on the southern shores of Lake Tanganyika in the northernmost tip of Zambia, the park covers an area of just over 2,000 square kilometres encompassing 100km of some of the most pristine shores of this vast lake. Its beauty ranges from sandy beaches, vertical cliffs, rocky coves and natural bays to the rugged hills and deep valleys of the interior. The Lufubu River winds its way through a valley flanked by 300-metre escarpments on either side.

THE COPPERBELT

Copper has been known and used in the region for centuries. The early European discoveries by prospectors like William Collier in 1902 (reputed to have made his discovery on the site where he had shot a roan antelope) had to await economic viability before any serious mining attempts were undertaken. It was only in the 1920s that a technical breakthrough was achieved that made the mining of the then Northern Rhodesia's 'red gold' highly profitable.

The initial boom in the industry was affected by the Great Depression of the 1930s. International gearing-up for the hostilities that resulted in World War II created the next boom which lasted until the early 1970s.

It was copper that motivated infrastructure development in Zambia, and that shaped colonial policies towards a federation with the then Southern Rhodesia (Zimbabwe) and Nyasaland (Malawi). It was also copper that created the social realities that fomented trade unions and the birth of Zambian Nationalism.

GETTING THERE

Zambian Airways and Proflight offer daily scheduled flights from Lusaka to Kitwe or Ndola (45 minutes flying). InterAir flies directly to Ndola from Johannesburg.

By road, the Copperbelt is easily reached from Lusaka. Take the Great North Road to Kabwe, Kapiri Mposhi, then Ndola (four-hour drive).

Ndola

Ndola lies some 320km north of Lusaka. It is the gateway to the mineral producing region of the country. Like Lusaka, the development of Ndola has been rapid and extensive.

There are many manufacturing industries and copper mines. Although copper is still Zambia's largest foreign exchange earner and the mainstay of the national economy, the city of Ndola has established itself as a commercial and light industrial centre of considerable importance, as well as being the junction and distribution centre for the Copperbelt complex.

Luanshya

Luanshya, to the left of Ndola, is the site of the oldest copper mine in Zambia. There is little of interest to the tourist here but its charms lie in the picturesque old colonial buildings on the main street. The Collier Monument here commemorates the site where William Collier discovered copper while hunting a roan antelope in 1902.

Chingola

Chingola is the most picturesque of the Copperbelt towns with a profusion of trees and flowers. Chingola is home to the biggest opencast mine in Africa, Konkola Copper Mines.

Kitwe

Sixty-four kilometres west of Ndola is Kitwe, the hub of the Copperbelt and the principal industrial and commercial centre of the area. The city owes its existence to the copper mining industry but a considerable number of secondary industries have been established. Planned on modern lines, Kitwe has a large shopping area with hotels, a cinema and theatre.

The good central position of the city in the Copperbelt area made it the most popular choice for industrial developers.

WHERE TO STAY

Arabian Nights
11 Mushitu Close, Parklands
Kitwe
Tel: +260-2-221097/229530
Email: shahida@zamnet.zm; dcole@zamnet.zm
A nice, cosy and comfortable place to stay with nicely furnished en suite bedrooms. Satellite TV but no Internet facilities. Also well known for its restaurants and excellent Indian food.

Copperfields Executive Guest House

48 Freedom Avenue, Parklands, opposite Kitwe Zoo
Kitwe
Tel: +260-2-230709/10
Fax: +260-2-231027

The guest house is a favourite with business travellers and offers a pick up/drop off service from either Ndola or Kitwe airport by arrangement. It has a full business centre. The rooms are en suite with satellite TVs. Traditional morning and afternoon teas with scones.

Eagle Guest House

Kitwe
Tel: +260-2-229748/230761
Email: gayatech@zamnet.zm

Homely, reasonably priced, private accommodation, bed and breakfast or full board, self-contained single and double rooms. Residents' bar, swimming pool. Satellite TV and phone in all rooms.

Edinburgh Hotel

Obote Avenue

Kalambo Falls

Kitwe
Tel: +260-2-222444
Email: edin@coppernet.zm
Fairly old-fashioned but clean and conveniently located. It has two restaurants, a casino and conference facilities.

Michelangelo
Plot 126 Broadway Road
Ndola
Tel: +260-2-620325/6
Fax: +260-2-620325
Email: vgstyle@zamnet.zm
An oasis in the Copperbelt, with 11 luxurious self-contained rooms set around a nice pool area. With satellite TV and Internet access in the rooms and wireless access in the common areas, it's an excellent choice for business travellers. Michelangelo is also well known in the region for its fine Italian food.

Mukwa Guest House
26/28 Mpezeni Avenue (off President Avenue)
Kitwe
Tel: +260-2-224266
Fax: +260-2-224266
Old colonial-style building with a nice garden and swimming pool. Satellite TV and fridge in the rooms. Also a good Indian/continental restaurant.

Mukuba Hotel
P O Box 72126
Alongside the Showgrounds, Industrial Area
Ndola
Tel: +260-2-651000/4/9
Email: mukhotel@zamnet.zm
52 rooms. Another possible choice for business travellers. Nice spacious rooms with satellite TV. A small herd of impalas reside in the hotel grounds.

New Savoy Hotel
12 Buteko Avenue
P O Box 71800, Ndola
Tel: +260-2-611097/8
Fax: +260-2-614001
154 rooms. Fairly old; go for a nice guest house if you can.

Michelangelo restaurant and lodge is an oasis in the Copperbelt

Protea Hotels
Chililabombwe
Tel: +260-2-312810
Fax: +260-2-313510
Email: protea@zamtel.zm
The famous chain has recently opened a new 40-room hotel in Chingola located in a residential area with a good restaurant and a lively bar. It has a swimming pool, Internet café, shops and an ATM machine and all rooms are air-conditioned. The hotel is only 1km from the Championship Golf Course.

WHERE TO EAT

RECOMMENDED

Arabian Nights Restaurant
11 Mushitu Close
Kitwe
Tel: +260-2-229530
Very famous in the region for its excellent Pakistani, Indian and continental food, in a nice semi-outdoor setting.

The Copperpot Restaurant
Copperfield Guest House
48 Freedom Avenue, Parklands, opposite Kitwe Zoo
Kitwe
Tel: +260-2-230709/10
Serving modern French cuisine. The restaurant offers anything from steak au poivre to chicken dishes and seafood delights flown in fresh from Mozambique. (Closed Sunday evenings only)

RECOMMENDED

Michelangelo
126 Broadway Avenue
Ndola
Tel: +260-2-620325/620476
Excellent Italian food with a nice Italian decor. Michelangelo's delicatessen offers excellent homemade cakes and pastries, and homemade cheeses. A must for the Copperbelt.

Hong Kong Restaurant
President Avenue North
Ndola
Tel: +260-2-514014
Chinese food.

Mona Lisa
Shop No. 3, Parklands
Kitwe
Tel: +260-2-229677
Cell: +260-96-785077
Pizza/Italian food. The food is not exceptional but there is a nice friendly atmosphere. Particularly good on Wednesdays.

Mukwa Restaurant
Mpezeni Avenue
Kitwe
Tel: +260-2-224266
Good variety of continental and Indian food.

WHAT TO DO

Mines

It is possible to visit the opencast mine. You need to get a permit from the Mine Office at the end of Fern Avenue.

Golf

If you're a golfing enthusiast, Nchanga Golf course in Chingola is one of the most beautiful and well-kept courses in Africa.

The Copperbelt Museum

Buteko Avenue, opposite the New Savoy Hotel

It has many interesting samples of the minerals found here as well as cultural arts and crafts. It is unfortunate that the exhibits are squashed into a small shop, but it's still worth a visit. It also sells local curios and copper items.

Chilengwa and Kashiba Sunken Lakes

Lake Chilengwa, lying about 16km southeast of Ndola,

is one of two sunken lakes found in the Copperbelt, the other being the 100-metre-deep Lake Kashiba, further south on the Kapiri–Mposhi road. Both lakes have local cultural significance. The lakes are formed by the collapse of surface rock into the underlying limestone. Lake Kashiba offers basic camping facilities, safe swimming and good birdwatching.

Makwera Falls and Lake

About 9km off the Kitwe–Ndola dual carriageway. The lake is a centre for fish farming. The Falls are small but quite picturesque as they tumble from a small river over a wider rocky outcrop before settling in a shimmering pool on the rock basement.

Dag Hammerskjold Memorial

Located 10km along the Ndola–Kitwe road, the memorial commemorates the sight where the United Nations Secretary General died in a plane crash during the Katanga crisis in Zaire in 1961.

Mindolo Dam

About 7km to the southwest of the city centre along Kalulushi road, it has a boating club, swimming pool and bar.

Chembe Bird Sanctuary

Thirty kilometres from Kitwe on the Kalalushi–Kasempa road is a very charming bird sanctuary run by the Wildlife Society. Thick woodlands surround a small lake and there are shady campsites at the water's edge. You can walk or drive around the lake and into the surrounding woodlands. Boats can be hired for fishing or birdwatching from the lake.

Chimfunshi Chimpanzee Sanctuary and Animal Orphanage

Friends of Chimfunshi
P O Box 3555, Kempton Park
1620 South Africa
Chingola:
Tel: +260-2-311293
Fax: +260-2-311100

On the headwaters of the Kafue River, 60km west of Chingola, lies the Chimfunshi Wildlife Orphanage. Aside from chimpanzees, Chimfunshi does have a host of other animals benefiting from the care of David and Sheila Siddle.

In 1983 Sheila received a young chimpanzee that had been confiscated from Zairean poachers. The chimpanzee wasn't expected to survive, but Sheila persisted and nursed the animal back to health. Since then, Chimfunshi has turned into an internationally recognized sanctuary and rehabilitation centre for this endangered species, hosting more than 50 chimpanzees. Plans for the acquisition of more land have developed into the formation of the Chimfunshi Wildlife Orphanage Trust. The Trust has purchased a neighbouring farm of 10,000 acres.

TRAVEL AGENCIES AND TOUR OPERATORS

Zambia National Tourist Board
Head Office, Lusaka Square, Cairo Rd
Box 30017, Lusaka
Tel: +260-1-229087
Fax: 260-1-225174
Email: zntb@zamnet.zm

ZNTB – Livingstone
Zambia Tourist Centre, Mosi-Oa-Tunya Road
Box 603432, Livingstone
Tel: +260-3-321404/5
Email: zntblive@zamnet.zm

ZNTB – USA
2419 Massachusetts Avenue, NW
Washington DC
Tel: +1-202-2659717
Fax: +1-202-3320826
Email: zntbusa@aol.com

ZNTB – United Kingdom
2 Palace Gate, Kensington
London, W85NG
Tel: +44-207-5896343/5896655
Fax: +44-207-5846346/5913975
Email: zntb@aol.com

ZNTB – South Africa
570 Ziervogel Street (off Hamilton Street)
Hatfield 0083, Tshwane
P O Box 12234, Pretoria
Tel: +27-12-3261947/3261854
Fax: +27-12-3262140
Email: zahpta@mweb.co.za

Gemistar Travel and Tours
Plot 4623, Mwaimwena Road, Rhodes Park
P O Box 50026, Lusaka
Tel: +260-1-254834
Fax: +260-1-254899
Email: gemistar@zamtel.zm

Imperial Travel
Valflax Plaza, Cairo Road
P O Box 380098, Lusaka
Tel: +260-1-232284/87
Cell: +260-95/96/97-772677
Tel/Fax: +260-1-232284
Email: imperialtravel@uudial.zm

Juls Limited
Plot 5507 Libala Road, Kalundu
Postnet # 79, Private Bag E891, Lusaka
Tel: +260-1-292979/293972
Fax: +260-1-291246
Email: julscar@zamnet.zm

Sunbird Travel and Tours Ltd
Plot 742 Ben Bella Road, on Caltex Filling Station
P O Box 33570, Lusaka
Tel: +260-1-226998/227064
Fax: +260-1-226998
Cell: +260-96-455137
Email: sunbird@zamnet.zm

Tara Travel and Tours
Plot 3512, House 13 Matandani Close, Rhodes Park
P O Box 30241, Lusaka
Tel: +260-1-252174/251564
Fax: +260-1-25371
Email: taratt@zamnet.zm

The Travel Shop
Shop 17A, Arcades Shopping Centre
Postnet Box 265, Private Bag E10, Lusaka
Tel: +260-1-255559/253194
Fax: +260-1-250746
Email: tsmarketing@microlink.zm

Topflight Travel
NSCB Building, next to Barclays Bank, North End
Private Bag E544, Lusaka
Tel: +260-1-224417/18/36/58
Email: topflight@zamnet.zm

Zambian Safari Company Limited
Central Park, Farmers' House, Cairo Road
P O Box 30093, Lusaka
Tel: +260-1-228682/3/231450/224616
Fax: +260-1-224915/222906
Email: reservations@zamsaf.co.zm

Voyagers
P O Box 37609, Lusaka
Tel: +260-1-253064
P O Box 70023, Ndola
Tel: +260-2-621333

BASIC VOCABULARY

Zambia has approximately 72 different languages; however, every province has a main language spoken by the majority. For instance, Lusaka province uses Chi Nyanja and Chi Bemba; Copperbelt uses Bemba; Western province is dominated by Chi Lozi; while Southern province uses Chi Tonga. Listed below are some phrases commonly used in Lusaka province.

WORD	CHI NYANJA	CHI BEMBA
How are you?	*Muli bwanji?*	*Mwashibukeni?*
I am fine	*Nili bwino*	*Eyamukwayi*
I am happy	*Ndine okondwela*	*Nintemwa*
Please	*Napapata*	*Napapata*
Thank you	*Zikomo*	*Twato te la*
I am sorry	*Muni Kululukile*	*Munje leleko*
My name is...	*Ndine...*	*Ninebo...*
What is your name?	*Ndimwe ba ndani dzina?*	*Niwebo ba nani eshina?*
Where are you from?	*Mwachoka kuti?*	*Mwafuma kwisa?*
Yes	*Inde*	*Eya ye*
No	*Iyaye*	*Awe*
Goodbye	*Baye*	*Baye*
How much is it?	*Zingati?*	*Shinga?*
It's too expensive	*Yadulisa*	*Nai dula*
Lower the price	*Chasani koni*	*Fumyeniko*
I cannot speak	*Sininga Kambe*	*Teti ndande*
Do you speak English?	*Mu kamba Chizungu?*	*Mula landa ichi Sungu?*
Let's go	*Tiyeni*	*Natuleya*
Stop	*Imilira*	*Iminina*
Slowly	*Pang'ono pang'ono*	*Panono panono*
Come here	*Bwelani kuno*	*Iseni kuno*
Help me	*Nitandi dzeni koni*	*Ngafweniko*
Drinking water	*Mazi akumwa*	*Amenshi ayakunwa*
Some food	*Chakudya*	*Ichakulya*

BIBLIOGRAPHY AND WEBSITES

The majority of the information compiled in this guide book is first hand information collected by our team in the country through a number of interviews

Zambia Review 2006

Bradt Guide Zambia

Export Review 2005

www.zambiatourism.com

www.times.co.zm

www.ebz.co.zm

www.zic.org.zm

www.zambiz.co.zm

www.zpa.org.zm

TOP COMPANIES
(in alphabetical order)

African Banking Corporation
African Life Financial Services
Alexander Forbes
Amanita Group
Aon Zambia
Armcor
Bank of Zambia
Barclays Bank of Zambia
Bata Shoes Company
BDO
BOC Gas
BP Zambia
British Airways
British American Tobacco
Caltex Oil
Cavmont Capital Bank
Celtel
CFAO
Chibuluma South Mine Ltd
Chilanga Cement
Citibank Ltd
Copperbelt Energy Corporation
Coppernet Solutions
Dana Holding
Deloitte and Touche
Development Bank of Zambia
DHL
Discount Steel
Dunavant Zambia
Engen
Equinox Minerals Ltd /Lumwana mining project
Fedex
Finance Bank Zambia
First Quantum Inc - Kansanshi Plc - Bwana Mkubwa Mine
Gemfields Holdings
Grant Thorton
Grizzly Mining
Holiday Inn
Indeni Petroleum Refinery
Indo-Zambia Bank
InterContinental Hotel
Investrust Bank
Kagem Mining
Kariba Minerals
Knight Frank
Konkola Copper Mines
Luanshya Copper Mines - Chambishi Metals
Lusaka Stock Exchange (LuSE)
Madison Insurance Company
Mopani Copper Mines
MTN
Nampack Zambia Ltd
Nanga Farm
National Airports Corporation Ltd
National Housing Authority
National Milling Corporation
National Pension Scheme Authority
National Savings & Credit Bank
Ndola Lime Company Ltd
Nico Insurance
Pangaea Partners
Par Excellence Safaris
Parmalat
Pharmanova / Malcom Group of Companies
Professional Insurance
Proflight Air Services
Railway Systems of Zambia
Saatchi & Saatchi
SDV- Delmas
SEEDCO
Stanbic Bank
Standard Chartered
Sun International
Swarp Spinning Mills
Taj Pamodzi Hotel
TAP Zambia
TATA Africa
Tazama Pipelines
Total
Unilever Zambia
Union Gold
Voyagers
York Farm
Zaffico
Zambeef Products Plc
Zambia Bureau of Standards
Zambia Electricity Supply Corp. (ZESCO)
Zambia Metal Fabricators
Zambia National Building Society
Zambia National Commercial Bank
Zambia National Tourism Board
Zambia Postal Services
Zambia Seed Company
Zambia State Insurance Corporation
Zambia Sugar Plc
Zambia Telecommunications Co
Zambian Airways
Zambian Breweries Group Plc
Zamnet Communication
ZCCM - IH

COMPANY INDEX

AGRICULTURE

ENERGY & MINING

FINANCE

COMPANY INDEX

INDUSTRY & TRADE

PUBLIC WORKS

TOURISM

TRANSPORT & COMMUNICATION

THE TOOL TO REACH
INTERNATIONAL BUSINESS GOALS...
ANGOLA
SYRIA
ZAMBIA
THE GAMBIA
KENYA
SUDAN
LIBYA
THE PREMIER GUIDEBOOK FOR BUSINESS GLOBETROTTERS
B.eBiz
eBiZ
guides
L.eBiz
All you need to know to do business and have fun
...AND ENJOY THE BEST LEISURE DESTINATIONS
TANZANIA
ALGÉRIE
MOZAMBIQUE
ETHIOPIA
EGYPT
CAMEROON
GHANA
NIGERIA